Birds in Our Lives

Dwelling in an Avian World

By Adam Davis and Mia Malloy
University of Georgia

cognella™

San Diego, CA

Bassim Hamadeh, CEO and Publisher
Christopher Foster, General Vice President
Michael Simpson, Vice President of Acquisitions
Jessica Knott, Managing Editor
Kevin Fahey, Cognella Marketing Manager
Jess Busch, Senior Graphic Designer
Zina Craft, Acquisitions Editor
Jamie Giganti, Senior Project Editor
Brian Fahey, Licensing Associate
Kate McKellar, Interior Designer

First published in the United States of America in 2013 by Cognella, Inc.

Illustrations by Matthew Kirkland Jones
Design and technical assistance for figures and anatomy photographs provided by Elizabeth Freeman.

Printed in the United States of America

ISBN: 978-1-60927-689-8 (pbk)

www.cognella.com 800.200.3908

CONTENTS

FOREWORD

Whether it is their ability to fly, utilization of sound and visual stimuli similar to us for communication, or their sheer number and presence on every continent, man's fascination with birds is well recorded throughout history. The relationship birds have with humans has resulted in these flying creatures becoming a key component of the global economy. Bird-watching and its associated ecotourism, as well as feeding and hunting wild birds, generate billions of dollars worldwide each year. Domesticated birds are popular pets across the globe. Meat and eggs produced by birds are the largest source of animal protein produced and eaten by humans. Other bird products like feathers, oils, leather, and feces are highly valuable in the clothing, pharmaceutical, cosmetics, or fertilizer industries. In addition, the value of bird service to humans through activities such as plant pollination, seed distribution, scavenging, consumption of insect pests—and as indicator species to the health of virtually every ecosystem present in the world—is absolutely invaluable.

This book will introduce you to the fascinating world of birds by providing you a basic understanding of avian biology through the exploration of topics such as bird evolution, anatomy, reproduction, nutrition, and sensory perception. You will also gain knowledge about the current status of the wild bird population, the threats birds are facing which are impacting their survival and well-being, and how you can help bird preservation. Finally, as commonly kept birds such as parrots, birds of prey, pigeons, ratites, game birds, and ornamental chickens are covered in the book, you will gain an appreciation for the role of birds in our lives as pets, as animals of vital economic importance, and as sources of entertainment through hobbies like falconry and homing pigeon racing.

I EVOLUTION & TAXONOMY

What is a bird? Today it can best be defined as any animal with feathers. This was not true in prehistoric times, as will be discussed later. The general public often tends to define birds using terms such as "animals with wings" or "animals that fly." Remember that bats fly, and although very different in structure and composition, they have wings. In addition, there are several animals that lay eggs, such as the duck-billed platypus, echidna, turtles, and crocodiles.

Despite a century and a half of previous research, the evolution, as well as the taxonomy of birds, is far from resolved. As new fossils are found and characterized and as new molecular studies provide insight into the phylogeny of both extant and extinct bird species, there is hope—especially given the rapidity of recent findings—that many of the unresolved issues will be clarified in the next one to two decades.

EVOLUTION

Our knowledge of bird evolution is based on fossils. Found fossils are dated for the most part based on stratigraphy (studying how deeply a fossil is buried in the rock strata) and radioisotope dating. Besides dating fossils, the morphology of any fossil is studied extensively to try and determine how it is evolutionarily related to other organisms that exist in the fossil record or is extant (living).

Finding even partial fossils of prehistoric birds is a rare event because typically their bones are relatively small in size and are thin and porous, which is great for reducing weight for flight, but poor for fossilization. Discovering an intact bird fossil becomes even more unlikely because, as prey animals, their remains can end up scattered and further scavenged by other animals.

The Solnhofen limestone quarry in Bavaria is known for its fine-textured limestone, the source of many exquisite fossils from hundreds of species. Often these fossils are of complete organisms that are very delicate in nature such as dragonflies, with even their wings preserved. When the limestone was formed, it occurred in protected salt lagoons that did not have exposure to strong currents or much water exchange. Thus, the bottom of the lagoons was anoxic, and as water evaporated from the lagoons between storms, the salinity increased to toxic levels for life. This created the perfect environment for the formation of fossils. Any organism that fell into the water would die or any organism washed into the lagoon by storms would settle to the bottom and not be scavenged by marine life or broken apart by strong currents as it was slowly covered by lime silt.

In 1861 arguably the most famous fossil from the Solnhofen quarry was found. The fossil was of an organism about the size of a pigeon that had a long tail like a lizard, a toothed jaw, front limbs that were modified to form wings, and most importantly, wing flight feathers that appeared

similar to those of modern-day birds and suggested rudimentary flight ability (Figure 1.1). *Archaeopteryx* was the name given to the organism, and the limestone from which the fossil was found was dated to about 150 million years ago, or the end of the Jurassic Period (Table 1.1). In subsequent years, several more complete *Archaeopteryx* fossils were found from this quarry. Because of *Archaeopteryx,* appearance it was classified as the most basal bird in the avian lineage, a distinction that has been challenged, but thus far has survived, as will be discussed in detail in the following sections

Another area proven as a rich source of fossils is Liaoning Province in northeastern China. Over a hundred million years ago, this was a forested area with lakes that provided an environment for a diverse array of organisms. The area also had active volcanoes that would periodically erupt, filling the local environment with poisonous gas and ash. The gas killed all living animals, which were then covered with fine ash that, in turn, enabled the formation of detailed fossils. Many early Cretaceous feathered dinosaur fossils have come from this location and have provided further insight into avian evolution. In addition, many early Cretaceous bird fossils have been found here, and some were preserved with gastrointestinal contents present such as seeds, fish, or stones.

FIGURE 1.1   *Archaeopteryx* fossil. Note the clear outline of feathers.

TABLE 1.1   *GEOLOGICAL TIME*

Era	Period	Date (millions of years ago)
Cenozoic		65.5 to present
	Quaternary	2.6 to present
	Tertiary[1]	65.5 to 2.6
Mesozoic		251.0 to 65.5
	Cretaceous	145.5 to 65.5
	Jurassic	201.6 to 145.5
	Triassic	251.0 to 201.6

[1] The Tertiary period has been renamed with the span being divided between the Paleogene (65.5 to 23 million years ago) and Neogene (23 to 2.6 million years ago) periods.

Thomas Huxley was the first to note the similarities between birds and dinosaurs and concluded that birds and theropods could be closely related (Huxley, 1868, 1870). In 1926, however, Heilmann's book, *The Origin of Birds*, was translated to English (Heilmann, 1926). Heilmann reported that birds were anatomically more similar to theropod dinosaurs than to any other fossil group. He indicated that birds and dinosaurs most likely evolved from a common ancestor in a group called Thecodonita (a term no longer used, but originally referred to a group of early archosaurs that gave rise to such things as dinosaurs, pterosaurs, and crocodilians). Although Heilmann recognized the similarity between theropods and birds, he erroneously hypothesized that the reduced clavicles of dinosaurs could not have evolved into the furcula (wishbone) in birds. Regretfully, this hypothesis was based on an assumption that an evolved characteristic could not disappear in a lineage and then reappear. In addition, several theropod fossils were subsequently found with well-preserved and defined furculae. However, the "theocont" evolution theory remained unchallenged for about 50 years; it is still accepted by some.

In the late 1960s and the 1970s, John Ostrom brought back the idea that birds were descended from theropod dinosaurs, based on morphological features that were similar between the two (Ostrom 1969, 1970, 1975, 1976). At the same time that Ostrom was publishing papers indicating that birds evolved from dinosaurs, the science of cladistics was born. What sets cladistics apart from other taxonomy classifications is that it focuses on identifying shared derived (new) characters (traits) among organisms. This focus on derived traits means that two groups of organisms that share these derived traits are more closely related to one another than they are to groups of organisms that display only original traits, but not the derived ones. Thus, traditional methods would likely exclude a species a group simply because it had traits not found in the other members of the group. In cladistics, this species with new traits would likely be considered an ancestor organism that founded a group (clade), having the derived characteristics not present in groups that evolved earlier. Thus, a clade would consist of this ancestor and all its descendants. Within a clade there can be subclades (subgroups).

The cladogram supporting birds being derived from theropod dinosaurs places *Archaeopteryx* at the base of the Aves (birds) clade (Figure 1.2). This clade consists of all other descendants of *Archaeopteryx*, which ultimately leads to modern birds. The *Archaeopteryx* clade is a subgroup of a broader clade consisting of maniraptoran theropods, which itself is a subgroup derived from more basal theropods, which, in turn, ultimately is derived from non-theropod dinosaurs. This indicates that birds are not only derived from dinosaurs, but are in fact dinosaurs, which are reptiles. It is important to remember that cladograms are not static—they change as fossils of new species are found and their morphology information is entered into data sets. In addition, individual cladograms can vary, depending on the morphology data utilized to make them; thus, this involves the scientist's judgment.

The use of cladistic analyses, combined with the discovery of many new theropod and bird fossils in the last 25 years, has provided more evolutionary steps in the transition of dinosaur to modern birds, as will be discussed below. Together, these new discoveries and the use of cladistics have led to near universal acceptance that birds evolved from dinosaurs. However, there are some paleontologists who do not accept this hypothesis and assume birds evolved from a more basal reptilian ancestor. Additionally, there are some issues yet to be resolved related to birds evolving from dinosaurs, which we will talk about later.

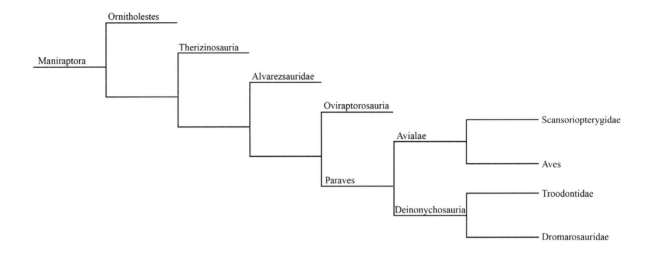

FIGURE 1.2.   Cladogram of the immediate precursors of *Archaeopteryx* (based on Zhang et al. (2008) and Zanno et al. (2009)).

EVOLUTION OF BIRDS

Theropod dinosaurs are characterized by being bipedal; most are carnivorous. *Tyrannosaurus*, *Spinosaurus*, and *Velociraptor* are popular examples of theropod dinosaurs. As reviewed by Zhou (2004), fossils from two clades of the theropod dinosaur lineage, the Deinonychosauria and the Oviraptorosauria (Figure 1.2), indicate that they had member species with feathers. These feathers can be roughly classified into two categories: dinosaur fuzz (non-branched, fluffy, fibrous feathers); and branching feathers of similar structure to flight feathers of today's birds. The filamentous hairlike feathers of *Sinosauropteryx* would fall into the first category, while *Microraptor gui*, *Caudipteryx*, *Pedopenna*, and *Protarchaeopteryx* had branching feathers more similar to present-day flight feathers. *Microraptor gui* and *Pedopenna* are interesting in that modern-type feathers are found on the forelimbs, hind limbs, and tail, giving them a biplane appearance (Xu et al., 2003; Xu and Zhang, 2005).

Initially, the finding of feathered theropod dinosaurs actually created a temporal paradox relative to *Archaeopteryx*, because the aforementioned feathered dinosaurs were all dated to the Cretaceous time period, while *Archaeopteryx* was from the end of the Jurassic period. Thus, how could *Archaeopteryx*, a bird, and a supposed feathered descendant from theropod dinosaurs, actually precede all other known birdlike feathered theropod dinosaurs? This argument was put to rest with the discovery of *Anchiornis huxleyi* (Figure 1.3), a feathered theropod fossil that predates *Archaeopteryx* by 5 to 10 million years (Hu et al., 2009; Xu et al., 2009b). *Anchiornis* is similar to *Microraptor* and *Pedopenna* in having a four-winged, or biplane, appearance with flight feathers on its forelimbs and hind limbs, as well as its tail. Subsequent research and hopefully more fossil finds will help rectify if this biplane arrangement was related to flight evolution (Witmer, 2009), or if it remains a simple curiosity that appeared in a few specimens, since flight-like feathers are not present in most of the birdlike dinosaurs.

As reviewed by Padian and Chiappe (1998), theropod dinosaurs also had several skeletal adaptations found in birds. Fossil evidence indicates theropod dinosaurs had hollow bones, like modern birds. The theropod dinosaurs that are closely related to the bird lineage also had hands that already consisted of only three fingers, which would eventually be fused together as birds evolved. Additionally, the theropod lineage leading to birds also started evolving elongated forelimbs, and *Archaeopteryx* had forelimbs that were longer than the hind limbs. The lengthening of the forelimbs allowed for a stronger flight stroke, and further extension occurred in flighted birds after *Archaeopteryx*. Theropods had long necks and fused clavicles forming the wishbone. They were bipedal with an upright stance, but held their back horizontally just as modern birds do. Finally, they walked on the three middle toes, with the fifth toe shortened and the first toe held higher than the three toes used in walking. Modern birds have very similar and more derived toe structure, as will be discussed in the bird anatomy section of Chapter 4.

Besides some theropod dinosaurs having feathers and many bone features similar to birds, they also had other anatomical and lifestyle similarities. Fossil evidence indicates at least some theropods laid eggs in nests, and likely defended these nests and were involved in brooding the eggs (Norell et al., 1994; Varricchio et al., 1997). A fossil of the theropod *Mei long* (Figure 1.4) shows it to be in the stereotypical sleeping or resting posture (head tucked under one forelimb) found in modern birds (Xu and Norell, 2004). There is also good evidence indicating that theropods had a respiration system that included air sacs similar to modern birds (O'Connor and Claessens, 2005; Sereno et al., 2008).

Although highly controversial, there is limited molecular biology evidence linking dinosaurs and birds (Organ et al., 2008; Schweitzer et al., 2009). In the first report (2008), protein sequences from bone-derived collagen from a 68-million-year-old *Tyrannosaurus rex*, a theropod, were most similar to those from birds. In the subsequent (2009) report, the same research team successfully extracted collagen protein material from an 80-million-year-old hadrosaur, indicating their procedure was repeatable. The new report also supported a molecular connection between birds and dinosaurs. The results have been met with skepticism, in large part because protein material is normally quickly degraded after an animal dies and is rarely found in fossils more than a few hundred thousand years old (Service, 2009). Additionally, there have been technical concerns raised about the research, as reviewed by Service (2009).

FIGURE 1.3   Depiction of *Anchiornis*, a pre-*Archaeopteryx* theropod with feathers.

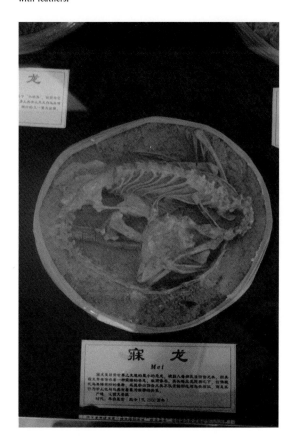

FIGURE 1.4   *Mei Long* fossil in sleeping position similar to modern birds.

EARLY BIRD FORMS THAT EVOLVED AFTER *ARCHAEOPTERYX*

While covering all the known birds that have been identified after *Archaeopteryx* is beyond the scope of this book, a selection of birds

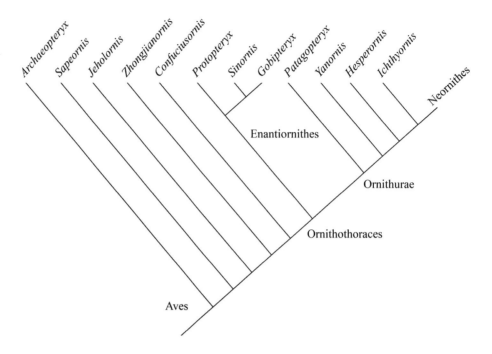

FIGURE 1.5 Phylogenic relationships of early birds, based on Zhou (2004); Zhou et al. (2008); Zhou and Li (2010). Note: Traditionally, *Jeholornis* has been listed as more basal than *Sapeornis* until the more recent phylogenic analysis that included *Zhongjianornis* (Zhou and Li, 2010).

will be covered to provide a road map to the evolution of modern birds (Figure 1.5). Unless otherwise noted, the descriptions for these birds are derived from Zhou (2004), Zhou and Zhang (2007), and Zhou and Li (2010). *Jeholornis* was about the same size as *Archaeopteryx*, but had longer wings and a longer tail containing more caudal vertebrae than *Archaeopteryx'* tail. It was not fully toothed and likely had a stronger flight capability than *Archaeopteryx*, but its rear facing toe (hallux) was not fully reversed. One specimen had preserved stomach contents consisting of several dozen seeds.

Sapeornis was slightly larger than *Archaeopteryx*, but had much longer wings which could have provided more flight capability. *Sapeornis* did not have teeth on its lower jaw and is the first basal bird to have a pygostyle. The pygostyle forms from the fusion of the final few caudal vertebrae into a single ossification that supports musculature and tail feathers. In basal birds, the pygostyle is longer and rod-shaped compared to the shorter plow-shaped form of Ornithurae. The shorter form, which is found in modern birds, allows the tail feathers to fan and retract.

Zhongjianornis, the most basal avian without any teeth in its pointed snout, had wing claws that were smaller and less curved than the proceeding basal birds, which may indicate that it did less climbing. Because the fossil specimen of this pigeon-sized bird did not contain the very rear portion, it is unclear if it had a pygostyle.

Confuciusornis (Figure 1.6) is the oldest bird known to have a horny beak. It lived 120–125 million years ago. However, several subsequent birds retained teeth. It was slightly smaller than *Archaeopteryx* and, as all subsequent birds, it had a pygostyle instead of a long skeletal tail. *Confuciusornis* had a pair of long central tail feathers. Based on the biomechanical (Wang et al., 2011) strength of their narrow primary wing feathers (Nudds and Dyke, 2010) and skeletal anatomy (Zhou and Zhang, 2007), it appears *Confuciusornis* was likely a glider. In fact, *Archaeopteryx*, *Jeholornis*, *Sapeornis*, *Zhongjianornis*, and *Confuciusornis* all had limited flight capability because they lacked the skeletal adaptations needed for sophisticated flight. Most likely they were all gliders; at best, they may have had very limited wing flapping ability during gliding.

Beyond the basal avian birds arose birds classified in the Ornithothoraces. These birds had superior flight capability compared to the basal avian species because of several anatomical changes. Anatomy will be covered in detail in Chapter 4, but ornithothoracines had elongated coracoid bones and a strengthened rib cage to provide skeletal strength for the physical stress of flight and a large keeled sternum to support flight muscles. The ornithothoracines are subdivided into two major groups: the enantiornithines and ornithurines.

The enantiornithine birds are all extinct, but they were the most numerous and widespread birds of the Mesozoic (Martin, 2011). Fossils have been found in North and South America, as well as Australia, Africa, Europe (Martin, 2011), and Asia. There are over 40 named species of enantiornithine birds, but many of the fossils from this branch of birds are just pieces and not complete. Even for the more intact specimens, complete descriptions have often not been made in the literature. Thus, the classification and taxonomy within the enantiornithines have been complicated, and changes often occur in the classifications of this diverse grouping of birds. Enantiornithine birds had more powerful and skilled flight compared to the basal birds, but still very poor flight compared to modern birds. They were smaller in size than the previous basal avian species, and all had a pygostyle, strut-like coracoids, a primitive keel, a compact wing with an alula, and a more elongated synsacrum. Their hallux was reversed and lowered toward the base of the bird leg to provide better perching capability than the basal avian species. Enantiornithines are separated into their own group from subsequent birds because the articulation of the shoulder bones (scapula and the coracoid) is reversed compared to all other birds, and the metatarsals are fused proximally to distally, which is also opposite of modern birds. *Protopteryx* is the oldest known member, with a fossil dating from 140 million years ago.

Ornithurines coexisted with enantiornithines. The Ornithurae lineage ultimately includes all modern birds. These birds had even more advanced flight than the enantiornithines, based on having a deep keel extending along the full length of the sternum, a much shorter pygostyle, and much more skeletal bone fusion. They likely were capable of powerful and skillful flight that was nearly equivalent to that of modern birds. The oldest ornithurines were small like the enantiornithines, but subsequent species became larger shortly thereafter. A few well-known species are briefly described.

Patagopteryx was actually a chicken- or small turkey-sized, flightless bird that had evolved from flighted ancestors (Alvarenga and Bonaparte, 1992; Chiappe, 1995).

Yanoris, dating back to about 120 million years ago, had well-developed flight capabilities similar to modern birds (Zhou and Zhang, 2001), but also was likely a shore wading bird. It was toothed and still retained two claws on each wing. Preserved fish remains in

FIGURE 1.6 This *Confuciusornis* fossil represents the oldest bird known to have a horny beak.

FIGURE I.7a   *Ichthyornis* skeleton restoration with teeth.

FIGURE I.7b and I.7c   Although no present birds have true teeth, the Common Merganser (b) and Keel-billed Toucan (c) have teeth-like ridges on their bills.

stomach, as well as gizzard stones and evidence of plant material, indicate a mixed omnivorous diet.

Hesperornis had a beak with teeth and was a flightless bird adapted for diving. It is assumed that it propelled its dives with its webbed, loon-like feet. Like modern penguins, *Hesperornis* had dense bone mass to reduce buoyancy (Chinsamy et al., 1998).

Ichthyornis fossils have been found from about 85 to 95 million years ago. *Ichthyornis* was about the size of a large pigeon and had a skeletal structure that indicates powerful flight. *Ichthyornis* had a long beak with curved teeth (Figure 1.7 a, b, c) that may have allowed the scooping of fish from or near the surface of water. *Ichthyornis* was widely distributed in North America (Chinsamy et al., 1998).

MODERN BIRD EVOLUTION

At the end of the Cretaceous period (Table 1.1), a large fraction of plant and animal life went extinct, including non-avian dinosaurs, pterosaurs, some bird families, and many fish families. This event is commonly referred to as the K-T or K-Pg extinction event. K is the original abbreviation for Cretaceous and T is the abbreviation for Tertiary—hence the K-T extinction event, which was renamed the K-Pg extinction event when the Paleogene (Pg) period became the official name for the first part of the Tertiary period.

There are many theories on the cause of this extinction, including a large asteroid(s) impacting the earth and/or massive volcano eruptions. Whatever the event or events, it is theorized that sea level and climate changes occurred. Based on current fossil records, the enantiornithes and basal ornithurines, which had radiated throughout much of the world by the end of the Cretaceous period, failed to persist beyond this period. Fossil beds in North America, which are dated to within 300,000 years of the K-T extinction event, indicate the presence of enantiornithes and basal ornithurines (Longrich et al., 2011). Neornithine bird fossils are extremely limited in the Cretaceous period and consist mostly of an array of fragments from many different specimens that cannot be conclusively identified (Mayr, 2009). At best, there may be evidence for the identification of early predecessors of water and game fowl as reviewed by Mayr (2009).

Of the ornithurine birds that survived the K-T extinction event, it was the Neornithes (modern birds) that adapted and radiated in the Paleogene period, and their abundant and diverse fossil record in the early Paleogene period supports this conclusion (James, 2005; Mayr, 2005; Mayr, 2009). Although different in morphology than the birds we see today, the early Paleogene fossils show characteristics of many of our present-day birds like ratites, waterfowl, penguins, and game birds. However, passerine (perching) birds—the most abundant of modern bird species, with over 5,000 known species—did not become abundant in the fossil record until the latter half of the

Paleogene period. Thus, most of the diversity seen within modern birds did not start to become established until after 33 million years ago, and modern species of birds mainly arose in the last 5 million years (James, 2005).

Interestingly, as we will cover shortly in the taxonomy section, there is not a consensus on the higher-level relationships between modern bird species. This lack of agreement on how modern birds relate to each other actually hinders the interpretation of the fossil record of the immediate precursors of modern birds, because the precursor skeletal morphology cannot be examined in relation to a unified data set from modern birds.

CONTROVERSIES AND UNANSWERED QUESTIONS

THE FINGERS OF DINOSAURS AND BIRDS

Paleontologists have traditionally labeled the digits remaining on bird wings (hands) as digits I-II-II. This nomenclature resulted because the fossil record indicated basal theropods traditionally had well-formed digits I-II-III with vestigial fourth and fifth digits, but as the theropod lineage evolves toward *Archaeopteryx*, only digits I-II-III remained. This strongly implied that these same three digits remained in living birds. In contrast, embryological studies on wing morphogenesis in present-day birds such as the chicken clearly indicated that the three remaining digits are II-III-IV (Figure 1.8), as reviewed by Burke and Feduccia (1997). Thus, one of the potential conclusions based on this opposing finger data was that modern birds could not have originated from a theropod lineage, despite the other evidence in favor of this theory.

In 1999 Wagner and Gauthier proposed a frame shift theory (Figure 1.9) as an alternative explanation that acknowledged the validity of both the I-II-III and II-III-IV digit observations (Wagner and Gauthier, 1999). In the frame shift hypothesis, it was assumed that during theropod evolution prior to the origin of *Archaeopteryx*, the embryonic mesenchymal condensations that originally develop into digits II-III-IV entered the developmental pathways of the digits anterior to them. This means that the morphological identity of the digits shifted, so that the embryonic mesenchymal condensations originally associated with digits II-III-IV began developing as digits I-II-III. Subsequent research provided support for the frame shift hypothesis (Vargas and Fallon, 2005; Vargas et al., 2008; Vargas and Wagner, 2009; Uejima et al., 2010). Gene expression data indicated that the most anterior digit (digit II of the II-III-IV) of the embryonic chicken wing has an expression profile that is diagnostic of digit I formation in other species. Experimentally, it was also shown that digits normally developing in positions II, III, and IV

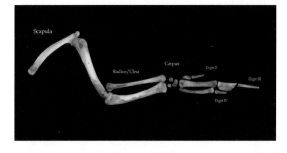

FIGURE 1.8 Modern bird wing and digits II-III-IV.

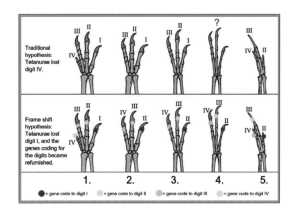

FIGURE 1.9 The Frame-shift Theory is one hypothesis describing how modern birds possess the II-III-IV digit arrangement.

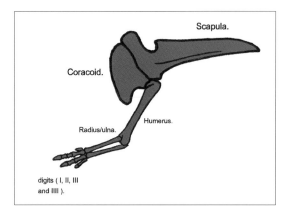

FIGURE 1.10   *Limusaurus* forelimb with reduced Digit I.

could be shifted, so that II and III developed in positions III and IV, and IV was lost, as is normal for position V. In addition, as reviewed by Bever et al. (2011), the Kiwi of New Zealand has only a vestigial wing made up of only two fingers (digits I and II of the I-II-III scheme), and interestingly, they can show a shift such that digit I of the I-II-III scheme can arise from position II or III of the II-III-IV scheme.

Recently, *Limusaurus inextricabilis* was discovered (Xu et al., 2009a). Presently it is the only known beaked herbivorous Jurassic period theropod. Although it is a theropod, it is in a basal lineage that is not one of the direct precursors to the *Archaeopteryx* branch of the theropod family. It has a very small, four-fingered hand consisting of digits I-IV, and digit I is incredibly reduced in size (Figure 1.10). The reduction in digit I suggests that it may have been subsequently lost in future descendants. This scenario provides the first indication that the three digits that were left in later theropods, such as the precursors of birds, were actually digits II, III, and IV, which would agree with the observations from embryonic morphology studies that digits II, III, and IV are the ones that developed in modern birds. In light of the implications of *Limusaurus*'s hand morphology and its evolutionary consequences, the developers of the original frame shift hypothesis have developed a new frame shift model called the Developmental Variability Model (Bever et al., 2011). As with their first hypothesis, the current model incorporates all the theropod digit morphology data and current embryo developmental data into a working hypothesis that will spur more research. Hopefully, in the next few years, the discovery of fossils from several new species of theropod dinosaurs will provide greater insight into the hand morphology of *Archaeopteryx*' immediate predecessors. Ultimately, a definitive answer will be unlikely due to the lack of theropod dinosaur embryology studies, which could indicate which digits were lost.

ARE SOME DINOSAURS FLIGHTLESS BIRDS?

Earlier in this chapter, it was discussed that several theropod dinosaurs had been discovered that had feathers, and that this strengthened the view that theropods were ancestors to *Archaeopteryx*. These feathered dinosaurs have also led to the argument that these dinosaurs actually represent flightless birds. In particular, dromaeosaurids, troodontids, and oviraptorosaurids have all been proposed as flightless birds (Feduccia and Smith, 2002; Paul, 2002). This proposal is also attractive for explaining why some advanced avian features like the pygostyle appeared in some feathered theropod dinosaurs, even though they are not found in all basal birds. If these selected theropods are accepted as flightless birds and not dinosaurs, this also means that *Archaeopteryx* is not the most basal bird, and that origin of birds has yet to be discovered. This is a legitimate hypothesis that currently has less fossil and cladistic support than the *Archaeopteryx* evolutionary lineage.

In part, the proceeding hypothesis also develops from the unease of some people in accepting that the *Archaeopteryx* evolutionary lineage leading to modern birds was occurring at the same time that other related lineages of dinosaurs were continuing to evolve (and in some cases becoming more birdlike) and proliferate. Thus, even if birds descended from one very specific branch of theropod dinosaurs, it does not imply that all of the other lineages of dinosaurs had to stop evolving or disappear from existence. That is the equivalent of saying that humans, as descendants of primates, would prevent the continued evolution or existence of all other primate lineages.

IMMEDIATE ANCESTOR OF NEORNITHES

The origin and the immediate ancestor of all extant bird groups has not been identified. Although many avian fossils have been found, there are still considerable gaps in the avian fossil record, and critical questions must be answered about the evolution and radiation of birds worldwide. Given that there have been more avian fossils found from the Cretaceous time period in the last 20 years than the previous 200 years, there is great optimism that the fossils needed will be found in the near future.

EVOLUTION OF FEATHERS

With the discovery of many feathered theropod dinosaurs that preceded basal birds such as *Archaeopteryx* and *Confuciusornis*, it is clear that feathers evolved before flight. Interpretation of feather fossil data in itself can be difficult for several reasons (Foth, 2011), but especially because the flattening of specimens during fossilization process amplifies the natural effect of overlapping among feathers and a loss of morphological detail, which can lead to misinterpretations. An evolutionary-developmental model for feather development has been established and modified (Prum, 1999; Prum and Brush, 2002) to suggest several stages of feather development, from early feathers consisting of a single filament (stage 1), to formation of a central shaft (stage 3), and finally, specialized feathers that resemble modern flight feathers (stage 5), which will be discussed in greater detail in Chapter 4.

Because the fossil record suggests flight developed well after the first appearance of feathers, the purpose or evolutionary advantage that feathers conferred to organisms is actively investigated. Likely, potential functions of early feathers include insulation, camouflage, and/or social signaling. A role for insulation is likely and would be closely allied with the attainment of thermoregulatory control of body temperature. Thermoregulation occurred during the transition from cold- to warm-blooded species of dinosaurs and likely preceded basal birds. The timing of this transition is hotly debated and beyond the scope of this book.

Besides insulation, feathers may have developed in some species for social signaling. *Beipiaosaurus*, a non-avian theropod, had single broad filament feathers that were most likely used for social signaling rather than insulation because their morphology and distribution was limited to the head, neck, and tail (Xu et al., 2009c). Additionally, the discovery that early feathers almost certainly contained melanosomes, which provided pigmented color and even iridescence to at least some early birds and non-avian dinosaurs (Li et al., 2010; Zhang et al., 2010; Li et al., 2012) also provides an indication that early feathers could have been used for social signaling or camouflage. An analysis of a fossilized *Archaeopteryx* feather (Figure 1.11) suggests that this feather was black in color (Carney et al., 2011).

In modern birds, specialized feathers serve functions that go beyond insulation and social signaling. Fossilized and preserved feathers from the Cretaceous period suggest that specialized feathers may have played such roles in earlier species. Until recently, it was widely accepted that *Confuciusornis sanctus* displayed sexual dimorphism, with males being larger in size and having a pair of elongated central tail feathers. This assumption was based on the fact that some modern-day birds exhibit this sort of sexual dimorphism. However, a recent reanalysis (Peters and Peters, 2009) of existing fossils indicated that the size dimorphism likely does exist, while it is unclear if the dimorphism is male or female

FIGURE 1.11 This *Archaeopteryx* feather fossil was found to contain black pigment.

biased. However, the central tail feathers exist in fossils of all sizes, but many fossils do not have them. The researchers suggest that they may have been used as an anti-predator defense mechanism, as stress-induced shedding of tail feathers can serve this purpose in modern birds. When a predator grabs a bird's tail the feathers fall out and the bird escapes. Additionally, some amber-preserved Cretaceous feathers display specialized features that would have allowed them to potentially absorb water, in a manner akin to the way similar specialized feathers absorb water in the plumage of grebes, to facilitate diving by modifying buoyancy (McKellar et al., 2011).

THE ORIGIN OF BIRD FLIGHT

Surprisingly, the origin of bird flight has been just as contentious as, or even more contentious than, the evolution of birds, as reviewed by Padian and Chiappe (1998) and by Zhou (2004). The arguments can be basically summarized into an arboreal or a cursorial hypothesis for the evolution of flight. As the name implies, the arboreal hypothesis indicates that the ancestors of modern birds lived in trees or climbed trees and started flying by gliding down from branch to branch or tree to tree. As feathers became more structured and stronger, flapping flight would have started to evolve during the gliding until birds had the flight muscles developed to sustain airborne flight. As discussed previously, many of the basal birds had wing structure to support gliding flight. Additionally, the claws that remained on their wings could have allowed them to climb trees much like the present-day hoatzin (Figure 1.12 a & b), a bird whose chicks still have claws on their first and second wing digits that help them climb about their surroundings (Burnham et al., 2010). However, in the case of *Archaeopteryx*, the fossils of this species have been found in environments that had plants no taller than a few meters making the arboreal hypothesis questionable. But as reviewed by Zhou (2004), there is evidence for a few arboreal theropods.

The cursorial hypothesis implies that basal bird species ran along the ground with their forearms outstretched for balance as they pursued prey or ran from predators. Forearms covered with feathers would have increased lift, and as these feathers grew longer and stronger, more lift would have been generated until the animal was off the ground. Then, as in the other hypothesis, full flight would have eventually evolved. This hypothesis is strengthened by the fact that theropod ancestors of birds were terrestrial, long-legged, bipedal, and lightweight.

In the end, the debate about whether flight developed from the ground or from trees does not matter, because it is impossible to prove definitively (Padian, 2003). Furthermore, there is no reason to assume that both hypotheses are not correct, because there is no evidence to suggest that any of the basal birds (*Archaeopteryx*, *Jeholornis*, *Sapeornis*, *Confuciusornis*) were skilled fliers, and thus

FIGURE 1.12a Adult Hoatzin.

FIGURE 1.12b The hoatzin chick has retained primitive claws on its wings to help it climb around in its surroundings.

strong flapping flight may have developed differently in different birds. As will be discussed in Chapter 4, flight in many large-bodied modern birds is also initiated based on a running start or jumping from an elevated position.

TAXONOMY

Taxonomy is the classification of organisms into categories based on the relationships among the organisms. Taxonomy depends heavily on phylogenetics, or phylogenetic systematics, which is the study of evolutionary relatedness among organisms. The relatedness of species is based on morphology and molecular genetic analyses. The classification of animal species uses taxonomic ranks, including domain (super kingdom), kingdom, phylum, class, order, family, genus, and species. The different ranks are used to signify evolutionary distances among organisms. Thus, two organisms which belonged to two different domains would be the most distantly related, while the relatedness of two organisms will increase if they are positioned together in each of the subsequent ranks.

TAXONOMY OF BIRDS

The taxonomy of a common North American bird, the Northern Cardinal (Figure 1.13), would be:

Domain	Eukaryota	an organism whose cells have a true nucleus and organelles that perform specific cellular functions
Kingdom	Animalia	Animals
Phylum	Chordata	animals with backbones
Class	Aves	animals defined as birds
Order	Passeriformes	perching birds
Family	Cardinalidae	all cardinals; there are 52 species
Genus	*Cardinalis*	similar cardinals; there are 3 species
Species	*Cardinalis cardinalis*	Northern Cardinal

FIGURE 1.13 Northern Cardinal, male.

The International Code of Zoological Nomenclature that regulates the scientific naming of organisms does allow the intraspecific rank within species of subspecies. For birds, subspecies are often designated within a species based on differences in size or plumage coloration, and subspecies are typically geographically isolated from one another. In our example of the Northern Cardinal, there are subspecies that are readily distinguishable based on plumage pattern and bill shape, such as the Eastern Northern Cardinal (*Cardinalis cardinalis cardinalis*) and the Southwestern Northern Cardinal (*Cardinalis cardinalis superbus*).

All other extant and recently extinct bird species would follow the same classification scheme presented in the example for the Northern Cardinal. However, while there will not be any disagreements among avian taxonomists for the categories of domain, kingdom, phylum or class, considerable disagreements can be found among experts when it comes to the categories of order, family, genus, and species.

BIRD SPECIES

The total number of species of birds varies slightly, depending on the authority composing the list and typically reflects whether something is classified as a subspecies or a distinct species. This book follows the number of species currently recognized by BirdLife International, because this is also the source for the current population status (extinct, threatened, etc.) of bird species used in subsequent chapters. BirdLife International recognizes a total of 10,052 bird species which are either extant or extinct in their searchable database (http://www.birdlife.org/datazone/species/search; searched 11/15/2011). Avian researchers that classify birds also disagree on the number of bird families that exist. BirdLife International recognizes 198 bird families.

BIRD ORDERS AND FAMILY CLASSIFICATIONS

There is also no agreement among bird phylogeneticists as to the number of bird orders. This is not surprising, because the science of how bird families relate to one another and for that matter, how individual bird species relate to one another, is rapidly evolving. Traditionally, bird species were classified based on morphological data, with those being most similar to each other grouped in the same genus, while those that were not similar were placed in a different genus. Similar genera are then placed in families, which are then placed in orders based on family similarities. These morphological studies continue, and one of the most exhaustive was completed by Livezey and Zusi, who developed a cladogram illustrating the interrelationships between bird orders and families (Livezey and Zusi, 2006, 2007). In addition to morphological analyses, molecular studies using DNA analyses are now being routinely completed, and several cladograms have resulted from a few extensive research reports (Sibley et al., 1988; Sibley and Ahlquist, 1990; Ericson et al., 2006; Hackett et al., 2008; Pacheco et al., 2011).

Although several cladograms based on morphology and molecular genetic studies have been produced, the nature of the relationships between bird families and orders is far from being completed. However, the availability of molecular genetic analyses to analyze mitochondrial and nuclear gene sequences across representatives from all bird families is quickly building a data bank that will solve the evolutionary interrelationships between bird orders and families.

CONVERGENT EVOLUTION

Ultimately, the hope is that far-reaching molecular genetic analyses in the number of genes and species from each bird family studied will define the evolutionary relationships among bird families and species. Such data, when it exists, will be superior to morphology analyses because it will not be influenced by the ecology and behavior of species. Convergent evolution—the evolution of similar traits in unrelated lineages—can obscure true evolutionary unrelatedness. For example, the platypus has a duck-like bill and is a mammal rather than a bird. Swifts (order: Apodiformes) and swallows (order: Passeriformes) both catch insects in flight and externally have a similar appearance (Figure 1.14 a & b), but they are not closely related. There are numerous other examples of convergent evolution (Fain and Houde, 2004). However, because molecular data sets are often very small at this stage, involving only a few genes, they can also lead to homoplasy, and thus lead to declarations of relatedness that do not exist (Mayr, 2011). As a result, currently the best approach to bird classification is still to utilize both morphological and molecular genetic data (Mayr, 2011).

TAXONOMY OF NEORNITHES

Amazingly, there is more agreement for the early evolutionary events of Neornithes, (modern birds, Figure 1.15) than later ones. It is generally accepted that the Neornithes can be divided into clades: the Palaeognathae and Neognathae. For extant birds, the Palaeognathae include the tinamous and the ratites. There is further agreement that the Neognathae group can be further subdivided into Galloanseres and Neoaves. The Galloanseres contain the sister groups of Galliformes (landfowl) and Anseriformes (waterfowl). Beyond this agreement, the interrelationships of bird orders and families remains to be completely defined, especially for the ratites of the Palaeognathae and within the Neoaves.

The following is a list of potential bird orders for modern birds.

FIGURE 1.14a   Barn Swallow. Swallows and swifts appear similar, yet they are grouped in separate orders.

FIGURE 1.14b   Horus Swift

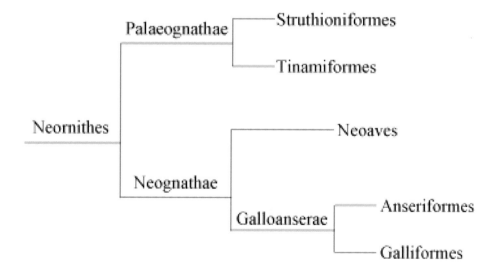

FIGURE 1.15   Phylogenetic relationship of modern birds.

PALAEOGNATHAE BIRD ORDERS:

Struthioniformes (Ostriches, Emus, Kiwis, Rheas, and Cassowaries)
Tinamiformes (tinamous)

NEOGNATHAE BIRD ORDERS:

WITHIN GALLOANSERAE:

Anseriformes (waterfowl: swans, geese, ducks, and allies)
Galliformes (landfowl: pheasants, grouse, quail, guinea fowl, and allies)

WITHIN NEOAVES

Sphenisciformes (penguins)
Gaviiformes (loons)
Podicipediformes (grebes)
Procellariiformes (albatrosses, shearwaters, storm-petrels, and allies)
Pelecaniformes (pelicans, cormorants, gannets, and allies)
Ciconiiformes (storks, herons, egrets, spoonbills, and allies)
Phoenicopteriformes (flamingos)
Falconiformes (falcons, hawks, eagles, and allies)
Gruiformes (cranes, rails, and allies)
Charadriiformes (plovers, gulls, sandpipers, and allies)
Columbiformes (pigeons, doves, and sandgrouse)
Psittaciformes (parrots and allies)
Cuculiformes (cuckoos)
Musophagiformes (turacos)
Opisthocomiformes (hoatzin)
Strigiformes (owls)
Caprimulgiformes (nightjars and allies)
Apodiformes (swifts and hummingbirds)
Colliiformes (mousebirds)
Trogoniformes (trogons)
Coraciiformes (kingfishers, rollers, and allies)
Piciformes (woodpeckers and allies)
Passeriformes (passerines)

This list was not presented in a cladogram because, as indicated previously, the evolutionary relationships between most of the orders are not well defined. Gerald Mayr recently reviewed (2011) the phylogeny of present-day birds and produced a tentative cladogram that depicts the evolutionary relationships between the orders and major families of birds, while accounting for both morphological and molecular genetic results, to reach evolutionary relationship conclusions.

Overall, the list of bird orders presented is conservative in total number, and balances morphology and molecular-based results. Potential differences (additions and subtractions) in this list of bird orders can be found in the literature, and the most notable potential differences will be highlighted. One of the most controversial classifications in bird taxonomy involves the order Struthioniformes (ratites), which includes Ostriches, Rheas, Cassowaries, Emu, and Kiwis. While there is general agreement that Cassowaries (Figure 1.16 a) and Emus (Figure 1.16 b) are closely related and are often grouped into an order named Casuariiformes, there is much debate about their relationship with other ratites (Ostriches, Rheas, and Kiwis) and the other ratites with each other. The orders Rheiformes (Rheas) and Apterygiformes (Kiwis) have also been named, leaving the order Struthioniformes with only Ostriches. Except for the small, flightless Kiwis, the other ratites are large flightless birds that may have similar morphological features due to convergent evolution. Thus, morphology-based analyses have not robustly conferred the relationships between ratites. Thus far, molecular DNA data has also not definitively defined the relationships between the ratites (Mayr, 2011). Therefore, the ratites remained as a single order in the above list, with the expectation that separation into additional orders will eventually be strongly supported as more molecular genetic studies are completed.

Similarly, the order Falconiformes is also very contentious. This order contains the families Cathartidae (New World vultures), Accipitridae (hawks, kites, eagles, Old World vultures, and allies), Sagittardiiae (Secretary Bird, Figure 1.17), and Falconidae (falcons and allies), which will all be discussed in the raptor chapter. Morphology data places the Accipitridae, Sagittardiiae, and Falconidae together (Livezey and Zusi, 2007). The New World vultures have always been problematic in their classification. While New World vultures share their carrion-feeding lifestyle and bare heads and necks with the Old World vultures, they differ significantly with regard to internal morphology and behavior (Ligon, 1967; König, 1982; Rea, 1983). In fact, some of these morphology and behavioral differences more closely align them with storks (Ciconiidae) than with Old World vultures. Initial molecular DNA research by Sibley and Ahlquist (1990) supported this link, and they were placed as a family in the Ciconiidae order (Sibley and Monroe, 1990). Subsequent molecular genetic research indicates that Cathartidae are not closely related to birds of the Ciconiidae order, but do have affinity with Accipitridae and Segittardiiae, but not Falconidae (Ericson et al., 2006; Hackett et al., 2008). This research also indicates that Falconidae also are not affiliated with the Accipitridae. Thus, the molecular data supports the formation of an Accipitriformes order made up of the Cathartidae, Segittardiiae, and Accipitridae, while the Falconiformes order retains falcons and their allies.

In some classifications, is not unusual to see the Musophagiformes order eliminated and instead be included as a family in the Cuculiformes order, based on morphology similarities. But genetic molecular analyses strongly support the separation of the Musophagiformes and Cuculiformes orders, as reviewed by Mayr (2011). It is also not uncommon to see sandgrouse separated

FIGURE 1.16a Southern Cassowary

FIGURE 1.16b Emu

FIGURE 1.17 Secretary Bird

into their own order, called Pteroclidiformes, instead of being listed as a family within the Columbiformes order. Morphology analyses highly support the placement of sandgrouse in the Columbiformes order, and some molecular analyses support the morphology-based conclusion, while other analyses show them to be separate orders, as reviewed by Mayr (2011). Puffbirds and Jacamars were given their own order, Galbuliformes, by Sibley and Monroe (1990) based on DNA analysis, but they are more typically placed with the Piciformes order, based on strong morphology similarities (Livezey and Zusi, 2007). Finally, it is not uncommon to find the tropicbirds (Phaethontidae) separated from the Pelecaniformes order into their own order, Phaethontiformes. The tropicbirds share strong morphological characteristics with the rest of the Pelecaniformes members, but sequence-based molecular data weakly separates the tropicbirds from other members of the Pelecaniformes, as reviewed by Mayr (2011).

SUMMARY

The evolution and taxonomy of birds is highly contentious. With the continued examination of extant birds with new molecular techniques and continued morphological characterization, there is no doubt that the relationships between all living birds will be characterized in the future. As further fossils are found, the evolution of birds will become clearer, but many mysteries—such as if the origin of flight was from the ground up or from the trees down, as well as the embryonic development of the hand in basal birds—are unanswerable and will simply be debated for years to come.

REFERENCES

Alvarenga, H. M. F. and J. F. Bonaparte. 1992. A new flightless landbird from the Cretaceous of Patagonia. Los Angeles: Natural History Museum of Los Angeles, Los Angeles.

Bever, G. S., J. A. Gauthier, and G. P. Wagner. 2011. Finding the frame shift: Digit loss, developmental variability, and the origin of the avian hand. *Evolution and Development* **13**:269–279.

Burke, A. C. and A. Feduccia. 1997. Developmental patterns and the identification of the homologies in the avian hand. *Science* **278**:666–669.

Burnham, D. A., A. Feduccia, L. D. Martin, and A. R. Falk. 2010. Tree climbing: A fundamental avian adaptation. *Journal of Systematic Palaeontology* **9**:103–107.

Carney, R., J. Vinther, M. Shawkey, L. D'Alba, and J. Ackermann. 2011. Black feather color in Archaeopteryx. *Society of Vertebrate Paleontology Annual Meeting Abstracts*:84.

Chiappe, L. M. 1995. The phylogenetic position of the Cretaceous birds of Argentina: Enantiornithes and Patagopteryx deferrariisi. *Courier Forschungsinstitut Senckenberg* **181**:55–63.

Chinsamy, A., L. D. Martin, and P. Dodson. 1998. Bone microstructure of the diving *Hesperornis* and the volant *Ichthyornis* from the Niobrara Chalk of western Kansas. *Cretaceous Research* **19**:225–235.

Ericson, P. G. P., C. L. Anderson, T. Britton, A. Elzanowski, U. S. Johansson, M. Kallersjo, J. I. Ohlson, T. J. Parsons, D. Zuccon, and G. Mayr. 2006. Diversification of Neoaves: Integration of molecular sequence data and fossils. *Biology Letters* **2**:543–U541.

Fain, M. G. and P. Houde. 2004. Parallel radiations in the primary clades of birds. *Evolution* **58**:2558–2573.

Feduccia, A. and K. G. Smith. 2002. Birds Are Dinosaurs: Simple Answer to a Complex Problem. *Auk* **119**:1187–1201.

Foth, C. 2011. On the identification of feather structures in stem-line representatives of birds: Evidence from fossils and actuopalaeontology. *Paläontologische Zeitschrift*:1–12.

Hackett, S. J., R. T. Kimball, S. Reddy, R. C. K. Bowie, E. L. Braun, M. J. Braun, J. L. Chojnowski, W. A. Cox, K.-L. Han, J. Harshman, C. J. Huddleston, B. D. Marks, K. J. Miglia, W. S. Moore, F. H. Sheldon, D. W. Steadman, C. C. Witt, and T. Yuri. 2008. A Phylogenomic Study of Birds Reveals Their Evolutionary History. *Science* **320**:1763–1768.

Heilmann, G. 1926. *The Origin of Birds*. H. F. & G. Witherby, London.

Hu, D., L. Hou, L. Zhang, and X. Xu. 2009. A pre-Archaeopteryx troodontid theropod from China with long feathers on the metatarsus. *Nature* **461**:640–643.

Huxley, T. H. 1868. On the animals which are most nearly intermediate between birds and reptiles. *The Annals and Magazine of Natural History* **4**:66–65.

Huxley, T. H. 1870. Further evidence of the affinity between the dinosaurian reptiles and birds. *Quarterly Journal of the Geological Society of London* **26**:12–31.

James, H. F. 2005. Paleogene fossils and the radiation of modern birds. *Auk* **122**:1049–1054.

König, C. 1982. Zur systematischen Stellung der Neuweltgeier (Cathartidae). *Journal of Ornithology* **123**:259–267.

Li, Q., K.-Q. Gao, Q. Meng, J. A. Clarke, M. D. Shawkey, L. D'Alba, R. Pei, M. Ellison, M. A. Norell, and J. Vinther. 2012. Reconstruction of Microraptor and the Evolution of Iridescent Plumage. *Science* **335**:1215–1219.

Li, Q., K.-Q. Gao, J. Vinther, M. D. Shawkey, J. A. Clarke, L. D'Alba, Q. Meng, D. E. G. Briggs, and R. O. Prum. 2010. Plumage Color Patterns of an Extinct Dinosaur. *Science* **327**:1369–1372.

Ligon, J. D. 1967. Relationships of the cathartid vultures. Occasional Papers of the Museum of Zoology **651**:1–26.

Livezey, B. and R. Zusi. 2006. Higher-order phylogeny of modern birds (Theropoda, Aves: Neornithes) based on comparative anatomy: I.—Methods and characters. *Bulletin of Carnegie Museum of Natural History* **37**:1–544.

Livezey, B. C. and R. L. Zusi. 2007. Higher-order phylogeny of modern birds (Theropoda, Aves: Neornithes) based on comparative anatomy. II. Analysis and discussion. *Zoological Journal of the Linnean Society* **149**:1–95.

Longrich, N. R., T. Tokaryk, and D. J. Field. 2011. Mass extinction of birds at the Cretaceous-Paleogene (K-Pg) boundary. *Proceedings of the National Academy of Science* **108**:15253–15257.

Martin, L. D. 2011. The other half of avian evolution: Cyril Walker's contribution. *Journal of Systematic Palaeontology* **9**:3–8.

Mayr, G. 2005. The Paleogene fossil record of birds in Europe. *Biological Reviews* **80**:515–542.

Mayr, G. 2009. *Paleogene Fossil Birds*. Springer, Heidelberg.

Mayr, G. 2011. Metaves, Mirandornithes, Strisores and other novelties: A critical review of the higher-level phylogeny of neornithine birds. *Journal of Zoological Systematics and Evolutionary Research* **49**:58–76.

McKellar, R. C., B. D. E. Chatterton, A. P. Wolfe, and P. J. Currie. 2011. A Diverse Assemblage of Late Cretaceous Dinosaur and Bird Feathers from Canadian Amber. *Science* **333**:1619–1622.

Norell, M. A., J. M. Clark, D. Demberelyin, B. Rhinchen, L. M. Chiappe, A. R. Davidson, M. C. McKenna, P. Altangerel, and M. J. Novacek. 1994. A Theropod Dinosaur Embryo and the Affinities of the Flaming Cliffs Dinosaur Eggs. *Science* **266**:779–782.

Nudds, R. L. and G. J. Dyke. 2010. Narrow primary feather rachises in *Confuciusornis* and *Archaeopteryx* suggest poor flight ability. *Science* **328**:887–889.

O'Connor, P. M. and L. P. A. M. Claessens. 2005. Basic avian pulmonary design and flow-through ventilation in non-avian theropod dinosaurs. *Nature* **436**:253–256.

Organ, C. L., M. H. Schweitzer, W. Zheng, L. M. Freimark, L. C. Cantley, and J. M. Asara. 2008. Molecular pylogenetics of Mastodon and Tyrannosaurus rex. *Science* **320**:499.

Ostrom, J. H. 1969. Osteology of *Deinonychus antirrhopus*, an unusual theropod from the Lower Cretaceous of Montana. *Bulletin of the Peabody Museum of Natural History* **30**:1–165.

Ostrom, J. H. 1970. Archaeopteryx: Notice of a "New" Specimen. *Science* **170**:537–538.

Ostrom, J. H. 1975. The origin of birds. *Annual Review of Earth and Planetary Sciences* **3**:55–77.

Ostrom, J. H. 1976. Archaeopteryx and the origin of birds. *Biological Journal of the Linnean Society* **8**:91–182.

Pacheco, M. A., F. U. Battistuzzi, M. Lentino, R. F. Aguilar, S. Kumar, and A. A. Escalante. 2011. Evolution of modern birds revealed by mitogenomics: Timing the radiation and origin of major orders. *Molecular Biology and Evolution* **28**:1927–1942.

Padian, K. 2003. Four-winged dinosaurs, bird precursors, or neither? *BioScience* **53**:451–453.

Padian, K. and L. M. Chiappe. 1998. *The Origin of Birds and Their Flight*. Scientific American. Nature Publishing Group, New York.

Paul, G. 2002. *Dinosaurs of the air: The evolution and loss of flight in dinosaurs and birds*. Johns Hopkins University Press, Baltimore, USA.

Peters, W. S. and D. S. Peters. 2009. Life history, sexual dimorphism and "ornamental" feathers in the Mesozoic bird Confuciusornis sanctus. *Biology Letters* **5**:817-820.

Prum, R. O. 1999. Development and evolutionary origin of feathers. *Journal of Experimental Zoology* **285**:291–306.

Prum, R. O. and A. H. Brush. 2002. The evolutionary origin and diversification of feathers. *Quarterly Review of Biology* **77**:261–295.

Rea, A. M. 1983. Cathartid affinities: A brief overview. Pages 26–54 *in* S. R. Wilbur and J. A. Jackson, editors. *Vulture Biology and Management*. University of California Press.

Schweitzer, M. H., W. Zheng, C. L. Organ, R. Avci, Z. Suo, L. M. Freimark, V. S. Lebleu, M. B. Duncan, M. G. Vander Heiden, J. M. Neveu, W. S. Lane, J. S. Cottrell, J. R. Horner, L. C. Cantley, R. Kalluri, and J. M. Asara. 2009. Biomolecular Characterization and Protein Sequences of the Campanian Hadrosaur B. canadensis. *Science* **324**:626–631.

Sereno, P. C., R. N. Martinez, J. A. Wilson, D. J. Varricchio, O. A. Alcober, and H. C. E. Larsson. 2008. Evidence for Avian Intrathoracic Air Sacs in a New Predatory Dinosaur from Argentina. *PLoS ONE* **3**:e3303.

Service, R. F. 2009. "Protein" in 80-Million-Year-Old Fossil Bolsters Controversial *T. rex* Claim. *Science* **324**:578.

Sibley, C. G. and J. E. Ahlquist. 1990. *Phylogeny and Classification of Birds: A Study in Molecular Evolution.* Yale University Press, New Haven, Connecticut.

Sibley, C. G., J. E. Ahlquist, and B. L. Monroe. 1988. A classification of the living birds of the world based on DNA-DNA hybridization studies. *Auk* **105**:409–423.

Sibley, C. G. and B. L. Monroe. 1990. *Distribution and Taxonomy of Birds of the World.* Yale Universitiy Press, New Haven, Connecticut.

Uejima, A., T. Amano, N. Nomura, M. Noro, T. Yasue, T. Shiroishi, K. Ohta, H. Yokoyama, and K. Tamura. 2010. Anterior shift in gene expression precedes anteriormost digit formation in amniote limbs. *Development, Growth & Differentiation* **52**:223–234.

Vargas, A. O. and J. F. Fallon. 2005. Birds have dinosaur wings: The molecular evidence. *Journal of Experimental Zoology* **304B**:86-90.

Vargas, A. O., T. Kohlsdorf, J. F. Fallon, J. V. Brooks, and G. P. Wagner. 2008. The evolution of HoxD-11 expression in the bird wing: Insights from Alligator mississippiensis. *PLoS ONE* **3**:e3325.

Vargas, A. O. and G. P. Wagner. 2009. Frame-shifts of digit identity in bird evolution and Cyclopamine-treated wings. *Evolution and Development* **11**:163–169.

Varricchio, D. J., F. Jackson, J. J. Borkowski, and J. R. Horner. 1997. Nest and egg clutches of the dinosaur Troodon formosus and the evolution of avian reproductive traits. *Nature* **385**:247–250.

Wagner, G. P. and J. A. Gauthier. 1999. 1,2,3 = 2,3,4: A solution to the problem of the homology of the digits in the avian hand. *Proceedings of the National Academy of Science* **96**:5111–5116.

Wang, X., R. L. Nudds, and G. J. Dyke. 2011. The primary feather lengths of early birds with respect to avian wing shape evolution. *Journal of Evolutionary Biology* **24**:1226–1231.

Witmer, L. M. 2009. Palaeontology: Feathered dinosaurs in a tangle. *Nature* **461**:601–602.

Xu, X., J. M. Clark, J. Mo, J. Choiniere, C. A. Forster, G. M. Erickson, D. W. E. Hone, C. Sullivan, D. A. Eberth, S. Nesbitt, Q. Zhao, R. Hernandez, C.-k. Jia, F.-l. Han, and Y. Guo. 2009a. A Jurassic ceratosaur from China helps clarify avian digital homologies. *Nature* **459**:940–944.

Xu, X. and M. A. Norell. 2004. A new troodontid dinosaur from China with avian-like sleeping posture. *Nature* **431**:838–841.

Xu, X. and F. Zhang. 2005. A new maniraptoran dinosaur from China with long feathers on the metatarsus. *Naturwissenschaften* **92**:173–177.

Xu, X., Q. Zhao, M. Norell, C. Sullivan, D. Hone, G. Erickson, X. Wang, F. Han, and Y. Guo. 2009b. A new feathered maniraptoran dinosaur fossil that fills a morphological gap in avian origin. *Chinese Science Bulletin* **54**:430–435.

Xu, X., X. Zheng, and H. You. 2009c. A new feather type in a non-avian theropod and the early evolution of feathers. *Proceedings of the National Academy of Sciences* **106**:832–834.

Xu, X., Z. Zhou, X. Wang, X. Kuang, F. Zhang, and X. Du. 2003. Four-winged dinosaurs from China. *Nature* **421**:335–340.

Zanno, L. E., D. D. Gillette, L. B. Albright, and A. L. Titus. 2009. A new North American therizinosaurid and the role of herbivory in "predatory" dinosaur evolution. *Proceedings of the Royal Society B: Biological Sciences* **276**:3505–3511.

Zhang, F., S. L. Kearns, P. J. Orr, M. J. Benton, Z. Zhou, D. Johnson, X. Xu, and X. Wang. 2010. Fossilized melanosomes and the color of Cretaceous dinosaurs and birds. *Nature* **463**:1075–1078.

Zhang, F., Z. Zhou, X. Xu, X. Wang, and C. Sullivan. 2008. A bizarre Jurassic maniraptoran from China with elongate ribbonlike feathers. *Nature* **455**:1105–1108.

Zhou, Z. 2004. The origin and early evolution of birds: Discoveries, disputes, and perspectives from fossil evidence. *Naturwissenschaften (The Science of Nature)* **91**:455–471.

Zhou, Z., J. Clarke, and F. Zhang. 2008. Insight into diversity, body size, and morphological evolution from the largest Early Cretaceous enantiornithine bird. *Journal of Anatomy* **212**:565–577.

Zhou, Z. and F. Z. Z. Li. 2010. A new Lower Cretaceous bird from China and tooth reduction in early avian evolution. *Proceedings of the Royal Society B: Biological Sciences* **277**:219–227.

Zhou, Z. and F. Zhang. 2001. Two new ornithurine birds from the Early Cretaceous of western Liaoning, China. *Chinese Science Bulletin* **46**:1258–1264.

Zhou, Z. and F. Zhang. 2007. Mesozoic birds of China—a synoptic review. *Frontiers of Biology in China* **2**:1–14.

II THE CURRENT STATE OF BIRDS

Because birds occupy nearly every ecological niche in the world, they are excellent indicators of environmental conditions. If the well-being and population of birds decreases in a given habitat, that can be a significant warning sign that the local ecosystem is not healthy. Therefore, current bird populations, as well as population trends of birds over time, are often closely monitored by environmentalists to help determine the quality of ecosystems. Ultimately, assuring the health of all the components of our environment is essential for our own well-being and survival.

MONITORING AND CLASSIFYING BIRD POPULATIONS

The International Union for Conservation of Nature (IUCN) is the world's oldest and largest environmental organization, whose mission is to influence, encourage, and assist societies throughout the world to conserve the integrity and diversity of nature. It supports scientific research, manages field projects and influences policy makers at the international, national, and company levels to promote and sustain biodiversity, fight climate change, and promote a greening of the world economy (http://www.iucn.org). One of IUCN's many functions is its role in the production of the IUCN Red List (http://www.iucnredlist.org). This list provides taxonomic, conservation status, and geographic distribution information for all known plants and animal species, with the hope of bringing attention to those species most in need of conservation and to the overall magnitude of threatened biodiversity.

One of the partners for the production of the IUCN Red List is BirdLife International, which helps assess the worldwide status of all bird species. This is reported in the IUCN Red List and is maintained in a searchable BirdLife International species data base (http://

FIGURE 2.1   The Bald Eagle was once listed as endangered on the IUCN Red List. Through captive breeding and management programs, the species thrived and was gradually downlisted to its current status, Least Concern.

www.birdlife.org/datazone/species/search). BirdLife International is a global partnership of conservation organizations whose mission is to conserve birds, their habitats, and global biodiversity. Their goals include preventing the extinction of any bird species, to maintain, and where possible, improve the conservation status of all bird species, and to conserve, improve, and enlarge habitats important to birds (http://www.birdlife.org/worldwide/index.html).

There are nine categories in the IUCN Red List system: extinct; extinct in the wild; critically endangered; endangered; vulnerable; near threatened; least concern; data deficient; and not evaluated. Species classified in the critically endangered, endangered, and vulnerable categories are considered threatened for extinction. Classification into the various categories is based on the risk of extinction, which is determined by population size, rate of population decline, area of geographic distribution, and the degree of population and geographic distribution fragmentation. A species is declared extinct only when exhaustive population surveys have been conducted throughout its entire historic range in its known habitat and at times when it should be present and active. The extinct-in-the-wild classification is used to describe a species which has been declared extinct in the wild, but for which individuals exist in captivity. Critically endangered species are those facing an **extremely high risk** of extinction in the wild, based on meeting one or more of the following Red List criteria:

1. Population decline >80% over ten years or three generations;
2. Having a range size <100 km2 and declining, severely fragmented, or restricted to one location;
3. Occupied range <10 km2 and declining, severely fragmented, or restricted to one location;
4. Population <250 mature individuals and declining with a specified population structure;
5. Population <50 mature individuals;
6. Quantified probability of extinction >50% in ten years or three generations.

Endangered species are those that still meet one of the criteria described for critically endangered species. However, endangered species are considered only to be facing a **very high risk** of extinction in the wild. Vulnerable species are equivalent to endangered species, except that they are only considered to be facing a **high risk** of extinction in the wild. Near-threatened species are those that currently do not qualify for being listed as critically endangered, endangered, or vulnerable and thus threatened, but are close to qualifying or are likely to qualify for one of the threatened designations in the near future. Species placed in the least concern category are those that are widespread and abundant. Species are listed as data deficient when there is not information available to make a direct or indirect assessment of the risk of extinction, because distribution and/or population abundance data is lacking.

DECLARING A SPECIES EXTINCT

The extinct declaration is very conservatively made because conservation funding is not targeted for species considered extinct, and also to minimize the occurrence of a species being considered extinct only to have it rediscovered at a later date. There are several notable bird species that were feared extinct only to be discovered later, such as the Banggai Crow ("Banggai Crow," 2012), Cerulean Paradise-flycatcher (Riley and Wardill, 2001), Cebu Flowerpecker, (Dutson et al., 1993), Forest Owlet (King and Rasmussen, 1998), Indigo-winged or Fuertes Parrot ("Indigo-winged Parrot," 2012), and Jerdon's Courser (Bhushan, 1986). All six of these species were rediscovered more than 80 years after the last record of their existence. Additionally, often the extensive definitive population surveys that are needed for the extinction declaration have not been completed or local and unconfirmed reports of the species have not been discounted (Butchart et al., 2006b). Therefore, within the critically endangered designation, a subcategory labeled as "possibly extinct" was established for bird species on the IUCN Red Book (Butchart et al., 2006b). To be considered for listing in this new category, Butchart and colleagues examined critically endangered species while considering factors that favored extinction: well-documented declines in population; severe threatening processes existed and were documented, such as intensive hunting or habitat destruction; the species possessed attributes known to predispose it to extinction, like having a tiny geographic range; and recent surveys were adequate to detect the species, but failed to do so. Butchart et al. (2006) also considered in their analysis factors against the extinction designation for each species, such as recent field surveys being inadequate to detect the species, the species is difficult to detect, suitable habitat for its existence remained and reasonably convincing reports of its existence or unconfirmed sightings existed. Finally, the factors considered for and against extinction were weighed in the context of the number of years (<10, >10, >50 or >100) since the last record of existence was documented, with the greater passage of time favoring extinction. Butchart et al. (2006) concluded that 15 bird species should be classified as possibly extinct.

BirdLife International currently recognizes 10,052 species of birds (Table 2.1). The number of described bird species is greater than the number of described mammalian (5,488), reptilian (8,734), and amphibian (6,347) species on the IUCN Red List. Despite having over 10,000 recognized species, birds are one of the best known and are the best-studied taxonomic groups, with less than 1 percent of bird species on the IUCN Red List having insufficient information available to be classified as data deficient (Vié et al., 2009). The 132 extinct bird species (Table 2.1) has been calculated from the year 1500. Obviously, the number of extinct birds from their initial evolution to present day is much higher, with hypothetical estimates indicating that possibly 150,000 bird species may have existed throughout history (Fuller, 1987) and 12,000 extinct species are known from the fossil records of birds (Harris, 2009).

TABLE 2.I CURRENT EXTINCTION THREAT LEVELS IN BIRDS

IUCN Red Book category	Number of bird species[1]
Extinct	132
Extinct in the wild	4
Critically endangered[2]	189
Endangered	382
Vulnerable	682
Near threatened	844
Least concern	7757
Data deficient	62
Total	10,052

[1]DATA FROM BIRDLIFE INTERNATIONAL AS OF II/I5/20II. (http://www.birdlife.org/datazone/species/search).

[2]WITHIN THE CRITICALLY ENDANGERED CATEGORY, I4 SPECIES ARE CONSIDERED POSSIBLY EXTINCT, AND ONE SPECIES IS CONSIDERED POSSIBLY EXTINCT IN THE WILD.

The percentage of threatened birds (extinct in the wild, critically endangered, endangered, and threatened) from the total of 9,920 living bird species is 12.67 percent—or roughly 1 out of every 8 bird species is facing a high risk of extinction. Furthermore, there are already 682 species of birds that are listed as vulnerable and could soon join the ranks of species facing a high risk of extinction.

Although over 85 percent of birds are not threatened, current population trends for all birds are reason for concern. Calculating the current bird population is an impossible task and relies on bird census data and the use of indicator species worldwide for given types of bird habitat. In 2002 Gaston et al. estimated the current world bird population, and then estimated that total bird populations had decreased 20 to 25 percent, based on changing patterns of land use by humans and the resulting habitat loss and degradation for birds. Worldwide, 40.3 percent of extant birds have declining populations, 44.4 percent have stable populations, and only 6.2 percent have increasing populations (Vié et al., 2009). The population trend for the remaining 9.1 percent is unknown. The water bird status index (percent of shorebird populations increasing, stable, or decreasing) has decreased overall by 33 percent since 1970, with an annual decrease of about 2 percent (Butchart et al., 2010). Mean population trends for terrestrial birds in Europe and the United States combined have decreased by 16 percent since 1970 (Butchart et al., 2010).

EVEN COMMON BIRDS ARE DECLINING

For the United States and Canada, excluding Hawaii and the boreal and arctic regions, data from the Audubon Society Christmas Bird Count and the U.S. Geological Survey's Breeding Bird Survey was analyzed from 1965 to 2005. The data indicates alarming declines for many common bird species (Butcher and Niven, 2007). Common bird species are those with populations over 500,000 and with a range over 997,145 km[2]. For the top 20 bird species in decline, each had suffered over a 50 percent decrease in population. The top three species in decline, the Northern Bobwhite Quail, Evening Grosbeak, and Northern Pintail (Figure 2.2) had seen an 82, 78, and 77 percent decrease, respectively, in their populations over the past 40 years (Butcher and Niven, 2007). For the top 10 bird species in steepest decline, the average population fell from 17.6 million birds to 5.35 million birds (Butcher, 2007). It should be noted that, although the focus of this study was to quantify declining common bird population, there were increases in the populations of some common birds.

Freshwater bird populations in North America and Europe have increased by 44 percent since 1980 due to wetland protection and management (Butchart et al., 2010).

Unlike wetland birds, the population of 39 percent of seabirds (those restricted to ocean habitats) in the United States is declining, while the population is stable for 37 percent, increasing for 12 percent, and not determined for 12 percent. There have also been overall declines in the populations of forest, arid, and grassland birds in the United States, based on data collected for the past 40 years on indicator species for each of these habitats. For arid regions of the United States like the Mojave and Great Basin deserts, 17 of 30 obligate indicator species have shown a steady population decline, totaling about 30 percent in the last 40 years. For grassland bird species, the population decline was nearly 40 percent over the last 40 years, based on 24 obligate indicator species. This population decline was not surprising, given that only about 2 percent of the tall grass prairie that existed in the early 1800s still exists today. Although there has been a significant overall decline in the numbers of forest bird species in the United States, this has been driven by a persistent decline that totals about 20 percent in eastern forest species, with only slight overall declines in western and boreal forest species. The overall population of urban bird species has increased in the United States over the last 40 years due in large part to population increases in a few highly opportunistic species like robins, House Finches, pigeons, House Sparrows, and Wild Turkeys (North American Bird Conservation Initiative, U.S. Committee, 2009).

THE REPERCUSSIONS OF REDUCED BIRD NUMBERS

Beyond the loss of birds indicating a degradation of original habitats, the decrease in bird populations has other serious implications. Birds play vital roles in our ecosystem and in our lives. A reduction in the numbers of raptors and scavengers would allow rodent populations to swell and a decrease in carcass cleanup, both of which could increase disease (rabies, hantavirus pulmonary syndrome, etc.) prevalence in humans. A decrease in frugivores will result in less seed dispersal, and in some cases, poorer germination rates for seeds distributed by fruit-eating birds. A reduction in the population of nectarivores will limit bird pollination of plants, which limits crop yields. Insectivores help control insect populations, so a decrease in these bird species will lead to more crop damage and lower yields, as well as potentially increasing the use of more pesticides. A reduction in guano, the feces and urine that has been deposited by large nesting colonies of seabirds, would occur if the population of these birds decreased, thus limiting an important source of fertilizer. For many humans, birds are a source of entertainment and recreation through

FIGURE 2.2a Even some common bird species have seen a drastic decrease in population over the past 40 years. The Northern Bobwhite Quail saw an 82% decrease in numbers.

FIGURE 2.2b Evening Grosbeak populations fell 78%.

FIGURE 2.2c Northern Pintail numbers fell 77%.

activities such as bird-watching, ecotourism, and wild bird feeding. A reduction in bird numbers would decrease the potential enjoyment derived from these activities.

WHERE BIRD SPECIES ARE CONCENTRATED IN THE WORLD

Even though birds can be found in all regions of the world, the highest numbers of bird species occur in the neotropics, especially in South America (Table 2.2), where Colombia supports 18 percent of the world's bird species. The United States has 857 bird species (http://www.birdlife. org/datazone/species/search). With nearly 10,000 species of birds present in the world, it is not surprising that in order to reduce competition with one another, they can be found in nearly every type of habitat. However, forests—especially tropical and subtropical forests—support over 75 percent of all bird species (Vié et al., 2009). Interestingly, forest habitat is followed by human-modified landscapes supporting 45 percent of all bird species. This demonstrates the adaptability of birds. Shrublands support 39 percent of all bird species, while grasslands, inland wetlands, and savannas each support about 20 percent of all bird species, followed by coastal, marine offshore, rocky, and desert habitats, each supporting less than 10 percent of bird species (Vié et al., 2009). Please note that most bird species utilize more than one habitat to survive and that is why the above percentages do not add up to 100 percent.

TABLE 2.2 COUNTRIES WITH THE HIGHEST NUMBER OF BIRD SPECIES[1]

Country	Number of bird species
Colombia	1808
Peru	1790
Brazil	1731
Ecuador	1582
Indonesia	1560
Bolivia	1418
Venezuela	1354
China (mainland)	1242
India	1168
Democratic Republic of Congo	1085
Mexico	1071
Tanzania	1048
Kenya	1029
Myanmar	1012
Argentina	1005
Uganda	988
Sudan[2]	929
Thailand	924
Angola	900
Panama	877

[1] SPECIES COUNTS FROM BIRDLIFE INTERNATIONAL INCLUDE EXTINCT IN THE WILD, CRITICALLY ENDANGERED, ENDANGERED, VULNERABLE, NEAR THREATENED, LEAST CONCERN, AND DATA DEFICIENT CATEGORIES (http://www.birdlife.org/datazone/species/search) SEARCHED 1/7/2012.

[2] DATA REFLECTS THE NUMBER OF SPECIES FOR BOTH SUDAN AND SOUTH SUDAN, WHICH RECENTLY BECAME AN INDEPENDENT COUNTRY.

ENDANGERMENT

PREDISPOSITION TO ENDANGERMENT

When the threat of extinction is considered for any animal, there are several factors that can predispose a species to extinction, as well as several things that can cause extinction. One factor that can predispose a species to endangerment is that it is considered dangerous. While this is not really applicable to any bird species, wolves have been persecuted heavily because they were considered dangerous. Animal species are also predisposed to endangerment if they are in competition with humans for resources. Many forest bird species have suffered as we have deforested large sections of the earth to have wood for building structures and a source of fuel for generating heat. Species are at risk for endangerment if they have something of value (as pets, furs/skin/feathers, or medicinal) to humans (Figure 2.3). This has been especially problematic for bird species that are members of the parrot and starling families, which make for high-quality pets, as will be discussed in subsequent chapters.

Other factors that can predispose a species to endangerment are having a specialized habitat or specialized diet. A classic case that involves both of these factors is the Everglades Snail Kite (Figure 2.4) of the United States. This kite is highly endangered. In the United States, the range of the Snail Kite is entirely restricted to watersheds in central and southern Florida. The Snail Kite also has a highly specific diet composed almost entirely of apple snails, and its slender curved bill has evolved to extract the snails from their shell. Urban development and agricultural activities have decreased the scope and quality of the watersheds in these areas of Florida—as a result, the population of apple snails has plummeted. Because there are no other suitable habitats available to support apple snails, the population of the snail kite has also plummeted. It is interesting to note that many other locations in Central and South America have the specialized habitats that support the Snail Kite, and in these areas it is not endangered.

Another factor that can predispose a species to endangerment is having a small geographical range. Because the population of the species is concentrated in one small area, it is susceptible to events that can quickly impact the survival of the species. The Cozumel Thrasher is endemic to Cozumel, Mexico, a small island in the Caribbean Sea off the eastern coast of Mexico's Yucatan Peninsula. This species of bird was common but became critically endangered after one of the most intense hurricanes ever recorded in the Atlantic Basin, Hurricane Gilbert, caused significant damage to the island in September 1988. Subsequently, the island has experienced three other significant hurricanes, Roxanne in 1995, Emily in 2005, and Wilma in 2005. The last definitive scientific record of this species was in 1995 (Macouzet and Escalante Pliego, 2001).

FIGURE 2.3 In the late 1800s, the demand for Ostrich feathers for fashion became so great that the species was nearly eradicated. Fortunately, Ostrich farming became popular and allowed for the plucking of domestic Ostriches, rather than hunting wild populations.

FIGURE 2.4 Snail Kites are vulnerable to extinction because they have a specialized diet, consisting mostly of snails. Its relatively thin bill and talons are adapted for extracting snails from shells.

FIGURE 2.5   Kiwis evolved in New Zealand, an island once free of mammalian predators. Today, with numerous introduced mammals, many kiwi populations are decreasing and vulnerable or endangered.

FIGURE 2.6   Domestic and feral cats are responsible for killing hundreds of millions of birds each year.

FIGURE 2.7   Originally from Europe, the invasive Rock Pigeon is now present in urban areas around the world.

A final predisposition to endangerment unique to birds is the inability to fly. There will be several examples of bird species scattered throughout this book (**Box 2.1, ratite and parrot chapters**) of birds that are extinct or highly endangered, as well as flightless (Figure 2.5).

CAUSES OF ENDANGERMENT

There are several general causes for species becoming endangered or extinct, and the major reasons will be described. Although these general categories apply to any animal and plant species, bird examples will be used. It is important to remember that normally, many factors contribute to the extinction of a species, and at least 48 percent of extinct birds have had multiple causes of extinction. This number could be an underestimate because of the lack of early records on historical extinctions (Butchart et al., 2006b). The leading cause for endangerment and extinction is habitat destruction, caused mostly by farming and logging. Habitat destruction deprives animals of a place to live and find food, and lowers reproductive success. Not only do logging, agriculture, and even urban development radically alter existing ecosystems and habitats, they also fragment existing habitats. Breaking habitats into small fragments is especially detrimental to species that rely on and exist in a large contiguous territory.

Invasive plants or animals are another major cause for extinction and endangerment of species. Invasive species are those that are not native to a location; once introduced, they proliferate and spread uncontrollably. Invasive non-native species threaten native bird species through reducing reproductive success by eating eggs and chicks, causing direct mortality by predation or disease introduction, and degrading existing habitats when invasive plants, insects, and herbivores alter the plant composition of a habitat. Introduced pathogens like avian malaria and avian pox transmitted by introduced mosquitoes on the Hawaiian Islands have contributed to the extinction of 16 avian species there (Butchart et al., 2006b). Worldwide invasive alien species negatively impact 52 percent of all critically endangered bird species, and for those species affected by invasive agents, the biggest impacts are from invasive mammals (88 percent), plants (31 percent), and diseases (24 percent) (BirdLife International, 2008). Cats and rats are typically the most invasive mammals, and in the United States, domestic and feral cats (Figure 2.6), kill hundreds of millions of birds each year (North American Bird Conservation Initiative, U.S. Committee, 2009).

Invasive species can also include birds. In the United States, Mute Swans introduced in the 19th century have overgrazed aquatic vegetation and been detrimental to the populations of other waterfowl. The common city Rock Pigeon (Figure 2.7), European Starling, House Sparrow, and Eurasian Collared Dove are all invasive species introduced to the United States to the extent that each now number in the millions and compete with native bird species for things such as food and nesting sites.

Overhunting/collection and human-caused catastrophes are two other mechanisms that lead to extinctions and endangerment. In North America, both the Passenger Pigeon and the Carolina Parakeet (Figure 2.8) went extinct in the early 1900s. These species were hunted for food and shot to protect crops, and these acts played a major role in their extinctions. Both of these species will be covered in subsequent chapters of the book. The endangered African Penguin that breeds only at 25 islands and four mainland sites in Namibia and South Africa ("African Penguin," 2012) has been jeopardized by two major oil spills in 1994 and in 2000, both of which resulted in penguin deaths. During the last oil spill, 19,000 oiled penguins were captured and treated, while another 19,500 birds were captured and moved to prevent them from becoming oiled (Wolfaardt et al., 2008). The decision to capture and move unoiled penguins to minimize their risk of getting oiled turned out to be highly successful and can be a response utilized for future oil spills that threaten this species.

The last major cause of extinction and endangerment is environmental contamination/pollution. For birds, the classic example is the insecticide dichlorodiphenyltrichloroethane (DDT). In the United States, the metabolites (breakdown products) of DDT caused the thinning of egg shells and increased reproductive failure for Brown Pelicans and several raptor species (Figure 2.9). These species suffered steep population declines, but population recovery gradually occurred in these species once DDT was banned for use in the United States in 1972. DDT will be discussed more in the raptor chapter of this book. It is also important to remember that many bird species are migratory. Thus, for example, although strict regulation of pesticide use and the banning of highly toxic pesticides has limited or eliminated the exposure of birds to harmful chemicals in the United States, many of these pesticides are available and used in Central and South America, where many bird species from the United States spend the winter.

CURRENT THREATS TO BIRDS

The leading current threats to birds were characterized for the IUCN Red List in conjunction with BirdLife International. Agriculture, logging, and invasive species were the top three threats affecting 87, 55, and 51 percent, respectively, of globally threatened species (Vié et al., 2009). These threats were followed in order by hunting and trapping, residential and commercial development, energy production (Figure 2.10), and mining, change in fire regimen, climate change and severe weather, pollution, human disturbance, transportation and service corridors, and fisheries (Vié et al., 2009). When just critically endangered species are examined, the threats are similar;

FIGURE 2.8   The Carolina Parakeet went extinct in the early 1900s.

FIGURE 2.9   The Osprey was one of the raptor species affected by DDT.

FIGURE 2.10   Many birds are killed each year by wind turbines. These structures are especially detrimental to bird populations when placed along migratory routes.

however, invasive species replaces logging as the second most critical threat, and climate change and weather moves up to position 6 in the list of greatest threats (BirdLife International, 2008). It is apparent from the list of threats that people are the driving force for birds going extinct and being threatened.

WHERE THREATENED BIRDS RESIDE

Although 97 percent of the world's countries and territories hold one or more globally threatened species (Vié et al., 2009) there are several countries in the Americas and Southeast Asia that have high densities of threatened bird species (Table 2.3). Sixty percent of threatened bird species are endemic to a single country, and the majority of these species have small ranges (Vié et al., 2009). In particular, islands have a high level of threatened species. Several island nations such as Japan, New Zealand, and the Philippines have a large number of threatened species even though they are not nations that possess the highest number of bird species (Table 2.2). The United States has a large number of threatened species in large part due to the number of threatened species in Hawaii. In fact, when looking at extinct birds, Hawaii, Mauritius, New Zealand, and the Reunion Islands have had 27, 18, 14, and 11 birds, respectively, become extinct on them (Butchart et al., 2006b) during the last 500 years. Since the first humans moderately colonized Hawaii in 300 AD, at least 71 species of birds have gone extinct. Currently, there are 10 bird species in Hawaii that are considered extinct, although not officially declared extinct (North American Bird Conservation Initiative, U.S. Committee, 2009).

The majority (over 88 percent) of known bird extinctions in the past 500 years have occurred on islands (Butchart et al., 2006b) even though over 80 percent of bird species live on continents. Bird species that evolved on islands often devoid of mammalian species have been no match to introduced invasive species like rats, cats, and goats that arrived with human settlement. Many of today's threatened birds are found on islands where the control of invasive species is critical to their survival, as is highlighted in **Box 2.1** for Mauritius and will be highlighted for New Zealand in subsequent ratite and parrot chapters.

Besides being prevalent on islands, extinctions in birds have also occurred disproportionately among some family of birds such as Rallidae (rails), Psittacidae (parrots), Drepanidae (honeycreepers), Columbidae (pigeons), Anatidae (ducks, geese, and swans), and Sturnidae (starlings). All of these bird families have had 23, 20, 16, 13, 7, and 5 extinctions within them, respectively (Butchart et al., 2006b).

TABLE 2.3. COUNTRIES WITH THE MOST THREATENED BIRD SPECIES[1]

Country	Number of threatened species[1]
Brazil	122
Indonesia	119
Peru	98
Colombia	94
China (mainland)	86
India	78
United States	76
Philippines	74
Ecuador	73
New Zealand	70
Mexico	56
Australia	52
Argentina	49
Russia[2]	49
Thailand	46
Malaysia	45
Myanmar	43
Vietnam	43
Tanzania	42
Japan	39

[1] THREATENED BIRDS INCLUDE THOSE EXTINCT IN THE WILD, CRITICALLY ENDANGERED, ENDANGERED, AND VULNERABLE. DATA IS FROM BIRDLIFE INTERNATIONAL (http://www.birdlife.org/datazone/species/search), SEARCHED 1/7/2012.

[2] THE TOTAL NUMBER FOR RUSSIA IS DERIVED FROM TOTALING THE NON-DUPLICATE SPECIES FROM THE RUSSIA EUROPEAN, RUSSIA ASIAN, AND RUSSIA CENTRAL ASIA CATEGORIES DESIGNATED BY BIRDLIFE INTERNATIONAL.

THE POTENTIALLY CATASTROPHIC EMERGING THREAT— CLIMATE CHANGE

BirdLife International (2008) reported that a total of 24 critically endangered species were threatened by climate change, with the biggest impacts coming from storms/floods and droughts, both of which have seemingly become more prevalent and severe over time. The long-term effects of climate change are hard to predict, but the negative impacts associated with it are likely to increase drastically. The bird species likely to be the most detrimentally impacted initially would be island-dwelling, oceanic, and coastal bird species, as well as Arctic and Antarctic bird species.

Oceanic bird species depend on marine food sources that could be affected by warming water temperatures, but more importantly, many of them utilize islands for nesting. Loss of nesting habitat due to rising ocean levels could be severe—especially for those species restricted to low-lying islands that could be completely or largely submerged as glacial ice and the polar ice caps melt due to increasing temperatures—and result in ocean levels rising. Similarly for birds living on islands and coastal birds, rising sea levels will submerge and flood much of their current habitat. In undeveloped coastal areas, the coastal habitats are likely to simply recede inland, but in developed areas near the coast this natural inland progression of the coast will not be allowed, decreasing the habitat acreage available to coastal birds. Additionally, coastal storms like tropical storms and

FIGURE 2.11 Emperor Penguin populations will likely plummet with global warming.

FIGURE 2.12 Some Brant Geese populations in Alaska are no longer migrating but instead remain in Alaska year-round.

hurricanes are expected to increase in frequency and intensity as ocean temperatures rise. Such storms can have devastating effects on bird populations as depicted earlier in the chapter for the Cozumel Thrasher.

As the polar ice caps melt, local habitats will change drastically. For the ice shelf-dependent Adelie and Emperor Penguins (Figure 2.11) of the Antarctic, large decreases in regional populations of both species have been observed, as well as a shift further southward for the range of the Adelie species (Parmesan, 2006). Some population and climate models for Emperor Penguins predict extreme declines by the year 2100, with a 36 percent likelihood of extinction (St. Claire and Boyce, 2009). In the Arctic, the landscape will change drastically as the amount of ice decreases and the permafrost thaws. With the thawing of the permafrost, the grasses, sedges, and dwarf shrubs of the tundra would be replaced by shrubs and trees. The higher ambient temperatures will increase evaporation, which could decrease tundra wetlands (North American Bird Conservation Initiative, U.S. Committee, 2010). Both of these changes will drastically influence open tundra and waterfowl breeding species.

A recent study that examined previous research on birds, mammals, arthropods, plants, reptiles, amphibians, fish, and mollusks from around the world determined that the combined distribution of all species examined is shifting to higher elevations at a median rate of 11 meters per decade and to higher latitudes at a median rate of 16.9 kilometers per decade, in association with climate warming (Chen et al., 2011). In the United States, there are already early warning signs that climate change is resulting in bird populations moving northward within their traditional ranges and in migrating species arriving earlier, as reported by Cornell's Laboratory of Ornithology (Garris, 2011). More specifically, robins arrive about 14 days earlier to their breeding grounds in the Colorado Rocky Mountains compared to 30 years ago (North American Bird Conservation Initiative, U.S. Committee, 2009) , while Tree Swallows have advanced their breeding date by up to 9 days from 1959 to 1994 (Dunn and Winkler, 1999). In western Alaska, ten times more Pacific Brant geese (Figure 2.12) are not migrating to the warm waters off Mexico's Baja Peninsula for the winter, but are instead remaining in Alaska (Ward et al., 2009). Using Christmas Bird Count data from 1966 through 2005, National Audubon researchers examined the range of 305 widely distributed species in North America, and discovered that 177 of the species had a significant shift north in their range, while 79 species had a shift to the south (Niven et al., 2009). Overall, the shift in range for all species was to the north by 34.8 miles during the 40-year study period. However, it is interesting to note that the bird species that did not show a significant shift north were water birds and coastally restricted birds, while land birds had a northward shift of almost 50 miles. Within land birds, grassland species did not show a significant shift northward, which is not surprising given the lack of grassland habitat. Finally, the shift north was not caused by the availability of food from yard feeders, as species that used bird feeders and those that did not both had a significant shift northward.

EXAMPLES OF SPECIES RECOVERY PROGRAMS IN THE UNITED STATES

WHOOPING CRANE

The Whooping Crane occurs only in North America. It is North America's tallest bird, with males approaching 5 feet (1.5 m) in height. Adult Whooping Cranes have white plumage highlighted with black primaries and a reddish head crown (Figure 2.13). In the wild, they live 25 to 30 years. Whooping Cranes reach sexual maturity at four to five years of age. They often mate for life but will find a new mate if one of the pair dies.

Although likely never abundant in population, fossil records indicate that the whooping crane was originally found in the eastern two thirds of the United States, but by the mid 1800s, its range had been reduced drastically, as settlers had drained wetlands and converted them into agriculture. Additionally, as they became rarer, they were shot by collectors. By 1865, only 700 to 1,400 birds were likely left. By 1938, only two small flocks remained: a migratory flock that nested in Canada and wintered in Texas and a non-migratory flock in southwest Louisiana. By 1941, the migratory flock contained 15 birds, and the non-migratory flock contained only 6 birds. Over the next few years, all of the Louisiana birds died. The wintering grounds of the migratory flock were protected in 1937 with the creation of the Aransas National Wildlife Refuge. The breeding grounds for the remaining birds remained elusive until discovered by chance in 1954 in Wood Buffalo National Park in Northwest Canada.

The discovery of this breeding ground has been pivotal in saving the species. In 1966 a young male crane with a broken wing was removed from the nesting area and brought to Patuxent Wildlife Research Center. The following year, one of two eggs started being removed from breeding pair's nests, as although two eggs were produced, only one chick would typically be raised. This practice of egg removal continued until 1996 and led to the establishment of a large captive population that has been and is presently the source of offspring for release programs (USFWS, 2012). The breeding program has kept detailed records to maintain genetic diversity as great as possible, given all descendants are from the original flock of 15 birds that only consisted of three breeding females.

They have also discovered that up to seven eggs will be produced by females if the eggs continue to be removed. Researchers have refined artificial incubation techniques and several methods are in place to prevent the young birds from imprinting on humans—for if this occurs, the imprinted birds will not reproduce with other Whooping Cranes as adults. These methods include the use of costumes, puppets, audio recordings, and live adult models to assure they imprint on other Whooping Cranes. Today, Whooping Cranes for reintroduction still come from the Patuxent Wildlife Research Center, but also the International Crane Foundation, the Devonian Wildlife Conservation Center (Calgary), Audubon Species Survival Center, and the San Antonio Zoo. Just over 150 birds are maintained in captivity.

Currently, the only self-sustaining population in the wild remains the Aransas Wildlife Refuge-Wood Buffalo National

FIGURE 2.13 Despite various breeding programs, Whooping Cranes are still considered critically endangered with only a few hundred individuals remaining.

Park migratory flock that currently numbers from 250 to 300 birds. Mortality for this flock includes natural predation from such animals as bobcats and coyotes. But the biggest source of known mortality for all fledged Whooping Cranes in the United States is collision with power lines. There has been progress in placing reflective objects on power lines in crane migration routes and in avoiding wetlands when placing new lines. There is concern about the development of wind farms in crane migratory routes, as there is potential for increased death rates from collisions with the turbine blades or the associated power lines. Finally, the fragility of the Gulf of Mexico coastline is an ever present concern.

Four other populations of Whooping Cranes have been introduced. The first introduced group, called the Rocky Mountain Population, resulted when Whooping Crane eggs were placed in Sandhill Crane nests at Grays Lake National Wildlife Refuge in Idaho, starting in 1975. Whooping Cranes were successfully raised by Sandhill Cranes and they migrated with them. However, when they reached sexual maturity, the Whooping Cranes were more interested in mating with Sandhill Cranes than fellow Whooping Cranes. The population of this group peaked at 33 birds in 1985. The project was terminated in 1989, and the last bird died in the spring of 2002.

In 1993 captive-raised Whooping Cranes were released in central Florida to establish a non-migratory flock. Between 1993 and 2004, 289 captive-born cranes were released. Only 11 chicks have ever been successfully fledged from this population. The program has been plagued by heavy natural predation and by the ongoing periodic droughts in Florida, which inhibit reproduction. In addition, land development in Florida continues to erode crane habitat. As of mid 2011, there were roughly 20 individuals left in this population, and the decision has been made not to pursue this recovery effort beyond monitoring the existing birds.

In 2001 a new migratory population was established using captive-reared and trained birds in Necedah National Wildlife Refuge, teaching them to migrate in the fall behind an ultralight plane to the central Gulf Coast of Florida. Operation Migration has continued ever since with new birds each fall (Operation Migration, 2012). Once the birds have completed the migration one time, they successfully complete it on their own in subsequent years. Wintering grounds for this population have expanded naturally to Alabama, South Carolina, and Tennessee. As of December 2011, this population numbered 106 cranes. Successful fledging of three chicks has occurred with this population. This population has had serious issues with nest abandonment, and the nest failure may be related to infestation with black flies or other biting insects causing parental nest abandonment. Research is currently ongoing to eliminate this problem, as nest attempts from 2005 to 2011 totaled an impressive 77.

Ten captive cranes were released in February 2011 in Louisiana to reestablish the traditional non-migratory population that once existed there. An additional 16 captive-reared birds were released in December 2011. The results with the original 10 birds released have not been encouraging, as one is presumed dead, one was likely eaten by a predator, one was euthanized because of respiratory infection and two were shot and killed (USGS, 2012). In just a little over a year, eight Whooping Cranes have been shot: two in Louisiana and six in the eastern migratory population (International Crane Foundation, 2012). The recovery of the Whooping Crane continues to be a slow and arduous process.

PEREGRINE FALCON

The Peregrine Falcon (Figure 2.14) has a nearly worldwide distribution, as it can be found on every continent except Antarctica. It is known for its rapid flight, reaching speeds slightly above 60 miles per hour (97 kilometers per hour) in direct pursuit of prey and for its dramatic aerial dives in pursuit of prey, in which it may reach speeds of 200 miles per hour (322 kilometers per hour).

Although never very abundant in the United States, the population of the peregrine falcon declined dramatically, with the eastern United States population becoming extinct in the 1960s. West of the Mississippi River, the population decreased by 80 to 90 percent, with a low of only 39 known pairs. The dramatic decline in the Peregrine Falcon's population was traced to DDE, a breakdown metabolite of the pesticide DDT. DDE caused Peregrine Falcon females to produce eggs with thin egg shells, which broke under the weight of the bird during incubation or led to embryo death due to improper moisture and gas exchange through the shell. Use of DDT was banned by the U.S. government in 1972. By the 1980s, DDT was banned almost worldwide.

FIGURE 2.14 Peregrine Falcons have adapted and thrived in man-made environments, utilizing tall buildings in cities as nesting platforms.

In 1970 Tom Cade at the Cornell Lab of Ornithology started the Peregrine Fund and started to breed Peregrine Falcons in captivity. Over the next 25 years, more than 4,000 Peregrine Falcons were released by this group. Many other similar programs were started around the world and in other parts of the United States, making the recovery a global effort. Dr. Cade's work depended in part on falconers, who use birds of prey for hunting purposes (Chapter 9). Falconers played a vital role in the recovery of the species, as they provided breeding birds and knowledge about captive management. They were needed as a source of birds, because once the U.S. government placed the Peregrine Falcon on the Endangered Species List in 1970, it became very difficult to obtain permits to capture wild birds for use even in recovery programs. Cade's group was highly innovative and smart, using artificial insemination and foster parents. They discovered that Peregrine Falcons were like many other bird species in that, if the first clutch of eggs produced by a pair were removed for artificial incubation, the pair would produce another clutch and sometimes a third clutch of eggs (Gallagher, 1999; Winter, 1999). Even when faced with Great Horned Owls and Golden Eagles catching newly released Peregrines in traditional habitats, the team adjusted and started to utilize urban areas, which had few predators, abundant food in the form of starlings and pigeons, and high-rise buildings and bridges with ledges that simulated the natural cliff edges they typically used for nesting. Furthermore, the constant news coverage of Peregrines in such cities as New York and Boston helped spread awareness and generate funds.

In 1999 the Peregrine Falcon was removed from the Endangered Species List of the United States, but it remains on many state endangered species lists to this day. In 2003 the population in the United States was estimated at 4,870 (the Peregrine Fund, 2012a). The worldwide population has also increased, and the Peregrine Falcon population status is classified as least concern by BirdLife International. With the success of the Peregrine Falcon recovery, the Peregrine Fund (http://www.peregrinefund.org/) switched its focus to conserving birds of prey worldwide. One of the many recovery programs they currently participate in is for the California Condor.

CALIFORNIA CONDOR

The California Condor is a New World vulture (Chapter 9) that has a wingspan of nine and half feet; it can weigh up to about 23 pounds (Figure 2.15). They can travel over 100 miles per day looking for dead carcasses of animals like deer, cattle, horses, and rabbits, or gut piles resulting from hunters cleaning the carcasses of killed animals. Over 10,000 years ago, their range extended on the West Coast of North America from Canada through Mexico and on the East Coast from New York to Florida. They also were found across the entire southern United States. However, this range was reduced to the West Coast inward to present-day Arizona by the time

FIGURE 2.15   Wild condors are monitored by noting the identification number on their wing bands.

of the European settlement of North America, and by the late 1930s, their range was reduced to just California. In 1982 only 22 California Condors existed, and the U.S. Fish and Wildlife service began a captive breeding program in 1983. Because of continued declines in the wild population, a decision was made to capture all remaining birds, such that all birds were held in captivity by 1987.

Condors become sexually mature at about six years of age and mate for life. Condors can live in the wild up to 60 years of age. In the wild, they typically produce one egg every other year, but sometimes will produce an egg in consecutive years. Young condors fledge at five to six months of age. Because their natural reproductive rate is slow, in captivity, the first egg produced by breeding pairs was taken for artificial incubation, which stimulated the production of a second egg, which could be taken as well, as on occasion even a third egg would be produced. Chicks resulting from eggs that were artificially incubated where fed by people using hand puppets shaped like a condor head (Figure 2.16), so that the chicks would not imprint on people.

Breeding was and is very successful in captivity, allowing California Condors to be reintroduced in the wild in 1992 in California and in Baja California, Mexico, and in 1996 in Arizona. The population of California Condors at the end of February 2012 was 386 birds, with 173 held in captivity and 213 in the wild (National Park Service, 2012). Of the birds in the wild, 118 were in California, 77 were in Arizona/Utah, and 18 were in Baja California, Mexico.

Captive birds are held at the World Center for Birds of Prey, the Oregon Zoo, San Diego Zoo Safari Park, Los Angeles Zoo, San Diego Zoo, Santa Barbra Zoo, and Chapultepec Zoo (Mexico City), with breeding programs at the first four locations providing birds for release. Released birds have successfully reproduced in the wild—of the total wild condors, 21 were wild-fledged birds in California and 7 were wild-fledged in Arizona (the Peregrine Fund, 2012b).

Released birds and even most of the wild-raised birds are now equipped with large numbered tags for identification and transmitters (Figure 2.17). The transmitters utilized are satellite-reporting GPS transmitters that allow for daily locations and movement to be tracked by field biologists. Released and wild-fledged birds face numerous threats, like being hit by cars while scavenging road kill, starvation, and even being shot by humans. But by far, the greatest threat is lead poisoning, which has killed numerous wild condors. Just from December 2011 to February 2012, three wild birds succumbed to lead poisoning; all three (two females and one male) were sexually mature, ranging in age from 9 to11 years (National Park Service, 2012). When hunters use lead shot to kill deer or elk, for example, the bullets tend to fragment into multiple (as much as hundreds) small pieces. Once the animal is hit, it may only be wounded and not found by the hunter, but instead will die of its wounds, only to be scavenged by California Condors. Even if the animal is killed instantly and found by the hunter, the hunter will dress the carcass, leaving a gut pile that has shards of lead in it. These gut piles are scavenged by California Condors.

Lead shot was banned by the U.S. government for waterfowl hunting about 20 years ago, as lead poisoning was a significant contributor to population declines in waterfowl. A similar ban does not exist for terrestrial animal hunting. California banned lead ammunition used for most hunting activities in the range of the California Condor in July 2008. Research evidence indicates that as a result of this ban, blood lead levels have declined significantly in two other carcass scavengers, the Turkey Vulture and the Golden Eagle (Kelly et al., 2011). Consequently, lead poisoning is less of a concern in the California population compared to the Arizona population, where lead poisoning continues to be a serious problem. Most wild condors in the Arizona population are now trapped twice a year so that blood samples can be obtained for lead concentration determination. Once lead levels are determined, many birds must undergo chelation treatment; in some cases, surgery is necessary to remove lead particles from the digestive tract. It is estimated that without these treatments, the death rate from lead might be four times higher than it currently is (Green et al., 2009). Massive public information campaigns in this area are waged to inform local hunters about the dangers of lead, trying to convince hunters to switch to other bullet forms such as steel, which does not pose a threat to condors and other birds.

REASONS TO BE OPTIMISTIC ABOUT BIRD CONSERVATION

FIGURE 2.16 Puppets are used for feeding young condors to prevent imprinting on their caretakers.

BirdLife International (2008) reported that 88 percent of critically endangered bird species have received targeted conservation action since 2004, and that over 70 percent of these species have seen beneficial results. Since 1988 at least 33 bird species have been down-listed to lower categories on the IUCN Red List (Butchart et al., 2010). From the period of 1994–2004, Butchart (2006a) determined that 16 bird species would have become extinct during this period if not for the establishment of conservations programs to help them. The conservation measures utilized for these 16 bird species included habitat protection and management for 12 of them, control of invasive species for 8 species, captive breeding and release for 6 of them, and translocation of individuals for 1 species (Butchart et al., 2006a). By the beginning of 2012, 8 of these original 16 bird species had been upgraded to endangered status, while the other species remained in the critically endangered category (http://www.birdlife.org/datazone/species/search searched 1/7/2012). Three successful interventions to save three endangered bird species in the United States are highlighted above.

Worldwide, land is being set aside by governments or purchased by conservation organizations in order to preserve critical habitats for wildlife. In the United States alone, more than 344 million hectares (850 million acres) of land and 5.6 million square kilometers (3.5 million square miles) of ocean are now publicly owned, which includes 1,600 Marine Protected Areas, 550 National Wildlife Refuges, 150 National Forests, about 400 National Park Service units and 6,000 State Park Units (http://www.stateofthebirds.org/introduction). Governmental regulatory measures are increasing throughout the world to minimize such things as pollution, oceanic bird by-catches during fishing, and the impact of renewable energy sources.

Public awareness of the plight of birds has increased tremendously through the education of the public by governmental—but more importantly—conservation-based organizations. This awareness has led to significant financial support of these organizations, allowing them to acquire and restore important habitats, sponsor conservation projects, and/or influence international and national policy to minimize further bird loss. Some of these organizations include the National Audubon Society, Parrots International, BirdLife International, the Peregrine Fund, the Nature Conservancy, World Wildlife Fund, International Crane Foundation, Natural Resources Defense Council, the Sierra Club, Royal Society for the Protection of Birds, Conservation International, American Bird Conservancy, Wildlife Conservation Society, and many others.

BOX 2.1 MAURITIUS ISLAND

The now extinct Dodo (*Raphus cucullatus*) once lived on Mauritius Island, located several hundred miles east of Madagascar in the Indian Ocean. Despite the controversy over its taxonomy due to limited descriptions and even fewer specimens, most scientists have agreed that the Dodo is a distant relative of the pigeon (Fuller, 1987). The first written account of the Dodo was in 1601; they were probably extinct by 1690 due to hunting and the introduction of invasive species such as monkeys and hogs that most likely contributed to the depredation of the Dodo ground nests. During those some 90 years, many travelers visited Mauritius, leaving with their own interpretations of this strange bird. They inhabited wooded areas and were described as large and fat, wobbling with their bellies scraping the ground, with small wings that rendered them completely flightless. Unfortunately, no skins remain to confirm this description. The only remains are a single preserved leg, a head and a few bones. Dodos were not, however, the only strange birds to vanish from Mauritius after the Europeans arrived. The Mauritius Red Hen (*Aphanapteryx bonasia*), a flightless bird presumed to belong to the rail family, was only depicted by rudimentary sketches and later confirmed by the finding of bones. The last live specimens were documented in 1693, and then were considered rare. The discovery that these birds made an easy meal for travelers to the island did not help the species' survivability. Avian species isolated to small islands are more susceptible to population declines due to the relatively small initial populations and the limited area, with little to no species immigration into the population. Several endemic species isolated to Mauritius Island have recently recovered from critically low population numbers, with the help of vital intervention of conservation programs. Without these management practices, these species would be extinct today.

The Mauritius Kestrel (*Falco punctatus*) is listed as vulnerable on the IUCN Red List due to its small population size on Mauritius and its susceptibility to a variety of threats. The kestrel's initial decline resulted from the island of Mauritius being deforested to 3 percent of its original woodland during colonial settlement. The more recent decline was due to organochloride pesticide exposure, which caused the thinning of egg shells, leading to eggs being crushed in the nest. Though conservationists have realized and eliminated the organochlorine threat, nests are still heavily preyed upon by introduced predators to the island. Conservation methods to help save the species include captive breeding and release, supplementary feeding, nest site provision, predator control, nest guarding, and disease treatment. The Mauritius Kestrel has undergone a drastic recovery, from only 4 birds in 1974 to a present-day population of 800–1000 mature individuals. Raptors often need large territories to find sufficient food. Though the numbers are increasing, the island has a small carrying capacity, and therefore the numbers are likely to remain small and keep the species at risk.

Once widely distributed across Mauritius, the Pink Pigeon (*Nesoenas mayeri*) is now listed as endangered. Populations are fragmented and small, with most of the species living in about 80 km². Main threats to the pigeon include severe habitat loss, predation of nests, and disease introduced by non-native pigeons. A captive breeding and reintroduction program is underway, in combination with habitat restoration, protected areas, control of exotic predators, disease management, and clutch fostering. The species only had 10 wild individuals in 1990, and without intervention, the pigeon would have gone extinct. Intensive management practices have brought the population to between 360 and 395 mature individuals, but the species numbers still fluctuate and rely on continued management practices.

The Echo, or Mauritius, Parakeet (*Psittacula eques*) was once common on Mauritius, but began to decline in numbers in the mid 1800s. By 1986, the population was estimated to be between 8 and 12 individuals. Through captive breeding, captive rearing, and intensive management, the wild population stood at 59–73 birds in 1998. By 2007, the population had grown to over 300 individuals in the wild. There are presently still only 50–249 mature individuals in the wild living in a small range on Mauritius. The species has been moved from critically endangered to endangered after its steady and prolonged increase in the wild population resulting from intensive recovery management. The Echo is 36 cm long, and green, with a long tail. It is easily confused with the smaller, paler, Rose-ringed Parakeet (*Psittacula krameri*), one of the most widespread parrots on continental Africa (Birdlife International).

These species probably would have gone extinct, but with intervention, the three species remain with small, but increasing, populations. Species that are isolated to islands are much more vulnerable to extinction due to their small population size and restricted habitats, so when a declining species is isolated to an island, drastic conservational efforts are made to try to save the remaining individuals (Butchart, 2006).

REFERENCES

"African Penguin." 2012. *BirdLife International Species fact sheet: Spheniscus demersus.* Downloaded from http://www.birdlife.org on 25/01/2012.

BirdLife International, (2012), "IUCN Red List for birds." Downloaded from http://www.birdlife.org on 09/01/2012.

Butchart, H. M., A. J. Stattersfield, and N. J. Collar. 2006. How many bird extinctions have we prevented? *Oryx* **40**(3), 266–278.

"Banggai Crow." 2012. *BirdLife International Species fact sheet: Corvus unicolor.* Downloaded from http://www.birdlife.org on 23/01/2012.

Bhushan, B. 1986. Rediscovery of the Jerdon's or Double-Banded Courser Cursorius bitorquatus (*Blyth*). *Journal of the Bombay Natural History Society* **83**:1–14.

Birdlife International. 2008. *Critically Endangered birds: A global audit.* Birdlife International, Cambridge, UK.

Butchart, S. H. M., A. Stattersfield, and Collar, N. J.. 2006a. How many bird extinctions have we prevented? *Oryx* **40**:266–278.

Butchart, S. H. M., A. J. Stattersfield, and T. M. Brooks. 2006b. Going or gone: Defining "Possibly Extinct" species to give a truer picture of recent extinctions. *Bulletin of British Ornithologists' Club* **126a**:7–24.

Butchart, S. H. M., M. Walpole, B. Collen, A. van Strien, J. P. W. Scharlemann, R. E. A. Almond, J. E. M. Baillie, B. Bomhard, C. Brown, J. Bruno, K. E. Carpenter, G. M. Carr, J. Chanson, A. M. Chenery, J. Csirke, N. C. Davidson, F. Dentener, M. Foster, A. Galli, J. N. Galloway, P. Genovesi, R. D. Gregory, M. Hockings, V. Kapos, J.-F. Lamarque, F. Leverington, J. Loh, M. A. McGeoch, L. McRae, A. Minasyan, M. H. Morcillo, T. E. E. Oldfield, D. Pauly, S. Quader, C. Revenga, J. R. Sauer, B. Skolnik, D. Spear, D. Stanwell-Smith, S. N. Stuart, A. Symes, M. Tierney, T. D. Tyrrell, J.-C. Vié, and R. Watson. 2010. Global Biodiversity: Indicators of Recent Declines. *Science* **328**:1164–1168.

Butcher, G. 2007. *"Wake-up call": Common Birds in Decline, A State of the Birds Report, Summer 2007.* National Audubon Society, New York.

Butcher, G. and D. K. Niven. 2007. *Combining Data from the Christmas Bird Count and the Breeding Bird Survey to Determine the Continental Status and Trends of North America Birds.* National Audubon Society, Washington, DC.

Chen, I.-C., J. K. Hill, R. Ohlemüller, D. B. Roy, and C. D. Thomas. 2011. Rapid Range Shifts of Species Associated with High Levels of Climate Warming. *Science* **333**:1024–1026.

Dunn, P. O. and D. W. Winkler. 1999. Climate change has affected the breeding date of Tree Swallows throughout North America. *Proceedings of the Royal Society B: Biological Sciences* **266**:2487–2490.

Dutson, G. C. L., P. M. Magsalay, and R. J. Timmons. 1993. The rediscovery of the Cebu Flowerpecker Dicaeum quadricolor, with notes on other forest birds on Cebu, Philippines. *Bird Conservation International* **3**:235–243.

Fuller, E. 1987. *Extinct Birds.* Facts On File Publications, New York.

Gallagher, T. 1999. Mission Accomplished. Cornell Laboratory of Ornithology, *Living Bird.* **18**(3):8–16.

Garris, A. 2011. The heat is on: From subways to dairy barns, is New York ready for climate change? *The Magazine of the College of Agriculture and Life Sciences.* Cornell University, Ithaca, NY.

Gaston, K. J., T. M. Blackburn, and K. K. Goldewijk. 2003. Habitat conversion and global avian biodiversity loss. *Proceedings of the Royal Society of London. Series B: Biological Sciences* **270**:1293–1300.

Green, R. E., Hunt, W. G, Parish, C. N. and I. Newton. 2009. Effectiveness of action to reduce exposure of free-ranging California Condors in Arizona and Utah to lead from spent ammunition. *PLoS ONE* 3(12: e4022.

Harris, T. 2009. *National Geographic Complete Birds of the World.* Brown Reference Group Ltd.

"Indigo-winged Parrot." 2012. *BirdLife International Species fact sheet: Hapalopsittaca fuertesi.* Downloaded from http://www.birdlife.org on 23/01/2012.

International Crane Foundation. 2012. Whooping Crane Shot in Indiana. Accessed 04/27/2012: http://www.savingcranes.org/whats-new/2012/01/whooping-crane-shot-in-indiana/

Kelly, T. R., P. H. Bloom, S. G. Torres, Y. Z. Hernandez, R. H. Poppenga, W. M. Boyce, and C. K. Johnson. 2011. Impact of the California Lead Ammunition Ban on reducing lead exposure in Golden Eagles and Turkey Vultures. *PLoS ONE* 6(4): e1656.

King, B. F. and P. C. Rasmussen. 1998. The rediscovery of the Forest Owlet Athene (Heteroglaux) blewitti. *Forktail* **14**:53–55.

Macouzet, F. T. and P. Escalante Pliego. 2001. Records of the Cozumel Thrasher Toxostoma guttatum after hurricane Gilbert. *Cotinga* **15**:32–33.

National Park Service. 2012. *California Condors.* Accessed 04/27/2012: http://www.nps.gov/grca/naturescience/california-condors.htm

North American Bird Conservation Initiative, U.S. Committee. 2010. *The State of the Birds 2010 Report on Climate Change, United States of America.* Department of the Interior, Washington, DC.

North American Bird Conservation Initiative, U.S. Committee. 2009. *The State of the Birds, United States of America, 2009.* Department of the Interior, Washington, DC.

Niven, D. K., G. S. Butcher, G. T. Bancroft, W. B. Monahan, and G. Langham. 2009. *Birds and climate change: Ecological disruption in motion.* National Audubon Society, New York.

Operation Migration. 2012a. "Ultralight-led Bird Migration." Accessed 04/27/2012: http://www.operationmigration.org/

Parmesan, C. 2006. Ecological and evolutionary responses to recent climate change. *Annual Review of Ecology, Evolution, and Systematics* **37**:637–669.

The Peregrine Fund. 2012. "Peregrine Falcon." Accessed 04/27/2012: http://www.globalraptors.org/grin/SpeciesResults.asp?specID=8248

The Peregrine Fund. 2012b. "Recent Raptor News: California Condor Update." Accessed 04/27/2012: http://www.globalraptors.org/grin/SiteNews.asp?lNewsType=1

Riley, J. and J. C. Wardill. 2001. The rediscovery of Cerulean Paradise-flycatcher Eutrichomyias rowleyi on Sangihe, Indonesia. *Forktail* **17**:45–55.

St. Claire, C. C. and M. S. Boyce. 2009. Icy insights from emperor penguins. *Proceedings of the National Academy of Sciences* **106**(6):1691–1692.

USFWS (U.S. Fish and Wildlife Service). 2012. "History of Whooping Cranes. Southwest Region 2. Aransas National Refuge Complex." Accessed 04/27/2012: http://www.fws.gov/southwest/refuges/texas/aransas/wchistory.html

USGS (U.S. Geological Survey). 2012. "Endangered Whooping Cranes Shot and Killed." Accessed 04/27/2012: http://www.usgs.gov/blogs/features/usgs_top_story/endangered-cranes-shot-and-killed

Vié, J.-C., C. Hilton-Taylor, and S. N. Stuart. 2009. *Wildlife in a Changing World: An Analysis of the 2008 IUCN Red List of Threatened Species*. Page 180. IUCN, Gland, Switzerland.

Ward, D. H., C. P. Dau, T. L. Tibbitts, J. S. Sedinger, B. A. Anderson, and J. E. Hines. 2009. Change in Abundance of Pacific Brant Wintering in Alaska: Evidence of a Climate Warming Effect? *Arctic* **62**:301–311.

Winter, M. 1999. Saving the Peregrine Falcon. *Cornell Focus* **8**(1):4–9.

Wolfaardt, A. C., L. G. Underhill, R. Altwegg, J. Visagie, and A. J. Williams. 2008. Impact of the Treasure oil spill on African penguins Spheniscus demersus at Dassen Island: Case study of a rescue operation. *African Journal of Marine Science* **30**:405–419.

III   INTERNATIONAL TRADE

ILLEGAL AND LEGAL IMPORTATION OF WILDLIFE

International trade in wildlife (live animals, parts, and products) is a key contributor to the endangerment and extinction of many animal species. In 2011 this threat was highlighted when the last Javan Rhinoceros was killed and its horn removed in Vietnam, leaving the only remaining population of less than 50 on the island of Java. In addition, the Western Black Rhinoceros was officially declared extinct in 2011. All remaining species of rhinoceros are in grave danger of becoming extinct as poachers kill them for their ivory horn, used for carving ornaments or ground for use in traditional Asian medicine, despite its having no known scientific medicinal value. Kruger National Park in South Africa is home to about 500 Black and 10,000 White Rhinoceroses (Figure 3.1) and despite having government soldiers helping to protect the animals in this park, a record 244 rhinoceros were killed there in 2011 (Associated Press, 2011).

It is estimated that the illegal trade in wildlife (Figure 3.2) generates at least $5 billion to over $20 billion annually (Wyler and Sheikh, 2008). Given the secretive nature of illegal wildlife trade, exact figures are unavailable, but there is a consensus that its value places it just behind the black marketing of drugs, weapons, and possibly human trafficking. As reviewed by Wyler and Sheikh (2008) for their congressional report, the United States is one of the leading importers of legal wildlife and wildlife products. There is also a demand in the United States for illegal wildlife due to the demand for exotic pets and hunting trophies. In addition, immigration to the United States has also increased the demand for illegal wildlife goods. For example, immigrants from Central America have created a demand that cannot be met legally for sea turtle eggs and meat, and immigrants from Asia have increased the demand for wildlife used in traditional Asian medicines (Wyler and Sheikh, 2008).

FIGURE 3.1 White Rhinos face extinction due to illegal poaching for their horn.

FIGURE 3.2 Various animal parts at a market in Myanmar.

THE THREATS FROM ILLEGAL WILDLIFE SMUGGLING

The international illegal trade in wildlife is considered a serious threat to the environmental and national security of the United States due to the potential introduction of invasive non-native species and disease transmission. In the United States, the introduction of non-native species is the second leading threat, behind habitat destruction to our nation's biodiversity, and this is especially the case with imperiled bird species (Wilcove et al., 1998). In addition, the biodiversity of the United States could be threatened if the demand for traditional medicines such as bear bile/gallbladders leads to increased exploitation here, since other world populations are becoming decimated or bear bile farming in Asia is outlawed. Finally, the danger of disease spreading to both humans and domestic animals from illegal wildlife trade is a potentially serious threat, but for the most part, it is unrealized. Customs officers in Belgium contracted psittacosis, a bacterial infection, from contact with illegally imported parakeets (De Schrijver, 1995), and the highly pathogenic Avian Influenza (H5N1) was confirmed in two Crested Hawk-Eagles confiscated from the hand luggage of an incoming Thai passenger at Brussels International Airport (Van Borm et al., 2005). If the birds had not been detected, they could have led to an outbreak of the H5N1 Avian Influenza in Belgium. Other disease concerns include monkeypox, Severe Acute Respiratory Syndrome (SARS), and Ebola hemorrhagic fever, all of which have confirmed or potential links to illegal bushmeat (meat from wildlife) trade.

REGULATION OF WILDLIFE IMPORTATION

Regulation of the legal import of wildlife (any living or dead wild animal, as well as captive-born and -bred wild animals, its parts, and products made from it) and the detection of illegal wildlife imports into the United States is under the control of the Fish and Wildlife Service (FWS). To facilitate inspection, the FWS has designated 18 ports across the United States through which most wildlife traffic is required to pass. If the origin of the wildlife is from either Mexico or Canada, there are some additional approved Mexican and Canadian border ports. Special ports are also in place and can be utilized if the final destination is Alaska, Puerto Rico, or Guam. Because of staffing limitations, only about 25 percent of declared wildlife shipments are inspected (Wyler and Sheikh, 2008). Undeclared shipments of wildlife receive even less attention unless illegal activity is suspected, and then specific shipments will be targeted. For the year 2008, the year-end number of inspectors was 117 individuals and the amount of declared wildlife shipments was 186,959 (U.S. Fish and Wildlife Service, 2008).

LEGAL IMPORTATION OF BIRDS

In addition to the FWS, legal import of birds into the United States also involves the United States Department of Agriculture (USDA) and the Centers for Disease Control and Prevention (CDC). The USDA Animal and Plant Health Inspection service (APHIS) regulates the import of animal and animal products that could harm agriculture or livestock. Birds fall into this category because the poultry industry in the United States generates hundreds of billions of dollars in revenue each year. The CDC takes the lead in protecting against communicable human diseases, and has recently been involved in bird import regulation due to the threat of the H5N1 Avian Influenza. There are currently a large number of countries from which no birds can be imported because they have had outbreaks of the H5N1 Avian Influenza (APHIS, 2011a).

For importation, the USDA defines commercial birds as those that are imported for resale, breeding or public display, or any other purpose, except pet birds, zoological birds, research birds, or performing or theatrical birds. The USDA also segregates out from commercial birds what is considered poultry. This includes chickens, doves, ducks, pigeons, geese, grouse, guinea fowl, partridges, pea fowl, pheasants, quail, swans, turkeys, and hatching eggs of these species (APHIS, 2011a). All bird species designated as poultry are not considered by the USDA to be pet birds. Personal pet birds are also given their own category and regulations for importation (APHIS, 2011b). In general, for the import of commercial birds and poultry, as well as pet birds, all importers must obtain an import permit, contact a USDA port veterinarian at least 72 hours before arrival of the bird(s), and secure a veterinary health certificate within 30 days of importation from a certified veterinarian of the exporting country. Upon arrival into the United States at a designated port, a port veterinarian will review all documentation and inspect the bird(s). All birds, except those from Canada, must be quarantined for a minimum of 30 days at one of the three USDA APHIS Import Centers located in New York, Miami, or Los Angeles, or placed in one of the privately owned quarantine facilities that have been approved by APHIS. During quarantine, all birds will be tested to determine if they are free of certain communicable avian diseases. Please note that each state also regulates animal importation and may have further requirements.

METHODS USED BY WILDLIFE SMUGGLERS

Wildlife smugglers first and foremost take advantage of the fact that only a small percentage of shipments are actually inspected. As previously mentioned, only about 25 percent of wildlife shipments are checked coming into the United States. Smuggled wildlife is often hidden in secret compartments of luggage, shipping containers, or clothing. In May of 2011, a man was arrested in Thailand after his suitcases were found to contain two baby macaques, two baby leopards, and one Malayan sun bear, all of which had been drugged and bound to keep them from being noticed (Babu, 2011). Smuggled wildlife is often deceptively declared on customs forms using look-alike, unprotected species as the listed species. Wild species are often declared as captive-bred species, which often exempts them from stringent regulations. Frequently, illegal species will be mixed with legal species or hidden in a shipment of legal species, especially if the legal species are venomous or dangerous, making the cargo less likely to be inspected. Often, the animals will be packaged in other containers, such as plastic detergent containers to be imported. Smuggling using the postal service, FedEx, DHL, and other similar carriers is often employed because these shipments are not subjected to as much scrutiny—the packages are simply labeled as merchandise like books, toys, or household goods. Finally, in the case of birds, the smuggling of collected eggs has become a huge problem. Smugglers will wear specially designed vests or underwear underneath their clothes to escape detection through airport security (Rosen and Smith, 2010 Coghlan et al.,

FIGURE 3.3   A passenger was caught by U.S. Customs attempting to smuggle rare birds into the country by taping them to his legs. One or two birds, with legs and beaks bound, were inserted into each tube.

FIGURE 3.4   Bali Mynah in captivity. This species of bird is critically endangered due to its demand in the illegal pet trade.

2011). This practice has been especially prevalent with eggs from cockatoo species, many of which are highly endangered, and has resulted in numerous arrests even here in the United States (United States Department of Justice, 1994, 1995, 1996).

Because the live, smuggled wild animals are often drugged to stay quiet and concealed tightly among clothes (Figure 3.3) or other goods and shipped under harsh conditions, many do not survive. It is estimated that up to 75 percent of smuggled wildlife die before reaching their destination (Seabrook, 2003). In the case of parrots, it has been estimated that up to 8 million parrots are captured for the pet trade each year and that 90 percent of these birds will die during the time from capture to reaching a final buyer (Nature, 2012). Despite the high death rate, the ultimate payoffs for the few that survive make it worthwhile for the smugglers. In the case of birds, a smuggled Black Palm Cockatoo egg can be worth $10,000, while a breeding pair is worth $25–80,000. A Mongolian Falcon can fetch $20,000, a Lear Macaw is worth $60–90,000, while a smuggled Hyacinth Macaw will be worth $5–12,000 (Wyler and Sheikh, 2008).

The following accounts provide a sampling of detected illegal trafficking of birds in the year 2011. In January, a pair of Bali Mynahs, four slow loris primates, and eight Pig-nosed Turtles were detected in the luggage of a Singaporean man at the Jakarta Airport. The Bali Mynah (Figure 3.4) is critically endangered, with only about 50 mature individuals in the wild ("Bali Mynah," 2012). In August, authorities boarded a boat in the Philippines and seized a critically endangered Red-vented Cockatoo, 71 Hill Mynahs, and 42 Blue-naped Parrots (Babu, 2011). International trade of both of the latter species of birds is highly regulated. In November, border police in Hungary seized about 10,000 dead songbirds close to the border with Romania (TRAFFIC, 2011). The birds were discovered in boxes in a refrigerated consignment that also consisted of legal boxes of meat and sausage products. In 2008, TRAFFIC published research that hundreds of thousands of wild birds were being illegally killed in Southeast and Central Europe and then smuggled to Italy to be sold as delicacies in restaurants (TRAFFIC, 2008).

PROGRAMS TO PREVENT AND PROTECT BIRDS IN INTERNATIONAL TRADE

CITES

The Convention on International Trade in Endangered Species of Wild Fauna and Flora (CITES) is an international agreement between governments that went into force in 1975 (www.cites. org). This agreement establishes international controls over trade in wild plant and animal species (as well as products derived from them) that are threatened or may be threatened due to excessive

III INTERNATIONAL TRADE 49

commercial exploitation. As of the end of 2011, 175 parties (countries) of the roughly 193 countries of the world have signed on to this international agreement (www.cites.org). Some notable countries that have not committed to this agreement are Angola, Western Sahara, Tajikistan, Turkmenistan, Lebanon, Iraq, North Korea, and East Timor (www.cites.org). Although CITES is legally binding on all signatories, it only provides the framework for implementation by each party, and each party has to adopt its own domestic legislation to ensure CITES is implemented. In the United States, the Endangered Species Act provides the framework for much of the implementation of CITES (U.S. Fish and Wildlife Service).

The species covered by CITES are listed in three appendices based on the degree of protection they need. Species included in Appendix I are threatened with extinction, and trade of specimens of species within this category is permitted only in exceptional circumstances (www.cites.org). Species of Appendix II are not necessarily threatened with extinction, but trade in these species is controlled to prevent utilization incompatible with their survival. Species are also included in Appendix II if they are difficult to distinguish from other species in this appendix, so that it is harder for illegal trade to take place through mislabeling and misidentification of shipments (Babu, 2011). An export permit (or re-export certificate from other exporting countries) from the country of origin is required, but an import permit is not required. In addition, any live animal or plant species in this appendix must be prepared and shipped in a manner to minimize risk of injury, damage to health, or cruel treatment (www.cites.org). Finally, species listed in Appendix III are protected in at least one country, which has asked other CITES signatories for assistance in controlling trade in this species. Imports require a certificate of origin, and if the importation is from a party that has included the species in Appendix III, then an export permit is required (Babu, 2011).

At the end of 2011, 156 species of birds and 11 subspecies of birds were listed in Appendix I of CITES. Appendix II included 1275 species and 2 subspecies of birds; 56 species of birds were listed in Appendix III. From a pet trade standpoint in the United States, almost all parrots are protected by CITES. However, the Budgerigar (Figure 3.5) (*Melopsittacus undulatus*), Cockatiel (*Nymphicus hollandicus*), Rose-ringed Parakeet or Indian Ringneck Parakeet (*Psittacula krameri*), and the Peach- or Rosy-faced Lovebird (Figure 3.6) (*Agapornis roseicollis*) are not listed by CITES. In the case of the Indian Ringneck Parakeet and Rosy-faced Lovebird, both have been listed on CITES Appendix III and Appendix II, respectively, in the past, but both were subsequently deleted as their populations in the wild increased. Furthermore, domestication and breeding of these species, especially for the cockatiel and budgerigar, is so widespread and successful that captive-bred populations are highly sustainable.

FIGURE 3.5 The budgerigar or "budgie," a common pet in the U.S., is not CITES protected.

FIGURE 3.6 The Rosy-faced Lovebird is one of four parrot species not protected by CITES.

OTHER LEGISLATION REGULATING BIRD IMPORTS

Besides CITES and the Endangered Species Act, bird trade in the United States is also regulated by the Wild Bird Conservation Act of 1992, which was passed to promote the conservation of exotic birds by ensuring that all trade of these species within the United States would only occur if such trade in these species was not detrimental to their survival and was biologically sustainable. Passage of this act halted the importation of wild-caught birds listed on any appendix of CITES, except under tightly regulated and approved exemptions by the U.S. Fish & Wildlife Service.

Two other acts that help conserve birds and limit bird trade and importation are the Migratory Bird Treaty Act of 1918 and the Lacey Act Amendments of 1981. The Migratory Bird Treaty Act originally covered migratory birds between Canada and the United States, but has subsequently been amended to include agreements of the United States with Mexico, Japan, and Russia. The provisions of these amendments prohibit, unless approved by the federal government of the signed parties, the pursuit, hunting, capture, killing, possession, buying, selling, and transport, as well as attempting any of these activities with regard to migratory birds, or any part, nest, or egg of any such bird. The Lacey Act Amendments of 1981 make it unlawful to import, export, sell, acquire, or purchase wildlife, fish, or plants taken, possessed, transported, or sold in violation of state, federal, tribal, and foreign laws. This act also gives the secretary of the interior the authority to prohibit the importation of wildlife that is deemed injurious to man, agriculture, or wildlife resources. The act also requires that all shipments of wildlife or wildlife products be accurately marked or labeled on the shipping containers. It also ensures the humane treatment of wildlife shipped to the United States.

FIGURE 3.7   African Grey Parrots are one of the most heavily internationally traded species of birds.

THE LEVEL OF INTERNATIONAL TRADE IN BIRDS IN THE LAST DECADE

The legal global trade in wild birds has declined from an estimated 7.5 million birds a year in 1975, when CITES came into effect, to about 1.5 million birds in 2007 (CITES, 2007). A worldwide overview of CITES species regulated international live bird trade from 2004–2008 indicates that captive-bred birds account for over 60 percent of the trade, while wild-caught birds account for over 30 percent of the trade volume (CITES, 2011). The most heavily traded family of birds worldwide during this time was by far the Psittacidae (parrots) family, followed by Estrildidae (finches). Members of the falcon and starling families were also heavily traded worldwide. Species such as the African Grey Parrot (Figure 3.7), the Java Sparrow, Peach-faced and Fischer's Lovebirds, and Eastern Rosella, Monk, and Senegal Parrots were also traded heavily. Mortality rates for birds during transport, as reported by CITES, is less than 1.5 percent (CITES, 2007),which is far better than the previously mentioned rates for illegally smuggled birds.

In the United States, legal importation of all wild parrots has stopped except for the exempt species discussed earlier. There is still substantial importation into the United States of wild birds that are not CITES-listed birds and unregulated birds bred in captivity from around the world to the United States.

AMERICAN FEDERATION OF AVICULTURE

The American Federation of Aviculture (AFA) defines anyone keeping exotic birds in captivity as an aviculturist. The purpose of this organization is to represent all aspects of aviculture and to educate the public about keeping and breeding birds in captivity. As part of their mission, AFA maintains a legislative awareness program that operates at the international, national, state, and local levels to keep their membership aware of current and proposed laws and regulations that impact aviculture (http://www.afabirds.org). It is interesting to note that this organization started in California in 1974 after an outbreak of exotic Newcastle's disease in the early 1970s, which resulted in the deaths of millions of chickens and thousands of exotic birds in private collections. While the outbreak in California was the most serious, there were several other smaller, localized outbreaks across the United States in the early 1970s. Many of these, like the California outbreak, were traced back to imported exotic birds (Walker et al., 1973). Because of the killing of healthy exotic birds and California's legislature introducing a plan to narrowly restrict or ban the ownership of exotic birds, private exotic bird owners and exotic bird clubs mobilized to form the AFA, which now has members from across the nation, as well as international members. California did not ban the ownership of exotic birds. Working with the AFA, the USDA implemented the quarantine for imported birds entering the United States in the early 1970s, thereby reducing the risk of legally imported birds spreading communicable diseases like Exotic Newcastle disease. As described previously, during the quarantine period, all imported birds are tested to determine if they are free of certain communicable avian diseases.

REFERENCES

"[APHIS] Animal and Plant Health Inspection Service. "2011a." Accessed December 31, 2011. http://www.aphis.usda.gov/import_export/animals/com_birds.shtml

"[APHIS] Animal and Plant Health Inspection Service. "2011b." Accessed December 31, 2011. http://www.aphis.usda.gov/import_export/animals/nonus_pet_bird.shtml

Associated Press. 2012. "South Africa says 25-year sentences for rhino poachers stiffest yet." *Washington Post*. Released February 1, 2012. Accessed February 1, 2012. http://www.washingtonpost.com/world/africa/south-africa-says-25-year-sentences-for-rhino-poachers-stiffest-yet/2012/02/01/gIQAZmlshQ_story.html

"Bali Mynah." *BirdLife International (2012) Species fact sheet: Leucopsar rothschildi.* Downloaded from http://www.birdlife.org on 01/02/2012.

Babu, N. B. *TRAFFIC Bulletin.* 2011. Seizures and Prosecutions. Vol. 23, no. 3.

[CITES] Convention on International Trade in Endangered Species of Wild Fauna and Flora. 2011. "CITES Trade Data Dashboards." Released January 11, 2007. Accessed December 29, 2011. http://cites-dashboards.unep-wcmc.org/global?id=Birds

[CITES] Convention on International Trade in Endangered Species of Wild Fauna and Flora. 2007. "News and Highlights: EU ban on wild bird imports 'disappointing.'" Accessed February 1, 2012. http://www.cites.org/eng/news/press/2007/070111_EU_bird_ban.shtml

Coghlan, M. L., N. E. White, L. Parkinson, J. Haile, P. B. S. Spencer, and M. Bunce. 2011. Egg forensics: An appraisal of DNA sequencing to assist in species identification of illegally smuggled eggs. *Forensic Science International: Genetics* http://dx.doi.org/10.1016/j.fsigen.2011.06.006.

De Schrijver, K. 1995. A psittacosis outbreak in Belgian customs officers. *Euro Surveill* **0**:173.

Nature. 2012. "The Real Macaw." Public Broadcasting Service. Accessed February 1, 2012. http://www.pbs.org/wnet/nature/episodes/the-real-macaw/ photo-gallery-discover-the-charm-of-macaws/2731/

Seabrook, C. 2003. Endangered creatures for sale. *Atlanta Journal Constitution.* Released December 21, 2003.

Rosen, G. and K. Smith. 2010. Summarizing the Evidence on the International Trade in Illegal Wildlife. *EcoHealth* **7**:24–32.

TRAFFIC. 2008. "The Illegal Trade in Wild Birds for Food through Southeast and Central Europe." *TRAFFIC. Wildlife Trade Monitoring Network.* Accessed February 1, 2011. http://www.traffic. org/home/2008/11/14/illegal-trade-in-wild-birds-highlighted-at-eu-wildlife-trade.html

TRAFFIC. 2011. "Hungarian police seize thousands of dead songbirds." *TRAFFIC, Wildlife Trade News, Wildlife Trade Monitoring Network.* November, 9, 2011. Accessed February 1, 2012. http://www.traffic.org/home/2011/11/9/hungarian-police-seize-thousands-of-dead-songbirds.html

U.S. Fish and Wildlife Service. 2008. "Annual Report FY 2008." Office of Law Enforcement, Department of Interior, U.S. Fish and Wildlife Service. Accessed February 1, 2012. http:// www.fws.gov/le/pdffiles/FinalAnnualReportFY2008.pdf

U.S. Fish and Wildlife Service. 2000. *Facts about federal wildlife laws.* Department of the Interior, U.S. Fish and Wildlife Service. Arlington, VA.

United States Department of Justice. 1994. "Florida Man Sentenced in Egg Smuggling Case." Released October 12, 1994. Accessed February 1, 2012. http://www.justice.gov/opa/pr/ Pre_96/October94/592.txt.html

United States Department of Justice. 1995. "Leaders of International Wildlife Smuggling Ring Sentenced." Released December 13, 1995. Accessed February 1, 2012. <http://www.justice. gov/opa/pr/Pre_96/December95/626.txt.html

United States Department of Justice. 1996. "Final Defendant in Cockatoo Egg Smuggling Ring Sentenced to Jail, Successful Nationwide Prosecution Complete." Released April 2, 1996. Accessed February 1, 2012. http://www.justice.gov/opa/pr/1996/April96/153.enr.htm

Van Borm, S., I. Thomas, G. Hanquet, B. Lambrecht, M. Boschmans, G. Dupont, M. Decaestecker, R. Snacken, and T. van den Berg. 2005. Highly pathogenic H5N1 influenza virus in smuggled Thai eagles, Belgium. *Emerging Infectious Diseases* **11**:702–705.

Walker, J. W., B. R. Heron, and M. A. Mixson. 1973. Exotic newcastle disease eradication program in the United States. *Avian Diseases* **17**:486–503.

Wilcove, D. S., D. Rothstein, J. Dubow, A. Phillips, and E. Losos. 1998. Quantifying threats to imperiled species in the United States. *BioScience* **48**:607–615.

Wyler, L. S. and P. A. Sheikh. 2008. International Illegal Trade in Wildlife: Threats and U.S. Policy. *Library of Congress, Washington DC. Congressional Research Service.* pp.1–51.

IV FLIGHT, FEATHERS, AND ASSOCIATED ANATOMY

As indicated in Chapter 1, warm-blooded animals have advantages over cold-blooded animals: they can be more active when the temperature is cooler, such as at dawn, dusk, and night, or on cloudy days and in temperate climates. However, maintaining body temperature in cooler and cold conditions comes at a large metabolic energy cost. The evolution of feathers may have occurred to provide insulation in some of the pioneering warm-blooded animals. In avian species, the development of highly functional feather-driven flight followed after the prior development of feathers in avian precursors. While not true in prehistoric times, today, all feathered animals are classified as birds. Flight development in birds offered the advantage of escape from predators, increased foraging opportunities, and the introduced opportunity to colonize new locations to alleviate competition for limited resources. But the costs of flight for birds have been significant in regard to energy demands and body size restriction.

THE COST OF FLIGHT

The energy associated with flight capability is tremendous. Flight muscles in birds with strong flight capabilities—such as hummingbirds and pigeons—account for up to 25 percent of a bird's total weight (Greenewalt, 1962; Tobalske and Biewener, 2008). Muscle tissue has a higher energy maintenance requirement than non-muscular tissue (McNab and Salisbury, 1995), so even at rest, birds have a very high metabolic rate. Just as airplanes use a tremendous amount of fuel during flight, birds must utilize a significant amount of energy to fuel their flights. Their metabolic rates exceed those of a running mammal of equal size, as will be discussed shortly in the cardiac section. To limit energy demands, many anatomical modifications have occurred in flighted birds to reduce flight load/

weight, as will be discussed shortly in the anatomy section. As a result, flighted birds show a very narrow weight range.

The smallest flighted bird and the smallest bird overall is the Bee Hummingbird of Cuba, which weighs 1.8 to 2 grams. The largest flighted birds (Trumpeter Swans, Andean Condors, and the largest species of pelican and bustard) weigh around 15 to 16 kilograms (33–35 pounds). This gives flighted birds a body mass ratio of 1 to 8888. In comparison, the smallest mammals are the Etruscan shrew and the Kitti's Hog-nosed bat, which both have weights similar to the Bee Hummingbird. The largest mammal, the blue whale, weighs on average 110,000 kilograms (the largest terrestrial mammal is the African bush elephant at 4,900 kilograms), which means the overall body mass ratio of mammalian species is an astonishing 1 to 61,111,111, or the size ratio between walking mammalian species is 1 to 2,722,222.

On the upper end of the weight scale, birds are limited in size simply by how much the bird can weigh and successfully get into the air for flight. Larger birds have larger wings compared to smaller birds, but the increase in wing size and body size is not linear. So in larger birds, the wing has to carry more weight relative to its size than the wing of a smaller bird. For example, the wing load (g of weight/cm² area of the wing) of the small Barn Swallow is 0.14, while in a large Mute Swan it is 1.66 (Frances and Larter, 2011). Making the wings even larger relative to body size in large birds would seem like the solution, but powering those larger wings would take more flight muscles, which adds more weight. The largest flighted birds already have skeletons with the most pneumatized (hollow) bones (Figure 4.1), and given that several different orders of birds have evolved to a maximum size of about 33 to 35 pounds (15–16 kilograms), with a few rare individuals approaching 38 to 40 pounds (17–18 kilograms), it would seem that this is the weight limit for avian flight. As such, the fossil evidence indicates that *Teratornis incredibilis* weighed potentially over 44 pounds (20 kilograms) and had a 16.4-foot (5-meter) wing span, while *Argentavis magnificens* had a wingspan of about 23–26 feet (7–8 meters) and may have weighed 154–165 pounds (70–75 kilograms). Both of these birds are believed to have possessed soaring flight. By comparison, the Andean Condor and Wandering Albatross both have the largest wingspans in present-day birds at 10 feet (3 meters).

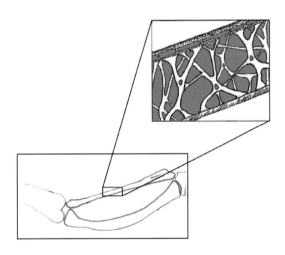

FIGURE 4.1 Flighted birds have various degrees of pneumatized or hollow bone to decrease their weight.

Birds are not smaller than the Bee Hummingbird because the energy required to maintain a high body temperature by endogenous heat production would simply be too great and would require constant feeding. As body mass decreases, the relative proportion of the body mass exposed as surface area increases. As the surface-to-body-mass ratio increases, heat loss increases. Thus, small birds lose heat to the environment at a faster rate than large birds and have to generate a lot more heat to keep their body temperature from falling. This means that small birds must eat a lot more relative to their body size than large birds. Hummingbirds consume an amount of nectar on a daily basis that is 1.6 to 5 times their body weight, depending on the sugar content of the nectar consumed and if their energy demands are increased, for example, by lower ambient temperatures (Beuchat et al., 1990; McWhorter and Martinez del Rio, 1999). So, without being able to feed 24 hours a day or giving up being warm-blooded, and thus becoming a flying insect, the size of birds is limited to just under 2 grams.

As it is, hummingbirds face tremendous pressure to get enough food to support their daytime activities and to accumulate sufficient energy reserves to survive the night with no food intake. To conserve energy, hummingbirds are capable of entering a state of torpor during the night (Lasiewski, 1963; Hainsworth et al., 1977). During torpor, the birds will decrease their heart rate and respiration rate and allow their body temperature to decrease to ambient levels, or a minimum for many species of about 20 degrees C or 65 degrees F (Perrins, 2009). However, as reviewed by McKechnie and Lovegrove (2002), the Andean Hillstar and Broad-tailed species of hummingbirds can reach a minimum temperature of 6.5 degrees C during their torpor. During torpor, hummingbirds are unable to react to external stimuli, and thus are at great risk of predation. There is also the risk that not enough energy reserve will be left when the sun comes up to initiate thermoregulatory mechanisms to return body temperature and muscle function back to normal so food consumption can start again. Thus, entering torpor may not occur and often does not occur on a daily basis in many species of hummingbirds (Hainsworth et al., 1977; McKechnie and Lovegrove, 2002), which allows them to avoid the risks associated with torpor. Torpor likely occurs only if energy reserves are depleted to some threshold level, and then, entering torpor extends the remaining reserves until food can be consumed again.

As reviewed by McKechnie and Lovegrove (2002), about 100 species of birds, including species other than hummingbirds, are able to enter into a regulated adaptive hypothermia. This number of species may be much greater, as the ability for adaptive hypothermia has not been widely investigated. Many of the species studied enter a shallow form of hypothermia, while a far fewer number are able to enter a pronounced deep hypothermia (torpor), where they are unresponsive to normal stimuli. Experts vary on their definition of what constitutes unresponsiveness, so different scientists give different numbers of bird species capable of a deep hypothermia.

Shallow hypothermia has been reported in such species as the Barnacle Goose, Black-capped Chickadee, Japanese Quail, and Bananaquit (Figure 4.2). The Greater Roadrunner of the southwestern United States is a desert dweller, and nighttime temperatures can get very low in this environment. The roadrunner, which has few predators in its desert environment, also enters into a shallow hypothermia in order to save energy (Ohmart and Lasiewski, 1971).

Bird species that experience torpor normally belong to families of birds that catch insects in the air or feed on nectar or fruit. The availability of these food supplies can be unpredictable, and most of the birds that utilize them are small in size. For example, some species of swifts will use torpor during the breeding season. If the weather turns cold, rainy, and windy during the nesting period, adults may be unable to obtain the flying insects they need to sustain themselves and their nestlings. During this time, the parents will lower their metabolic rates and body temperature and remain roosted at the nest site until warm weather returns. The early-developing nestlings, which can fast for

FIGURE 4.2 The Bananaquit is a bird species that has been known to enter into a light hypothermia during sleep.

days, enter a profound torpor and appear dead. However, if the weather improves and the parents are once again able to provide food and warmth, the chicks can successfully fledge.

The Common Poorwill is a small, insectivorous member of the nightjar subfamily and a year-round resident of the southwestern United States. It is the only species of bird that is known to become torpid and immobile for days at a time and potentially even months during the winter to conserve energy (Woods and Brigham, 2004). The Hopi Indians referred to the Common Poorwill as "the sleeping one," and given the duration that it can remain in a deep torpor, it is often considered the only hibernating bird species.

FLIGHTLESS BIRDS

The evolution in birds of the inability to fly has typically occurred on islands where natural predators were limited. Many flightless birds developed on New Zealand, where, other than a

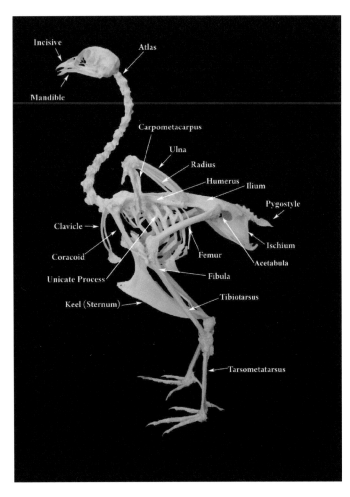

FIGURE 4.3   Skeleton of an adult chicken.

couple species of bats, humans were the first mammalian inhabitants. On New Zealand and other islands, where there was less pressure from predators, it makes sense biologically to "de-evolve" and become flightless. By being flightless, the muscle mass needed to support flight can be lost. This is significant, as flight muscles account for on average about 17 percent (Butler, 1991) of a flighted bird's mass and may approach 25 percent (Greenewalt, 1962; Tobalske and Biewener, 2008). Muscle tissue is very energetically expensive to maintain. Thus, for two bird species that weigh the same amount, one being flighted and the other one not, the amount of energy needed to simply maintain the flighted bird—even if it is not flying—is considerably greater than for the one that is not flighted and has lost the muscle mass associated with flight. With predators removed from the equation, the bird without flight capability now has a survival advantage over the flighted bird, because it needs to acquire less food. Of course, as discussed in Chapter 2, once humans and their associated animals like cats and rats arrived and settled on these islands, flightless birds were at great peril. Consequently, they account for a majority of the extinct bird species.

The limitations on body size disappear with being flightless. Several flightless birds such as the Ostrich, Emu, and Rhea have become very large, with male Ostriches weighing around 300 pounds or 140 kilograms. As adults, these large birds have far fewer natural predators than smaller birds and they have fast running abilities (Emus and Ostriches can run 30–35 miles per hour). Large ratites also have powerful kicks which can inflict deadly wounds, as will be discussed in the chapter on ratites.

The final category of birds where the evolved inability to fly has tended to occur is waterbirds. Several species of penguins exist, and all are flightless. Other examples include the Junín and Titicaca Grebes, the Galapagos Cormorant, the extinct Great Auk, and several duck species like the Fuegian Steamer Duck.

SKELETON

The skeletons (Figure 4.3) of birds show remarkable adaptations for flight. In general, the adaptations can be categorized into (1) changes that place the center of gravity in the center of the body underneath the wings; (2) changes that make the skeleton lightweight; and (3) those changes that provide overall strength for this lightweight skeleton. Having the center of gravity near the center of the body underneath the wings is an essential adaptation for flight. To accomplish this center of gravity position, the skull has been greatly reduced in size and weight. Jaw bones and teeth have been replaced by a light weight bill. The size of the head has been greatly reduced, such that the eyes often take up over 50 percent of the cranial space. The eyes are immobile in almost all birds, because the muscles to move them have been lost to reduce the overall weight of the head. The bones of the skull are lightweight and thin compared to those of mammalian species. Birds also have replaced long, bony tails with a pygostle to reduce weight and move the center of gravity to the middle of the bird. To understand the adaptations to the tail and the head as related to flight, consider the bird as an airplane: Just as planes cannot be nose or tail heavy and successfully fly, neither can a bird. The flight load needs to be near the center associated with the wings for successful, efficient, and highly maneuverable flight.

To reduce the overall weight, many of the bones of the skeleton are hollow (pneumatized), with internal struts for structural strength (Figure 4.1). In general, as flighted birds get larger, more bones become pneumatized. Many of the bones of the bird's skeleton have also been fused together so large muscles and ligaments are not needed to hold them together as in mammalian species. To reduce weight in the wing, the equivalent of our arm and hand, digits 4 and 5 have been lost. In addition to skeletal changes to reduce weight, other anatomical changes have occurred. For example, birds have no urinary bladder, as we will see in Chapter 5, and in most females, only the left ovary and oviduct develop, as will be discussed in Chapter 6.

One notable exception where the bird has more bones than mammals is in the neck. Cervical vertebrae in mammals always total seven. Obviously, the length of these seven vertebrae varies tremendously in mammalian species when you consider the length of the giraffe's neck relative to a human's neck. In birds, the number of cervical vertebrae varies from the low teens to the mid twenties, based on the length of the neck. The uppermost cervical vertebrae, the atlas, articulates with the occipital condyle at the lower back portion of the skull. The skull in birds has a single occipital condyle, which theoretically allows for nearly a 360-degree turning of the head; in contrast, mammals have two occipital condyles, which only allow turning the head 180 degrees.

Despite being lightweight in construction the skeleton is very strong in order to withstand the forces of flight. Much of this strength comes from the fusion of bones. For example, the vertebrae of the back are fused together to form the thin elongated, but rigid, synsacrum. Birds are unique in having fused clavicles (wishbone or furcula) and a keeled sternum (breastbone). The keel provides the location for the attachment for the large breast muscles needed to power flight. The ribs of almost all species of birds have unicate processes, backward-curved projections of bone that link individual ribs together and provide extra strength. The coracoid bones of birds have been elongated and strengthened into struts that prevent the collapse of the skeletal system during the powerful downstroke of flight. Each wing articulates at a point where the coracoid, wishbone, and scapula (shoulder blade) join one another to form the pectoral girdle, which is relatively immobile and provides a great deal of structural integrity.

The feet of birds are typically well placed under and straddling the center of gravity, which provides balance and stability in perching. Some ducks, loons, and other foot-propelled, swimming waterbirds have feet positioned more toward their rear, leaving them less balanced when walking, but making them excellent swimmers. In birds, the acetabula—the equivalent of our hip socket—is located toward the rear of the bird (Figure 4.3), away from the center of gravity and the large muscles and skeleton adaptations for flight. The top of the femur attaches to the hip socket bone and the femur projects forward, toward the center of gravity; it is fairly immobile. The bottom of the femur and the top of the tibiotarsus come together at the equivalent of our knee. This joint, along with the femur and hip joint, are typically hidden by body feathers and not visible to us when we look at birds.

The parts of the leg that are typically visible are the tibiotarsus, tarsometatarsus, and the foot. The junction of the tibiotarsus with the

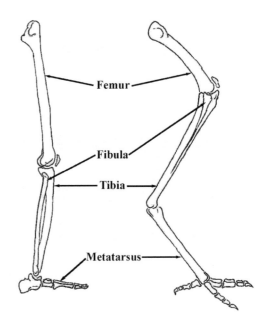

FIGURE 4.4 Comparison of the bone arrangement in the human leg and foot (left) with that of a bird (right). Note that the junction of the tibia (called tibiotarsus in birds) with the metatarsus (called tarsometatarsus in birds) at the ankle in humans is equivalent to the knee in birds and that the bird's foot is the equivalent of the human toes.

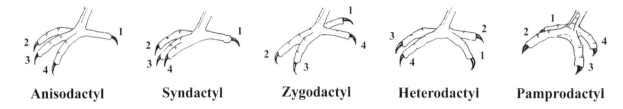

Anisodactyl   **Syndactyl**   **Zygodactyl**   **Heterodactyl**   **Pamprodactyl**

FIGURE 4.5   The different toe arrangements seen in birds.

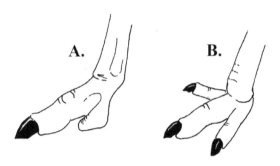

FIGURE 4.6   Ratites have an unusual number of toes for birds, with Ostriches having 2 toes (a) and Emus, Cassowaries, Kiwi, Rheas having 3 toes (b).

FIGURE 4.7   The Northern Jacana has very large feet proportioned to its body for walking in mud and upon floating plants in wetland environments. By distributing their weight over the wide surface area of their feet, they do not sink into the mud or water.

tarsometatarsus is equivalent to our ankle. Therefore, what looks like the knee in birds is really equivalent to the ankle in humans. Because the foot bones (tarsals) in birds are fused to one another and with the metatarsals to form the tarsometatarsus, birds are walking on their toes rather than our equivalent foot bones (Figure 4.4).

Leg length and strength varies tremendously in birds. Wading birds like storks, flamingos, and cranes have long legs. The large ratites have long, powerful legs designed for running. Penguins have very short legs relative to body size and have a distinctive waddling gait. Despite the appearance that the waddling walk of penguins is energy intensive, research actually indicates that waddling reduces a penguin's energy expenditure (Griffin and Kram, 2000). Even with this savings, penguins with their short legs still use twice as much metabolic energy when compared to other similar-sized terrestrial animals walking the same distance.

There are a variety of toe arrangements in birds. Most perching birds have anisodactyl feet, with three toes pointing forward and one rear pointing toe, but other arrangements are seen (Figure 4.5). Woodpeckers, parrots, cuckoos, and owls have zygodactyl feet, with the two outside toes pointed backward and the middle toes pointing forward. Trogons also have a zygodactyl arrangement of toes, but for them toes 1 and 2 point backward and toes 3 and 4 point forward, an arrangement that is termed heterodactyl. In a pamprodactyl arrangement, all the toes point forward, and this has been reported to be found in mousebirds and some swifts. However, in reality, this arrangement is rarely seen in mousebirds, and in the case of swifts, is better described as a lateral zygodactyl arrangement (Collins, 1983). In the syndactyl foot, the arrangement of toes is the same as in anisodactyl, but with two toes fused from the base partway up their length. This arrangement is found in Coraciiformes (kingfishers and allies). Ratites are tridactyl (three toes), except for Ostriches, which are didactyl (Figure 4.6). The reduced number of toes and shortened toes of ratite feet lend themselves to fast running, as will be seen in the ratite chapter.

Further adaptations are seen in the feet of birds to fit lifestyle needs. The long toes of the Jacana are ideal in spreading the weight of the bird over a large surface area so that it can hunt for food while walking on floating water lily pads (Figure 4.7). Many water birds have webbed feet, and a few birds such as grebes and coots have rounded lobes on their toes to facilitate swimming (Figure 4.8 a & b). Webbed feet can be further characterized as totipalmate: fully webbed foot involving all 4 toes; palmate: fully webbed but only involving three toes; and semipalmate: the webbing only extends partway up the toes from their base (Figure 4.9). Further adaptations to the feet of raptors will be discussed in the chapter on raptors.

The feet of birds are covered in scales and these scales extend up the leg. The amount of the expansion of scales up the legs of birds varies between species. Scales are made of keratin, the same protein that is used to make feathers. Scales provide mechanical protection.

Many birds grip food with their feet and utilize their feet as hands. Most species of parrots are well known for this practice. Birds that use their feet like hands are actually similar to humans in that they show a preference for utilizing their right or left hand/foot. African Grey Parrots are roughly equal in being either left- or right-handed, but in other avian species, left-handers outnumber right-handers by 3 to 1 (Frances and Larter, 2011).

THE PHYSICAL PRINCIPLES OF FLIGHT

In general, flight in birds is very similar to the flight principles governing airplanes. The two forces needed for flight are lift and thrust. Lift is provided naturally by the shape of the bird's wing in flight (Figure 4.10 a & b). The front of the wing is the thickest portion of the wing, as the wing bones and most of the musculature are located here. The back of the wing is thin and lightweight, as it only consists of a single thin layer of the ends of the primary, secondary, and tertiary wing feathers (Figure 4.11). The wing also gently curves downward so the back of the wing is lower than the front. As air moves against the thick front of the wing, it is either deflected over the wing or under the wing. The air that is deflected over the top of the wing creates a suction that helps lift the wing up. The air that is deflected underneath is inhibited by the downward curve of the wing feathers and pushes the lightweight feathers up. Finally, because the air flowing over the top of the wing is moving faster than the air underneath the wing, it exerts less pressure than the slower-moving air under the wing. As a result, the wing is pushed or lifted upward by the difference in pressure between top and bottom (Bernoulli effect). The next time you have the opportunity to look at the wing

FIGURE 4.8 American Coots (a) and grebes (b) (Western Grebe shown with foot outstretched) have specialized lobate feet for swimming.

Palmate

Semipalmate

Totipalmate

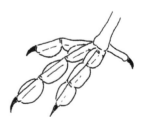

Lobate

FIGURE 4.9 Various types of webbed feet adapted for aquatic habitats and lifestyles.

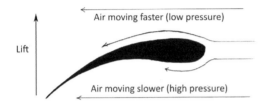

FIGURE 4.10 Falcon in flight (a). This image (b) depicts a cross-section of a wing with the leading edge being thicker than the trailing edge. The back of the wing curves downward. Both of these factors help move air faster over the top of the wing, creating lower pressure, while slower-moving air below the wing creates higher pressure. Lift is established when the higher pressure air below pushes the wing upward towards lower pressure air.

of an airplane, you can see the same design principles present in bird wings.

THRUST AND FLIGHT MUSCLES

With the lift naturally provided by the shape and anatomy of the wing, to move forward, the bird must provide thrust. The thrust is provided by flapping the wings, utilizing the flight muscles. Each wing is powered by a pectoralis major and minor muscle (supracoracoideus) that are connected by a tendon that forms a rope-and-pulley system (Figure 4.12). On the downstroke, the pectoralis minor relaxes and the pectoralis major contracts, pulling the wing down and forward, creating forward propulsion. The downward stroke is the most energy demanding and utilizes the larger of the pectoralis muscles, because it takes a lot of effort to displace the air that is beneath the wing. The upstroke occurs when the pectoralis major relaxes and the pectoralis minor pulls the wing back up. This stroke takes much less effort, as indicated by the much smaller size of the pectoralis minor. During the upstroke, the tips of the primary flight feathers separate, allowing air to pass through them; this reduces friction (drag).

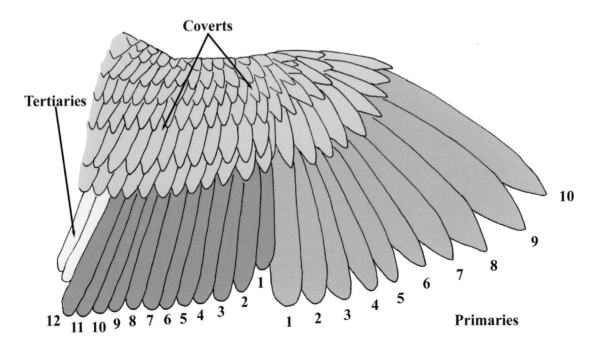

FIGURE 4.11 The different wing feathers on a bird wing.

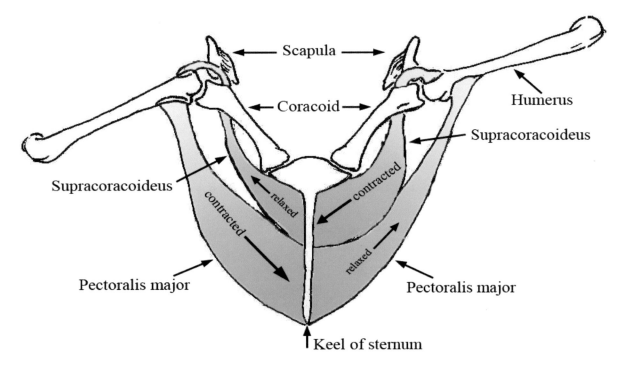

FIGURE 4.12   The pectoralis muscle and the supracoracoideus muscle are connected as a rope and pulley system, which means the wing moves upward when the supracoracoideus muscle contracts and moves downward when the pectoralis muscle contracts.

DRAG

Moving through the air during flight creates friction on the bird's body, and this is called drag. To prevent excessive drag—which would make flight even more energetically demanding—birds are very streamlined and aerodynamic. During flight, the bird presents a very sleek profile, and feathers are perfectly contoured to the body, making the bird very aerodynamic. The legs are stretched backward and held close to the body to further reduce drag. Additionally, the tail region forms a triangular shape, with the tail feathers the point of the triangle. This shape allows air flow to proceed smoothly beyond the wings with little additional friction. However, the tail feathers can be spread to provide maneuverability that can turn the direction of flight to allow the movement around objects. The amount of drag increases with bird mass and varies based on wing shape.

WING SHAPE

Gliding birds, such as albatrosses, have long but narrow wings that are ideal for gliding. Soaring birds, like vultures, have large, long wings like gliders but they are also broad in width. Often, the feathers of these high-lift capable wings will be slotted at the tips of the wings during flight, which helps reduce drag at slow flight speeds associated with soaring. The rounded nature of these wings also provides some maneuverability. Wings short in length, but rounded in shape, are typical of many songbirds and provide the highest degree of maneuverability. Sharp turns in flight while fleeing predators or while maneuvering within trees and bushes are characteristic of these birds. The pointed and backswept wings of swifts and swallows are narrow and can be flapped rapidly to provide for rapid flight with minimum drag. Penguins have stiff, compact wings that they use like flippers for underwater swimming.

TAKE-OFF AND LANDING

Getting into the air is the most energy-demanding moment of flight, as the bird has to accelerate rapidly to pass stalling speed. For lighter-weight birds like songbirds, this is accomplished by springing into the air, with the legs providing most of the initial thrust and velocity followed by wing flapping. With the first few flaps, the position of the bird is more perpendicular to the ground, so these flaps are producing vertical lift and the primary wing feathers are spread apart to reduce turbulence. Once into the air, the bird leans forward to initiate the flight mechanics discussed above.

For larger birds like swans, grebes, albatrosses, and many ducks and geese, flight must be initiated by running along the ground or on water to generate enough speed to create the lift necessary for take-off. This maneuver replicates exactly what airplanes have to do to take off. For large birds, flight can also be initiated by taking off from an elevated position such as a cliff along the seacoast. Gamebirds, which are fairly large, have an explosive flight that is rapidly initiated from the standing position to avoid predators. This flight is fueled by very large flight muscles, and the flight only lasts for a short distance.

Landing, like take-off, requires a great deal of energy compared to cruising flight, because the forces of friction are much greater in association with slower speeds. Landing takes much more skill to be done smoothly than take-off. To land, a bird will drop its air speed until it is about to stall. Then it will increase the angle of its wings, lower and spread its tail so that lift is decreased and drag is greatly increased. This brings the bird basically to stop. The legs and feet are extended and the bird lands (Figure 4.13). Birds can also land by targeting a spot lower than their intended final perch and then when they reach this lower point, they will brake by swooping upward so

FIGURE 4.13   When a bird lands, it brings its wings nearly vertical, acting as brakes, and extends its feet.

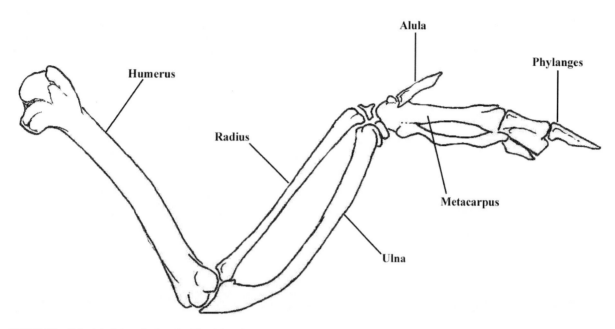

FIGURE 4.14   Skeletal depiction of avian wing. The alula and its associated feathers can assist with maintaining smooth airflow over the wing.

their forward speed is zero by the time they reach their intended perch. Swans are some of the heaviest flighted birds, and thus have lots of forward momentum and land on water using their large webbed feet as brakes, as they skid along the surface of the water as their speed slows.

At the low speeds associated with take-off and landing, the alula (Figure 4.14) plays a critical role in maintaining smooth airflow over the wing. The alula feathers (3 to 4), attached to the first digit of the wing, can be raised and help maintain lift by ensuring smooth airflow over the wing, thus preventing stalling when the angle of the wing is very elevated during landing or take-off (Figure 4.13).

ECONOMICAL FLIGHT

It is not unusual to see large birds of prey such as hawks, eagles, and vultures soaring high in the sky in a circular motion as they look for their next meal. These birds are taking advantage of the thermals created when the sun heats the ground. The heating of the earth's surface is uneven, with fields or areas of sparse vegetation heating up more quickly than areas with trees and/or water. As the air above an area of heated ground warms, it becomes lighter and rises relative to the surrounding cooler and denser air, creating a thermal. Birds will ride a thermal, gaining elevation within the thermal, until the warm air begins to cool with elevation and stops rising. Soaring birds with large, broad wings that provide for lots of lift will descend slowly like a glider based on their body weight, but typically find the next rising thermal to repeat the process before reaching a landing altitude. The disadvantage for birds depending on thermals is that they do not form until well after sunrise, once the sun has warmed the ground sufficiently for thermals to form. Use of thermals for flight is done with minimal or no flight powered by wing flapping. Wind is deflected upward by mountain ranges, which also will create rising air for lift, and it has the advantage of being present with or without the heat of the sun.

Dynamic soaring is seen in albatrosses and related birds. In this form of soaring, the bird extracts lift energy without flapping its wings by repeating a cycle of 180-degree turns at two different elevations above a large body of water (Sachs, 2005). The shear wind near the surface of the ocean has a velocity that is considerably less than at elevation, as wind speed increases loga-rithmically with altitude. Thus, for the albatross, the cycle consists of a windward climbing flight, generated by the increase in wind speed, followed by change of flight direction to the leeward. During the leeward descent flight, the bird simply glides, powered by the effects of gravity on its own weight. As it nears the water surface it will change direction to the windward, which starts the cycle over again. By repeating this cycle, a wandering albatross can cover 6,000 to 12,000 miles (9,700 to 19,300 kilometers) of ocean over a 10- to 20-day period obtaining food (Frances and Larter, 2011).

Flying in formation can also save energy if the birds are positioned correctly to take advantage of it. This type of flight is probably most synonymous with geese flying in a V-formation, but it occurs in other species as well with birds such as pelicans and cranes. A bird behind another bird in formation will have a reduction in wind resistance created by the bird in front, and flying in this reduced-resistance zone saves energy that has been estimated at 11 to 14 percent in pelicans (Weimerskirch et al., 2001). The lead bird is not receiving this energy savings benefit, and that is why changes in the lead bird are often witnessed.

HOVERING

Hovering is seen in relatively few birds because it is energetically the most costly form of flight (Dial et al., 1997). For most birds, such as kestrels, hovering flight is accomplished by flying into a head wind at a speed equal to that of the wind so there is no net forward movement. Hummingbirds are the only truly specialized hovering birds, as they are the only birds that can hover in place based totally on their own wing-generated power. To accomplish this feat, the wings of humming birds are shaped slightly differently than other birds and operate differently. The wings of a humming-bird move incredibly rapidly (roughly 12 beats per second for large hummingbirds to a little over 80 beats per second for small hummingbirds [Feo and Clark, 2010]) and in a figure-eight pattern. This wing movement provides lift on both the downstroke, like other birds, but also on the upstroke, which is not birdlike but rather like the flight of insects (Warrick et al., 2005). With weight support provided by both the down- and up-stroke, hummingbirds can hover. Not only does the specialized flight of hummingbirds allow them to hover, but it also allows hummingbirds to fly backward—the only birds physically able to do so.

HEART

Flighted birds have an aerobic metabolic capability that is about twice that of running mammals of equal size. During flight, oxygen consumption in birds increases by 5 to 14 times the value at rest to meet the significantly increased metabolic rates (Milsom, 2011). This need for more oxygen is delivered in part by a five- to six-fold increase in heart rate (Milsom, 2011) and the heart muscle of birds is better adapted with greater blood flow, muscle fiber number, and better oxygen extraction capability to sustain long-term exercise than comparable mammalian hearts (Bishop, 1997; Peters et al., 2005, as reviewed by Gill, 2007). The respiratory system and its increased efficiency in birds relative to mammalian species will be covered in Chapter 5.

The heart is similar in form and function to ones found in mammalian species. The avian heart has four chambers, but it is larger compared to a mammalian species of the same body mass—not surprising given the aerobic needs associated with flight. Larger birds tend to have proportionally smaller hearts relative to body size than smaller birds. Hummingbirds have proportionally the largest hearts relative to body size compared to all other birds, and this results from their highly energy-demanding flight that requires a great deal of hovering flight while feeding. Birds have bigger stroke volumes than a mammal of corresponding size, but at rest, they have slower heart rates than an equal-sized mammal. Cardiac output reflects the combination of stroke volume and heart rate. Although heart rate is lower, the difference in stroke volume is great enough such that cardiac output adjusted to equal body mass is higher than in mammalian species (Lasiewski and Dawson, 1967; Calder, 1968; Grubb, 1982, 1983).

FEATHERS

Feathers, like the other epidermal appendages of the bird—such as claws, scales, and beak—are constructed of a unique fibrous protein called beta-keratin. Beta-keratin is used in the construction of scales and claws in reptiles, and overall, the molecular evolution of beta-keratins parallels the evolution of birds and reptiles (Greenwold and Sawyer, 2011). In birds, the beta-keratin multigene family has diverged into four major subfamilies: scale, claw, feather-like, and feather. The avian scale subfamily of beta-keratin genes are closely related to the beta-keratins of crocodilians and are more basally derived than the avian feather beta-keratin subfamily of genes (Greenwold and Sawyer, 2011). Although derived from the same protein family, molecular evidence does not indicate that feathers evolved directly through morphological changes to scales, and a number of theories have been proposed for the evolutionary origin of feathers. The evolutionary stages of feather development were covered in Chapter 1.

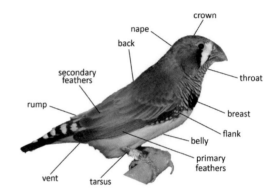

FIGURE 4.15 Feather coloration of birds is often used for identifying species in the wild. It is therefore important to know the different feather locations on the body.

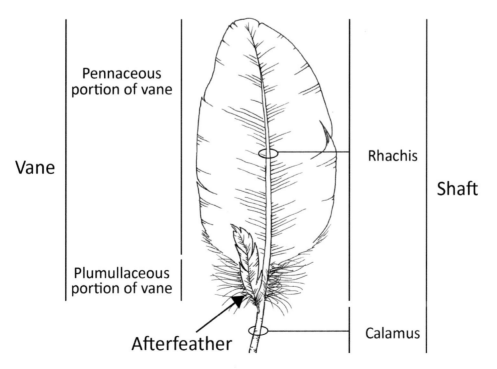

FIGURE 4.16 The various parts of a feather.

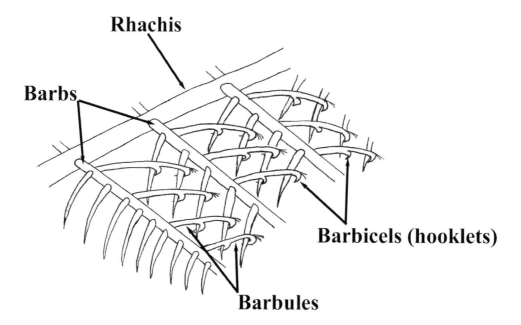

FIGURE 4.17   An enlarged version of the parts of a feather. Many feathers can be "zipped" back together if they are comprised of barbs, barbules, and barbicels that can hook together, ensuring a smooth, aerodynamic surface for flight.

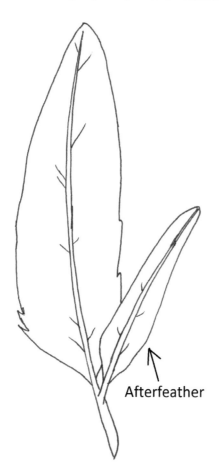

FIGURE 4.18   In some bird species, the afterfeather is very enlarged which will give the bird a shaggy appearance as is seen in many ratites.

FEATHER STRUCTURE AND FUNCTION

Birds have several types of feathers which provide for a highly aerodynamic exterior (Figure 4.15) and superior insulation capabilities. In some flightless birds, the aerodynamic feather exterior has been lost and this is commonly seen in ratites; we will explore this further in the chapter on ratites. Feathers are produced by feather follicles located under the skin, and the growth of feathers will be discussed in a later section of this chapter. Feather follicles are arranged in specific tracts called pterylae, and in between these are featherless areas called apteria. A feather shaft can be broken into two distinct parts. The smooth, strong base of the feather that extends under the skin is called the quill or calamus (Figure 4.16). The portion of the center feather vane above the skin from which the lateral branches extend is called the rachis. The lateral branches/filaments that project from each side of the rachis are called barbs. In larger structured feathers, the barbs have two sets of microfilaments projecting from their sides; these projections are called barbules. The upper row of barbules from one barb cross over and hook with the lower barbules from the barb positioned above it (Figure 4.17). The tiny hooklets are called barbicels. The latching of the barbicels forms a feather that is smooth and well held together to meet the demands of flight. The barbicels are like Velcro in that they can come detached, but can easily be reattached when the bird preens its feathers.

The section of the feather that consists of the rachis with barbs is called the vane. At the base of large body feathers, there is typically an afterfeather, (Figure 4.16), which looks like a miniature version of the full-sized feather. It can provide some insulation, and in a few birds, the afterfeather is full sized (Figure 4.18), giving the bird a shaggy appearance, as will be discussed in the ratite section. Finally, feathers with barbules and barbicels are considered pennaceous feathers, while fluffy feathers without barbules and barbicels are called plumulaceous feathers. In reality, pennaceous feathers have a plumulaceous portion that varies in size at their bottom portions.

There is tremendous variation in feather types and structure within an individual bird and between species of birds. The remiges are the primary, secondary, and tertiary flight feathers (Figures 4.19 and 4.11). There usually are ten primary feathers (the number can be more or less in a few species) at the end of each wing, and they are involved in generating the forward thrust of flight. The barbs on each side of the rachis are not symmetrical, with the leading (exterior) edge being narrower (Figure 4.20), as it is the portion that cuts through the air in flight. The total number of secondary and tertiary flight feathers varies from species to species, with hummingbirds having less than ten and albatrosses having four times that many (Gill, 2007). The secondary flight feathers function in providing the lift associated with flight, while the tertiary feathers help prevent turbulence by providing a smooth confluence between the wing and the body. The large flight feathers are covered by several sets of successively smaller feathers (coverts) arranged like roofing shingles to provide a smooth, un-gapped, highly aerodynamic structure (Figure 4.21).

Retrices are the tail feathers (Figure 4.22) that attach to the pygostyle. Their structure is similar to the flight feathers, except they are more symmetrical in shape. These feathers are used like a rudder and a brake in flight as discussed above. The typical number of tail feathers is 12, but there is species variation in this number. In many species, the tail feathers are highly specialized social signaling instruments (Figure 4.23) for attracting mates (Figure 4.24). The

FIGURE 4.19 The primary, secondary, and tertiary feathers of a macaw wing.

FIGURE 4.20 The primary feathers found in flighted birds have assymetrical barbs on each side of the rachis with the leading (exterior) edge being narrower.

FIGURE 4.21   Covert feathers cover the large flight feathers and help create a streamline arrangement between the wing and the body.

FIGURE 4.22   A retrix, or tail feather, of a macaw.

rachis of the tail feathers in woodpeckers is exceptionally thick and strong. The undersides of these strong tail feathers are held flush to the tree to provide support for the wood-pecking activities of the bill (Figure 4.25).

Contour feathers (Figure 4.26) are the major externally visible feathers covering the body, and they tend to be pennaceous for the part that is externally visible and plumulaceous near the body to provide insulation. They overlap one another so the external body covering of the bird is streamlined and aerodynamic.

Semiplume feathers (Figure 4.27) have a large rachis with loose plumulaceous vanes. They have a varied appearance based on their intermediate structure between down and contour feathers, with the fluffy appearance of down feathers but the length of contour feathers. They provide insulation, but are often specialized display feathers used for attracting mates.

Down feathers (Figure 4.28) are soft, fluffy feathers that are underneath the contour feathers and are not visible externally. The fluffy structure of these feathers typically results from a lack of a central rachis with flexible barbs and barbules, instead extending directly from the calamus. The loose structure of the down feathers allows them to trap a layer of insulating air near the skin surface. Additionally, many bird species will utilize down feathers to line the insides of their nests in order to provide insulation for the eggs and hatchlings.

Filoplume feathers (Figure 4.29) are hairlike feathers scattered throughout the plumage of the bird. They consist of a thin rachis that ends with a tuft of barbs with barbules at their follicular base, and they are associated with sensory corpuscles at their follicle. Given their structure, filoplume feathers are not easily visible even when they extend past contour feathers, and they are unable to trap air for insulation. However, they are perfectly suited in structure to monitor the movement and position of adjacent veined feathers and to relay this information to the muscles at the base of the monitored area, which then may contract or relax to change a feather's position.

Bristle feathers are typically located near the eyes and bill (Figure 4.30) and may serve as eyelashes (as will be covered in Chapter 5), or for a host of other hypothesized functions. These functions include food collection in birds that eat flying insects, protection of the eyes from struggling insect prey during handling, protection of the openings of the nose and ears from particle entrance, and sensory perception. However, accumulated research evidence is limited for any of these suggestions. In captive Willow Flycatchers, removal or taping of bristle feathers did not affect their ability to capture live houseflies (Conover and Miller, 1980). Cunningham et al. (2011) recently examined the feather histology and morphology of bristle feathers in five insect-eating birds in New Zealand, and found that they were associated with vibration and pressure-sensitive mechanoreceptors. This suggests that the bristles have a tactile function that could be involved in prey detection, prey handling, or gathering information for navigation in nest cavities, in flight or on the ground.

In addition to the functions of flight, insulation, food collection, and sensory reception, feathers also play vital roles in social signaling, camouflage, and in some species, sound collection. The roles of feathers in social signaling will be presented in Chapter 5 with visual communication and in Chapter 6 with mate selection. The role of feathers in camouflage will be discussed in subsequent sections on feather coloration and molting. Finally, the importance of feathers in hearing will be discussed in Chapter 5.

FIGURE 4.23 The Turquoise-browed Motmot has unique tail feathers that it uses for social signaling.

FIGURE 4.24 In the case of the male peacock, it is a fan of enlarged tail covert feathers that provides for a stunning display to attract females.

FIGURE 4.25   Woodpeckers and woodcreepers have exceptionally thick and strong tail feathers used for support while pecking and prying for food.

The amount of feathers covering the body varies incredibly based on species and geographic location. Birds living at high latitudes have more feathers than those in tropical climates. Overall, feathers typically constitute anywhere from 5 to 15 percent of the total body weight of birds, and often outweigh the mass of the skeleton sometimes by as much as twice.

FEATHER COLORATION

There is an immense array of colors that are found in the plumage of birds. These colors result from pigments, feather structure, or a combination of the two. A detailed examination of feather color in birds is provided in the book *Bird Coloration, Mechanisms and Measurements*, by Hill and McGraw (2006). Pigments are chemicals that absorb and emit wavelengths of visible light. The resulting colors are produced by pigments dependent on the structure and concentration of the pigment. Except for albinos, all birds have some melanin coloration, making it the most widespread pigment coloration seen in birds. It is responsible for all black coloration and for most of the brown, rufous, gray, and buff colors seen in birds. Just as in humans, it also provides skin color in birds. Melanin pigments are all synthesized in the bird by cells called melanocytes, utilizing the essential amino acid tyrosine as a base molecule. Because the melanocytes are synthesizing and releasing the pigment into the developing feather cells, precise genetic-based control is possible and this is why banding (bars) and spotting patterns seen in plumage (Figure 4.31) involve

FIGURE 4.26 Contour feathers overlap one another all over the body to keep the bird streamline for flight. The feathers may come in various shapes to cover different parts of the body. Contour feathers are pennacious for the part that is externally visible and plumaceous near the body to provide insulation.

black, brown, and other melanin-based colors. Melanin deposition into the feather appears to strengthen them both structurally and by making them more resistant to microbes that digest (and thus degrade) feathers. This strengthening effect is hypothesized to be the reason why many generally all-white birds have black tips on their flight feathers, which experience a great deal of friction-based wear in flight (Figure 4.32). Melanins are also often added to feathers to shade or provide a background for other colors.

Carotenoid pigments are the second most prevalent family of pigments found in birds and are responsible for most of the red, orange, and yellow colors of plumage. Well-known examples of plumage color derived from carotenoids include those of the flamingo, Roseate Spoonbill, Scarlet Ibis, Common Canary, and Northern Cardinal. In addition, the red, yellow, and orange leg and bill colors of many birds, including ducks, geese, and chickens, are also derived from carotenoids. Birds cannot synthesize these pigments, so they have to be ingested either directly by eating algae, fungi, or plants or indirectly by ingesting prey animals such as insects, vertebrates, and crustaceans that contain them through dietary acquisition. As carotenoids are obtained from the diet, there is often a huge variation in color based on intake of individual birds of a species, as well as differences in color based on season, age, and sex differences. Because carotenoids are deposited into feathers based on their absorption from the blood, the precise control for

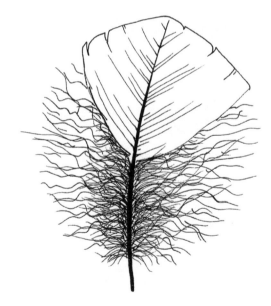

FIGURE 4.27 Semiplume feathers have a large rachis with loose plumulaceous vanes. They provide insulation, but are often specialized display feathers used for attracting mates.

FIGURE 4.28   Down feathers are soft, fluffy, insulating feathers that are underneath the contour feathers and are not visible externally in adult birds.

FIGURE 4.29   Not easily visible, filoplume feathers are hair-like feathers scattered throughout the plumage of the bird.

barring and striping in feathers seen with melanin is not possible. Carotenoids are also antioxidants that protect cells from oxidative stress. Therefore, they are important in the health of birds and provide a basis for the association that bright plumage coloration in an individual of a species indicates that the bird is in good health, as will be discussed further in Chapter 7. Because of their antioxidant properties, carotenoids are deposited in the yolks of eggs by females to give their offspring optimal development.

There are a couple of other pigment classes that have been identified for providing color in some birds. Porphyrins are common pigments, as both chlorophyll (the green of plants) and heme (blood color pigment) are pigments belonging to this family. In birds, the brown and rufous color of the feathers of several birds, most notably in bustards, owls, and nightjars, are porphryin based. Additionally, turacin, a red pigment, and turacoverdin, a green pigment, both found in most turaco species (Figure 4.33), are porphyrins complexed with copper. Porphyrins are synthesized by the bird. The red combs and wattles of birds are mostly colored by blood, which gets its color from the porphyrin heme; but in some cases, the red color is derived from both blood coloration and red carotenoids. Brown, blue, olive, and bluish-green colored egg shells also owe their color to porphyrins, with the blue and green colors coming from heme that has been degraded to form biliverdin.

Parrots synthesize psittacofulvins, which are pigments that are responsible for the red, orange, pink, and yellow colors exhibited by several species in this family (Figure 4.34). Undoubtedly, other

FIGURE 4.30   Bristle feathers are typically located on the face, as seen on this owl, possibly for sensory reception. On the right and an illustration of an individual bristle feather. An illustration of an individual bristle feather is represented on the right.

feather pigments await identification, so the list presented will likely increase. In fact, the yellow/orange color found in several penguin species (Figure 4.35) is from a pigment that does not match any currently described pigment. Finally, a few species add color to their feathers from external sources like soil or secretions from the preen gland. Male Great Hornbills, for example, use a vivid yellow secretion from their preen gland to stain white feathers on their wings and neck.

Structural colors are also widespread in bird plumage. These colors are produced by the physical interaction of light waves with the structure of the feather that causes the light to be scattered. How the light is scattered depends on the refractive indices of the feather structures with which it interacted. In general, structural colors are produced by three classes of feather anatomical structures. White color is produced by incoherent scattering of all visible wavelengths of light from the unpigmented feather component beta-keratin. Structurally colored feather barbules typically produce iridescent structural colors by scattering light coherently from arrays of highly organized melanin granules, suspended in the beta-keratin of feather barbules. Iridescence is an optical phenomenon in which there is a change in color based on a change of the angle of observation or angle of illumination. Hummingbirds are characterized by having iridescent colors, especially on their throats. At certain angles, little or no light will be reflected back to the observer and the throat feathers of a hummingbird can appear black, but as the viewing angle changes, the refracted light becomes visible in glowing and shimmering iridescence. Finally, non-iridescent blues, violets, and greens can be created when feather barbs that are spongy in structure (organized air pockets or channels intermixed with the beta-keratin) scatter light coherently. The blue color of the Indigo Bunting (Figure 4.36) is an example of this type of structural color.

In addition, many plumage colors arise from the combination of different pigments or pigments and structural colors. Green, for example, is a very common plumage color in birds, and except for species of turaco, it results by combining yellow carotenoid or yellow psittacofulvin pigmentation with blue structural colors. Olive green can result from a combination of carotenoids and melanins. Additionally, a melanin-based color normally underlies many structural colors; this can be seen by backlighting a feather which eliminates the reflectance of the structural color so it is no longer seen leaving only the plumage color from melanin (Figure 4.37).

FEATHER USE BY HUMANS

Just as down feathers are used by birds for insulation, harvested down feathers often taken from geese have a soft texture and wonderful insulation capabilities, making them ideal in the manufacturing of winter external clothing, pillows, blankets, and sleeping bags. Colorful and/or ornate feathers have been heavily used in fashion

FIGURE 4.31 Banding or barring on feathers, as seen on this Barred Rock Rooster, is an example of a plumage pattern precisely controlled by genetics.

FIGURE 4.32 Many white birds, such as this White Pelican, have melanin pigment on their wing tips, giving these feathers strength to account for the wearing that occurs during flight.

FIGURE 4.33   The red and green colors of most Turaco species are derived from porphyrins complexed with copper.

FIGURE 4.34   Psittacofulvins are pigments synthesized by parrots and they are responsible for the red coloration found in this female eclectus.

throughout the years, especially in the 18th, 19th, and 20th centuries. These feathers were typically used on women's hats. The display plumes of the Snowy and Great Egrets were highly coveted, and this demand nearly caused their extinction. The exploitation of birds for feathers for the sake of fashion led in part to the passage of the Lacey Act in the United States, as discussed in the last chapter. Although similar legislation at national levels and CITES at the international level protect endangered birds, the plumage from commercial and unprotected wild birds is still used as a fashion accessory around the world.

In sport, feathers have long been used for fletching arrows and in fishing lures. Feathers from Ostriches, which are fluffy and lack barbicels, have often been used in feather dusters. In earlier times, larger, quilled feathers were used as writing instruments, and the word pen is derived from the Latin word *penna*, which means feather. Feathers from birds killed for human consumption are collected and typically turned into feather meal. Poultry is the most widely consumed farm animal meat in the world. In the United States alone, there are over two billion pounds of feathers available for feather meal production each year. The feathers are heated under pressure to partially hydrolyze them, and then they are ground to make feather meal. Although not the most digestible feed ingredient available, it is often incorporated into animal and pet feeds, or used as an organic fertilizer.

Around the world, certain bird feathers can have significant cultural or spiritual value. An illustrative case of this is the recent decision by the United States Federal Government to grant a permit for the killing of up to two federally protected Bald Eagles to an Indian tribe in Wyoming for religious purposes (Ahtone, 2012). Many Native American tribes utilize Golden and/or Bald Eagle feathers in religious ceremonies. In recognition of this, a clause permitting the harvesting of these eagles was originally placed in the Bald and Golden Eagle Protection Act. Finally, feathers can be used in the biomonitoring of heavy metal and other pollutants in environments. Birds exposed to high levels of these compounds will produce feathers that have elevated levels of these pollutants.

FEATHER MAINTENANCE

Bathing (Figure 4.38) is routinely done by birds to clean feathers, and when water is readily available, it can happen daily. When water is not available, birds will resort to bathing in dried, loose particles of dirt—a dust bath which is the only form of bathing practiced by some bird species. The purpose of a dust bath is obviously not the removal of dirt, but may be useful in dislodging lice, ticks, and mites that may be feeding at the skin of the birds. Dust bathing can also physically remove or rub off oils on the feather surface.

Even more important than bathing is feather preening. On average, birds spend 8.5 percent of their day grooming (Cotgreave and Clayton, 1994) using their bills, heads, or their feet to preen and manipulate feathers. For the Sword-billed Hummingbird, which has the longest beak in relation to body size, feather preening can only be accomplished using its feet, and in other species, the feet are often used for preening the head feathers. Preening allows birds to remove any debris from their feathers, to adjust any misplaced feathers, and to reattach any barbicels that have become dislodged from adjacent barbs. These actions ensure that the external feather plumage is highly aerodynamic for flight. The next time you have the opportunity to hold a wing or tailfeather, pull apart the barbs to create a ragged appearance. Then, with one hand holding the quill, take two fingers from your other hand and slide them with the feather in between them away from your other hand. When you do this, your fingers are acting like the bill of a bird—you can observe that this action has reattached many of the barbicels to barbs. With a couple repetitions of this action, the feather will return to its original, smooth, and aerodynamic state.

Most bird species have a uropygial gland (preen gland) located at the base of the tail on the lower back (Figure 4.39). Some notable exceptions of birds without a preen gland are species of ratites and parrots. The preen gland produces a lipid-based secretion that is applied to feathers while birds are preening. The oily secretion is released through a nipple-like opening at the top of the gland. Application of this oil is accomplished using the bill, or birds will rub their head feathers on the preen gland and then transfer the oil from these feathers to feathers on other areas of the body. This oil makes the feathers more waterproof and flexible and inhibits feather wear and breakage.

Some species of birds also have powder feathers that are specialized modified down or pennaceous feathers that can be found scattered in the plumage or concentrated in dense patches, as reviewed by Delhey et al. (2007). These feathers grow continuously, with small pieces of the ends of the barbs or barbules breaking off and disintegrating into a fine talcum-like powder. This powder is applied to the rest of the plumage by the bill or with the head feathers similar to preen oil. The function of the powder seems very similar to that of preen oil in maintaining and waterproofing the feathers, and the uropygial gland is absent or very reduced in many species with well-developed powder feathers. The powder can also change the appearance of feather color by enhancing sheen and diluting dark colors, and thus plays a role in social signaling. Some birds that have powder feathers are species of parrots, pigeons, and herons. Several species of parrots have powder feathers, which can cause allergy issues in some humans who keep them as pets, as will be discussed in the chapter on parrots.

Feather-degrading bacteria do exist, but the ability to digest/ break down beta-keratin, the main structural component of feathers, is uncommon in bacteria species. There is now evidence that the preen oil produced by some birds contains bactericides that offer protection against some of these bacteria (Shawkey et al., 2003;

FIGURE 4.35 The yellow pigment found in penguin plumage has yet to be identified.

FIGURE 4.36 The blue color of the Indigo Bunting is a result of structural color, not a blue pigment.

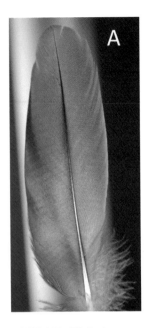

FIGURE 4.37 This feather possesses structural colors as well as melanin-based pigments. This image shows the same feather under normal, reflective light (a), reflecting the structural blue and green colors and portraying the colors we see. When the feather is backlit (b), only the brown, melanin-based colors remain.

FIGURE 4.38 Most birds bathe daily in either water or dust to maintain their feathers. Here a Crimson Rosella is bathing in a waterbath.

Martín-Vivaldi et al., 2009). Interestingly, the antimicrobial chemicals contained in Hoopoe preen oil secretions are actually produced by symbiotic bacteria residing in the preen gland (Martín-Vivaldi et al., 2009).

Another unusual behavior documented for at least a few hundred species of birds is anting. During this behavior, birds rub insects (typically ants) onto their feathers. The purpose of this behavior is unknown. One common hypothesis regarding this behavior is that the birds are inducing the ants to discharge defensive secretions such as formic acid onto their feathers. These secretions may then serve as an insecticide, miticide, and/or a bactericide that inhibits feather degrading bacteria. Anting behavior has also been documented with birds using snails and fruit, as reviewed by Gunderson (2008).

FEATHER REPLACEMENT

Worn and damaged feathers need to be replaced. Typically, at least once a year, birds will replace old feathers with new feathers in a process called molting. Molting of damaged and worn feathers ensures that birds will be able to maintain or regain flight ability throughout their adult lives. This is an adaptive advantage, as bats that suffer badly damaged wing membrane(s) have no ability to regain flight. Molting also allows for seasonal changes in appearance for mating or camouflage purposes. The White-tailed Ptarmigan, which is white in winter to blend in with the arctic snow, replaces these feathers with mottled brown-colored feathers in the spring to blend in with ground-level vegetation, where it spends its time during the day foraging for food.

Molting is a highly regulated process due to the energy involved in making new feathers and the energy costs associated with inefficient insulation and flight when feathers are missing. The timing, frequency, and the extent of molt varies widely from species to species, and the physiological regulation of molting is poorly understood and may well differ between species. Most parent birds are challenged to provide enough food and are often unable to provide sufficient food for all of their offspring to survive the brooding period. Therefore, during this period, parent birds want to be at peak flight performance; thus, high levels of sex hormones are thought to prevent feather molt. In non-breeding periods, feathers are molted, and this can be accomplished rapidly, or slowly over time. For example, ducks, swans, and geese that breed at the high latitudes will, at the end of the breeding period, shed all of their primary flight feathers at the same time and will be unable to fly for a few weeks. This rapid molting process in these birds allows them to have a complete set of new, highly efficient feathers by the time that they need to migrate south for the winter. In other species that cannot afford or survive being flightless, the molting process is accomplished in an orderly sequential pattern over a much longer period of time, until all feathers of the body are replaced. This ensures functional, but less efficient flight, as the feathers are slowly replaced a few at a time.

FEATHER GROWTH

Feathers develop from feather follicles located underneath the skin with an opening at the skin surface. Feather follicles have a rich blood supply that is heavily utilized during feather growth, as a great deal of energy is needed for the feather growth process and for the delivery of the amino acid building blocks used to construct the beta-keratin protein-based feather. As the new parts of the feather are being constructed at the follicle base, it pushes recently completed parts upward, and this pushes the old feather out of the follicle. Growing feathers are tubular in structure, with the outer layer as the sheath. The tubular feather surrounded by its sheath emerges through the skin as a pinfeather (Figure 4.40) and continues to extend further as more cells are added at the follicle base. The sheath eventually ruptures at its end, allowing the feather to unfurl, and when the feather's growth is complete, the sheath completely falls away from the entire length of the feather. Given this growth pattern, it means the tip of the feather is the oldest part of the feather, while the root of the feather is the youngest part. It is the same pattern as the growth of your hair and fingernails. However, unlike your hair and fingernails, the feather does not continue to grow. When the feather is fully grown, the living pulp of the feather base is reabsorbed, leaving a completely dead structure.

MIGRATION

WHY BIRDS MIGRATE

The term "migration" may evoke visions of honking geese flying over in a V-formation. These geese are an example of a large-scale, annual movement, or migration, between breeding and non-breeding grounds. Some animals hibernate in order to endure severe seasons, but animals that migrate are allowed year-round activity. In general, birds migrate from areas of low or decreasing resources to high or increasing resources. Though not all birds migrate, thousands of avian species split time in two locations in order to exploit seasonal feeding opportunities in favorable climates throughout the year. Though escaping cooler weather is a motivating factor to migrate, many birds species could survive the freezing temperatures as long as an adequate food supply is available. Birds also migrate to reach adequate nesting sites that include ample space, protection, and resources to raise young.

FIGURE 4.39   The uropygial or preen gland is located just above the tail.

FIGURE 4.40   These pin feathers on the wings of a young Blue and Gold Macaw are filled with a rich blood supply as they grow.

There seem to be no absolute parameters that determine whether a species migrates. It has been argued that neotropical migration evolved from frugivorous diets or habitat choice (Levey and Stiles, 1992). However, recent analysis of 379 species supported these two factors being related to migration, but in more complex ways than proposed (Boyle and Conway, 2007). Food availability, which depends on various factors, has been named the main factor in predicting whether a particular species will migrate. Birds that engage in flocking behavior are also less likely to migrate. When birds band together to search for food, the group is more efficient than a lone individual. Therefore, when faced with a food shortage, the birds can either forage in groups or migrate (Boyle and Conway, 2007). Ultimately, birds migrate in order to take advantage of milder climates and increase their food resources throughout the year. But why haven't all bird species evolved to migrate? One possibility is that certain traits make some species more likely to migrate, and research is slowly providing some light on which traits encourage migratory behavior.

TYPES OF MIGRANTS

Until recently, researchers have been unable to track individual birds moving between their breeding and wintering grounds, and therefore there is relatively little known about which particular birds travel where. There is even less known about events that occur between these two locations. Now, through modern techniques such as chemical isotope analysis, molecular genetic markers, and radio telemetry, scientists are gaining insight into where certain birds go for a good portion of the year.

Not all birds migrate, and the birds that do may not travel that far. Non-migratory birds are called permanent residents. These birds are able to thrive in one habitat for the duration of the year. There are several types of migrants, classified according to the distance they migrate. Short-distance migrants may only move from lower to higher elevations on a mountainside with the season, while medium-distance migrants travel several hundred kilometers. Long-distance migrants travel thousands of kilometers to reach their wintering grounds. Many long-distance migrants have ranges extending from Canada and the northern United States in the summer to Mexico and Central America in the winter. The Arctic Tern makes the furthest yearly journey of any bird, flying 40,000 km (25,000 miles) from its Arctic breeding grounds to winter in Antarctica. These classifications, however, do have some variations and can even vary within species. Some populations within a species, such as the Hairy Woodpecker or the Northern Bobwhite, are short-distance migrants, while the rest of the species remain permanent residents of an area year-round (Cornell Lab of Ornithology, 2012). These categories can vary, but in general, they help divide the many migratory birds into behavioral and natural history classifications that can be useful in conservation planning.

TRIGGERS AND CUES FOR MIGRATION

Birds must time migration with annual cycles of various factors. Migration is a predictable, seasonal cycle corresponding to favorable climate or food availability. There are many innate and external cues that signal a bird's physiology to begin preparing for migration. Birds have instinctive circadian (24-hour cycle) rhythms and circannual (cycle of Earth's rotation around the sun) rhythms that can influence physiological changes and do not require the cue of external factors to maintain. Studies performed on starlings, housed without natural daylight cycles, still came into breeding plumage and molt at a similar time as comparable wild starlings (Gwinner, 1977). In nature, migratory birds are cuing off of their environment through factors such as daylight length, weather, genetic disposition, and food availability, all of which can trigger daily departures and rest stopover sites. Birds will try to avoid flying into headwinds and will sometimes wait for tailwinds in the weather to help conserve energy. The time in which certain cues will trigger individual birds does vary, with different species and even different segments of a population following different migratory patterns.

Once a bird is cued to begin preparing for migration, it may exhibit some degree of restlessness, called zugunruhe, leading up to migration, as well as begin frantically gorging itself on food and eating constantly. This gorging state is called hyperphagia and occurs several days or weeks before beginning migration. During this period, the bird will increase its weight by up to 36 percent, storing enough excess fat to be converted to energy during the long journey (McLandress and Raveling, 1981). In addition, some species switch their diet to nutrient-rich food in order to deal with the stresses of journey.

HOW BIRDS NAVIGATE

Migrating birds are able to travel the same course for thousands of miles each season to and from their nesting and non-breeding grounds, often without deviating far from the same route. First-year birds are able to migrate unguided by elders to wintering grounds that they have never seen before and then return to where they were hatched. Many of the mechanisms for how birds are able to do this remain a mystery—however, birds do seem to utilize a combination of several techniques such as navigating by the stars or the sun, sensing the earth's magnetic field, landscape recognition, and even by smell. Navigation techniques will be covered more thoroughly in Chapter 10 on pigeons.

THE COST OF MIGRATION

In addition to having physiological requirements, migration comes at a cost. Time spent migrating is time that could be used for breeding; however, year-round resident species face the harshness of winter and tend to have a lower survivability (Cornell Lab of Ornithology, 2012). Though overall survivability increases with the option of migration, the journey is not without its hazards. Birds undergo a great deal of physiological stress during the trip, where they may be deficient in food supplies or fly into inclement weather. They also risk exposing themselves to predators.

Some species, especially waterfowl and shorebirds, follow specific flight paths year after year, stopping at certain stopover sites to refuel and rest. These sites often contain vital food items that must be gathered in order to continue the bird's journey. About 80 percent of the North American Red Knot (Figure 4.41) population stop in Delaware Bay during their migration, to feed specifically on horseshoe crab eggs, fattening their bodies for the rest of the trip (Cornell Lab of Ornithology, 2012). The harvesting of horseshoe crabs in the bay has severely affected the Knot population, and management efforts are now in place to increase the crab population (Karpanty et al., 2011). It is important to learn more about the migratory pathways and stopover sites in order to assist, rather than hinder, an already energetically expensive and dangerous endeavor undergone by thousands of bird species biannually.

SUMMARY

Highly specialized feathers allow birds to fly, which allows escape from predators and the colonization of new areas. But the costs of flight to birds are enormous, both from an anatomical and physiological perspective and considering the energy intake required to fuel flight. Feathers are

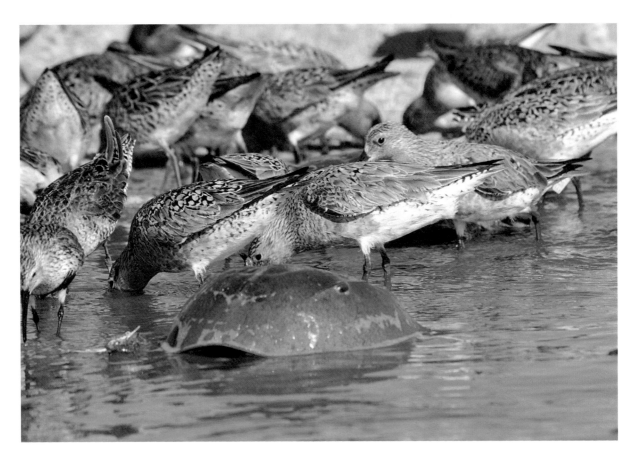

FIGURE 4.41   Red Knots at their migratory stopover site in the Delaware Bay, feeding on horseshoe crab eggs.

used by birds for many other purposes like insulation, social signaling, and camouflage. Feather colors are derived from pigments, their microscopic structure, or a combination of these two. Maintaining feathers in their highly functional state requires birds to spend a good portion of their day completing grooming activities, such as preening and bathing. However, the maintenance of the feathers ensures that they function efficiently, which can be the difference between survival and death. This feather maintenance is vital for events like migration. Not all birds migrate, and the costs and benefits must be weighed as to whether a species or population will migrate. Though often energetically expensive, migration coincides with many benefits when birds are flying to destinations with a more reliable food supply, more space for breeding territory, or a more desirable climate during a particular season of the year.

FURTHER READING

Chu, M. 2007. *Four Seasons in the Lives of Migratory Birds*. Walker Publishing Company, Inc. New York.

REFERENCES

Ahtone, T. 2012. "Wyoming Tribe Wins Right to Hunt Two Bald Eagles." National Public Radio. Accessed 04/23/12: http://www.npr.org/2012/03/19/148919990/wyoming-tribe-wins-right-to-hunt-two-bald-eagles

Beuchat, C. A., W. A. Calder, and E. J. Braun. 1990. The integration of osmoregulation and energy balance in hummingbirds. *Physiological Zoology* **63**:1059–1081.

Bishop, C. M. 1997. Heart mass and the maximum cardiac output of birds and mammals: Implications for estimating the maximum aerobic power input of flying animals. Philosophical *Transactions of the Royal Society of London. Series B: Biological Sciences* **352**:447–456.

Boyle, W. A. and Courtney J. Conway. 2007. Why Migrate? A Test of the Evolutionary Precursor Hypothesis. *The American Naturalist* **169**:344–359.

Butler, P. J. 1991. Exercise in Birds. *Journal of Experimental Biology* **160**:233–262.

Calder, W. A. 1968. Respiratory and heart rates of birds at rest. *Condor* **70**:358–365.

Collins, C. T. 1983. A reinterpretation of pamprodactyly in swifts: A convergent grasping mechanism in vertebrates. *Auk* **100**:735–737.

Conover, M. R. and D. E. Miller. 1980. Rictal bristle function in Willow Flycatcher. *Condor* **82**:469–471.

Cornell Lab of Ornithology. 2012. "All About Birds: Migration." Accessed 03/24/2012: http://www.birds.cornell.edu/AllAboutBirds/studying/migration/

Cotgreave, P. and D. H. Clayton. 1994. Comparative analysis of time spent grooming by birds in relation to parasite load. *Behaviour* **131**:171–187.

Cunningham, S. J., M. R. Alley, and I. Castro. 2011. Facial bristle feather histology and morphology in New Zealand birds: Implications for function. *Journal of Morphology* **272**:118–128.

Delhey, K., A. Peters, and B. Kempenaers. 2007. Cosmetic coloration in birds: Occurance, function, and evolution. *American Naturalist* **169**:S145–S158.

Dial, K. P., A. A. Biewener, B. W. Tobalske, and D. R. Warrick. 1997. Mechanical power output of bird flight. *Nature* **390**:67–70.

Feo, T. J. and C. J. Clark. 2010. The displays and sonations of the Black-chinned Humingbird (Trochilidae: *Archilochus alexandri*). *Auk* **127**:787–796.

Frances, P. and S. Larter. 2011. *Illustrated Encyclopedia of Birds*. BirdLife International. Dorling Kindersley Limited, London.

Gill, F. B. 2007. *Ornithology. 3rd edition*. W. H. Freeman and Company, New York.

Greenewalt, C. H. 1962. Dimensional relationships for flying animals. Smithsonian Miscellaneous Collections **144**:1–46.

Greenwold, M. J. and R. H. Sawyer. 2011. Linking the molecular evolution of avian beta (β) keratins to the evolution of feathers. *Journal of Experimental Zoology Part B: Molecular and Developmental Evolution* **316B**:609–616.

Griffin, T. M. and R. Kram. 2000. Penguin waddling is not wasteful. *Nature* **408**:929–929.

Grubb, B. R. 1982. Cardiac output and stroke volume in exercising ducks and pigeons. *Journal of Applied Physiology: Respiratory, environmental, and exercise physiology* **53**:207–211.

Grubb, B. R. 1983. Allometric relations of cardiovascular function in birds. *American Journal of Physiology: Heart and Circulatory Physiology* **245**:H567–H572.

Gunderson, A. R. 2008. Feather-degrading bacteria: A new frontier in avian and host-parasite research? *Auk* **125**:972–979.

Gwinner, E. 1977. Circannual Rhythms in Bird Migration. *Annual Review of Ecology and Systematics* **8**:381–405.

Hainsworth, F. R., B. G. Collins, and L. L. Wolf. 1977. The function of torpor in hummingbirds. *Physiological Zoology* **50**:215–222.

Hill, G. E. and K. J. McGraw. 2006. *Bird Coloration, Mechanisms and Measurements*. Harvard University Press, Cambridge, MA.

Karpanty, S. M., J. Cohen, J. D. Fraser, and J. Berkson. 2011. Sufficiency of Horseshoe Crab Eggs for Red Knots During Spring Migration Stopover in Delaware Bay USA. *Journal of Wildlife Management* **75**:984–994.

Lasiewski, R. C. 1963. Oxygen consumption of torpid, resting, active, and flying hummingbirds. *Physiological Zoology* **36**:122–140.

Lasiewski, R. C. and W. R. Dawson. 1967. A re-examination of the relationship between standard metabolic rate and body weight in birds. *Condor* **69**:13-23.

Levey, D. J. and F. G. Stiles. 1992. Evolutionary Precursors of Long-Distance Migration: Resource Availability and Movement Patterns in Neotropical Landbirds. *American Naturalist* **140**:447–476.

Martín-Vivaldi, M., A. Peña, J. M. Peralta-Sánchez, L. Sánchez, S. Ananou, M. Ruiz-Rodríguez, and J. J. Soler. 2009. Antimicrobial chemicals in hoopoe preen secretions are produced by symbiotic bacteria. *Proceedings of the Royal Society B: Biological Sciences* **277**:123–130.

McKechnie, A. E. and B. G. Lovegrove. 2002. Avian facultative hypothermic responses: A review. *Condor* **104**:705–724.

McLandress, M. R. and D. G. Raveling. 1981. Hyperphagia and Social Behavior of Canada Geese Prior to Spring Migration. *Wilson Bulletin* **93**:310–324.

McNab, B. K. and C. A. Salisbury. 1995. Energetics of New Zealand's temperate parrots. *New Zealand Journal of Zoology* **22**:339–349.

McWhorter, T. J. and C. Martinez del Rio. 1999. Food ingestion and water turnover in hummingbirds: How much dietary water is absorbed? *Journal of Experimental Biology* **202**:2851–2858.

Milsom, W. K. 2011. Cardiorespiratory support of avian flight. *Journal of Experimental Biology* **214**:4071–4072.

Ohmart, R. D. and R. C. Lasiewski. 1971. Roadrunners: Energy conservation by hypothermia and absorption of sunlight. *Science* **172**:67–69.

Perrins, C. 2009. *The Princeton Encyclopedia of Birds*. Princeton University Press, Princeton, NJ.

Peters, G. W., D. A. Steiner, J. A. Rigoni, A. D. Mascilli, R. W. Schnepp, and S. P. Thomas. 2005. Cardiorespiratory adjustments of homing pigeons to steady wind tunnel flight. *Journal of Experimental Biology* **208**:3109–3120.

Sachs, G. 2005. Minimum shear wind strength required for dynamic soaring of albatrosses. *Ibis* **147**:1–10.

Shawkey, M. D., S. R. Pillai, and G. E. Hill. 2003. Chemical warfare? Effects of uropygial oil on feather-degrading bacteria. *Journal of Avian Biology* **34**:345–349.

Tobalske, B. W. and A. A. Biewener. 2008. Contractile properties of the pigeon supracoracoideus during different modes of flight. Journal of Experimental Biology **211**:170–179.

Warrick, D. R., B. W. Tobalske, and D. R. Powers. 2005. Aerodynamics of the hovering humming-bird. *Nature* **435**:1094–1097.

Weimerskirch, H., J. Martin, Y. Clerquin, P. Alexandre, and S. Jiraskova. 2001. Energy saving in flight formation. *Nature* **413**:697–698.

Woods, C. P. and R. M. Brigham. 2004. The avian enigma: "Hibernation" by Common Poorwills (Phalaenoptilus nuttalli). Pages 129–138 *in* B. M. Barnes and C. Carey, editors. *Life in the cold: Evolution, mechanisms, adaptation and application.* 12th International Hibernation Symposium.

V SENSES, SOUND PRODUCTION, AND RESPIRATION

Part of people's fascination with birds is undoubtedly related to the fact that they are similar to us in the way that vision and hearing play critical roles in their lives. For the most part, birds, like us, are active during the day and perceive their surroundings primarily through sight and secondarily through auditory signals. Furthermore, they communicate with one another through visual displays and vocal communication. In our daily lives, it is often very easy for us to witness, appreciate, and even understand birds' visual and vocal interactions—and that is why bird-watching is one of the most common hobbies of humans. Our shared dependence with birds on the senses of vision and hearing also explains in part why birds are popular pets. The scent-dominated world of cats and dogs is hard for humans to comprehend and appreciate because our sense of smell, like that of most bird species, is relatively undeveloped compared to our primary senses of vision and hearing.

VISION

Despite being highly visual ourselves, our vision pales in comparison to birds. An indication of the importance of vision in birds is that, relative to their overall body size, birds have very large eyes. This is easily appreciated by the fact that the eyes of large eagles and owls approach or equal the size of human eyes. The terrestrial vertebrate with the largest eye is the Ostrich, not a large mammal such as the elephant or rhinoceros. It is not uncommon for avian eyes to occupy 50 percent or more of the cranial volume, so there is little room left for musculature to move avian eyes. Thus, avian eyes are relatively immobile, but birds make up for this deficiency by having heads that can readily and swiftly turn at least 270 degrees.

Other than being large, the overall structure and function of the avian eye is not really different from humans. Incoming light passes through the cornea, the anterior chamber, the lens, and the vitreous body. These components act to magnify and focus an image onto the retina, where photoreceptors convert light energy into electrical impulses that are processed by the central nervous system. Because the overall design and function of the avian eye is similar to humans, our focus will be to point out important differences in avian vision relative to humans. Excellent reviews of avian vision have been written by Waldvogel (1990) and Jones et al. (2007). The reader is encouraged to refer to these for further details on the mechanics of avian vision.

EYE SHAPE AND POSITION

Eye shape varies among birds. Most birds have flat eyes which allow for a large field of view, but decrease resolution a bit. Tubular-shaped eyes are found in nocturnal species such as owls, and they provide for increased light to be acquired for vision in low-light situations. Finally, spherical or globose-shaped eyes are common in daylight hunters like raptors, and they provide for better visual acuity at the expense of some field of vision.

Eye position in the head of a bird varies as well. Woodcocks have eyes located very high up on the sides of their heads, which gives them a 360-degree visual field. Most diurnal birds have eyes positioned on the side of their heads, but they are positioned more in the center of the head. This positioning, when combined with their flat eyes, results in visual fields that are not as impressive as the woodcock, but are in the 300-degree range. Raptors and insect-eating birds, like swallows, that catch flying insects have eyes that are still located on the side of the head, but moved forward toward the beak. With this eye positioning and globose eye shape, they gain much visual acuity, but sacrifice some on visual field. Finally, owls have eyes positioned similarly to humans in the front of their heads, which restricts their visual field, but provides for greater light-gathering ability since twice the amount of light is gathered from an object within view of both eyes.

COMPONENTS OF THE EYE

FIGURE 5.1   Ostriches are one of the few bird species that possess specialized feathers around their eyes, similar to our eyelashes.

Like humans, birds possess both upper and lower eyelids which can be closed during sleep. The eyelid, when closed, can provide mechanical protection for the eye. Eyelids in birds may or may not contain specialized hairlike feathers that are similar to our eyelashes, but a few species such as Ostriches and raptors do possess these feathers (Figure 5.1). Some birds like the Ostrich, Black-Browed Albatross, and night heron species have enlarged eyebrows (Martin and Katzir, 2000), and most raptors are well known for their distinctive supraorbital ridge: a bony ridge covered with feathers that extends above and in front of the eye (Figure 5.2). As in humans, the presence of eyelash feathers and eyebrow structures are thought to reduce glare from the sun and to protect the eye from wind and debris such as dust.

Unlike humans, birds have a nictitating membrane, which is a transparent/translucent third eyelid that lies beneath the other two eyelids. It can be rapidly swept across the eye to clear the surface of the eye of any debris and to moisten the eye (Figure 5.3). It can also provide mechanical protection to the eye. In owls, the nictitating membrane is opaque and thicker in construction and moves slowly across the eye.

Eyes are moistened by secretions from Harderian and lachrymal (or lacrimal) glands.

The iris is muscular tissue that controls pupil size, and the pupil regulates the amount of light reaching the retina. Iris color in birds varies from the more typical deep browns to bright red to include yellow, white, pale blue, and green. Most birds have large pupils, so more light strikes the retina in birds than in mammalian eyes of the same size. Pupils dilate to gather more light when looking at distant objects, and the pupil constricts when looking at close objects. In dim light or darkness, pupils also dilate to let in more light. The pupil opening is round in almost all birds except skimmers (Rynchopinae subfamily, within the Laridae [gull and tern family]), which have a vertically slit pupil in bright light that becomes rounded in dim light (Zusi and Bridge, 1981).

Birds active at night have an eyeshine when bright light is focused on them, resulting from the reflection of the light from the tapetum lucidum membrane. This membrane naturally reflects visible light back through the retina, increasing the light available to the photo-receptors, which improves vision in low-light conditions. Because humans can readily detect eyeshine, ornithologists will often use spotlights to create the eyeshine when trying to detect nocturnal birds in the field.

The avian retina, unlike the retina of mammals, is avascular, which is thought to have evolved to prevent shadows and light scattering. This makes nutrient uptake more of a challenge in bird retinas. However, birds have a unique black-pigmented, pleated structure known as the pectin. Containing many blood vessels, the pectin is located in the eye's posterior chamber and projects towards the retina. The exact purpose of the pectin is unknown, but one of the hypothesized functions is to deliver nutrients and oxygen to the internal portion of the eye.

Like the human retina, the avian retina contains both cone and rod cells. Cone cells are responsible for color vision and sharp visual acuity, functioning best in daylight. Rod cells produce black-and-white vision and are needed for night vision, as these photoreceptors respond to light of lower brightness. Thus, nocturnal birds possess rod-dominant retinas, as opposed to the heavy concentration of cone cells in the retinas of diurnal birds. Cone cells in birds have some unique features. First, they can contain an oil droplet, and avian cone cells can either be single-celled (as in humans) or double-celled functional units. The purpose of the double cells is not well understood. The number of cones in birds can easily be double to five times greater than the number found in human eyes per square millimeter, accounting for birds' superior vision.

COLOR AND ULTRAVIOLET VISION

All diurnal birds appear to have excellent color vision that most likely far exceeds our own color vision in discriminating subtle color

FIGURE 5.2   Most raptors have a boney protuberance over their eye called a supraorbital ridge.

FIGURE 5.3   The nictitating membrane is a third translucent eyelid in birds that can be seen covering half of the eye of this Naked-Neck Rooster.

FIGURE 5.4   The Blue Tit can be found in a number of countries in the Eastern Hemisphere and is especially well-known in Britain. To human eyes, males and females look similar, but to bird eyes, which are sensitive to UV light, the males have brilliant purple crowns.

differences. Humans have three cone photopigments, but birds may have more. The human retina is trichromic, as it contains cones that respond to wavelengths of 560 nm (red cones), 530 nm (green cones), and 420 nm (blue cones). So when light with a wavelength of 530 nm strikes the retina, the green cones respond the strongest, and the object from which the light emanated is perceived as green. Different color hues are perceived when the light wavelength stimulates the three spectral classes, for example, a wavelength of 490 would generate a submaximal response from all three cone types to varying degrees, such that the mixed response would be perceived as purple (Jones et al., 2007). Bird cones have similar spectral sensitivity to red, green, and blue. But many species have a fourth spectral class in the ultraviolet or near-ultraviolet range (roughly 300 to 400 nm), with peak sensitivity in the near-ultraviolet part of the electromagnetic spectrum at a wavelength of about 365–370 nm for passerine species (Vorobyev et al., 1998). This means that most bird species have visual capability in the ultraviolet range. Many fruits reflect in the ultraviolet range, and plumage can appear very colorful with ultraviolet reflection. For example, the colored throat patches of common pet budgerigars reflect ultraviolet light, and thus glow to the eyes of birds. The crests of Blue Tits (Figure 5.4) look similar between males and females to our eyes, but with ultraviolet visual sensitivity, the males have a brilliant purple crown patch and females prefer the males with the brightest crown. Many other examples of ultraviolet light perception by birds have been discovered, as reviewed by Rajchard (2009).

As mentioned earlier, the cone cells of birds often contain oil droplets. The exact purpose of these oil droplets has not been elucidated. The appearance of these oil droplets varies, based on the concentration and type of carotenoid pigments that it has. In cone cells containing an oil droplet, light must pass through this droplet before striking the cone photoreceptor. Thus, the ultimate response of a given cone cell can vary not only on the spectral sensitivity of its photopigment, but also on the transmittance characteristics of its oil drop. Therefore, the typical avian retina is capable of discriminating among many more wavelengths of light than humans and is likely to perceive even the slightest color differences.

VISUAL FIELD

Birds have a large part of their visual field, perhaps about 20 degrees, sharply in focus at any one moment—compared to the 2–3 degrees that humans can focus on sharply (Perrins, 2009). The overall visual fields of birds vary a great deal based on the position of the eyes on the head and the shape of the eye as already discussed. The visual field is made up of both monocular vision (vision with one eye) and binocular vision (vision with both eyes due to the overlap between the visual fields of the individual eyes). For birds with forward-facing eyes such as owls, the visual field may be around 150 to 200 degrees, with 45 to 70 degrees of this total being binocular vision (Figure 5.5b). On the other extreme is the American Woodcock, which has flat eyes located laterally and close to the top of the head, which gives it a 360-degree visual field with limited binocular vision in front and in back of its head (Figure 5.5c). For the woodcock, which spends much of its time on the ground probing for food, this visual field allows it to detect potential predators sneaking up on it from the sides and from behind. All other birds fall between these extremes. Typically, most birds have laterally placed eyes on the side of the head like the pigeon, which has a 300-degree visual field (Figure 5.5a). Raptors and birds that catch insects in the air such as swifts and swallows have more forward-facing eyes, which provides greater binocular vision than most other birds, but less than owls'. Thus, excluding owls, most other birds fall into the range of 15 to 30 degrees of binocular vision, with raptors making the upper end of this range.

Monocular vision and its association with wide visual fields allows birds to detect motion and potential predators for their survival. Behavioral studies indicate that many avian species prefer monocular vision for fixating and inspecting distant objects, as indicated by them turning their heads sideways to the object. Birds have very good lateral (monocular) visual acuity.

Binocular vision is excellent for depth perception, and thus, judging distance, as the input from both eyes is needed to compute the distance of a visual target. As reviewed by Martin (2009), binocular vision in birds is primarily used for the control of the bill or feet position in foraging and/or feeding young. It can also be used by some species to inspect items held in the bill, such as during the building of nests. Finally, it is used for flight control, obstacle avoidance when flying or running, and precise landing at the end of a flight. Interestingly, only 5–10 degrees of binocular vision are needed for the control of locomotion.

VISUAL ACUITY

For many birds, visual acuity, which reflects the degree of resolving power of the visual processing system, is 2.5 to 3 times better than ours; this is especially true for the raptors. Thus, most birds can resolve the details of an image that is about three times further away from them in distance than we can. The American Kestrel's visual acuity is astounding, as it is capable of discriminating 2 mm insects from 18-meter treetops (Fox et al., 1976), which helps explain the hunting prowess of this raptor. Raptors achieve this acuity by having large pupils and a higher-than-average density of cones in the retina compared to other birds. Birds with exceptionally large visual fields have less visual acuity, and their visual acuity may not be much greater than that of humans.

DETECTING MOTION

Motion sensitivity in birds is much better than that of humans. The frequency at which motion can no longer be resolved is called the flicker-fusion frequency. Humans have the ability to resolve sequential moving images only at frequencies less than 60 hertz, while birds are able to resolve movements faster than 100 hertz. For us, images projected at frequencies above 60 hertz blend together to create continuous movement that motion pictures depend on for seamless viewing. At higher frequencies of 80 hertz or greater, the motion becomes erratic to human eyes, as the viewed image does not have time to register, but this would not be the case for birds. Put another way, birds can easily distinguish the individual flashes

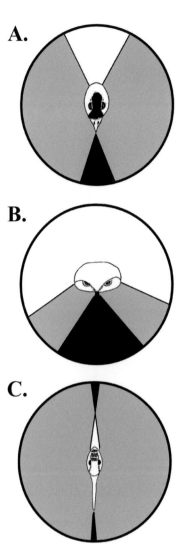

FIGURE 5.5 A comparison of visual field among three types of birds: pigeon (a), owl (b), and woodcock (c). In the figure white shading indicates no vision present, light purple shading indicates the monocular visual field and dark purple shading indicates the binocular visual field.

FIGURE 5.6   The male Resplendent Quetzal can grow a tail longer than 3 feet (91 cm).

FIGURE 5.7   Normally lying flat, the brilliant crest of the Royal Flycatcher protrudes forward to communicate or convey aggression.

of a fluorescent light bulb oscillating at 60 hertz, while we would see continuous light. The sensitivity of birds to motion is critical as they maneuver with agile precision around obstacles during rapid flight, and the detection of movement is critical for many species in obtaining food and avoiding becoming food.

Besides allowing them to resolve rapid movement, the retina of birds also allows them to detect slowly moving objects. As was discussed in the migration section of the flight chapter and in the upcoming pigeon chapter, birds are able to detect the movement of the sun traveling through its daily arc or the rotation of other celestial bodies and constellations, while we cannot. Birds use this ability for migration, navigation, and homing ability.

UNIHEMISPHERIC SLOW-WAVE SLEEP

Unihemispheric slow-wave sleep in birds is characterized by sleeping with one eye open and half of the brain awake. It allows birds to detect approaching predators while still getting rest. Dolphins, whales, seals, and manatees also exhibit unihemispheric slow-wave sleep, as it allows them to sleep and swim to the surface to breathe. Birds seem to be unique in that they can elect at will to sleep with both halves of the brain asleep or half the brain asleep. When there is more risk of predators, the proportion of unihemispheric slow-wave sleep increases (Rattenborg et al., 1999). In research with sleeping rows of Mallard ducks, Rattenborg et al. (1999) discovered that birds on the end of the row were more likely to utilize unihemispheric slow-wave sleep, and for 86 percent of the time, the eye remaining open was the one oriented away from the group's center.

VISUAL COMMUNICATION

Vision is used for visual communication, flight, foraging, and predator detection. Visual communication is highly effective in birds and visual signals are used to attract mates, ward off enemies. and provide recognition. Visual communication is based primarily on plumage color and shape, but beak and leg coloring are also used to communicate messages, especially for mating purposes. The plumage and tail feathers of the Resplendent Quetzal (Figure 5.6), for example, visually communicate to female quetzals his suitability and fitness as a potential mate. Many birds will raise their head feathers to convey aggression (Figure 5.7) and the Sunbittern can transform itself to appear like a large eyed monster by spreading its wings (Figure 5.8). Many ground-nesting birds such as the killdeer, found throughout much of North America, visually communicate to threatening nest predators. In order to lead the predator away from their nest, they will pretend to have a broken wing by fluttering it helplessly as they walk away from the nest site.

HEARING

Vocalizations are used by birds to communicate important messages such as alarm and food source location, but they are also used for echolocation in dark caves, to attract mates, and to defend territory. Bird communication utilizing calls and songs is something we can easily hear on a daily basis. For birds, vocal communication has advantages over visual communication, in that it can be transmitted for longer distances and can be transmitted while the sender and receiver both can be hidden in vegetation. Booming sounds produced by large species of bitterns or by the Kakapo Parrot can be heard up to three miles away. Similarly, the bell-like "bonk" of the male Three-wattled Bellbird (Figure 5.9) breeding in Costa Rica is one of the loudest bird songs produced and can be heard for at least a mile.

To hear vocalizations produced by other birds and other noises in their environment, birds have a hearing capability roughly equal to ours, except that many species may not be able to hear low frequency sounds as well as humans. However, birds can distinguish sounds that are very much closer in time than humans, such that what a human hears as one note may have been heard by a bird as up to ten separate notes (Perrins 2009).

ANATOMY AND HEARING BASICS

Birds have none of the external ear components which are found on mammalian species. A bird's ear openings are typically funnel shaped and hidden beneath plumage, behind and below each eye. The ear openings can be easily seen in scaleless chickens (Figure 5.10), which have been bred for their lack of scales and, thus, feathers. In other birds, the ear is typically covered by specialized feathers called auricular feathers that are adapted to minimize flight turbulence, while not impeding sound transmission. Specialized reflector feathers that are dense enough to influence the path of sound can be positioned to reflect and amplify sound entering the ear, as is the case in Barn Owls (Figure 5.11). Owls have acute hearing abilities that exceed those of humans and allow them to locate and catch prey that is moving on the ground. Owl ear openings are often asymmetrical, located so that the source of sound can be better pinpointed based on the differences in intensity and timing of sounds heard between the two ears. This allows owls to capture prey in total darkness, unassisted by vision (Frances and Larter, 2011).

The middle ear in birds consists of one middle ear bone called the columella instead of consisting of three bones (Figure 5.12), as is the case in mammals. The inner ear of birds consists of a cochlear organ and a vestibular organ that are part of the bony labyrinth (a network of bony passages or canals) of the inner ear. The saccule and utricle are part of the vestibular organ, which is involved in maintaining balance and equilibrium. The cochlea, which is not coiled as it is

FIGURE 5.8 Sunbitterns may fan their wings out in a defense posture in order to appear larger. The spots resemble giant eyes.

FIGURE 5.9 The Three-waddled Bellbird's call can be heard from great distances.

FIGURE 5.10 The ear opening can be easily visualized in this scaleless, and therefore featherless, chicken.

FIGURE 5.11 Like many owls, the Barn Owl has specialized feathers around its face that form a disc shape which funnels sound to its ears.

in mammals, is involved in converting sound waves into neuronal impulses that are translated as sound in the brain.

In general, hearing is accomplished by airborne sound waves entering the ear and impinging on the tympanic membrane (eardrum) of the ear. Movement (vibration) of the tympanic membrane is translated to the inner ear via the ossicle of the middle ear. This cartilaginous and bony ossicle is called the columella in birds. The end of the columella fits into the oval window of the cochlea of the inner ear, so movement of the columella causes oscillations of the inner ear fluid. In the inner ear, oscillations of the inner ear fluid cause movement of the basilar membrane, which leads to the mechanical movement of hair cells whose excitation, in turn, allows chemical transmission of information from the auditory nerve to the central nervous system. From there, the information is processed and the bird hears. In mammals, loss or damage to the hair cells results in hearing loss that is irreversible. At least in some species of birds, hair cells have the ability to regenerate after damage or loss, as reviewed by Dooling and Dent (2001).

ECHOLOCATION

Echolocation occurs in two families of birds: the Steatornidae (oilbirds) and Apodidae (swiftlets) and is used for orientation in dark caves. Oilbirds (Figure 5.13) roost and nest deep within caves; these birds feed during the night and are typically not exposed to daylight. Visually, oilbirds have large pupils that allow for the highest light-gathering capability of any bird (Martin et al., 2004). Additionally, the rod cells within the eye are banked three deep, with a density of one million per square millimeter. The stacked arrangement of rod cells results in a loss of temporal and spatial resolution, so they depend on emitted vocal clicking noises for echolocation within the caves they use for nesting and roosting.

SMELL

Overall, the sense of smell is not as well developed in most bird species as the senses of vision and hearing. Air passes through the external nares located on a bird's bill through two sequential nasal chambers that lead to a third chamber. Olfactory sensory neurons in the olfactory epithelium lining this third chamber detect odors and conduct impulses via the olfactory nerves to the olfactory bulb of the brain, which, in turn, sends neural messages to higher brain centers for odor perception. Traditionally, it has been thought that birds have a limited sense of smell because they do not display behaviors indicative of a reliance on olfactory cues. Typically, you do not observe birds with their noses to the ground smelling as they walk like you see with dogs, nor do you see them stretching their nostrils in the air sniffing for scents as you do in other animals. Furthermore, in birds studied thus far, the olfactory bulbs varied widely in size and many of them were small, which contributed to the perception that the sense of smell was not well developed in birds. This traditional perception is changing, as more research indicates that several bird species have a very well-developed sense of smell as reviewed by Caro and Balthazart (2010). Tubenoses (Procellariiformes) like petrels and albatrosses have tubular nostrils (Figure 5.14) and a highly developed sense of smell that they use to locate food in water. Similarly, the Kiwi has nostril openings at the tip of its long bill, and the sense of smell plays an important role in Kiwis locating food. New World vultures have perforated nostrils (Figure 5.15), and some of them, such as the Turkey Vulture, locate decaying flesh based on smell, as will be discussed in Chapter 6.

Further indication that the ability of birds to smell was underestimated previously has come from research involving olfaction in birds unrelated to them foraging for food. As we will discuss in Chapter 10, homing pigeons use olfactory cues in order to return home. Additionally, sensitivity to pheromones (volatile hormones that bind to receptors in the nasal passages of the receiver, causing a response or communicating information) has been documented and suggested in several bird species (Caro and Balthazart, 2010). The combined research evidence indicates that the role of smell in birds needs to be further researched, and that the decades-long assumption that the bird's sense of smell was not developed or utilized needs to be clarified across the broad spectrum of bird species.

TASTE

Taste does not appear to be well developed in birds. Birds have relatively few taste buds compared to other animals. For example, the number of taste buds found in chickens, Blue Tits, bullfinches, Japanese Quail, starlings, and parrots was 24, 24, 46, 62, 200, and 350, respectively (Mason and Clark, 2000; Frances and Larter, 2011). This compares to 9000, 15,000, 17,000, and 100,000 taste buds for humans, pigs, rabbits, and catfish, respectively (Mason and Clark, 2000). The taste buds in birds are primarily located on the caudal (rear) surface of the tongue and have a structural biology similar to the taste buds found in other vertebrate animals.

Despite having relatively few taste buds, birds are capable of sensing the four basic taste sensations of sour, bitter, sweet, and salty, as reviewed by Mason and Clark (2000). Many species will show a preference to water containing natural sugars, and this response is strongest in nectar feeders. Some grain-eating birds and some omnivores reject sugar solutions especially if they contain sucrose, as it is thought that at least some of these species lack the enzyme sucrase to digest it. Birds are tolerant of acidic and alkaline solutions, and this probably explains the tolerance by many birds of unripe, sour fruit

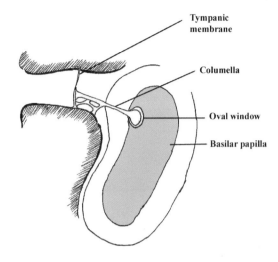

FIGURE 5.12 The avian ear.

FIGURE 5.13 Highly nocturnal and roosting in caves, the Oilbird uses echolocation to navigate.

FIGURE 5.14 Albatrosses are "tube-nosed" birds, with elongated nostrils that assist in finding food through scent.

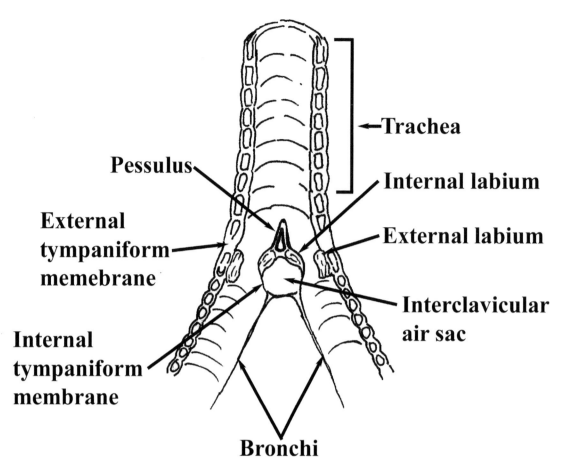

FIGURE 5.15   The syrinx is positioned at the point where the trachea bifurcates into the primary bronchi that go to the lungs. The syrinx contains two halves, each of which consist of internal and external labium and tympaniform membranes.

as a food source. Bitter responses by birds are variable. Some compounds that are very bitter to humans are readily accepted by birds, but often many of the things found bitter by humans are also avoided by birds. Many plants produce bitter phenolic compounds, which are thought to inhibit predation by birds. Some insects also contain these compounds, making them unpalatable to many birds. Salt tolerances are highly variable in birds, but they have a specific appetite for dietary salt if they are deficient in this essential mineral. As will be discussed in Chapter 6, birds vary in their ability to excrete ingested salt, which probably plays a significant role in the acceptance or avoidance of salt solutions beyond the nutritional requirement.

OTHER FACTORS

Water temperature drastically influences water consumption in domestic fowl, which can discriminate a temperature difference of 3 degrees C (5 degrees F). Voluntary intake decreases as water temperature increases above ambient temperature. Chickens will suffer from acute thirst rather than drink water 10 degrees F above their body temperature of about 105 degrees F or 40.5 degrees C (Kare and Rogers, 1976). Red-winged Blackbirds have also been shown to reject water of higher temperature in favor of cooler water (Mason and Maruniak, 1983).

Birds have very specific appetites for certain required nutrients. Research with domestic fowl indicates they select diets that provide the correct levels of essential nutrients such as sodium, calcium, and essential amino acids and avoid feeds that have the wrong balance or excessive levels of essential nutrients. Domesticated birds also consume diets based on energy needs and tend not to overconsume nutritionally balanced diets that are provided to them ad libitum. Caged pet birds like finches and parrots or domesticated fowl like pheasants and ornamental chickens are typically maintained with constant food availability. Even with excessive amounts of food available, these birds self-regulate their intake to meet their daily energy needs without eating an excess to cause weight problems. In animals, hormonal regulation of food intake to accommodate energy needs is extensive and works well to maintain appropriate weight. However, these natural mechanisms to balance food intake with energy needs can be lost in domesticated animals such as chickens that have been genetically selected for rapid growth. These regulatory mechanisms may be lost over time in domesticated pet birds without the natural, genetic selection pressure that maintains these traits in the wild.

SOUND PRODUCTION

Unlike humans who have vocal cords associated with their larynx, in birds, the larynx simply opens into the trachea through its slit-like glottis. The laryngeal muscles contract with breathing to open the glottis, which is closed to prevent food and water from entering the respiratory tract. The trachea has complete, cartilaginous rings around it in most species of birds and is lined with abundant smooth muscles. Penguins are unusual in having a double trachea that is divided into two tubes by a medial septum.

The syrinx is positioned at the point where the trachea bifurcates into the primary bronchi that go to the lungs (Figure 5.15). The syrinx is made up of tracheal tissue in antbirds and neotropical woodcreepers, bronchial tissue in cuckoos, nightjars, and owls, or both tissue types in most birds (Gill, 2007). The structure of the syrinx varies considerably among species, from being essentially absent in New World vultures to being highly complex structures in many songbirds. The syrinx contains two halves, each of which consists of internal and external labium and tympaniform membranes (Figure 5.15). Pairs of muscles control the tension of the membranes and the position of the internal and external labium. The internal labium and internal tympaniform membranes are also stretched from pressure generated by the interclavical air sac. As expired air's movement is restricted by the membranes and labia, it creates vibrations in these structures, and sound is produced. Songbirds have many more pairs of syringeal muscles than non-songbirds in order to create more tension manipulations of the membranes and labia. In songbirds, the two sides of the syrinx can act together or independently to produce sound. Thus, the two sides may generate different sounds simultaneously (Suthers, 1990; Suthers et al., 1999). The tone and pitch of the sound depends on the precise tensions of the labia and their vibrations (Suthers et al., 1999). Species that lack functional syringeal musculature like storks, Ostriches, and New World vultures, can only grunt or hiss. The temporal pattern of the vocalization is determined in large part by contraction of thoracic and abdominal muscles that control the airflow coming from the respiratory system that passes through the syrinx.

The quality of the sound produced by the syrinx can be further influenced or modified by the length of the trachea and the tightening or relaxation of the cartilage rings of the trachea to change air pressure. Furthermore, it appears that much like humans, birds further influence the sound they make, based on tongue and beak gape position during the sound production. Birds also can breathe and sing at the same time by taking short shallow breaths, which allows for the production of long, continuous songs.

The neural pathways that control song production at the syrinx, as well as song memory and learning, are well mapped. Song production can be inherited and/or learned. Inherited vocalizations occur in birds whether they have heard that vocalization or not. Learned vocalizations involve listening to the song followed by practicing them. Typically, listening to adults sing provides the necessary examples to follow. A lot of learning and practice is needed before the refined ability develops in young songbirds that have complex songs to master. The learning of vocalizations occurs in parrots, hummingbirds, and oscine songbirds (passerine songbirds with a highly developed syrinx). For some birds, lifelong learning occurs, as illustrated by the male Marsh Warbler's ability to learn to mimic the songs of up to 80 other species of birds during their lifetime or by Northern Mockingbirds that can learn to mimic the songs of up to 30 species (Frances and Larter, 2011). For parrots, mynahs, and the superb lyrebird, mimicry can involve the sounds of machines, humans, and other animals. Parrots learning human speech will be discussed in Chapter 8.

Recent research (Abe and Watanabe, 2011) with Bengalese finches indicates that they have the ability to discriminate syntactic rules. Humans process language communication based on specific rules of word organization and can quickly distinguish syntactically incorrect sentences that disrupt these grammatical rules. Bird songs can be viewed as being like a sentence, with the different sounds being like words. Researchers played jumbled-up songs to male finches and discovered that they could use syntactical information to process songs and reorder them logically to discriminate novel auditory information. Thus, humans are no longer unique in being the only animals able to order sound communication logically.

Male sex hormones play critical roles in bird vocalizations. As will be discussed in Chapter 7, males often use song to attract females for reproductive purposes. Thus, it is not surprising that song production increases in some species during the breeding season in correlation with testosterone levels. Furthermore, males outside of the breeding season—and even females—can be induced to sing by giving them testosterone injections. In domestic poultry, if hens are given sufficient testosterone they will crow like roosters.

MECHANICAL SOUNDS

In addition to vocally produced sounds, birds also produce sounds mechanically that can be used for communication purposes. A few examples of these mechanical noises will be highlighted. Wing clapping/drumming is common in birds and can be simple, as seen in pigeons, to very elaborate, as in the Ruffed Grouse. In order to attract females and to proclaim his territory, the Ruffed Grouse makes a loud drumming noise by beating his wings very rapidly against the air. Woodpeckers produce loud drumming sounds with their beaks on trees to announce territory or communicate, while storks commonly clatter their long lower and upper bills together to generate noise. Male White-collared Manakins produce loud snapping and popping noises by rubbing together specialized wing feathers (Figure 5.16).

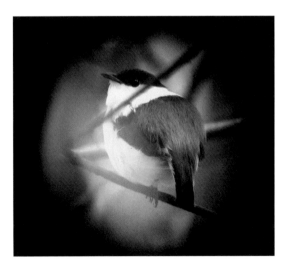

FIGURE 5.16   Manakins are a unique family of birds known for their elaborate courtship displays. The male White-collared Manakin has specialized feathers on his wings that he snaps together, creating loud popping and snapping noises for his display.

RESPIRATION

As discussed in the preceding chapter, the metabolic rates of flighted birds are over 75 percent greater than would be found in a mammal of the same mass and body temperature. The oxygen demands to support active flight are tremendous. Additionally, birds have been recorded flying at or above 10,000 meters, or about 33,000 feet. At this elevation, humans would need supplemental oxygen to maintain consciousness. As altitude increases, the percent concentration of oxygen in the air remains the same, but the pressure of the atmosphere decreases, leaving the air less compressed, and the number of oxygen molecules available to be taken in per breath is reduced. Birds are able to function at high elevations and meet their oxygen needs for metabolism, because they have a respiratory system that is much more efficient than that of humans.

THE LUNG

Inspired air travels down the trachea, which divides at its base into two primary bronchi that lead to the lungs. The primary bronchus of each lung actually extends through the entire length of the lung and ends at the opening of an abdominal air sac (Figure 5.17). The primary bronchus branches off into secondary bronchi along its entire length in the lung. The secondary bronchi

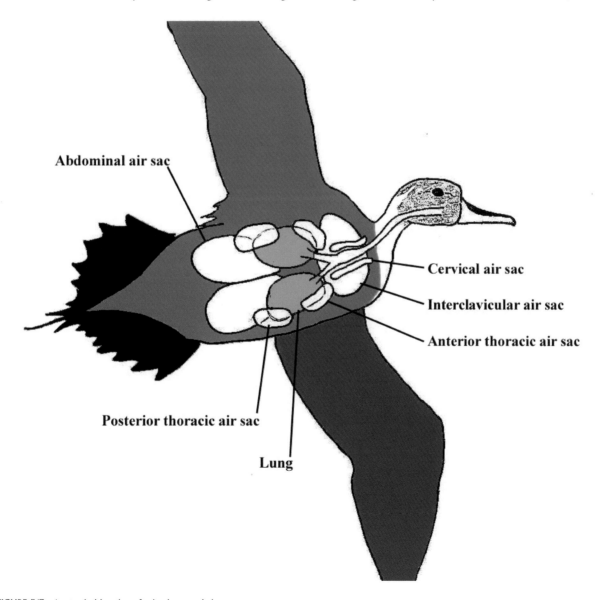

FIGURE 5.17   Anatomical location of avian lungs and air sacs.

then branch off into parabronchi. The primary and secondary bronchi do not participate in gas exchange, and some of the secondary bronchi lead to openings of the thoracic and cranial air sacs. The parabronchi are the functional units for gas exchange, and most of the parabronchi are organized as a series of several hundred tubes. The parabronchi connect at both ends with secondary bronchi allowing for unidirectional airflow through them. This collection of parallel parabronchi is referred to as paleopulmonic parabronchi. Some of the parabronchi are not organized as regular parallel stacks and have a random organization, and these are referred to as neopulmonic parabronchi. There are species variations in the amount of neopulmonic parabronchi, with penguins having none, and no species having over 25 percent of their parabronchi arranged as neopulmonic parabronchi (Powell, 2000).

AIR SACS

The number of air sacs varies across bird species. There are 6 in weavers, 7 in loons and turkeys, and at least 12 in shorebirds and storks (Gill, 2007). However, most species have 9 air sacs. The cervical air sacs, anterior thoracic air sacs, abdominal air sacs, and posterior thoracic air sacs are each paired with one on either side of the bird's midline (Figure 5.17). The interclavicular air sac is not paired and is the one mentioned previously because of its association with the syrinx. The air sacs are avascular, thin-walled transparent structures that extend throughout the body cavity and into the wings and leg bones. The fact that the air sacs are intimately associated with the viscera and bones of the bird explains why inhaled irritants or pathogens can have devastating effects on birds. Respiratory diseases are among the most common in birds and many of them are associated with exceedingly high mortality rates. The role of inhaled irritants in feather picking in parrots will be discussed later in the chapter on parrots. The contact of the air sacs with the visceral organs and the movement of air to and from the air sacs also allow for the dissipation of core body heat to prevent overheating.

The air sacs themselves are not involved in the direct exchange of oxygen and carbon dioxide. Instead, they act as bellows that hold air and allow for the highly efficient, continuous unidirectional flow of air through the lungs. The air sacs directly connect with the primary and secondary bronchi. Inspired air actually takes two full respiratory cycles before it is expired (Figure 5.18). During inhalation 1, the air that comes in moves down the primary bronchi, bypassing the cranial (forward) secondary bronchi openings, and instead fills the caudal (rear) secondary bronchi and rear air sacs. The air that enters the caudal secondary bronchi proceeds through the paleopulmonic parabronchi to enter the cranial air sacs. With exhalation 1, the anterior and posterior air sacs compress, with air in the forward air sacs expelled out the trachea to the environment, the air in the rear air sacs moving forward into the paleopulmonic parabronchi. During inhalation 2, the anterior and posterior air sacs expand again. Air from the lungs moves forward into front air sacs, while new air brought in moves to rear air sacs and the rear secondary bronchi. Finally, during exhalation 2, some of the original air brought in during inhalation 1 that entered the rear sacs is now in the forward air sacs, and it moves out the trachea and mouth into the environment.

Air flow through the paleopulmonic parabronchi is always unidirectional from caudal to cranial during both inspiration and expiration,

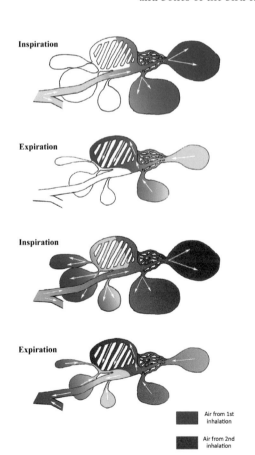

Inspiration

Expiration

Inspiration

Expiration

Air from 1st inhalation

Air from 2nd inhalation

FIGURE 5.18   In birds, inspired air takes two full respiratory cycles before it is expired.

which enhances oxygen delivery to the blood as will be described below. Airflow though the paleopulmonic parabronchi is constantly occurring. In contrast, airflow in the neopulmonic parabronchi is cranial to caudal during inspiration and caudal to cranial during expiration, and thus bidirectional.

GAS EXCHANGE EFFICIENCY

The lung only serves as a gas exchanger in birds and does not play a role as a mechanical ventilator as it does in other species. Thus, the lung is compact, rigid in structure, and fixed in position. Avian lungs are actually about 27 percent smaller in volume compared with a non-flying mammal of similar size (Maina, 1989; Maina et al., 1989). However, the entire volume of the respiratory system of the bird, including the lungs and air sacs, is three to five times greater than the volume of the lung of a mammal of equal size (Tenney and Remmers, 1963; Lasiewski and Calder Jr., 1971). But more important than total volume, the air sacs allow for the lungs to be constantly bathed in oxygen-rich blood during both inspiration and expiration, which maximizes gas exchange relative to mammals, where the lung is both a gas exchanger and a ventilator.

Efficiency of gas exchange is further increased based on the structure of the gas exchanging tissue. From the parabronchi lumen, atria project outward, giving rise to the infundibulae, which in turn give rise to air capillaries. The air capillaries heavily anastomose and intertwine with the blood capillaries for gas exchange. The blood capillaries and air capillaries are arranged so that there is the inward flow of deoxygenated blood through the blood capillaries and the outward flow of air through the air capillaries. This countercurrent arrangement maximizes gas exchange by diffusion (Figure 5.19). Additionally, the respiratory surface area where gas exchange can occur is greater in birds—especially small birds—than a comparable-sized mammal; the pulmonary capillary blood volume is also 22 percent greater than a non-flying mammal (Maina et al., 1989; Maina, 2006). Finally, the thickness of the blood gas barrier through which oxygen and carbon dioxide have to diffuse is 56 to 67 percent thinner in birds than it is in mammals (Maina, 2006), thus enhancing exchange efficiency.

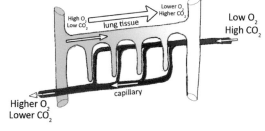

SUMMARY

The respiratory system in birds is very efficient to allow them to meet the gas exchange needed to support their very high metabolic rates that result from being small flighted animals. In birds, vocalizations are created by the syrinx utilizing air flow from the respiratory system. Some bird species also create mechanical-based sounds to communicate. Birds have excellent vision that is characterized by superb visual acuity, and in most species, a very large visual field. Because birds are highly visual and auditory animals, the senses of smell and taste are relatively less developed; taste does not seem to play a huge role in their lives. The sense of smell does play a large role in the lives of many bird species with regard to locating food, social communication, and navigation. Communication by visual displays, as well as by sound, plays essential roles in reproduction, which is the focus of Chapter 7.

FIGURE 5.19 Counter current exchange. Air and blood flow in opposite directions to maximize oxygen and carbon dioxide exchange. Blood returning from the body that is low in oxygen and high in carbon dioxide passes next to air that has already passed through much of the air capillary system. Thus, the concentration of oxygen has already been decreased and the carbon dioxide concentration has been increased, but there is still sufficient oxygen and a low enough carbon dioxide level to allow for diffusion with the returning blood. As the blood moves forward, it gains progressively more oxygen and loses more carbon dioxide, but it interacts with air capillaries with progressively more oxygen and less carbon dioxide, which allows diffusion of these two gasses along the entire exchange surface. This active diffusion gradient between air and blood is not found in mammalian lungs, where, in contrast, air ebbs into the alveoli exchange area and sits until it is expired out the same way it entered.

REFERENCES

Abe, K. and D. Watanabe. 2011. Songbirds possess the spontaneous ability to discriminate syntactic rules. *Nat Neurosci* **14**:1067–1074.

Caro, S. and J. Balthazart. 2010. Pheromones in birds: Myth or reality? *Journal of Comparative Physiology A: Neuroethology, Sensory, Neural, and Behavioral Physiology* **196**:751–766.

Dooling, R. J. and M. L. Dent. 2001. New studies on hair cell regeneration in birds. *Acoustical Science and Technology* **22**:93–99.

Fox, R., S. Lehmkuhle, and D. Westendorf. 1976. Falcon visual acuity. *Science* **192**:263–265.

Frances, P. and S. Larter. 2011. *Illustrated Encyclopedia of Birds*. BirdLife International. Dorling Kindersley Limited, London.

Gill, F. B. 2007. *Ornithology. 3rd edition*. W. H. Freeman and Company, New York.

Jones, M. P., K. E. Pierce Jr., and D. Ward. 2007. Avian Vision: A Review of Form and Function with Special Consideration to Birds of Prey. *Journal of Exotic Pet Medicine* **16**:69–87.

Kare, M. R. and J. G. Rogers. 1976. Sense Organs. Pages 30–52 *in* P. E. Sterkie, editor. *Avian Physiology*. Springer-Verlag, New York.

Lasiewski, R. C. and W. A. Calder Jr. 1971. A preliminary allometric analysis of respiratory variables in resting birds. *Respiration Physiology* **11**:152–166.

Maina, J. N. 1989. The morphometry of the avian lung. Pages 307–368 *in* A. S. King and J. McLelland, editors. *Form and Function in Birds, vol. 4*. Academic Press, London.

Maina, J. N. 2006. Development, structure, and function of a novel respiratory organ, the lung-air sac system of birds: To go where no other vertebrate has gone. *Biological Reviews* **81**:545-–579.

Maina, J. N., A. S. King, and G. Settle. 1989. An allometric study of pulmonary morphometric parameters in birds, with mammalian comparisons. *Philosophical Transactions of the Royal Society of London. Series B, Biological Sciences* **326**:1–57.

Martin, G., L. Rojas, Y. Ramírez, and R. McNeil. 2004. The eyes of oilbirds (*Steatornis caripensis*): Pushing at the limits of sensitivity. *Naturwissenschaften* **91**:26–29.

Martin, G. R. 2009. What is binocular vision for? A bird's-eye view. *Journal of Vision* **9**.

Martin, G. R. and G. Katzir. 2000. Sun shades and eye size in birds. *Brain, Behavior and Evolution* **56**:340–344.

Mason, J. R. and L. Clark. 2000. The Chemical Senses in Birds. Pages 39–56 *in* G. C. Whittow, editor. *Sturkie's Avian Physiology, 5th edition*. Academic Press, San Diego, CA.

Mason, J. R. and J. A. Maruniak. 1983. Behavioral and physiological effects of capsaicin in Red-winged Blackbirds. *Pharmacology Biochemistry and Behavior* **19**:857–862.

Perrins, C. 2009. *The Princeton Encyclopedia of Birds*. Princeton University Press, Princeton, NJ.

Powell, F. L. 2000. Respiration. Pages 233–259 *in* G. C. Whittow, editor. *Sturkie's Avian Physiology*. Academic Press, San Diego, CA.

Rajchard, J. 2009. Ultraviolet (UV) light perception by birds: A review. *Veterinarni Medicina* **54**:351–359.

Rattenborg, N. C., S. L. Lima, and C. J. Amlaner. 1999. Half-awake to the risk of predation. *Nature* **397**:397–398.

Suthers, R., F. Goller, and C. Pytte. 1999. The neuromuscular control of birdsong. *Philosophical Transactions of the Royal Society of London. Series B: Biological Sciences* **354**:927–939.

Suthers, R. A. 1990. Contributions to birdsong from the left and right sides of the intact syrinx. *Nature* **347**:473–477.

Tenney, S. M. and J. E. Remmers. 1963. Comparative quantitative morphology of the mammalian lung: Diffusing area. *Nature* **197**:54–56.

Vorobyev, M., D. Osorio, A. T. D. Bennett, N. J. Marshall, and I. C. Cuthill. 1998. Tetrachromacy, oil droplets and bird plumage colours. *Journal of Comparative Physiology A: Neuroethology, Sensory, Neural, and Behavioral Physiology* **183**:621–633.

Waldvogel, J. A. 1990. The Bird's Eye View. *American Scientist* **78**:342–353.

Zusi, R. L. and D. Bridge. 1981. On the Slit Pupil of the Black Skimmer (Rynchops niger). *Journal of Field Ornithology* **52**:338–340.

VI NUTRITION

Whether it is pigeons in cities or penguins and snowy owls at polar extremes, birds utilize almost every terrestrial ecosystem throughout the world. However, given that there are nearly 10,000 species of birds that coexist with each other in these varied habitats throughout the world, it is not surprising that a plethora of food items are utilized by birds to reduce their competition with one another.

WHAT BIRDS EAT

Plant material is the most common food item for birds and includes items such as grass, leaves, buds, flowers, nectar, sap, seeds, and fruit. Seeds and fruit are the most commonly consumed plant material. In temperate zones, fruit availability is seasonal and often widely available at the end of the growing season. In the fall, many birds, including those that are typically insect eaters, consume fruit as they build body energy stores for fall migration or as a food source during migration. In the tropics, fruit is available year-round and is the primary staple food source for many species of birds called frugivores. As a rich source of nutrients, fruit is produced by plants to attract animals, because the fruit is associated with the seed(s) of the plant. Animals are excellent at ingesting and dispersing these seeds. Many bird species drop the seeds after consuming the flesh or they regurgitate or defecate intact, whole seeds, all of which helps to ensure the propagation of the plant species to new locations.

For many bird species, seeds are the primary source of their nutrition, and they are collectively termed granivores. With these species, the seeds are destroyed as they are hulled by a bird's beak and/or degraded by the digestive tract of the bird. Thus, the plant's ability to propagate is being diminished. Thus, plants have counteracted the predation of

FIGURE 6.1 The Sword-billed Hummingbird has a specially adapted bill to reach the pollen in tubular flowers, such as the *Brugmansia* flower.

FIGURE 6.2 *Brugmansia* flower.

seeds by altering their morphology, such as making them small or hard, and in many cases, as will be discussed in the parrot chapter, it is not unusual for plants to lace their seeds with toxic compounds to discourage their consumption and digestion.

More than 1,500 species of birds feed on nectar (nectivores or nectarivores) and pollen (Frances and Larter, 2011), including hummingbirds, honeyeaters, sunbirds, and lories. The relationship between hummingbirds and plants can be taken to coevolutionary extremes, as illustrated by the Sword-billed Hummingbird (Figure 6.1) and one of its primary nectar sources, *Brugmansia* flowers (Figure 6.2). Plants prefer hummingbirds over insect pollinators, because they are relatively long lived, able to fly long distances, and thus pollinate at greater distances. To attract hummingbirds more exclusively, the plants produce flowers with no landing platform and with long tubular necks, which produce large amounts of relatively dilute nectar. Similar patterns of flower evolution can be seen with other nectar feeders like the sunbirds.

Invertebrates both aquatic and terrestrial are abundant and diverse, and thus are the most commonly used item of food for birds after plant material. Even plant-eaters supplement their diets with insects to meet protein intake requirements. This is especially true during the breeding season when females lay protein-laden eggs and when parents have to meet the protein requirements of rapidly growing altricial chicks. Even nectar feeders like hummingbirds supplement their nectar-based carbohydrate diet with insects for protein. Birds that eat invertebrates may focus on particular prey such as the Black-billed Cuckoo found in North America, which has a preference for large, spiny caterpillars, or the Snail Kite that feeds almost exclusively on apple snails. Swifts, swallows, nightjars, and kites are some of the birds that specialize in the pursuit, capture, and ingestion of insects in the air. Other species such as flamingos specialize in obtaining and eating aquatic invertebrates, and many songbirds pursue and feast on invertebrates caught on the ground.

The meat (carnivores) and fish (piscivores) eaters are diverse and widespread. Owls, hawks, and falcons are well known for their pursuit and capture of prey, while vultures are synonymous with the consumption of carrion, and osprey, pelicans, and puffins are fish hunters. The raptors will be covered extensively in a subsequent chapter. Finally, there are many species of birds—such as gamebirds, starlings, crows, toucans, and water birds—that consume a large variety of the foodstuffs already mentioned. These species are called omnivores. Such birds will be covered in more detail in subsequent pages and chapters.

OBTAINING FOOD

USING SENSES

All birds use their senses in obtaining food, but for many species a sense has become highly honed for food acquisition. Most people think of owls hunting by sight, and although they do have very good vision, it is their sense of hearing that is critical for hunting. This becomes readily apparent in northern climates, where owls can be observed catching prey they cannot see underneath a blanket of snow. Similarly, the North American Robin uses its keen sense of hearing to locate earthworms moving in the soil. Vocal communication is used by many species to alert family or other group members to the location of food.

The sense of smell is highly developed in some bird species, such as Kiwis and some New World vultures. The Turkey Vulture, for example, can detect decaying flesh that is hidden under the tropical rainforest canopy and then further hidden under leaf litter from kilometers away, with their acute sense of smell. Kiwis are well known for locating food by smelling with nostrils on the tip of their long, probing beaks.

The ends of bills can be very sensitive to touch, especially in wading and shore birds, which can feed in muddy water or soft mud, where food items cannot be seen but only touched. As Avocets move their upturned bills through the water in a sweeping motion back and forth looking for food, they clamp their bills around anything edible that it touches within 1/50th of a second (Frances and Larter, 2011). Spoonbills and ibis (Figure 6.3 a & b) use the same technique of feeding in shallow water. The use of touch allows these birds to feed in turbid water that could not be used if they were dependent on sight. Curlews have long bills that they use to probe into mud and the tip of the bill is highly sensitive, allowing the curlew to detect invertebrate prey. Recent research evidence indicates that some bird species like the Northern Island Brown Kiwi (Cunningham et al., 2009) and Madagascar Crested Ibis (Cunningham et al., 2010)—and likely many other birds that utilize touch in feeding—have remote touch capabilities. Remote touch capabilities are mediated by the tips of bills being packed with sensory receptors such as Herbst's corpuscles. These receptors allow, from a distance, the detection of both vibrotactile signals from invertebrates burrowing through the substrate or pressure disturbances caused by prey that are not moving in the substrate.

As discussed in Chapter 5, birds are highly visual, and vision is commonly used by birds in locating food. Several bird species have evolved specialized vision-based techniques in acquiring food. As discussed previously, birds have vision in the ultraviolet range, and kestrels use this visual sensitivity to locate voles, which mark their trails with urine and feces. These excretory signposts are highly visible in ultraviolet light, allowing the kestrels to target the location

FIGURE 6.3 Roseate Spoonbills (a) and ibises (b) both have a very strong sense of touch in their bills in order to feed in turbid water.

of their prey. Old World vultures scan the ground for carcasses, and when they locate a carcass, they start a slow, circular descent to the carcass. This circular descent is noticed by other vultures, which are then attracted and converge at the food location.

SPECIALIZED ANATOMY AND FOOD GATHERING

Birds have evolved a multitude of specialized anatomical features beyond digestive tract anatomy to help them obtain or transport food. Webbed feet are common in water birds and aid in swimming. Osprey have nostrils with valves that close when they dive in the water to catch fish, and the bottom of their feet are covered with spiny projections that allow them to securely grip slippery fish. Penguin wings appear and function more like flippers rather than wings; unlike most modern birds, penguins have regained bone density to reduce their buoyancy during dives and underwater swimming.

Even in desert areas, the sandgrouse is able to successfully reproduce because it has specialized feathers. Sandgrouse are native to desert and semiarid regions of the Old World, in particular, Africa, the Middle East, and Southeast Asia. They may live up to 50 miles away from water (Harris, 2009), the most important nutrient. Sandgrouse chicks are dependent on their father for water delivery until they are able to make the daily flight to a water source. Every day, to accomplish this water delivery, the male will fly to the nearest watering hole and then rub his belly feathers vigorously in sand or dry soil to remove the waterproofing preening oil from them. Once this is accomplished, the male will wade into the water while holding his wings and tail feathers up out of the water. He will then move his belly up and down to incorporate water into specially adapted belly feathers that wick up the water. Once the feathers are saturated he flies back to the chicks and stands over them as they drink the water from his feathers. Once they are finished drinking, he will rub his feathers on the dry earth again to remove any remaining water so he is not weighed down by the water weight.

FIGURE 6.4 Lammergeiers are vultures that specialize in consuming bones. They will drop bones on rocks from great heights in order to break them apart.

USE OF TOOLS IN GATHERING FOOD

Birds can be ingenious in their use of tools to obtain food. Egyptian vultures will pick up stones and toss them onto Ostrich eggs in order to break them to get the rich nutrients of the internal egg contents (Thouless et al., 1987). Lammergeiers or Bearded Vultures (Figure 6.4) are vultures that specialize in eating bones, which make up 70 to 90 percent of their diet (Perrins, 2009). To break bones into smaller, edible pieces and to gain access to the highly nutritious marrow in the center of bones, these birds will carry the bones high in the air and then drop them at breaking areas littered with rock, called ossuaries. Bones that do not break on the first drop have the dropping process repeated until they do shatter.

Galapagos Finches and New Caledonian Crows are notorious for selecting cactus spines or small stems and twigs to use for probing and removing insects and more typically insect larvae out of wood. In both cases, these bird species are taking advantage of the fact that these isolated islands have not been populated by woodpeckers that would normally be utilizing this food source. The Green Heron is known to conceal itself near the water's edge and then throw earthworms, insects, and other bait onto the surface of water to attract minnows that it then catches.

Shrikes are relatively small birds that weigh between 20 and 100 grams, depending on the species (Figure 6.5 a). They hunt insects and small vertebrates and are known for impaling their prey on barbed wire or the thorns of trees, or even hanging it in forked branches (Figure 6.5 b). This allows them to dismember and eat small vertebrates that they could not hold in place with their feet, and this provides food storage that can be utilized when hunting is not good. Food storage is not widespread in the bird world, but is practiced by members of the crow family (such as crows, ravens, jays, nutcrackers, and magpies). Members of this family not only store vast quantities of food, especially in northern areas where winters are harsh, but they conceal their stored food in several locations. Members of this family have excellent memories, not only for remembering the location of their stashes, but also what is hidden where and will utilize the most perishable items or preferred foods first (Perrins, 2009).

USE OF OTHER ANIMALS FOR FOOD GATHERING

The Brown-headed Cowbird is well known in North America for following livestock such as cows and horses as they feed in pastures. The birds forage on the ground for insects disturbed by the livestock. Antbirds (Figure 6.6), on the other hand, got their name based on following swarming army ants. Although antbirds do not eat the ants, they do prey on the invertebrates that are flushed from cover and are fleeing the approaching ants.

Oxpeckers in Africa rarely leave the backs of their large mammalian animal hosts like wildebeests, zebras, and impalas. They feed on parasites like ticks on the hides of these animals. They also eat dandruff and earwax, but primarily feed on blood from their hosts. The blood not only comes from the bloated ticks that they consume, but also is taken directly from bleeding cuts and scrapes from their hosts that the birds make sure do not heal.

Sapsuckers in North America cut holes into trees and then feed on the sap, which collects in these wells, and to a lesser degree the insects that get caught in the sap. But many other birds such as orioles, warblers, and hummingbirds will also feed on the sap, an important source of nutrition for these birds in the spring before other food sources utilized by these birds are widely available.

A few species of birds such as gulls, skuas, and frigatebirds are classified as kleptoparasites, which means they engage in the stealing of food that has already been caught by another bird (Vickery and Brooke, 1994; Bélisle and Giroux, 1995; Miyazaki, 1996; Perrins, 2009). Frigatebirds (Figure 6.7) are among the most specialized kleptoparasites. Frigatebirds are seabirds but their feathers are not waterproof, and their legs and feet are unsuited for swimming or wading. Thus, they hunt by swooping down near the water surface, lowering their heads so their bills can snatch at the surface flying

FIGURE 6.5 Despite its small size, the Loggerhead Shrike is a fierce predator (a). It will capture insects and small vertebrates and then impale them on branches, thorns, or, in this case, barbed wire fencing (b).

FIGURE 6.6 Immaculate Antbird. Native to the tropics, antbirds specialize in following army ant swarms through the forest. As the ant swarms move, insects flee upward, allowing the antbird to capture an easy meal.

FIGURE 6.7   Magnificent Frigatebird. Although frigatebirds are oceanic dwellers their feathers are not waterproof which means they are incapable of swimming or diving for prey. Instead, they must either pluck fish from the water's surface, a difficult task to perfect, or resort to stealing the food of other seabirds.

fish or squid that are fleeing predators. This hunting technique is difficult to perfect, so frigatebirds also perfect robbing food of other seabirds in flight, often by upending them so they regurgitate their prey. Vickery and Brooke (1994) determined that individual Great Frigatebird specialists obtained 40 percent of their daily energy needs by kleptoparastism. In addition to kleptoparasites, it is not unusual for larger birds to opportunistically steal prey from smaller birds. This is often seen in raptors.

ANATOMY OF THE DIGESTIVE TRACT

The digestive system (Figure 6.8), like so many other systems in the bird, has been adapted for reducing weight for flight. Modern birds, unlike many prehistoric birds, do not have teeth, and lack heavy jaw bones and extensive jaw musculature. Food items are swallowed

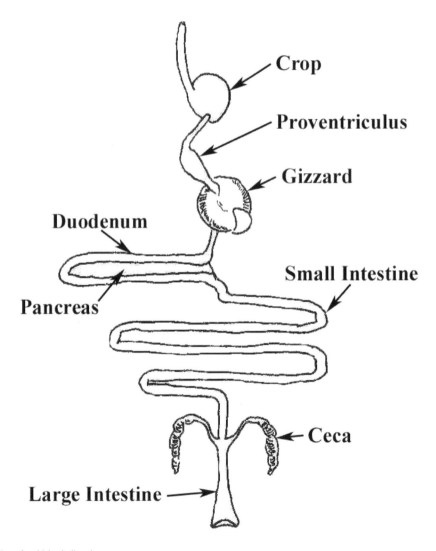

FIGURE 6.8   Illustration of a chicken's digestive system.

whole and then broken down by a muscular gizzard that is located more centrally to help keep the bird's center of gravity near the wings.

THE BILL OR BEAK

Bills are important tools used by many species for preening feathers, building nests, social signaling, and/or aggression. But most importantly, bird beaks are efficient tools for the acquisition of food. They vary greatly in size, shape, and function to allow birds to utilize a plethora of food items. The bill can be viewed as an extension of the skull. Its structural framework, especially at its base, is made up of bone covered by a thin layer of blood vessels, nerves, and keratin-producing cells. The outside of the bill is made up of keratin, which is a hard structural protein that is comparable to, but harder than, your fingernails. The tip of the bill is made up of keratin with no bone structure. In some birds, only the tip of the bill is hard, while the rest of the bill is relatively soft, as is seen in many waterfowl like ducks and geese.

Just as your fingernails grow throughout your lifetime, so too does the outside covering and tip of the bill. The continual growth of the outer bill and its tip in wild birds simply serves to replace the keratin being lost by normal wear and tear of the bill. Thus, there is typically no net growth of the bill in adult birds. However, it is not unusual for birds kept in captivity to suffer from an overgrowth of the tips of the bill due to a lack of wear and tear, and this excess growth must be ground (filed) down by a veterinarian or trained bird specialist.

In many bird species, both the upper (maxilla) and lower (mandible) bills are hinged, allowing both to be opened. This allows for a very wide gape to swallow food whole or for the manipulation and breaking of large food items such as nuts with their beak. In contrast, in mammalian species such as humans, only the lower part of the jaw moves when the mouth is opened, which limits the gape that can be achieved.

For birds like raptors and owls, the beak is very efficient at tearing meat into small pieces that can be swallowed. Many birds also use their beaks to shell seeds. For seed-eaters, the bills are often stout and strong. In many species of seed-eaters, the upper bill will have a grooved edge that the bird uses to crack and separate the husk of the seed as the bird manipulates the seed around the grooved edge with its lower beak and tongue. The seed kernel is swallowed, and the husk is discarded. In the case of some parrots, the upper mandible has a ridge across the interior. which allows the seed to be wedged and held as the lower mandible applies pressure to crack the shell.

Bird bills come in a variety of shapes and sizes to assist with food gathering (Figure 6.9). The form and function of beaks often allow a large number of bird species to live in the same specialized habitat without competing with one another for food. Shorebirds and waders—which include sandpipers, curlews, snipes, and woodcocks— all share the same real estate, but their bills vary greatly in length and shape (Figure 6.10), which allows them to not compete with one another for food while being densely packed in the same ecosystem. Waders with short bills will eat surface prey, while those with increasingly longer bills are able to probe increasingly deeper for prey, while still others have short, thick bills, specialized for turning over stones to find prey. In the birds with long bills that probe moist soil for food, the tips of their bills can separate while the rest of the bill remains closed, which allows for grasping the prey without filling the entire beak with dirt. Similarly, the bills of different finch species show a wide range of shapes and sizes. Some finches, like American Goldfinches (Figure

FIGURE 6.9 Bird beaks come in a variety of shapes and sizes to assist with food gathering and utilization.

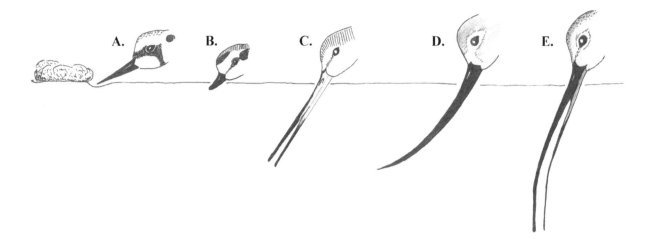

FIGURE 6.10   Shorebird bills vary imensely, reducing the amount of competition for food. Ruddy Turnstones (a) feed at the surface of the mud, often turning over stones to look for prey. Snowy plovers (b), using their short bills, rely on prey just under the surface of the mud. Longer bills, such as the Marbled Godwit (c), American Avocet (d), and Long-billed curlew (e), can access prey deep in the mud.

FIGURE 6.11   The American Goldfinch (a) has a small bill ideal for picking small seeds from seed heads while the bill of the Red Crossbill (b) is ideal for extracting seeds from pine cones.

6.11 a), have long narrow beaks that they use like tweezers to extract small seeds from seed heads. Different-sized species of crossbills, on the other hand, use the different sizes of their unique bills to obtain seeds from differently sized conifer cones (Figure 6.11 b). Other finches such as the Hawfinch (Figure 6.11 c) have relatively larger and thicker beaks that are powerful, allowing them to break very hard seeds. Grosbeaks (Figure 6.11 d), on the other hand, have rounder bills with sharp edges that are used to obtain berries and buds.

Flamingos are highly specialized filter feeders with a unique bill structure (Figure 6.12). As they feed with their beak upside down in the water, they use their tongues like a piston to rapidly suck and expel muddy water through their bills, which are lined with tiny projections called lamellae that filter out particles of foods. The edges of their tongues have bristles to assist in the filtering. Several other water birds are also able to filter feed with lamellae on their bills.

Pelicans have one of the largest bills of any bird, but more importantly, the mandible has sides which are springy and flexible, allowing them to expand outward and fill with water when a pelican dives into the water for fish. Thus, the pelican is not the most precise fish catcher, but rather it scoops up a large volume of water, which then drains from the pouch of the lower bill, leaving behind any caught prey. In contrast, anhingas (Figure 6.13) are highly accurate fish catchers that swim underwater to pursue and spear fish with their pointed bill. Once the impaled fish is brought to the surface, it is tossed off the bill into the air and then swallowed headfirst and whole. Anhingas are one of the few birds that have wettable feathers. This means that the air normally trapped in the down feathers is pushed out by the water, so the birds are not as buoyant and can effectively swim underwater.

TONGUE

The tongue in birds varies in structure based on its involvement in collecting, manipulating, and swallowing food. Some bird species like woodpeckers and hummingbirds have very long tongues that can be extended out of the bill to extract insects from holes in wood or obtain nectar from the bases of flowers. The woodpecker tongue acts like a spear in obtaining insects. Until very recently, it had been traditionally thought that the tongue of hummingbirds acted like a capillary tube when obtaining nectar from a flower. However, a recent reevaluation indicates that the bifurcated tips of the hummingbird tongue have membranous edges, fringed with lamellae that extend on contact with nectar and then roll inward, trapping the liquid as the tongue is removed from the nectar (Rico-Guevara and Rubega, 2011). Lories, members of the parrot family, also consume nectar and pollen with specialized tongues that are tipped with tiny, thin papillae projections. These projections are normally sheathed unless their owner is actively feeding on nectar or pollen from flowers, and then these projections act like a brush that sops up the nectar and pollen.

Tongues that are used to manipulate food and simply for assisting in swallowing are non-protruding and have varying degrees of coverage of stiff, caudally directed papillae. For filter feeders, the edge of the tongue is typically lined with papillae that work with the lamellae to strain food particles from water.

The distinction between the pharynx and the mouth of birds is not as distinct as it is in mammalian species. The combined oral and pharyngeal cavities are referred to as the oropharynx. As covered previously in the respiration section, the palate contains a longitudinal slit called the choana, which links the nasal and oral cavities. Right behind the tongue is the laryngeal mound, which opens into the trachea through the slit-like glottis. The salivary glands vary tremendously across bird species, from being well developed in granivorous birds but absent or poorly developed in many piscivores, because fish need little additional lubrication to be swallowed whole. Woodpeckers also have well-developed salivary glands, as the saliva helps prey stick to the tongue.

THE ESOPHAGUS AND CROP

The tongue aids in moving food back to the esophagus, a thin-walled, highly distensible tube that transports food from the pharynx to the stomach. The esophagus contains a number of longitudinal folds, making it highly distensible, thus allowing birds to swallow their food whole. The food swallowed can be very large such as the whole fish swallowed by herons, cormorants, and anhingas. The esophagus lacks both the upper and lower esophageal sphincters present in mammals and is divided into a cervical and thoracic region. The

FIGURE 6.11 The strong bill of the Hawfinch (c) is designed to crack hard seeds while the rounder bill of the Rose-breasted Grosbeak (d) is ideal for obtaining buds and berries.

esophagus has mucus-producing glands, especially in the thoracic region.

In many species, the cervical esophagus will form an out-pocketing at the base of the neck called the crop. The structure of the crop varies widely between birds, which reflects different feeding habits and differences in the need to store food. The crop can be unilobed, bilobed, spindle shaped, and even absent in bird species (Figure 6.14). The crop serves as a temporary storage place for ingested food. During the day, many species of birds feed rapidly out in the open, storing large volumes of food in the crop, then these birds return to more sheltered and protected areas away from predators to slowly release the food from the crop to digest. Birds can often be seen at dusk feeding before it gets dark. In species with well-developed crops, food can be stored and then subsequently digested, which reduces the length of the nighttime fast—which can be critical for some species of birds, given their high metabolic rate and relative lack of body energy stores compared to unflighted, larger animals (as discussed in Chapter 4). Finally, the crop can be used to transport food and water to nestlings, and in a limited number of species, the crop actually produces nutritive crop milk that is fed to nestlings, as will be discussed later in the chapter on pigeons.

FIGURE 6.12   Flamingos have uniquely-shaped bills for filter feeding.

FIGURE 6.13   With their spear-like bills, anhingas are able to impale fish underwater, swim to the surface and toss the fish into the air, swallowing it whole.

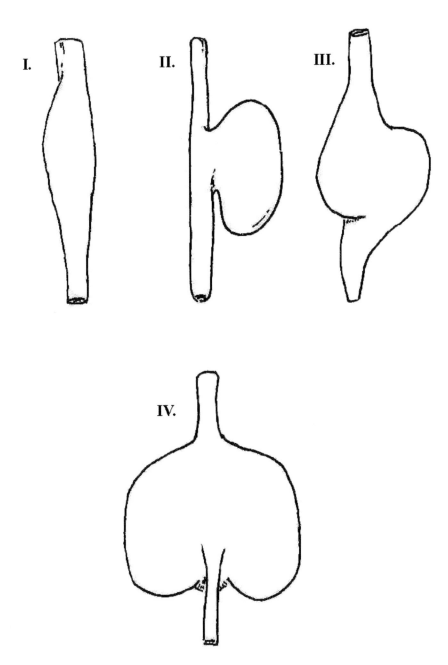

FIGURE 6.14   Crops vary greatly among birds. They can be nearly absent (I), unilobed (II), spindle shaped (III), or bilobed (IV).

PROVENTRICULUS

Beyond the crop, the thoracic esophagus continues to connect with the proventriculus, which is the first chamber of the stomach, followed by the gizzard, which is the second stomach chamber in birds. The proventriculus is often referred to as the true stomach or glandular stomach in birds because its function is comparable to its mammalian counterpart. The proventriculus varies in size in bird species. It is well developed in many carnivores and piscivores and less developed in granivores, herbivores, and nectivores. The proventriculus is highly glandular and secretes hydrochloric acid, pepsinogen, and mucous. The pH of the secreted gastric juices is between 0.2 and 1.2 (Gill, 2007). Pepsinogen is converted to pepsin, a protein-digesting enzyme. Both pepsin and hydrochloric acid are critical for protein digestion, and even ingested bones. Bearded Vultures can digest ingested cow vertebrae in two days (Gill, 2007).

GIZZARD

The gizzard (Figure 6.15) or ventriculus functions in mechanical digestion and is the site for gastric proteolysis (protein breakdown). Its structure and size also varies greatly among different bird species. In omnivores, herbivores, and granivores, it is highly developed for the mechanical breakdown of tough, hard foods. However, in nectivores, the gizzard is weak and thin walled, as there is little need for mechanical breakdown of their diet except for the insects that are consumed for protein. Similarly, the gizzard is not very muscular in fish-eating birds. In some species, the gizzard is positioned as an out-pocketing allowing soft material such as fruit to bypass it, while harder food items such as insects enter the gizzard (Gill, 2007). In species with well-developed, powerful gizzards, the gizzard consists of two pairs of opposing muscles termed thick and thin (Figure 6.15). To assist these muscles in the mechanical breakdown of food, many birds, especially seed-eaters, consume grit, which can be the size of pebbles in larger birds. Over time the grit is worn/broken down into fine particles that pass on through the digestive tract. Thus, these species must continually consume grit throughout their lives. As the intake of food items needing mechanical breakdown is increased or decreased, the size (musculature) of the gizzard responds accordingly among bird species (Piersma and Drent, 2003).

The interior surface of the gizzard is lined with a thick cuticle (Figure 6.15), which is produced by the mucosal glands of the gizzard. The cuticle is essential in protecting the muscular (protein) tissue of the gizzard from the acid and proteolytic enzymes secreted by the proventriculus to break down ingested protein. The cuticle also protects the muscular tissue from injury during the

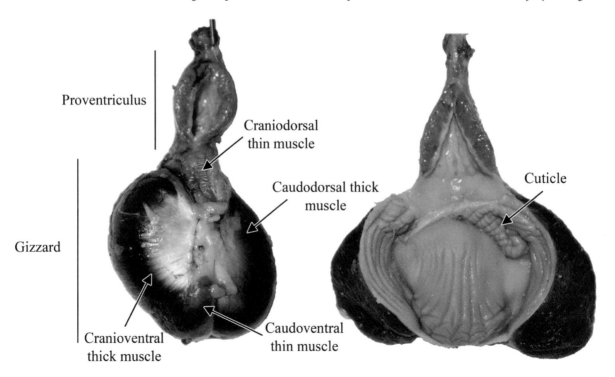

FIGURE 6.15   An external and internal view of the proventriculus and gizzard of an adult chicken. The craniodorsal thin muscle is continuous with the cranioventral thick muscle. The cranioventral thin muscle is continuous with the caudoventral thick muscle. These muscles provide for the mechanical breakdown of ingested food.

grinding of hard- and sharp-edged food items. The greenish brown color of the cuticle is due to the reflux of bile pigments from the duodenum, the first section of the small intestine.

In predatory birds such as owls, the gizzard collects indigestible remains like fur and bones and compresses them into compact pellets that are then brought back up through the proventriculus, esophagus, and bill. These pellets can provide important details on the types of prey animals consumed by predatory birds.

SMALL INTESTINE

The fine mushy paste of food particles produced by the gizzard then passes into the small intestine. The small intestine is often divided into three segments called the duodenum, jejunum, and ileum, but their separation is not based on significant histological differences. The first segment is the duodenum, and there is a distinct duodenal loop (Figure 6.16). The yolk stalk, also called the diverticulum vitellinum, or Meckel's diverticulum, is often used to distinguish the separation of the jejunum and ileum, the second and third segments of the small intestine, respectively. The yolk stalk is a remnant from embryonic development, when it served as a conduit for the source of nutrients in the yolk of the egg to the digestive system of the developing embryo. The overall length of the small intestine varies across different birds species. It tends to be shorter in frugivores and insectivores, for example, while it is longer in herbivores, carnivores, and granivores. The small intestinal wall is lined with projections called villi, which themselves are also covered with projections called microvilli. The villi and microvilli greatly increase the absorptive surface area of the small intestine to help ensure all available nutrients are absorbed.

The diffuse pancreatic tissue of the bird is found spread within the duodenal loop (Figure 6.16). As it does in other species, the pancreas plays a key role in digestion, in addition to being critical as the source of the key glucose-regulating hormones, insulin and glucagon. The pancreas secretes liquid into the duodenum via a pancreatic duct(s) (Figure 6.17), which typically drains into the ascending portion of the duodenum loop. The pancreatic liquid contains buffers, carbohydraes, lipases, and proteases. The bicarbonate buffers raise the pH of the highly acidic digesta that arrives from the gizzard to a more neutral pH, at which the digestive enzymes of the small intestine function most efficiently. The carbohydrases digest carbohydrates, while the lipases and proteases digest lipid (fat) and protein, respectively. In addition to the digestive enzymes contained in the pancreatic secretions, the cells lining the small intestine contain within them, or attached to their luminal surface, digestive enzymes that further break down partially digested nutrients.

The liver produces bile acids that are stored in the gallbladder in most bird species, but some bird species do not have gallbladders, such as some pigeon and parrot species. Regardless of having a gallbladder or not, bile acids are continuously secreted by the liver and released into the duodenum via the bile ducts (Figure 6.17). For species with a gallbladder, the presence of food in the duodenum stimulates the production of hormones that, in turn, stimulate the contraction and release of bile from the gallbladder into the duodenum. Bile emulsifies fats into tiny particles that can be absorbed and digested by lipases.

While the gizzard is responsible for mechanical digestion, the small intestine is the primary site for the chemical digestion started in the proventriculus and the absorption of nutrients. The enzymes break the complex proteins, carbohydrates, and lipids contained in the mechanically digested digesta into simpler absorbable components such as

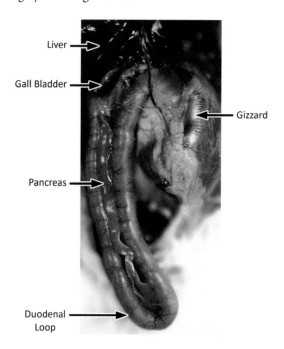

FIGURE 6.16 The duodenum loop surrounding the pancreas.

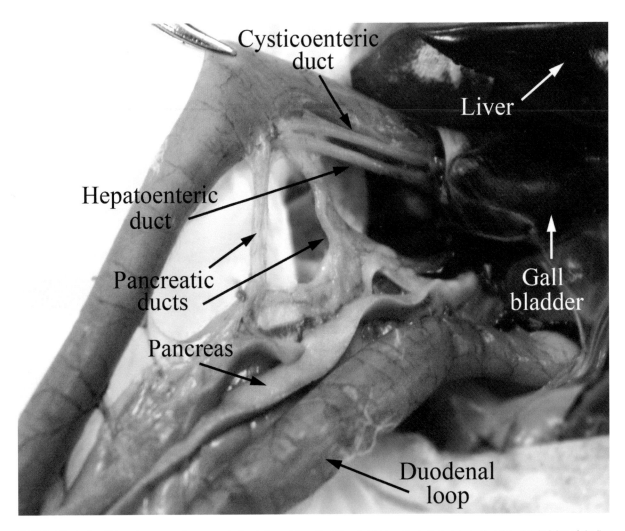

FIGURE 6.17 In the chicken, the common hepatoenteric duct is formed from the left and right hepatic ducts that drain the left and right lobes of the liver. The right hepatic duct has a branch that empties into the gallbladder. Stored bile in the gallbladder is released upon stimulation into the duodenum via the cysticoenteric duct. For species of birds without a gallbladder, the left and right hepatic ducts each drain directly and into the duodenum.

monosaccharides, amino acids, and fatty acids, the respective building blocks of carbohydrates, proteins, and lipids. Other components like vitamins and minerals are also liberated from the digested food and then absorbed. Indigestible food components pass through the small intestine.

CECA

At the junction of the ileum and large intestine are the ceca (Figure 6.18). These blind pouches are typically paired but can be a single pouch. Ceca size, histology, and function vary widely between different species of birds, as reviewed by Clench (1999). There are several classifications of ceca. Intestinal ceca are histologically similar to the small and large intestine and can range from large to vestigial in size. Intestinal ceca are found in such species as chickens, pheasants, grouse, ducks, geese, Ostriches, loons, and cranes. The function of intestinal ceca is the further digestion and fermentation of food particles, in particular leafy plant material. This material is digested through the action of cecal secretions, bacteria, and fungi. Water, digested nutrients, and fermentation end products such as volatile fatty acids are absorbed across the ceca.

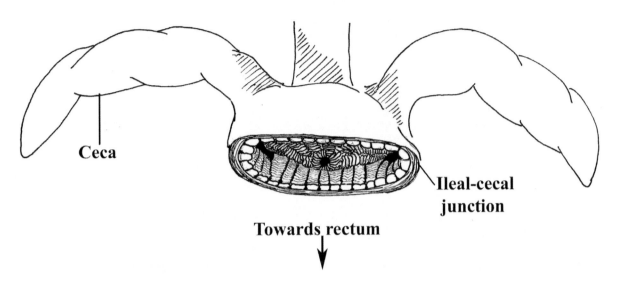

Small intestine

Ceca

Ileal-cecal junction

Towards rectum

FIGURE 6.18 The ileal-ceca-rectal junction of a chicken.

Ceca classified as glandular tend to be large and are found in relatively few birds, such as owls and nightjars. The function of glandular ceca is unknown but may be important in maintaining water balance in owls. Lymphoid ceca tend be small and vestigial and contain many lymphocytes, and thus may serve a role in immune function. Lymphoid ceca are found in passerine birds, pigeons, falcons, and flamingos. Ceca are absent in many bird species like parrots, woodpeckers, hummingbirds, and swifts.

LARGE INTESTINE

The size of the large intestine or colon of birds varies across different species. In almost all bird species, it is relatively short, but in a few species such as the Ostrich, its length has been increased dramatically to provide a location for the further digestion of fibrous plant material. In all species, the large intestine is an important location for water and electrolyte absorption. The large intestine does not need to be long in birds because it contains minimal indigestible waste, as birds void waste as quickly as possible to reduce their flight weight. In fact, transit times through the digestive tract are very fast in birds compared to most mammalian species, with transit times of many ingested materials being less than an hour for nectarivores and some frugivores to a few hours for granivores (Karasov, 1990; Klasingm 1998; Gill, 2007).

CLOACA

The cloaca is where the urinary, digestive, and reproductive tracts all come together into a common pathway that allows for the exit of products out of the body (Figure 6.19). It contains three chambers: the coprodeum, urodeum, and proctodeum. The large intestine leads into the coprodeum, which is followed by the urodeum. The urinary and reproductive tracts empty into

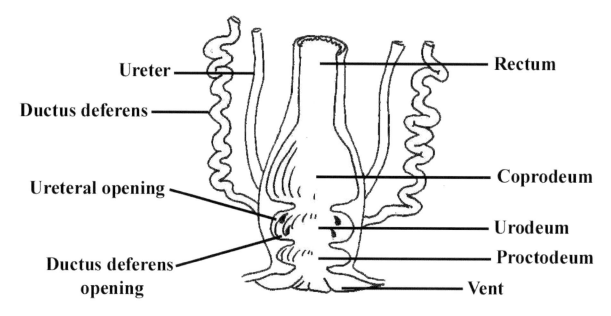

FIGURE 6.19   The cloaca is the common area where the urinary, digestive and reproductive tracts empty and then exit through the vent of the bird.

the urodeum. The final chamber is the proctodeum, which opens externally through the anus. The bursa of Fabricius projects dorsally into the proctodeum and is most prominent in young birds. The bursa of Fabricius is critical in immune function, as it is an area where B-lymphocytes—cells that produce antibodies—are generated.

Bird excrement voided by the cloaca is a combination of urinary and fecal waste. The kidneys of birds extract nitrogenous waste from the blood, but instead of excreting it as urea dissolved in water to produce urine as mammals do, birds excrete the nitrogenous waste in the form of uric acid. Uric acid is white in color and has a very low solubility in water. Thus, the material delivered to the cloaca by the ureters is white and pasty. Urinary waste is constantly delivered to the cloaca, as birds do not have the equivalent of a urinary bladder. Therefore, voided feces have a brownish green component from the intestine and a white, urinary component. In the chapter on parrots, monitoring the appearance of pet birds' feces will be discussed as a diagnostic for health status.

A few species of birds (Anna's Hummingbirds, Palestine Sunbirds, and Yellow Vented Bulbuls) appear to primarily excrete ammonia rather than uric acid under conditions when water intake and availability for excretion of highly toxic ammonia are high (Preest and Beuchat, 1997; Roxburgh and Pinshow, 2002 Tsahar et al., 2005). Furthermore, in at least some of these species, uric acid was the major nitrogen waste form in the urine, but not in the feces, indicating post-renal modification (Roxburgh and Pinshow, 2002; Tsahar et al., 2005). As discussed and reviewed by Tsahar et al. (2005), research supports the bacterial breakdown of uric acid in the ceca and/or the reabsorption of uric acid by birds. Although hummingbirds, sunbirds, and bulbuls have no ceca or tiny vestigial ceca, in other bird species with large ceca, the breakdown of uric acid by microorganisms within the ceca is significant, as is the potential reabsorption and conservation of this nitrogen by the bird. Thus, urinary waste that enters into the cloaca can undergo reverse peristalsis (refluxing) and enter the large intestine and ceca. Once in these locations, as already mentioned, the nitrogen from the uric acid can be utilized by bacteria and recycled. But more importantly, the water component of the urinary waste can be reabsorbed, leading to water conservation when needed.

DIGESTION OF FIBROUS PLANT MATERIAL

Starch is a highly digestible plant carbohydrate nutritional reservoir due to its chemical alpha 1-4-linkages of glucose. However, cellulose is the major structural polymer of plants and consists of glucose molecules linked together by beta 1-4-linkages. Birds, like mammalian species, cannot digest the structural fibers of plants because they do not produce cellulases, the enzymes necessary to digest cellulose into its individual glucose units. However, bacteria do exist that can digest cellulose, and such bacteria are found in the rumen of ruminant animals, such as cows and deer. In ruminants, the bacteria readily proliferate in the rumen by digesting for energy the ingested structural plant material consumed by the ruminant in the form of grass, leaves, etc. The bacteria produce volatile fatty acids, which are absorbed and used as an energy source by the ruminants. In addition, bacteria pass from the rumen, through the ruminant's true stomach and small intestine and are easily digested and highly nutritious.

Birds that eat plant material such as grass and leaves are called herbivores. Herbivorous birds use one of a few general strategies or a combination of these strategies to meet their energy needs. One strategy is to eat buds, or new sprouts of vegetative material, which are much more digestible, as they do not yet contain high levels of insoluble structural cellulose. Another strategy is to eat a high volume of plant material, digest and absorb the limited amount of nutrients that are highly digestible, and excrete the indigestible portion. This is the strategy adopted by Canada Geese in North America—they eat grass voraciously but digest little of it and quickly pass out the rest as feces. The South American Hoatzin, on the other hand, is the only known bird with an enlarged crop that it uses as a rumen (Figure 6.20 d). The hoatzin's crop is full of bacteria that digest the cellulose of the consumed plant material; thus, the hoatzin's digestion and derived nutrition from plant material follow the description above for a ruminant. In other species like the Rhea, the cecum is the location where fibrous plant material is digested by bacteria (Figure 6.20 a). In the Ostrich, the cecum is present, but it is a greatly enlarged large intestine that provides for the digestion of structural plant material (Figure 6.20 b), making it more equivalent to the horse, which is also a hind-gut digester of plant material.

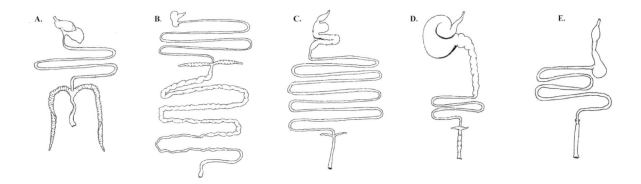

FIGURE 6.20 Structural differences in the digestive tract of the large ratites, the hoatzin and a meat-eating hawk. The Rhea (a) is largely vegetarian, eating primarily leaves and grasses that are digested in the ceca. The Ostrich (b) eats grasses, seeds leaves and flowers and has an enlarged large intestine to help digest this structural plant material. The Emu (c) of Australia is unlike the other two large ratites in that it eats highly digestible, fruits, flowers, seeds and young shoots. The hoatzin (d) has an enlarged crop that acts like a rumen in digesting the leafy plant material it consumes. The meat-eating hawk (e) uses its specialized beak to tear pieces of meat from prey and will have an enlarged proventriculus and relatively weak gizzard. Proventriculus function is critical, given the high protein content of the diet, while gizzard strength can be reduced because mechanical grinding is not necessary, rather simple mixing of the meat-based diet with the acid and pepsin from the proventriculus is needed (Adapted from Stevens and Hume 1998). Not drawn to scale.

WAXES

Waxes are also very hard to digest, but some species of birds will eat such things as wax-coated berries, honeycomb, and ear wax from animals. Some bird species metabolize the wax compounds produced by marine crustaceans. Ingested waxes, together with bile and pancreatic secretions, will be recycled several times to the gizzard and proventriculus to break down the complex fatty acids into digestible components.

FEEDING BIRDS IN CAPTIVITY

As illustrated throughout the section on the anatomy of the digestive systems of birds, the anatomy varies greatly across bird species. This diversity makes it absolutely critical that research be completed prior to feeding bird species held in captivity for display, as pets or for recovery purposes. Innumerous birds have died in captivity as a result of being fed improper diets. When at all possible, the research conducted before captive feeding needs to include the detailed examination of the digestive tracts of specimens that have died. Structural examination of the proventriculus and gizzard, as well as noting the presence or absence of the ceca, for example, can provide valuable clues to the diet of a bird and what it is capable of digesting (Figure 6.20). Needed research also includes extensive field studies to determine in detail what a species in the wild consumes for food. If the food being consumed cannot be provided in captivity, then detailed nutrient analyses of the food consumed in the wild must be completed. This will allow for the replication of this wild diet, as far as providing the correct nutrient levels. Such research is routine today, but in the past, it could have ensured that no nectar-feeding lories would have ever been fed seeds simply because they are parrots. It also would have ensured that all Hyacinth Macaws were fed an unusually high fat diet to replicate what they consume naturally.

WATER

Although often overlooked as an essential nutrient, water is the most important nutrient. Dehydration will kill before starvation. For hummingbirds, which consume a liquid-based diet, the physiological goal is to get rid of enough water. To accomplish this goal, their intestinal tract selectively absorbs the carbohydrates derived from nectar, while allowing most of the water to pass unabsorbed. They also have the highest evaporative water loss of any bird species. For birds that eat meat, insects, or fruit, large amounts of water are ingested as part of their food. For seed-eaters, the need for water intake is greater because seeds are low in water content. Birds will consume water from streams, puddles, dew, raindrops, snow, etc. Birds also produce more metabolic water than most vertebrates due to their high metabolic rate. Metabolic water is produced in the body as a by-product of the oxidation of organic compounds containing hydrogen. So burning (oxidizing) fuels such as carbohydrates and fats in the body generates water, and birds burn a lot of fuel, as discussed in Chapter 4. Consequently, for some bird species, the combination of metabolic water and the water consumed in food is enough to meet their water needs.

WATER CONSERVATION

Water conservation can be very significant in birds. As already discussed in the cloaca section of this chapter, the need for water in birds is also lowered because (1) they excrete uric acid rather than urea; and (2) they extract the water from urinary waste once it enters the cloaca. Furthermore, oceanic birds can actually drink salt water because they, like other birds that need to conserve water or consume a salty diet, have salt glands located on their head near the eye which drains out the nostril. The excreted solution, formed by the glands by filtering the bird's blood, can contain as much as 5 percent salt (Gill, 2007), which exceeds the 3 percent salt content of seawater and negates the bird from having to excrete excess salt via the kidneys and increase urinary output. In bird species where the kidneys are solely responsible for excreting salt, the ingestion of seawater would cause dehydration as it does in humans that drink seawater. This is because the amount of water needed to form the urine to excrete the salt contained in seawater would be over one and a half times the amount of the seawater consumed.

As previously discussed in Chapter 4 birds have an extremely high metabolic rate, resulting in a high body temperature. As a result, birds in many situations will be losing heat to the environment. However, if faced with high environmental temperatures that push them above their thermoneutral comfort zone, birds will react the same way as we do by seeking out shade, bathing in cool water, reducing physical activity, and losing heat by evaporative cooling. Evaporative cooling through water loss can occur directly through the skin (birds do not have sweat glands) or through respiration (Gill, 2007). Birds will also pant to increase evaporative cooling losses through respiration. However, evaporative cooling means the loss of water. If water needs to be conserved, some birds facing heat stress will undergo controlled hyperthermia and thus raise their body temperature a few degrees, so that they are once again losing body heat to the environment instead of utilizing evaporative cooling (Gill, 2007).

SUMMARY

With nearly 10,000 different extant bird species, it is not surprising that nearly every terrestrial ecosystem is utilized by species of birds. To further reduce their competition with one another, birds seemingly use every imaginable food source and have evolved a plethora of ways to obtain and utilize these varied food sources for their nutritional needs. Such diversity is part of what attracts us to birds—but this diversity is of upmost importance in conserving all ecosystems for the continuation of all bird species.

REFERENCES

Bélisle, M. and J.-F. Giroux. 1995. Predation and Kleptoparasitism by Migrating Parasitic Jaegers. *Condor* **97**:771–781.

Clench, M. H. 1999. The avian cecum: Update and motility review. *Journal of Experimental Zoology* **283**:441–447.

Cunningham, S. J., I. Castro, T. Jensen, and M. A. Potter. 2010. Remote-touch prey detection by Madagascar Crested Ibises Lophotibis cristata urschi. *Journal of Avian Biology* **41**:350–353.

Cunningham, S. J., I. Castro, and M. A. Potter. 2009. The relative importance of olfaction and remote touch in prey detection by North Island Brown Kiwis. *Animal Behaviour* **78**:899–905.

Frances, P. and S. Larter. 2011. *Illustrated Encyclopedia of Birds*. BirdLife International. Dorling Kindersley Limited, London.

Gill, F. B. 2007. *Ornithology. 3rd edition*. W. H. Freeman and Company, New York.

Harris, T. 2009. *National Geographic Complete Birds of the World*. The Brown Reference Group Ltd.

Karasov, W. H. 1990. Digestion in birds: Chemical and physiological determinants and ecological implications. *Studies in Avian Biology* **13**:391–415.

Klasing, K. C. 1998. *Comparative Avian Nutrition*. CAB International, New York.

Miyazaki, M. 1996. Vegetation Cover, Kleptoparasitism by Diurnal Gulls, and Timing of Arrival of Nocturnal Rhinoceros Auklets. *Auk* **113**:698–702.

Perrins, C. 2009. *The Princeton Encyclopedia of Birds*. Princeton University Press, Princeton, NJ.

Piersma, T. and J. Drent. 2003. Phenotypic flexibility and the evolution of organismal design. *Trends in Ecology & Evolution* **18**:228–233.

Preest, M. R. and C. A. Beuchat. 1997. Ammonia excretion by hummingbirds. *Nature* **386**:561–562.

Rico-Guevara, A. and M. A. Rubega. 2011. The hummingbird tongue is a fluid trap, not a capillary tube. *Proceedings of the National Academy of Sciences* **108**:9356–9360.

Roxburgh, L. and B. Pinshow. 2002. Ammonotely in a passerine nectarivore: The influence of renal and post-renal modification on nitrogenous waste product excretion. *Journal of Experimental Biology* **205**:1735–1745.

Stevens, C. E. and I. D. Hume. 1998. Contributions of microbes in vertebrate gastrointestinal tract to production and conservation of nutrients. *Physiological Reviews* 78(2): 393–427.

Thouless, C. R., J. H. Fanshawe, and C. R. Bertram. 1987. Egyptian Vultures Neophron percnopterus and Ostrich Struthio camelus eggs: The origins of stone-throwing behaviour. *Ibis* **131**:9–15.

Tsahar, E., C. Martínez del Rio, I. Izhaki, and Z. Arad. 2005. Can birds be ammonotelic? Nitrogen balance and excretion in two frugivores. *Journal of Experimental Biology* **208**:1025–1034.

Vickery, J. A. and M. D. L. Brooke. 1994. The Kleptoparasitic Interactions between Great Frigatebirds and Masked Boobies on Henderson Island, South Pacific. *Condor* **96**:331–340.

VII   REPRODUCTION

E fficient reproduction is essential to the survival of a species. However, reproduction is not essential for the survival of an individual. Thus, sexually mature females or males only proceed to produce eggs or sperm if they have the excess energy intake and body reserves to support a reproductive effort. This is especially true in vertebrate female species, where the metabolic demands for reproduction are greater than in males, because there are high energy demands associated with the production of either large eggs or with gestation.

VIVIPAROUS, OVIPAROUS, AND OVOVIVIPAROUS

Vertebrate animals show a wide range of reproductive strategies. In ovuliparity, there is a release of ova from the female reproductive tract, followed by fertilization within the external environment. With internal fertilization, the development of the embryo and fetus may occur within the female, with a close vascular connection between fetus and mother—this is termed viviparous. All placental mammals are viviparous, and more specifically, hemotrophic viviparous species. There are a few histotrophic viviparous species (some fish and at least one salamander) in which the developing embryo(s)/zygote(s) develops in its mother's oviduct, but is nourished not by the mother's blood, but rather by eating subsequently released ova (oophagy) or by consuming developing siblings (intrauterine cannibalism). Oviparity also occurs with internal fertilization, but the development of the embryo occurs outside the mother's body within an encased egg that provides the nutrients for its development and growth. All birds are oviparous, as are some reptiles and some mammals (echidna and duck billed platypus). Interestingly, there are some fish, reptiles, and amphibians that are ovoviviparous in which fertilization is internal, but development of the offspring occurs from the nourishment of an encased egg that is within the female's body—or in some cases, the male's body—for protection. In ovoviviparity, there is no nourishment provided by the parent during development.

SEASONALITY

Female birds lay eggs and young are hatched at a time of year that will maximize the chance of offspring survival. This corresponds primarily to food availability, as obtaining and delivering enough food to meet the nutrient demands of their growing offspring are the main problems facing parent birds of many bird species. However, it takes several weeks for the avian gonads to grow from a regressed, non-functional state to a fully functional state. Therefore, birds use environmental cues to regulate the reproductive cycle, such that they produce offspring during the best time for offspring survival. The best time to reproduce varies from one environment to another, between individual species and their environment, and between different geographic populations of the same species.

Environmental cues for reproduction can be characterized as long, medium, and short term. Increasing day length is a long-term cue in temperate environments. As the length of daylight (photoperiod) increases in the spring, birds perceive this increase in day length and respond by initiating the first stages of reproduction. Typically, about 12 hours or more of light are needed to stimulate reproduction in both male and female birds. Birds that respond to increasing day length as a cue to initiate reproduction are called long-day breeders. Emperor penguins are unusual in the bird world, as they are short-day breeders and initiate reproduction in response to decreasing day length in the fall.

Increasing day length is followed by increasing environmental temperatures and increased food supplies in temperate regions. Establishing a territory and having an adequate food supply are medium-term cues for reproduction. If both of these cues are positive, preparation for reproduction continues with further development of the gonads. The growth of the testes, and especially the ovarian follicles and oviducts, is energy and nutrient demanding and will not occur without adequate nutrition. For birds that live closer to the equator where day length does not fluctuate greatly throughout the year, increasing day length cannot be used as a long-term cue. In these species, medium-term cues are more important. Other environmental cues such as rainfall may signal the initiation of reproduction in anticipation of the increased food supply the rains will bring.

The final cues for reproduction are short term and include such things as having a nest site and mate, as well as courtship. In general, long-, medium-, and short-term cues all must be positive for reproduction to proceed to the laying of fertile eggs. If a long-term cue initiates development of the reproductive system, but appropriate medium- and short-term cues are lacking, reproduction will be blocked. Similarly, if long-term and medium-term cues are appropriate, but short-term cues are lacking, reproduction is blocked.

Environmental cues are perceived by sensory organs or directly by the brain. The hypothalamus is the key brain structure that receives all of the inputs regarding reproduction. In birds, day length is perceived directly in the hypothalamus, as light can pass through the thin skulls of birds and directly stimulate photopigments in the hypothalamus. In contrast, mammalian eyes are the only source of light detection, and day length is translated by the pineal gland, which produces the hormone melatonin in response to darkness. Melatonin is only produced during darkness, so its levels decrease as the days get longer. In addition to directly stimulating the hypothalamus, light influences the production of melatonin in birds, as it does in mammalian species. In addition to light, the hypothalamus also receives information about nutritional status via hormones produced in response to daily energy intake and the quantity of body stores of energy, particularly fat mass available to support reproduction.

In response to meeting a threshold of light (typically about 12 hours or more) and having adequate nutrient intake and/or body stores of nutrients, the hypothalamus produces and releases gonadotropin-releasing hormone (GnRH). GnRH is released into the blood and travels a short distance to stimulate the anterior pituitary gland to synthesize and release follicle-stimulating hormone (FSH) and luteinizing hormone (LH). FSH and LH travel in the blood to the gonads, where they stimulate the growth and development of the gonads (Figure 7.1). Hormones produced and released by the gonads stimulate growth of the reproductive duct systems, control reproductive behavior, and in females, stimulate many of the reproductive processes required for egg production.

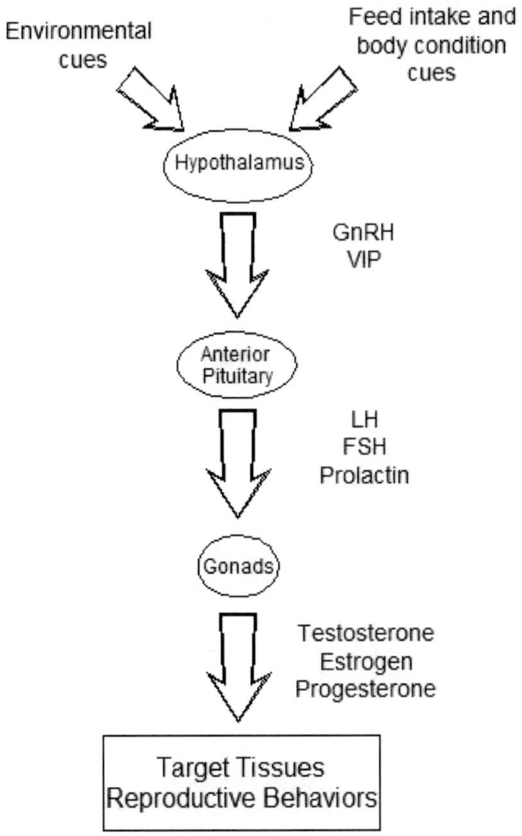

AVIAN FEMALE REPRODUCTIVE ANATOMY

In the vast majority of birds, only the left ovary and left oviduct develop. The lack of the right ovary and oviduct is hypothesized to be a weight-reduction mechanism that developed for flight purposes. The right oviduct is present in a very rudimentary form. In some raptor species, both the right and left oviduct are present, as will be discussed in the chapter on raptors (Chapter 9). There is a massive growth of the ovary and oviduct during the reproductive season. For example, in a large, non-reproductive chicken, the ovary and oviduct will each weigh less than a couple of grams, but within a matter of weeks, the ovary

FIGURE 7.1   The hypothalamus-pituitary-gonadal axis.

and oviduct can grow and weigh about 60 and 70 grams, respectively. Both the ovary and oviduct shrink back to their prereproductive size once egg production has concluded for the reproductive season. The regression of the ovary and oviduct is thought to be an adaption to minimizing flight weight.

THE OVARY

The ovary of the sexually mature bird typically consists of a visually evident hierarchy of follicles relative to size and time to ovulation. The size of this hierarchy and the time that it is present depend on the number of eggs the female will produce before incubation commences, which ends follicular development. In most birds, there are commonly four or so large yellow, yolk-filled follicles, termed hierarchical follicles. These follicles are accompanied by several small yellow follicles, in which yellow yolk deposition has begun, and a large number of even smaller white follicles that have not started the uptake of yellow yolk. The larger yolk-filled follicles are named according to size and time to ovulation. The largest follicle is termed the F1 follicle and will ovulate within the next 24 hours (Figure 7.2). The next largest follicle is named the F2 follicle; it will typically ovulate 24–48 hours after the ovulation of the F1 follicle. The remaining large yolk-filled follicles are named accordingly (F3–Fn). With each ovulation, all the hierarchical follicles advance one position forward in the naming hierarchy, and a new follicle enters into the hierarchy from the pool of small yellow follicles. In addition, some of the larger white follicles will start the uptake of yellow yolk and become small yellow follicles. A vast majority of the small yellow and large white

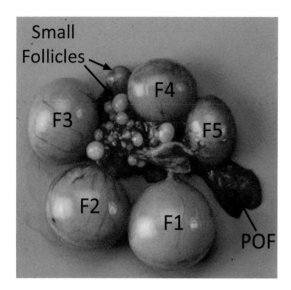

FIGURE 7.2   The follicular hierarchy in a chicken ovary.

follicles will never be selected and advance into the hierarchy, but will instead die in a process typically referred to as follicular atresia. Although seemingly wasteful, follicular atresia occurs in all species, as initiating growth of a number of follicles at one time ensures that at least one of them will successfully grow and advance to ovulate at the appropriate time, and there will be backup follicles progressing in case the development of the selected one fails. With typically fleeting favorable conditions for reproduction, it is essential that the female bird produces the egg(s) for incubation without delay.

Each preovulatory follicle has distinct tissue layers that surround the yolk-filled oocyte. The developing oocyte is first surrounded by its plasma membrane, then the inner perivitelline layer, followed by the granulosa cell layer, a basement membrane, and theca tissue layers (Figure 7.3). The theca tissue is highly vascularized, in contrast to the avascular granulosa cell layer, and facilitates the transfer of yolk precursors from blood plasma to the developing follicles in the ovary. Follicular maturation is regulated by the two pituitary hormones, LH and FSH. Both LH and FSH promote granulosa cell proliferation and maturation and thus follicular growth. They also stimulate production of estrogen and progesterone. The theca cells of the small yellow and white follicles are the primary source of plasma estrogen. Estrogen plays critical roles in stimulating the development of the oviduct, stimulating the liver to synthesize egg yolk components, stimulating the oviduct cells to produce the egg albumen and shell, and promoting sexual behavior in female birds. Progesterone is produced primarily by the granulosa cells of the

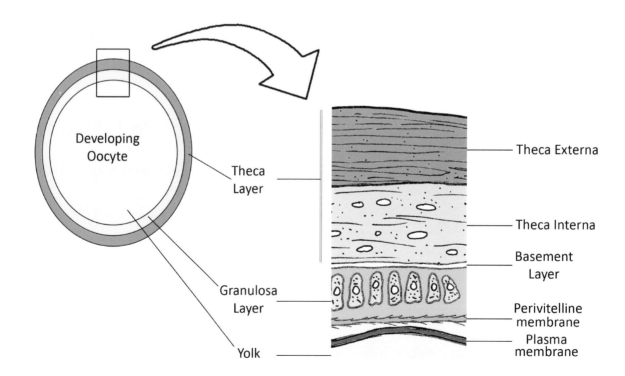

FIGURE 7.3   The various layers of the developing oocyte or follicle.

largest preovulatory follicle in the hours preceding ovulation. It is essential for the stimulation of the LH surge necessary for ovulation. Progesterone and LH both stimulate the breakdown of the stigma, which is a less vascularized and weaker constructed portion of the follicle through which the ovum will ovulate (Figure 7.4). Progesterone also stimulates the oviduct to produce albumen components of the egg.

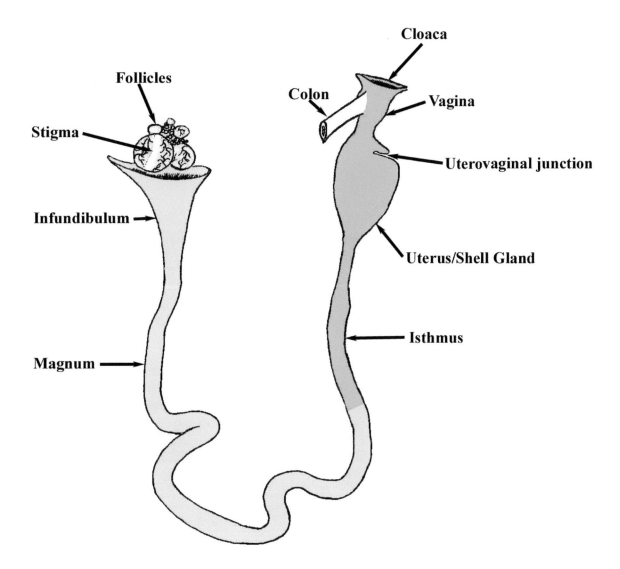

FIGURE 7.4 The avian oviduct. The infundibulum captures the freshly ovulated ovum and is the site of fertilization. The follicle is only in the infundibulum for 15–30 minutes. The magnum is where most of the egg albumen is synthesized and added to the forming egg with this process taking 2 to 3 hours. For the next 1 to 2 hours, the isthmus produces the inner and outer shell membranes of the developing egg. The developing egg enters the uterus as a membranous sac that is not full. In the first part of the uterus, water and electrolytes are added to the egg so that the internal contents fill the membranous sac completely to provide a smooth taut surface upon which the shell will be deposited. The deposition of the shell occurs in the last portion of the uterus. The egg remains in the shell gland for 18 to 26 hours in most species. Passage through the vagina to the cloaca only lasts about 15 minutes. The whole process of forming of the rest of the egg around the yolk after ovulation takes about 24–30 hours in most species.

THE OVIDUCT

In birds, the term oviduct refers to the whole tubular reproductive tract of the female, in contrast to mammalian species, where it refers only to the short portion of the tubular tract from the ovary to the uterus. The oviduct's growth is stimulated by sex hormones, particularly estrogen. The oviduct in birds is composed of several distinct regions that include the infundibulum, magnum, isthmus, uterus, uterovaginal junction, and vagina (Figure 7.4). The infundibulum captures the freshly ovulated ovum, is the site of fertilization, and functions as a secondary site for sperm storage. The magnum is where most of the egg albumen (egg white) is synthesized and added to the forming egg. The isthmus is where inner and outer shell membranes are synthesized around the developing egg. The developing egg enters the uterus as a membranous sac that is not full (Figure 7.5). Think of it as a water balloon that is three quarters full, with a wrinkly, non-turgid skin. In the first part of the uterus, water and electrolytes are added to the egg so that the internal contents fill the membranous sac completely to provide a smooth, taut surface (a now-filled water balloon), upon which the shell will be deposited. The deposition of the shell occurs in the last portion of the uterus. The uterovaginal junction is the primary storage site for sperm. The vagina is the passageway to the cloaca and the site of sperm selection. The whole process of forming the rest of the egg around the yolk after ovulation takes about 24–30 hours in most species.

SPERM STORAGE

The capacity to store sperm in birds most likely evolved for a number of reasons. First and foremost, birds have an unusually short fertilization window compared to most vertebrate species. Fertilization occurs in the infundibulum, and sperm must make contact with the freshly ovulated ovum within about 15 minutes after ovulation before the ovum passes to the caudal region of the infundibulum. As the ovum passes the caudal region of the infundibulum, two protein layers—the middle continuous layer and outer perivetilline layer—are added around the egg, which mechanically blocks sperm from contacting the ovum for fertilization. After the addition of these two layers,

FIGURE 7.5   A membrane egg lacking its shell is shown on the right. Note the wrinkled appearance as fluid has not been added to the egg to completely stretch the shell membranes. For comparison, an egg complete with shell is shown on the left.

albumen also starts to be added around the ovum in the last portion of the infundibulum and then subsequently in the magnum, and sperm are unable to penetrate the albumen. Additionally, birds, unlike some other animals, do not have an estrus cycle, so there no synchronization between mating and ovulation. In birds studied, copulation does not induce ovulation; thus, sperm storage helps ensure that sperm are available when an ovum is ovulated.

Sperm storage also eliminates the need for repeated copulations while ensuring the fertility of eggs, which are often ovulated on a daily basis for several days. In some bird species in which the female provides all the parental care, sperm storage allows the female to just mate once with the male during a breeding season and produce an egg or several sequential eggs that are fertile. In some bird species, eggs produced as many as six weeks after a copulatory event will be fertilized with stored sperm (Hatch, 1983; Bakst, 1988). However, for most birds studied, the duration of fertility after copulation is in a range of seven to 14 days. As will be discussed later, copulation in birds puts them at risk for predator attack, so sperm storage also can limit the number of copulations needed and as such, lowers the risk of predation. Finally, the evolution of sperm storage has led to sperm selection, as will be discussed below.

Sperm storage tubules in the bird species examined occur primarily at the uterovaginal junction. However, there is evidence of sperm storage capacity in domestic poultry in the infundibulum (Howarth, 1990), but the sperm storage tubules located here have not been isolated. Sperm storage tubules can be viewed as isolated compartments, as even spermicide introduced into the oviducts of hens does not have any effect on the sperm located in the tubules (Walton and Whetham, 1933). Inside the tubules, an environment is provided that keeps the sperm quiescent and stable, as reviewed by Bakst et al. (1994), which maintains their viability for extended periods of time.

SPERM SELECTION

To get to the sperm storage tubules, the sperm have to be able to swim through the vagina. Vaginal secretions contain a lot of non-specific immunoglobulins that will attach to sperm. They seem to preferentially attach to sperm that are defective or have surface characteristics that have more antigenicity with the female's immune system. Consequently, sperm from one male may be perceived as more foreign and attract more immunoglobulins than this same sperm would attract in another female. Immunoglobulins that attach to sperm act like anchors, making it hard for the sperm to move forward. The fastest forward-moving sperm that attract the least amount of immunoglobulins will reach the sperm storage tubules first, and the tubules appear to fill on a first-come, first-served basis. The storage tubules closest to the vent fill first, followed by those progressively moving toward the cranial portion of the oviduct. Once all the sperm storage tubules are filled, any subsequent sperm without storage opportunity simply swim out of the infundibulum into the body cavity, where they will die, as reviewed by Bakst et al. (1994). This means that the sperm from the first insemination have an advantage in filling the storage tubules and siring any produced offspring, compared to males with subsequent inseminations.

Overall, in a given female, live sperm that have the least amount of structural defects (bent tails, two tails, two heads, etc.), have the appropriate surface characteristics, and have the fastest forward movement, are the sperm that reach the sperm storage tubules first and are then stored. Total storage capacity is limited in the sperm storage tubules, and probably less than 2 percent of sperm from an initial insemination are stored, based on research in domestic fowl (Bakst et al., 1994). Sperm competition and selection has been documented frequently in research, as reviewed by Bakst et al. (1994). The significance of sperm selection can be seen in the following example: 70 percent of the offspring produced from turkey hens artificially inseminated with pooled semen from 15 males, each contributing the same amount of sperm, were fathered by two of the males, based on genetic fingerprinting.

AVIAN MALE REPRODUCTIVE ANATOMY

In avian species, paired internal testes are located along the dorsal body wall below the spine and cranial to the kidneys (Figure 7.6). This internal location means that spermatogenesis occurs at 41 degrees C in avian species, as opposed to the scrotal temperature of about 25 degrees C in other animals. Because spermatogenesis occurs at an elevated temperature in birds, there is a higher mortality rate for the developing sperm; however, this increased rate of mortality is negated by the higher synthetic capacity of birds to produce more sperm per weight of testes compared to other

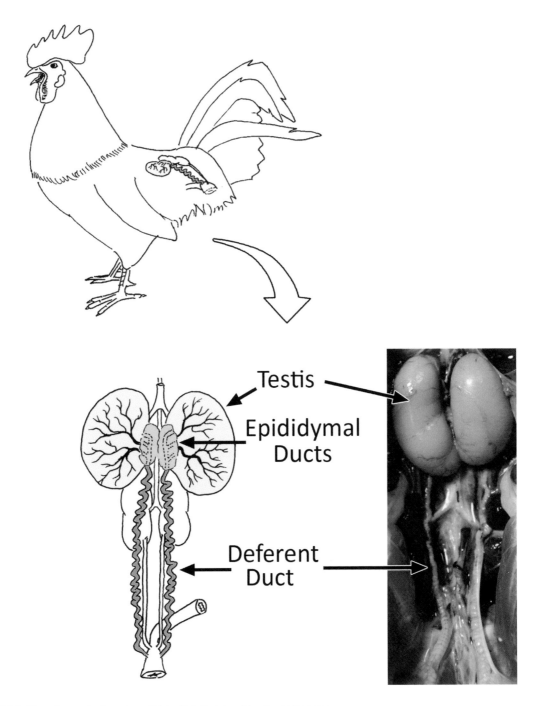

FIGURE 7.6   The male reproductive system of birds. Note the internal location of the testes.

animals (Bearden and Fuquay, 1984; Howarth, 1995). The sensitivity to high temperatures also results in decreased semen quality and fertility in birds exposed to heat stress (McDaniel et al., 1995; McDaniel et al., 1996; Jiang et al., 1999; Karaca et al., 2002). The higher synthetic capacity of birds to produce sperm also makes up for their limited storage capacity, as they have small epididymal ducts compared to mammalian males.

Avian species also lack the accessory reproductive organs, such as the bulbourethral glands, seminal vesicles, and prostate, which are common in mammalian species. The absence of the secretions from these accessory organs results in avian semen being much less voluminous and more concentrated than semen produced by mammalian species. In an evolutionary context, this is important, as the transfer of this concentrated semen can occur very rapidly when the male copulates with a female. As prey animals, most bird species want copulation to occur as fast as possible. During copulation, the male is typically trying to balance on the back of the female, often fluttering his wings for balance, which attracts predator attention. Once positioned, the male moves downward and to one side of the female's back and tail to contact his cloaca with that of the female to transfer semen. The actual cloacal contact is typically less than half a second.

Each individual testis is composed primarily of two types of tissue: the interstitial tissue and seminiferous epithelium. The interstitial tissue is dispersed in the spaces between the seminiferous tubules and contains blood and lymphatic vessels, nerves, and Leydig cells. The Leydig cells, stimulated by LH, produce testosterone. Thin, concentric layers of myoepithelial cells (also called myoid cells or peritubular contractile cells), fiberblasts, and connective tissue overlie the basal lamina separating the interstitial and seminiferous epithelium (Figure 7.7 a). The seminiferous epithelium is composed of spermatogonia and Sertoli cells (Figure 7.7 b), which completely line the circumference of each seminiferous tubule. The Sertoli cells are large cells that project from the basal lamina to the lumen of the seminiferous tubule. Sertoli cells provide a microenvironment in which spermatogenesis—the transformation of spermatogonia to a functional sperm—occurs. They produce androgen-binding protein, which binds testosterone and sequesters it near developing sperm cells for their normal growth and maturation. The Sertoli cells also transfer nutrients to the developing sperm cells. Given the vital functions Sertoli cells play in sperm development, it is not surprising that the number of Sertoli cells present in the testis is proportional to testicular size, and thus sperm production.

Fully developed sperm are released into the lumen of the seminiferous tubules. The seminiferous tubule network merges into the rete testis followed by the efferent ducts, connecting ducts, the epididymal duct (commonly referred to as the epididymis in mammalian species), and finally the deferent duct (or vas deferens in mammalian species). The caudal end of each deferent duct expands into the receptacle of the deferent duct, which opens into the cloaca via a papilla. The papilla of the paired deferent ducts is located next to the rudimentary phallus, for most bird species lack an intromittent phallus, as will be discussed shortly. The phallus of most male birds is very small and is not a true intromittent phallus. Instead, the phallus nonprotrudens is located ventromedially in the cloaca on the ventral lip of the vent. When erected with lymph fluid produced by the paracloacal vascular bodies, the lymphatic folds of the phallus form a median groove that facilitates the flow of semen to the outside of the vent for copulation (Figure 7.8).

Testosterone in the adult male is necessary for spermatogenesis, maintenance of the excurrent ducts, and behavioral aspects such as crowing, territorial aggressiveness, and mating behavior. Testosterone is the precursor of estrogen, which is involved in the growth, differentiation, and function of male reproductive tissues. It plays vital roles in spermatogenesis. Estrogen also plays a pivotal role in the development of the specialized feathers in male birds to attract females.

Spermatogenesis, the formation of spermatozoa from a spermatogonia (germ cell), is four to six times more rapid in avian species than in humans and other farm animals (de Riviers, 1968; Takeda, 1969; Howarth, 1995). Thus, functional sperm, ready for ejaculation and fertilization, are produced in about two weeks in birds, versus over a two-month time period in humans. This

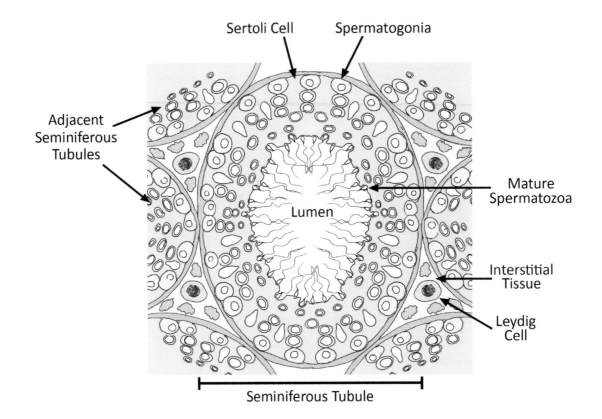

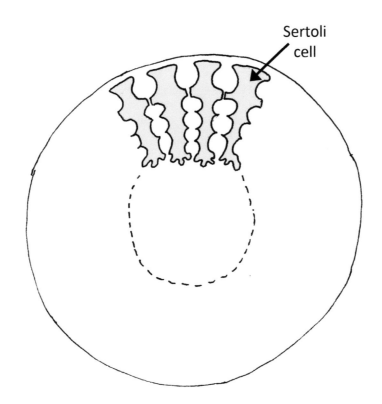

FIGURE 7.7 The internal anatomy of the testes showing the placement of seminiferous tubules and interstitial tissue in the top figure. A seminiferous tubule showing a few of the Sertoli cells that completely line the circumference of each seminiferous tubule to illustrate their size (bottom figure).

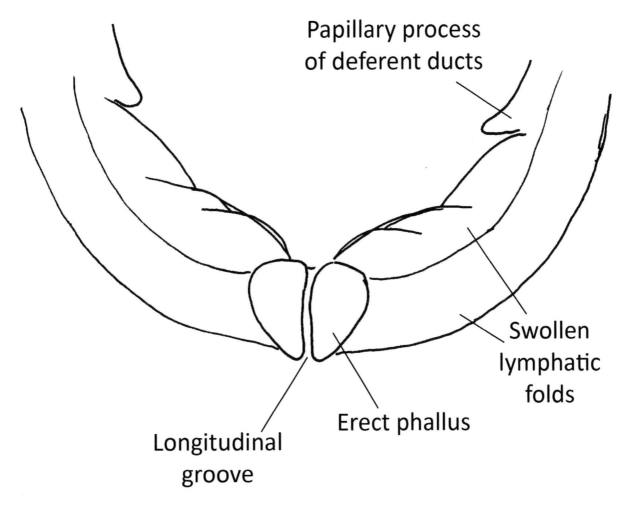

FIGURE 7.8   The phallus of most male birds is very small and is not a true intromittent phallus. Located in the ventral lip of the cloaca, the phallus can be erected with lymph fluid to form a median groove that facilitates the flow of semen during copulation.

fast maturation of sperm in birds is necessary so they can rapidly take advantage of favorable environmental conditions for reproduction before these favorable conditions are gone. For example, in an arid environment, the arrival of rain will bring an abundance of food and will stimulate reproduction in bird species. If, however, the male birds had to wait for over two months for sperm to mature once reproduction was stimulated, the food supply could already be running out before fertilized eggs are even produced. Instead, with many passerine species, a pair can produce fertilized eggs within a couple of weeks of correct environmental conditions, then incubate these eggs and have hatchlings in another couple of weeks, and finally have fledged offspring leave the nest in about three more weeks.

LACK OF INTROMITTENT ORGAN

Of the roughly 10,000 species of birds, only about 250 species have an intromittent organ, or penis, for copulation. Intromittent organs are housed in the cloaca and extend out from the cloaca, once erected with lymph fluid (Figure 7.9). As reviewed by Briskie and Montgomerie (1997), it is typically agreed that the loss of the intromittent organ has occurred over time, an idea supported

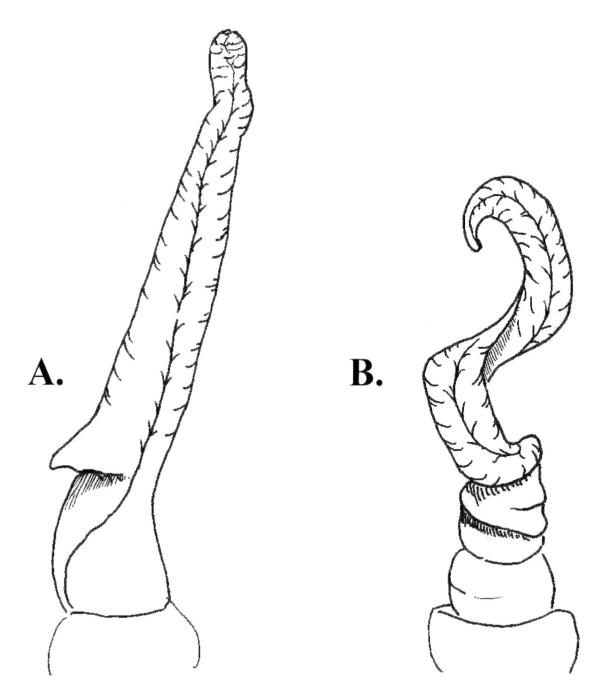

FIGURE 7.9 Few birds species have an intromittent organ. The Rhea (a) and the Long-tailed Duck (b) are two examples that have retained their intromittent organs over evolutionary time.

by the fact that male common feral pigeons have an intromittent organ during embryonic develop-ment, but it is reabsorbed before hatch. For species without an intromittent organ, copulation is accomplished by simple cloacal contact, commonly referred to as a cloacal kiss, between the everted cloaca of a male and a female bird. The cloacal kiss in most bird species is incredibly rapid (less than half a second), and thus necessitates the males having a highly concentrated ejaculate, as discussed previously. For those bird species with an intromittent organ, the male inserts the organ briefly into the female's vagina. Again, even when males have intromittent organs, copulation is still accomplished very quickly. Copulation duration between bird species, where males have or do not have intromittent organs, are equal (Briskie and Montgomerie, 2001).

Species in which the males have retained intromittent organs are confined to several species of water birds, the ratites, tinamous species, and members of the Cracidae family (guans, curassows, and chachalacas). An intromittent organ is also found in male Vasa Parrots, and the only passerine species to have an intromittent organ are male buffalo weavers. In species of buffalo weavers, the organ acts as a stimulatory organ and does not have ducts for sperm transfer (Briskie and Montgomerie, 1997; Winterbottom et al., 1999).

The absence of an intromittent organ is highly unusual for species that have internal fertilization, like birds. This, combined with the fact that less than 3 percent of bird species have retained an intromittent organ, has led to several hypotheses to explain the presence or lack of an intromittent organ in male birds, as reviewed by Briskie and Montgomerie (1997, 2001) and Wesolowski (1999). The two most prevalent ideas for the retention of an intromittent organ involve water damage prevention and sperm competition (Briskie and Montgomerie, 1997). Many of the birds that have retained intromittent organs are water birds. Copulation on water occurring by a cloacal kiss could result in the sperm being washed away from the female's cloaca by water or having sperm come into contact with water, causing sperm damage (osmotic shock). If the male had an intromittent organ, this would be avoided. In support of this theory, the vast majority (over 90 percent) of water birds that copulate on water have an organ, while the vast majority of water birds that copulate on land do not have an organ.

The sperm competition hypothesis is based on the fact that, for male birds that incubate and care for their offspring, the investment is only worthwhile for the male if the offspring represent his genetics. In almost all the ratite species (except for Ostriches and some Kiwi species) and many tinamous species, the male incubates the eggs and provides all the parental care that is given. Intromittent organs are found in both ratites and tinamous, and moreover, these organs are typically large and unusually shaped, with papilla and groves. In these species, males may use their intromittent organ to deliver sperm to the female beyond a point where she can eject it (see below), but also may use it to scrape away stored semen present from a previous male, thus ensuring his paternity. Interestingly, forced copulations in duck species are very common, and competition among males is very keen for breeding opportunities. Ducks also have fairly large intromittent organs, with the male Argentine Lake Duck having an organ that can reach over 16.5 inches (42 cm) in length (McCracken et al., 2001). Male duck copulatory organs also have unusual shapes and can contain brush-like papillae. Although female ducks have extended and convoluted vaginas that have co-evolved along with the male's copulatory organ (Brennan et al., 2007), the ridges and brush-like papillae may serve to remove the sperm of competitors (McCracken, 2000).

For the loss of an intromittent organ in 97 percent of bird species, there is less conclusive evidence for hypotheses. One hypothesis involves the avoidance of sexually transmitted diseases. Because birds have a cloaca which houses the openings to the urinary, digestive, and reproductive tracts, the bacteria and pathogens associated with the digestive tract could be more easily introduced into the female reproductive tract when the male's intromittent organ passed through the cloaca and entered the reproductive tract. In addition, the male would be exposed to these potential pathogens, as well. Although plausible, this theory cannot explain why an intromittent organ has been retained in some of the most long-lived birds and almost universally absent in short-lived birds. If avoidance of sexually transmitted disease vectors were the goal, the opposite would be expected.

Female birds typically have the heavy reproductive investment in producing the eggs and caring for young. The females typically choose their mates based on which mate will provide the best genetics for her offspring. If males had intromittent organs, forced copulations would be possible. With the cloacal kiss copulatory event, females have to be willing partners if the sperm is going to be transferred successfully. More importantly, because the semen is placed at the cloaca, the female can eject the semen if the copulation is coerced or if she does not want the semen. Female chickens eject the sperm of subdominant males who have coerced copulation (Pizzari and Birkhead, 2000). Female Dunnocks, small ground-dwelling birds, are often polyandrous, breeding with two males. Both males will help feed the chicks. The female can eject sperm and a male will peck at the cloaca to stimulate the ejection of sperm from a previous male (Davies, 1983). Thus, the female can choose the paternity of her offspring based on who she believes offers the best genetics by ejecting unwanted sperm, but have the benefit of two males feeding her offspring. Based on avoiding unwanted copulations and having the ability to eject sperm, it is hypothesized that over time, females selected males with smaller copulatory organs until they became non-existent.

MATING

The vast majority of bird species (over 90 percent) are typically monogamous. A pair of birds will function as a unit in raising offspring. The duration of this partnership varies from one breeding attempt, to a breeding season, or even a lifetime, as is the case in such species as swans and many of the parrot species. Forming a monogamous pair does not mean that extra pair copulations do not occur if the opportunity arises to mate with a dominant/genetically superior individual, or that pairs will not divorce if reproductive efforts fail or one of the partners has the opportunity to trade up to a more genetically fit partner. Although not always true, the male and female of monogamous species tend to look the same or almost the same in physical appearance. Monogamy seems to be so prevalent in birds because reproductive success depends on both parents working to provide enough food for the survival of their offspring. Passerine parent birds typically make several hundred trips back to their nests each day feeding nestlings.

Polygamous birds, which have several partners in a breeding season, typically take the form of polygyny (one male mating with multiple females), but polyandry (one female with two or more males) does occur. With polygyny, the males typically have no further role in reproduction beyond providing sperm. In these species, the males often look very different visually compared to the females. In the Northern and Grey species of phalaropes, the roles of the sexes in reproduction are reversed. The females are more brightly colored than the males, and one female will mate and lay eggs for two males that incubate the eggs and care for the young. For reasons not understood, a very high proportion of the polygamous species consumes fruit or leaves as their main food sources (Perrins, 2009).

Cooperative breeding is seen in at least 300 species of birds (Frances and Larter, 2011). This breeding pattern has become more widely recognized and is utilized by more bird species than previously thought. Cooperative breeding occurs when territory is not available for all pairs of a species to breed, and in some species, it is used to help ensure the survival and fledging of the breeding pair's offspring when food is not abundant. In some species of shrikes, a varying number of helpers will assist the breeding pair of the group to raise the nestlings. More often, the helpers are relatives, in particular, offspring from previous broods, as is seen in some species of tyrant flycatchers and puffbirds. In hornbills, the helpers may be either accessory males or juveniles that help the dominant pair.

During courtship, females almost always choose the male based on who she thinks will provide her offspring with the best genetics, thus resulting in the continuation of her genes. Factors used to attract females are typically visual and/or acoustic based. Visual displays can take the form of dazzling feathers, as seen in peacocks, birds of paradise (Figure 7.10), or pheasants. Visual displays can take different forms other than the presence of colorful feathers. Inflated throat pouches are common, and nothing can rival the inflated scarlet throat pouch of the male Magnificent Frigatebird, which he uses to attract females (Figure 7.11). In species of bower birds of New Guinea and Australia, males are polygamous and advertise to perspective females by building large bowers that each male decorates with brightly colored fruits, flowers, dead insects or insect wing casings, pebbles, etc. Each bower reflects the male's own unique decorating style. Females inspect different bowers and mate with male(s) that impress her. Attracting females by song is also common, and the courtship calls or songs performed by many songbirds are heard by humans during the breeding season. One of the best vocals, based on complexity, are the songs created by Lyrebirds (Figure 7.12), whose songs incorporate mimicked versions of 30 or more songs from other species. Song is also used by many male birds to establish and maintain breeding territories.

Many polygamous male birds perform and breed with attracted females at leks. At lekking grounds, males will gather in numbers ranging from one to several dozen, depending on the species. They will often use loud booming calls to attract females. When the females have gathered, the males will put on elaborate displays that often include vocalizations, feather displays, strutting, and/ or flight displays. Females will evaluate the males to determine the most suitable male. Often, the dominant male chosen by the females will have almost more mating partners than he can handle, while males deemed less genetically fit will have no mating opportunities. Physical fighting for reproductive rights at a level to cause death or serious injury is relatively rare in the bird world, but does occur in some species of Galliformes (grouse, pheasants, and allies).

In monogamous species, pair formation and the cementing of the relationship involves such things as the giving of food gifts, courtship dances, and courtship aerial displays. The water courtship dances in grebes are especially elaborate, as are the aerial courtship displays of several large raptors. If these courtship displays do not go smoothly within a few attempts, the relationship will likely end. Mutual preening is very common in pair formation in parrots and some species of finches (Figure 7.13).

Although the stunning visual feather displays, the calls and songs produced, and the flight and dancing displays all awe humans, they serve an important biological purpose in allowing a female—and in a some cases, a male bird—to determine the fitness of a future mate. For example, as indicated in Chapter 4, feathers are made of protein and are very costly in energy to make, and the carotenoid pigments that produce many feather colors are obtained from dietary sources. As a result, males with the largest and most colorful feather displays are the ones with excellent foraging skills and are the healthiest and most robust. Similarly, the elaborate displays require a great deal of stamina and energy and can provide a female an indication of the male with the highest quality genetics to be passed on to her offspring, in particular, her male offspring, as will be discussed in the next section.

FIGURE 7.10 Raggiana Bird of Paradise

FIGURE 7.11 Male Magnificent Frigatebirds inflate their red throat pouch to attract females.

FIGURE 7.12   The male Superb Lyrebird uses amazing vocals to attract females.

FIGURE 7.13   Mutual preening is often an important component of pair formation, as seen in these Scarlet Macaws.

SEX RATIO MANIPULATION

In 1973 Trivers and Williard theoretically predicted that offspring sex ratios might be skewed in response to available resources (food) such that, when resources were abundant, a bias toward the production of the most costly sex would be favorable. Typically, males are the most costly because they are larger in size, but they can also often sire multiple offspring with different females, thereby providing the most benefit to their mothers in passing their genes on to future generations. Subsequently, as scientific evidence started to prove this theory, it was expanded to include other aspects like social hierarchy and mate attractiveness. Females lower in social structure or in poorer body condition would be anticipated to invest more in female progeny, as their daughters are likely to have greater lifetime reproductive success. Put another way, a male produced by a female in poor body condition and/or of low social structure status is likely to be small in size and unlikely to become a dominant male. As a non-dominant male, he is unlikely to have any mating success in a situation where males compete for mating opportunities. Therefore, in this situation, the mother would be smarter to produce a female that would at least produce some offspring and spread the mother's genetics. A mother that is socially dominant and in good body condition with abundant food resources, on the other hand, would benefit by producing a son who is likely to become a dominant male and sire abundant offspring in the future and distribute her genetics widely. Similarly, females mating with attractive males would be expected to produce more sons. Because of the expectation that the sons would inherit their father's attractiveness, they would have greater reproductive success with multiple mates and produce more grandchildren than daughters could.

In the last 10 to 20 years, a plethora of examples in which female birds have manipulated offspring sex ratios has been scientifically documented. Excellent detailed reviews on sex ratio manipulation in birds have been written (Pike and Petrie, 2003; Alonso-Alvarez, 2006; Rutkowska and Badyaev, 2008). A few illustrative examples are provided to offer context. Female Lesser Black-backed Gulls (Nager et al., 1999) and domestic pigeons (Pike, 2005) both produce significantly more females than male hatchlings when food resources are limited. Females of the critically endangered Kakapo Parrot produce more male offspring when they are provided supplemental food, as will be discussed further in the chapter on parrots (Sutherland, 2002). Female Blue Tits mated to attractive males, which have brighter blue crests in the ultraviolet spectrum, bias their offspring sex ratio toward male (Sheldon et al., 1999). The brightness of the blue crest in Blue Tit males is correlated with a significantly greater likelihood of survival to the next breeding season and an increased ability to acquire extra-pair copulations with other females. Finally, in the Seychelles Warbler, daughters from previous broods may serve as helpers to their parents in raising their new brood. These helpers are beneficial if the parents have a high-quality territory, but are a hindrance (consuming valuable, limited food) if the parents have a low-quality territory. Thus, on high-quality territories, pairs produce 87 percent female offspring, while pairs on low-quality territories produce 77 percent male offspring (Komdeur et al., 1997; Komdeur et al., 2002).

Typically, the bias in sex ratios is more subtle, like 60/40 or 65/35, and not as drastic as seen in the Seychelles Warbler. Additionally, generalizing the reasons for deviations in sex allocation in birds is difficult. With so many bird species, there are a multitude of reproductive strategies. Species may also be widely distributed, and the quality of local environmental resources varies, so alterations in sex ratios seen in one species may vary in one location from another and from year to year. Finally, the relative value of females and males varies from species to species.

MECHANISMS

With birds, the female is the heterogametic sex possessing a Z and W sex chromosome, while males have two Z sex chromosomes. Thus, unlike mammalian species, the female determines the sex of produced offspring based on whether a Z or W sex chromosome is present in the ovulated ovum. During the completion of division I of meiosis, half of the replicated chromosomes of an ovum are retained with the ovum, while the other half is eliminated in the first polar body (Figure 7.14). If the replicated Z sex chromosome is in the half of the chromosomes placed in the first polar body, then the ovum will contain the replicated W sex chromosomes, and the offspring produced will be female (ZW). This is because in division II of meiosis, half of the chromosomes of the ovum will again be placed in a second polar body, leaving the ovum with half the chromosomes (haploid state) necessary to make a new individual. But this half of the chromosomes will contain a W sex chromosome. Because males only have Z sex chromosomes, sperm always contain the Z sex chromosome. Consequently, when the egg is fertilized by a haploid sperm that contains the other half of the chromosomes needed to make a new individual, the new individual would have W and Z sex chromosomes, making it a female. On the other hand, if the replicated W sex chromosomes are placed in the first polar body, then the ovum will carry a Z sex chromosome that will combine with the Z sex chromosome of the sperm, making a new individual that is male (ZZ).

The production of the first polar body, and thus sex determination, occurs within two hours prior to ovulation. Current research suggests that hormone profiles, particularly progesterone, testosterone, and/or corticosterone in the female bird at the time of the production of the first polar body, determine which pair of replicated sex chromosomes is placed in the polar body. Experimental elevation of each of these hormones in female birds at this time is associated with dramatic shifts in the sex ratio of the resulting offspring. Several research groups are now focused on determining the exact method by which maternal hormones could lead to the preovulatory segregation distortion of the sex chromosomes at the first meiotic division, such that the production of one sex is favored.

In addition to preovulatory segregation distortion of the sex chromosomes at the first meiotic division, other mechanisms of sex ratio manipulation do occur after the egg is produced. Eclectus Parrots have been documented to adjust the sex ratio of offspring by selectively killing male offspring early in the rearing period (Heinsohn et al., 2011). The Australian Brush-turkey, a member of the family Megapodiidae, utilizes the heat from mounds of decaying organic material on top of their eggs to incubate the eggs. Based on the incubation temperature in early incubation, a biased sex ratio of the offspring can result (Göth and Booth, 2005). If the incubation temperature is 96.8 degrees F (36 degrees C), more females hatch; if the temperature is 87.8 degrees F (31 degrees C), more males hatch. And if the temperature is 93.2 degrees F (34 degrees C), the sex ratio is equal. However, the altered sex ratios at the high and low temperatures are associated with correspondingly higher embryonic mortality. In both of these cases and in other cases where sex ratios develop secondarily after the laying of the eggs, the cost of this manipulation is very high, as

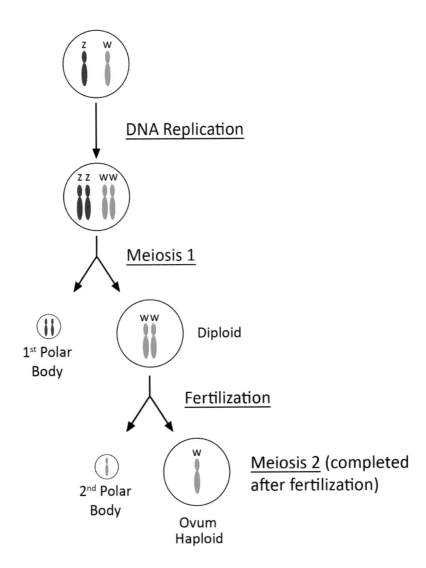

FIGURE 7.14   Sex determination in birds. Refer to text for details. Note that all of chromosomes are replicated, but for simplicity, only the two sex chromosomes in the female bird, the Z and the W chromosomes, are shown.

a great deal of energy was expended by the female to produce the egg, and a significant amount of energy was typically expended to incubate eggs from one or both parents. Thus, primary sex ratio manipulation—most likely through segregation distortion of the sex chromosomes—is probably more widespread than secondary sex ratio manipulation, because there is not a great deal of wasted energy associated with this method.

MATERNAL EGG PROVISIONING

In addition to manipulating the sex ratio of produced offspring, female birds can also influence the potential success of the produced offspring based on adding extra provisions into the produced egg. A few illustrative examples of many will be highlighted. Raptors often exhibit reverse sexual dimorphism, in that females are considerably larger than males, especially in many falcon species. This size difference is seen in nestlings, and female nestlings often outcompete males. American Kestrel females compensate for this by producing larger eggs, and thus bigger chicks when the sex of the offspring in the egg is male (Anderson et al., 1997). In the domestic laying hen, Müller et al. (2002) reported that the dominant hen (highest on the pecking order) provisions her eggs containing male embryos with extra testosterone, compared to those containing females. This makes it more likely that he will become a dominant male in the future. In contrast, female hens at the bottom of the social hierarchy tended to provision their eggs containing female embryos, relative to those containing male embryos, with extra testosterone. This potentially was done with the hope of improving the female offspring's growth and size, so she would not be the most subordinate female like her mother. Finally, female house finches mated with less attractive males compensate by depositing more testosterone and antioxidants into their eggs than if mated to attractive males (Navara et al., 2006). As a result, the female potentially counteracts the male's deficiencies with these additives to improve the growth and health potential of the offspring.

EGG COMPOSITION

YOLK

It is always important to remember that the yolk of an egg is one incredibly large single cell, the female gamete or ovum. So, the yolk is surrounded by a lipid bilayer plasma membrane, which is covered by the inner perivitelline layer, which in turn contains sperm-binding (receptor) sites necessary for fertilization. This large cell is packed with yolk, which is made up primarily of water, lipid, and protein. The vast majority of the protein and the lipid contained within the yolk is synthesized in the liver and then is transported in the blood to the growing ovum. Estrogen stimulates the liver to produce and release vitellogenin, the protein component, and very low-density lipoproteins (VLDLs), the lipid component. Both of these components are then taken up from the blood by the growing follicles. Maternal antibodies are also passed to the yolk. The yolk contains most of the vitamin content and much of the mineral content of the egg. The rich, yellow/red color of the yolk is provided by carotenoid pigments, which serve as antioxidants for the ovum and later for the developing embryo. The color of the yolk varies widely across and within species, depending on the amount and type of carotenoids consumed by the female bird producing the egg. While most people associate egg yolk with lipid, and all but a trace of the lipid found in the egg is in the yolk, the yolk also contains about half of the protein content of the egg in most bird species.

In the small white follicles, the yolk composition is mostly water with some protein and lipid. As the follicle grows, the lipid and protein components from the liver are added around this white yolk core, and the water, lipid, and protein composition of the egg changes from 87, 4, and 5 percent, respectively, to 45, 37, and 15 percent, respectively, as reviewed by Etches (1996). The central white yolk core remains, but some of the white yolk rises to the top of the surface of the yolk, and the cellular organelles and the maternal chromosomes of the ovum are located here in what is termed the germinal disc (Figures 7.15 and 7.16). The organelles of the ovum and the early developing embryo remain in this white yolk, as it is similar in composition to the normal cytoplasm of the cell, unlike the lipid-rich yellow yolk.

The amount of yolk relative to the total weight of the egg varies across species. The more yolk that an egg contains, the more advanced in maturity the chick is at hatch, as we will see later in this chapter.

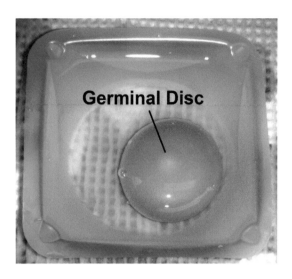

FIGURE 7.15   The germinal disc contains the female genetic material of the single-celled egg.

ALBUMEN

Albumen is secreted as a uniform mixture of proteins and water and is primarily produced by secretory epithelial cells of the magnum. As the egg rolls down the oviduct, the albumen separates into thin and thick albumen layers (Figure 7.16). The inner and outer thin layers contain a higher proportion of water-soluble proteins and more water. These thin albumen layers increase in amount as the egg ages, and the thick albumen layer disintegrates over time. Commercial eggs stored over time decrease in quality for some cooking purposes as the thick albumen disintegrates. Fresh eggs that still have high levels of thick albumen are ideal in cooking applications where the egg whites need to be whipped. Thick albumen will hold a great deal of air, meaning the eggs whites will become light and fluffy as they are beaten, which allows angel food cakes, for example, to be light and fluffy when made with fresh eggs. Thin albumen will incorporate very little air when whipped. In a fresh chicken egg, of the total amount of albumen, about 57 percent is thick, 17 percent inner thin, and 23 percent is outer thin albumen. The other 3 percent is the chalaziferous layer of albumen that surrounds the yolk. This layer is composed of structural proteins that form the fiber like chalazae (Figure 7.16). The spiral rotation of the yolk will twist the chalazae, which project through the inner thin albumen into the thick albumen. The chalazae maintain the position of the yolk in the center of the

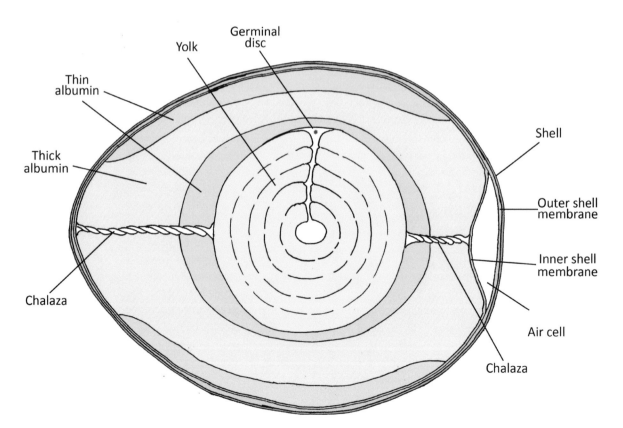

FIGURE 7.16   The major components of the egg.

egg, which is essential, as the early embryo develops because the lipid content of the yolk would naturally cause the yolk to float to the top of the egg. This could result in the germinal disc region, where the embryo develops, to contact the shell of the egg, resulting in abnormal development of the early embryo mass as it was compressed and shaped by the shell. Because the chalazae on each end of the yolk are twisted in opposing directions, you cannot spin an egg like a top unless you hard boil the egg, which denatures the protein of the chalazae.

Albumen is the major water reservoir for the egg and contains about half of the total protein content of the egg. It also has about one third of the mineral content of the egg. The protein constituents of albumen, besides providing amino acid building blocks for the growth of the developing embryo, also serve vital functions in protecting the egg from bacterial invasion. The egg is a nutrient-packed ideal food that is highly coveted as a food source for many vertebrate animals, including humans. It is also an ideal medium for bacterial proliferation, with the yolk being the ultimate nutrient prize. However, albumen proteins such as ovalbumin and ovomucoid are effective protease inhibitors. Proteases are the enzymes that break down protein into fragments and ultimately individual amino acids, which bacteria could utilize for growth and metabolic energy. Albumen also contains lysozyme, which lyses (destroys) gram positive bacteria. Other albumen proteins such as ovotransferrin and avidin sequester vital minerals and vitamins needed for metabolic energy production, making them unavailable for bacteria utilization. Finally, other albumen proteins such as ovomucin give the albumen insoluble gel-like qualities that make it very difficult for bacteria to penetrate.

SHELL MEMBRANES

The inner and outer shell membranes are secreted by the epithelial cells of the isthmus. The membranes consist of interwoven fibers, which are made up of protein, collagen, and glycoproteins. The membranes are permeable to gases like oxygen and carbon dioxide and crystalloids. The outer membrane is fairly porous to bacteria, but the inner shell membrane—especially the surface in contact with the albumen—has fibers that are much more tightly woven and contain lysozyme. The outer shell membrane contains the cores upon which the shell will be formed (Figure 7.17). The outer and inner shell membranes are only separated from one another at the air cell (Figure 7.16). The air cell is a pocket of air that grows in size during incubation as water evaporates from the egg. The air cell provides the first air for pulmonary respiration when the chick pierces it as it starts to hatch.

SHELL

The shell is deposited in the shell gland and is 94 percent calcium carbonate. The shell consists of crystals of calcium carbonate stacked on mammilary cores of the outer shell membrane. The initial portion of this shell, the cone layer, is constant in composition, while the depth of the stacked crystals in the palisade layer of the shell can vary, leading to differences in shell thickness (Figure 7.17). The stacked crystals of calcium carbonate can be separated by pores. All shells contain pores, but the number of pores differs across species, in part based on the ease of water evaporation across the shell in a given geographic location, as will be discussed later in the incubation section. The pores are also essential as a conduit for oxygen uptake and carbon dioxide removal for the embryo's respiration. The shell is the source of calcium

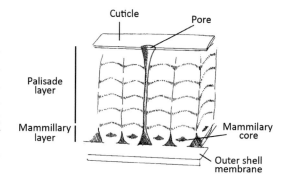

FIGURE 7.17 The outer shell membrane contains the mammilary cores upon which the shell will be formed. The palisade layer consists of stacked crystals of calcium carbonate and this stacking can vary in depth, leading to differences in shell thickness.

in the egg and during incubation, calcium carbonate crystals are pulled from the shell to provide the calcium needed by the developing embryo for such things as bone formation. The shell also provides mechanical protection for the egg. It is surprisingly durable. To see the durability of the egg, you can take an egg with no shell cracks and place it vertically between the palms of your two hands and apply pressure. Most people cannot generate the strength needed to break the egg as long as the egg remains vertical; if the egg shifts at all to a horizontal position, it is much easier to break.

In the female bird's oviduct, the calcium for egg shell formation comes from the absorption of calcium by the epithelial cells of the small intestine from digested food or from the breakdown of medullary bone. Estrogen stimulates the formation of medullary bone in female birds. This highly labile bone forms in the hollow cavities of long bones such as the femur. Shell formation typically occurs in female birds in the overnight hours, when the calcium to make this shell is unavailable from intestinal absorption acquired from food. Thus, medullary bone will be broken down to release its major constituent—calcium—which is then transported by the blood to the shell gland for use in shell formation.

CUTICLE

The cuticle is the thin coat placed on the egg just before it is laid. It contains protein, polysaccharide, and lipid. The cuticle can easily be rubbed off the egg. Its function is unclear. But it is hypothesized that by covering the pores in the shell, it may provide a mechanical block to bacteria entry into the egg right after the egg is laid and cooling from an internal temperature of about 107 degrees F (41.7 degrees C), to ambient temperature.

EGG COLOR

After the shell is formed, pigment glands present in the uterus may add pigment to the outside of the shell. Egg colors result from porphyrin pigments that were discussed previously, as they also provide plumage color. Many species lay white eggs, which are devoid of pigment. The brown, blue, olive, and bluish green colored egg shells owe their color to porphyrins, with the blue and green colors coming from heme (a porphyrin) that has been degraded to form biliverdin. Non-pigmented, white eggs also may become stained after they have been laid by mud, contained in the nest or from incubating parents' feet, or they may become stained by decaying vegetation contained within the nest. Typically, ground-nesting birds will lay mottled colored eggs so that they will be camouflaged and very hard for predators to observe (Figure 7.18). Colored patterns produced by a female within a species are also unique to the female that produced them, and this allows the females of species like the Common Murre that nest in colonies with closely packed nests to identify their eggs (Perrins, 2009).

Commercially produced chicken eggs are either white or brown. The color of the shell does not affect the flavor, nutritive value, quality, or cooking characteristics of the egg.

FACTORS INFLUENCING EGG SIZE AND COMPOSITION

Eggs are fairly resistant to changes in composition. Biologically, this makes sense, as the female bird would not want to expend the significant energy investment in producing an egg that is lacking an essential constituent needed for the successful development and hatch of a chick. If a female

FIGURE 7.18 Ground-nesting birds, such as quail, can lay eggs with a variety of mottled color patterns to assist in camouflaging the nest to predators. Note the very different patterns of these Japanese Quail eggs, each produced by a different female.

bird's intake of an essential nutrient such as an amino acid or fatty acid is marginally deficient for the production of an egg, the female will compensate by producing a slightly smaller egg, as the embryo developing in this egg will be smaller and the requirement of this essential nutrient will be less. However, if the deficiency of a required nutrient is greater than marginal, egg production will typically cease.

Body weight influences egg size to some degree within a species but not across species. For example, the largest bird, the Ostrich, produces the largest egg in the bird world (Figure 7.19), but the weight of this egg relative to total body weight is only 1.3 percent. In contrast, the Kiwi produces an egg that is 25 percent of its body weight. Within a species, smaller females will produce smaller eggs than larger birds. This association between egg size and female mass is also often manifest based on age. Young females that are sexually mature but have not quite reached mature body size produce smaller eggs than they will once mature body size is obtained.

Finally, the size and composition of the egg varies, depending on how well developed the chick will be at hatch according to species, as we will discuss further below. But in general, the more mature the chick is at hatching, the greater the size of the egg and the larger the yolk proportion of the egg.

FIGURE 7.19   Ostriches lay the largest egg of any bird, yet due to the bird's enormous size, their eggs are some of the smallest avian eggs in proportion to their bodies. The photo shows an Ostrich egg next to a Gouldian Finch egg for comparison.

FACTORS INFLUENCING CLUTCH SIZE

A clutch is the number of eggs produced by a female in a given breeding attempt. Clutch size varies widely across species and can vary within species. For example, the Kiwi produces a clutch consisting of one egg, while the common feral pigeon produces a clutch of two eggs; many waterfowl and game fowl produce clutches with egg numbers in the teens. Within a species, clutch size can vary, based on such things as nutrition, territory size, time of year, and health. Clutch size across species varies for many reasons. Birds like the Kiwi, which produce incredibly large eggs relative to body size that are energy dense, tend to produce small clutches. Clutch size may also be limited by how many eggs the bird can physically cover and incubate. In addition, eggs remain viable for only so long. With egg storage, the likelihood of an egg successfully hatching starts to decrease after a few days, and this decrease in hatching ability increases for each subsequent day that the egg is stored and not incubated. Thus, for a bird producing a large clutch, there can come a point of diminishing returns, in which the first eggs would no longer be viable as subsequent eggs were produced. In general, long-lived species also tend to have smaller clutches than short-lived species, but over time, their total reproductive efforts equal.

Jetz et al. (2008) examined global variation in clutch size across 5,290 bird species, and over half of the bird species produced clutches of two or three eggs. Clutch size was significantly larger in species that hatched more developed and more independent offspring (precocial offspring, discussed later) than those that hatched helpless (altricial) chicks that require a great deal of after-hatch care. Cavity nesters have larger clutch sizes than open nesters, which probably reflects the lower nest predation experienced by cavity nesters, and thus their willingness to take a greater risk in producing a larger clutch. Geographical location and seasonality also play important roles in predicting clutch sizes, as clutch sizes are larger in species breeding at high latitudes compared to those near the equator. Clutches are also larger for birds that nest in areas with highly seasonal food abundance. Migrating birds also tend to produce larger clutches than non-migrating species, because they face a greater mortality risk associated with migration. Similarly, year-long residents in temperate areas produce large clutches because they face greater death rates associated with cold temperatures and less food availability in the winter—they may only have one reproductive opportunity.

This difference in clutch size between higher latitudes with distinct seasons and middle latitudes and/or less seasonal variation also plays a role in the propensity for nest abandonment. Ghalambor and Martin (2001) determined that on average birds in the Northern Hemisphere tend to lay more eggs than similar species in the tropics and the Southern Hemisphere. Furthermore, based on predation risk, Southern Hemisphere birds, which produce fewer eggs per nest, are also more willing to sacrifice their offspring. For the Northern Hemisphere, for birds that may only get one breeding attempt due to not surviving another winter, the investment in larger clutch sizes and doing everything possible to ensure their success makes sense. In contrast, it makes sense for birds from the Southern Hemisphere, which will have more lifetime breeding opportunities, to value their own survival and future reproductive attempts rather than sacrificing heavily or focusing exclusively on the survival of one reproductive attempt.

INDETERMINATE VERSUS DETERMINATE LAYER

Females in some species of birds can produce a second clutch of eggs if a predator consumes the first clutch of eggs. Producing this second clutch of eggs is termed double clutching. Birds that can produce a second clutch of eggs are termed indeterminate layers, and these birds also may produce a second clutch of offspring in the same season if environmental factors are still favorable after the first clutch fledges or fails. Determinate layers, on the other hand, describe female bird species that enter the reproductive season with a set number of eggs that will be produced. If their clutch of eggs is destroyed, they must wait until the next reproductive season to produce more eggs. In species recovery programs, greater population gains can be made with indeterminate layers, as the eggs from the first clutch can be removed for artificial incubation or foster parent incubation and rearing, and the parents will produce a second—or in some cases, a third—clutch to rear. The commercial egg production industry also takes advantage of this, as laying hens will continue to lay eggs because their eggs are removed each day. In addition, through genetic selection, almost all commercial laying hens no longer have the desire to incubate eggs and do not become broody.

NESTS

Because eggs are nutrient-dense and well balanced in all of the building blocks needed to make a new individual, they are a highly sought-after food by some birds, snakes, lizards, and small and large mammals, such as raccoons and primates. Nest sites are often selected and nests are often constructed to minimize egg predation. Cavities in trees are highly desirable and defended once obtained, as they provide good protection from the elements and predators. Cavity nests are also carved out in sandy cliffs or in the soft mud along riverbanks or burrows made into the ground. For predator protection, it is not unusual for birds to build nests in trees over water or to place their nest near wasp nests. Others will build an open cup nest that remains empty, while the real nest is underneath accessed by a hole on the side of the nest. Most hornbill species are cavity nesters that take nesting security to the extreme. In all but a couple of ground-nesting species of hornbills, the female will seal herself in the nest cavity, except for a narrow vertical slit through which the male can pass food and the female can pass back debris. The female uses mud, feces, and leftover food items to form the cavity seal. In some species of hornbills, the female will have to break out of the cavity when the chicks are half grown to help the male feed the chicks. Once the female is out, the seal is not reformed in some species, but in other species, the chicks reform the seal and only break it later when they are ready to fly.

Seabirds such as terns typically nest in dense colonies, but colony nesters also include terrestrial birds, such as some swallows and weavers. Seabird colony nesters such as Common Murres often nest out in the open and may not even construct much of a nest, as the large number of birds that are nesting together form a formidable defense against predators. In some cases, the colonies are so large that it offers protection by simply satiating local predators by the sheer number of eggs and chicks available. Thus, the overall sacrifice of some provides protection to the majority. Typically, the highest ranking individuals nest in the center of the colony, which provides maximum security for their eggs.

Nests come in all sizes and shapes and can be architectural masterpieces, like those constructed by weaverbirds or oropendolas (Figure 7.20). Nests are constructed from a host of materials, such as sticks, twigs, feathers, grasses, and mosses (Figure 7.21). Many birds use saliva to help glue nests to a surface (Figure 7.22), and tailorbirds use stitching made out of spider webs. Songbirds typically build a new nest for every reproductive attempt, while many raptors simply refurbish their old nest each year. Ground nesters in open habitats often have simple nests that may be no more

FIGURE 7.20   Chestnut-headed Oropendulas make long, pendulum nests to protect their eggs.

FIGURE 7.21   Using an array of materials, bird nests are made in a variety of sizes and shapes according to the bird species.

than scrapes in the ground, as the key to their success is camouflage and avoiding detection. For birds that nest in temperate locations, nests tend to be thicker in construction and well-insulated to help reduce the energy cost of providing heat during incubation. In these colder environments, birds will also nest in protected areas or even in man-made structures, in order to gain protection against wind chilling and/or warmth from building structures. These locations can sometimes also have the added benefit of reduced predation risk.

INCUBATION

PROLACTIN

Incubation and parental behavior are stimulated by the production of the protein hormone, prolactin. This is the same hormone that stimulates lactation in animals such as humans, domestic livestock, and pets. Prolactin also stimulates the production of crop milk in a limited number of bird species, as will be discussed in the pigeon chapter. Prolactin is produced and released by the anterior pituitary gland under the control of vasoactive intestinal peptide (VIP) released from the hypothalamus (Figure 7.1). In most bird species, prolactin levels are higher in the sex that invests more in parental duties. It typically reduces the circulating concentrations of FSH and LH, which results in gonad regression and focuses birds on incubation and parental care rather than sexual behaviors. During incubation, the production of prolactin in birds peaks, and the production is maintained at high levels by a positive feedback loop in which prolactin production is promoted by visually seeing the nest, eggs, an incubating mate, or babies. The produced prolactin makes the parent stay at the nest and incubate, thus providing more stimulation for continued prolactin production.

Prolactin promotes the formation of the brood patch in many bird species. Feathers on the breast will be lost, exposing the skin for direct contact with the eggs for incubation. Without the feathers, direct transfer of heat by conduction from the skin to the eggs will be more efficient. Blood vessel number and diameter will increase to the skin of the brood patch to increase blood flow, and thus available heat for transfer to the eggs. Depending on the species, the temperature at the surface of the brood patch is typically one to five degrees higher than the egg temperature. If the eggs are not being maintained at a warm enough temperature, the bird responds physiologically by increasing available heat through cold vasodilatation. Normally, animals respond to cold by decreasing blood flow to the skin in order to maintain core body warmth, and only increase blood flow (vasodilate) to skin blood vessels when body heat needs to be lost. In the incubating bird, this normal physiology is ignored and the blood vessels of the brood patch vasodilate in response to cold, in order to deliver more heat to keep the eggs warm. In conditions in which the eggs get too warm, the incubating bird will lessen blood flow to the brood patch, stand over, or leave the nest to allow the eggs to cool.

Transfer of heat to the eggs is most difficult during early incubation because heat has to be transferred by conductance to heat the entire egg contents, but especially to the center of the egg where the developing embryo is located on top of the yolk. Rotating the incubating eggs with their feet assists the incubating bird in providing even heating throughout each egg. As the embryo develops, it will generate more and more heat through its own metabolism, but more importantly, its circulatory system—part of which is located close to the shell of the egg—will distribute heat throughout the egg. So, once the circulatory system is well developed, heat transfer from the incubating parent becomes much easier, as heat only has to transfer by conductance through the shell instead to the middle of the egg, as it did in the first few days of incubation.

FIGURE 7.22 Barn Swallows will use mud and saliva to attach their nests to substrates, often utilizing buildings or bridges for added shelter.

ENERGY DEMANDS OF INCUBATION

In addition to it being more difficult to transfer heat to the eggs in early incubation, the efficiency of heat transfer diminishes with decreased ambient temperatures and with increased clutch size. Ideally, the incubating bird would have enough stored body energy reserves so that it did not have to leave the nest, as this would ensure the eggs did not cool and minimizes the potential for predators to notice movement to and from the nest. But having this level of energy stores is a rarity. When both parents are involved in incubating, they can take shifts incubating the eggs, or, in some species, the males bring food to the incubating female. For species of birds in which one parent is left to handle all of the parental duties (typically the female, but males in a few species), judicious choices must be made. Typically, given the difficulty of warming eggs early in incubation (as discussed above), energy reserves are utilized in early incubation to minimize or prevent nest non-attendance. As energy reserves are depleted, the conflict between energy intake of the parent and providing heat to the embryo increases and can be exacerbated by cold ambient temperatures. The cost of a parent having to leave the nest to find food is that with each nest non-attendance, the eggs cool, with the degree of cooling depending on the time gone. Rewarming the eggs back to incubation temperature costs the parent a great deal of energy when it returns, which simply increases the amount of food needed to be consumed. With the eggs cooling and embryo development slowing, the total amount of incubation time before hatching will increase, and there will be a decrease in the percent of embryos successfully developing and hatching. The likelihood of nest abandonment by the parent or nest failure (no hatching eggs) increases as nest attentiveness decreases. As a result, those birds with the greatest body energy reserves will have the greatest reproductive success during incubation.

Besides stimulating incubation and parental behavior, prolactin, in conjunction with corticosterone, may work in balancing parental effort, energy status, and parental survival during incubation and brooding (Angelier and Chastel, 2009). Corticosterone is a stress hormone, and levels of it increase during stress and incubation can be viewed as a chronic stressor. Corticosterone promotes the use of body energy stores. During incubation, metabolism is dependent on the utilization of body stores, with an overriding metabolic focus on supporting this dominant physiological state, even to the detriment of the parent bird. To illustrate the interplay of metabolism and behavior during incubation, two examples will be given. Female Golden Pheasants in captivity may not eat, drink, or move off their nests for the entire 22-day incubation period of their eggs (Perrins, 2009). In these females, brooding behavior (staying at the nest) is overriding normal homeostatic controls to seek food, while energy needs are being met through body energy stores such as fat; total energy expenditure is being limited by lack of movement.

A similar, but even more drastic, interplay between parental behavior and parental investment is seen with Emperor Penguins (Robin et al., 1998; Lormée et al., 1999; Groscolas and Robin, 2001). Male Emperor Penguins will fast for about 120 consecutive days as they complete courtship, incubate the resulting egg, and then walk back to water for feeding once their mates arrive to relieve them and care for the newly hatched chick. During this fast, they will typically lose over half of their body mass, going from about 88 to 39 pounds (40 to 18 kilograms). During incubation, which lasts 64 days, the males become very docile, with low locomotor activity which conserves energy. In this behavioral modification, prolactin likely plays a role here, as it does in the Golden Pheasant. If a penguin's mate does not arrive back as expected, he will ultimately abandon his chick and start walking to the sea, so he will be able to obtain food. However, this is not done until a point where he is running out of fat and is actively breaking down protein (muscle) for energy. If he did not leave at this point, he would starve to death. The decision to leave is correlated with elevated plasma corticosterone and decreased plasma prolactin concentrations, which indicate parental desire is ultimately outweighed by parental survival.

METHODS OF INCUBATION

Different species of birds provide the heat for incubation in different ways. For most bird species, the parents build a nest, and either the female, male, or both transfer body heat to the egg(s) by sitting on them (Figure 7.23). For most birds, this is accomplished with heat transfer from the bare skin of the brood patch, but in a few birds like pelicans and Blue-footed Boobies, heat is transferred via their webbed feet. In some penguins such as the Emperor and King Penguins, a single egg is held on top of the feet and then covered by a roll of abdominal skin backed by fat. For the roughly 20 species of megapodes distributed in Australia, Southeast Asia, and some Pacific islands, eggs are laid by the female in burrows or under mounds of vegetation. Incubation heat is then provided either by the sun, thermal vents, or the heat of decaying vegetation.

Brood parasitism describes the practice of a female bird placing an egg in another bird's nest for the other bird to incubate with its own eggs. This incubation strategy takes one of two forms. Obligate brood parasites place their eggs in other birds' nests because they are no longer evolutionarily capable of successfully raising their own offspring. Non-obligate brood parasites will lay eggs in the nests of conspecifics, but typically will successfully produce offspring from their own nests as well. The goal of the non-obligate brood parasite is to increase their reproductive output beyond what they are capable of by themselves, and this type of parasitism is seen in over 200 species of birds (Yom-Tov, 2001). It is seen in some species of ducks, starlings, and moorhens.

Species dependent on obligate brood parasitism have, over evolutionary time, lost the ability to raise their own young. This type of parasitism is seen in about 80 species of birds, including many—but not all—species of cuckoos and cowbirds. The war between obligate brood parasites and their victims is ongoing, with hosts coming up with ways to prevent the parasitism and the parasites coevolving to maintain the advantage or finding new host species (Moskat, 2005). For example, several of the cuckoo species have the shortest incubation periods before hatch of any bird species. So the cuckoo can remove

FIGURE 7.23   This Clay-colored Thrush in Costa Rica is sitting on her nest, incubating her eggs. Prolactin is the hormone responsible for encouraging brooding behavior like this.

an egg from a hosts nest and replace it with one of its own and be assured that its egg will be the first or one of the first to hatch. In several of the obligate brood parasitic species of cuckoo, once the baby cuckoo hatches, although blind and not well developed, it has the strength to push out anything it contacts in the nest. So, the host's eggs and nestlings are pushed out of the nest to die, leaving the parasitic offspring to receive all of the food from the parents (Figure 7.24). Brood parasite offspring often are very effective at mimicking the calls of what would have been the host's offspring.

Victims of obligate brood parasites also wage war on the parasites. Some species of weaverbirds have learned to construct entrance tubes to their nests that are small enough in diameter to prevent parasitism by the Diederik Cuckoo. Other species of birds are intelligent enough that if they recognize a foreign egg, they will abandon their nest or eject the egg. For example, the Village Weaver has evolved the ability to lay eggs across a broad range of colors and patterns to combat brood parasites and make identification of its own eggs easy (Cruz and Wiley, 1989; Lahti and Lahti, 2002).

HEAT, WATER LOSS, AND EGG ROTATION DURING INCUBATION

The critical components during incubation are water loss, adequate heat, and egg rotation. Water loss is essential during incubation, but too much loss is detrimental. If not enough water is lost, the air cell will be small, and the chicks will be soft and flabby, hatch early, and have a higher rate of mortality. If too much water is lost, the egg dries out, and the chicks will be small and feeble with underdeveloped kidneys and have a high rate of mortality. Although general guidelines are always risky, given that there are almost 10,000 species of birds (and many have no incubation data), the total amount of water loss needed as a percent reduction in egg weight from the time it was laid until it starts to hatch is 11–15 percent (Figure 7.25). This critical loss of water weight is why eggs incubated from endangered species are weighed every day so that the water loss can be monitored. If water loss is determined to be occurring to quickly, the humidity in the incubator will be adjusted upward, and if the water loss is not proceeding as fast as necessary to reach the target loss, the humidity of the incubator will be adjusted downward. Water loss is a function of shell thickness and the number of pores. In the wild, these two factors are adjusted, such that birds in hot dry climates produce eggs with thicker shells and fewer pores, so water loss is not too great. This is why, for example, Ostrich eggs need to be incubated in a commercial incubator at a much lower humidity than chicken eggs to achieve the correct water loss.

Optimal temperatures for incubation vary across species, but they tend to fall in a range from about 95 to 100 degrees F (35 to 37 degrees C). If temperatures are slightly above optimum throughout incubation, the incubation period until hatch will be shortened.

FIGURE 7.24 The Reed Warbler is often a victim of brood parasitism by cuckoos.

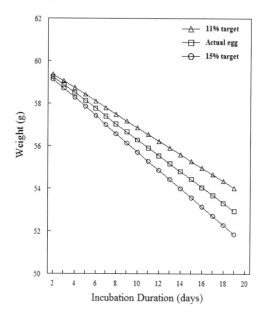

FIGURE 7.25 Water loss in an egg with a 21-day period incubation with hatching initiated (pipping) on day 19. Ideally, eggs need to lose between 11 and 15 percent of their mass as evaporated water from incubation onset to the initiation of hatch. To make sure water loss is proceeding at an appropriate rate, the egg was weighed each day and its weight plotted. If water loss had been proceeding too quickly, the humidity of the incubator would have been increased. If, on the other hand, water loss was not happening at a great enough rate, then the incubator humidity would have been decreased.

Similarly, if the incubation temperature is one or two degrees below optimum, the normal incubation period before hatch will be increased. In both cases, the percent of eggs successfully hatching would decrease, as embryonic mortality would increase. Typically, a slight increase or decrease in the optimal incubation temperature throughout the entire incubation period is going to be rare in the wild and more likely to occur under artificial incubation. In nature, it is more likely that the incubating eggs will be exposed to periods of more extreme heating or cooling. Embryonic death susceptibility to either critically low or high temperatures varies across species and with the developmental stage of the embryo within a species. In general, developing embryos are more sensitive to overheating than to cold, and the sensitivity to both high and low temperature extremes decreases as embryonic development increases. For example, in developing chicken embryos, exposure to 46.4 degrees F or 8 degrees C (optimum incubation temperature is 99.5–99.75 degrees F or 37.5–37.6 degrees C) is survivable, even if the heart stops beating until the embryo is rewarmed, for one day when the embryo is six days into its 21-day incubation period. However, at 20 days of incubation, the survivability is only a few hours (Tazawa and Whittow, 2000). In contrast, chicken embryos have a tolerance before death of about 100 minutes if exposed to 114.8–116.6 degrees F (46–47 degrees C) at 12 days of incubation, and this tolerance decreases to 50 minutes at day 20 of incubation (Tazawa and Whittow, 2000). Overheating is a common problem, especially with open ground nests, nests in the tops of trees, or on exposed cliffs. With the sunlight shining on the eggs in these nests, they can quickly overheat. To prevent this, the parents will provide shade by standing over the nest with outstretched wings, and if necessary, will provide evaporative cooling by soaking their feathers in water and sitting on the eggs or by showering the eggs with regurgitated water. White- or light-colored eggs absorb less radiant heat from the sun and are typically produced by species facing overheating problems.

When birds incubate their eggs, they actively rotate the eggs in their nests with their feet. In the wild, egg rotation helps in warming the eggs evenly, but it serves other important functions as well. The importance of these other functions has been underscored in developing artificial incubation protocols in domestic fowl, where the amount and degree of rotation has had to be determined in order to optimize hatchability. These experiments indicate that a lack of rotation decreases gas exchange by the developing embryo with the environment. Additionally, a lack of sufficient egg turning is detrimental to extraembryonic membrane development and is associated with poor embryo growth and decreased hatchability. Although egg rotation is critical throughout the incubation period, it seems especially critical during early incubation (the first third).

DURATION OF INCUBATION

Incubation duration varies widely across species. For example, incubation is 11 days in Black-billed and Yellow-billed Cuckoos, with many small passerine birds also having a similarly short 10–12 day incubation period. In contrast, the Wandering Albatross and Brown Kiwi both have incubation periods over 80 days. Many gamebirds, water birds, parrots, and raptors have incubation ranges from 20 to 40 days. In general, the larger the egg, the longer the incubation period, and this also correlates with the development of the chick at hatch. Chicks that are more developed at hatch had longer incubation periods than chicks that hatch less developed.

HATCHING

PRECOCIOUS VERSUS ALTRICIAL

When chicks hatch, they are classified based on visual appearance as either precocious or altricial. At hatch, precocious chicks (Figure 7.26) are covered with feathers, their eyes are developed and functional, and they have walking locomotion. They typically hatch in nests on or in the ground and leave the nest site within 24 hours of hatching. They may or may not have parental contact. Nutrient energy consumed by these chicks is used for things like locomotion, maintaining body temperature, and finding food, with what is left over utilized for growth. Consequently, although precocious chicks are born more mature, their maturation rate after hatch tends to be slow and they do not reach adult size for many weeks to months. Precocious chicks hatch from relatively large eggs that have low water content (low 60s as a percent of total composition) and are mostly yolk-filled (65–70 percent of total egg mass in Kiwis and some megapodes). The parental investment lies with the female in producing the large, energy-dense eggs. Prolactin production steadily decreases in birds that produce precocial chicks after the chicks hatch.

Altricial chicks (Figure 7.27) hatch naked without feathers. Eye development is not complete, so their eyelids are not open. They are helpless and huddle in their nests with little movement and depend typically on both parents for protection, nourishment, and warmth. Altricial chicks have large mouths and well-developed digestive tracts. Thus, they readily digest food, and almost all of the energy derived from that food is utilized for growth, since not much is needed for locomotion and warmth. So, although less mature at hatch, altricial chicks mature rapidly and fledge as flighted adults in a matter of weeks—in some cases, in under two weeks. They are typically hatched in protected, elevated nests and hatch from relatively smaller eggs containing higher water content (typically greater than 80 percent) and less yolk (around 16–20 percent of egg content). Because parents are providing for all of their needs and the eggs are less nutrient-dense, the parental energy investment comes after hatch and is almost always shared by both parents. Prolactin production in birds that produce altricial chicks steadily decreases after brooding.

SYNCHRONOUS VERSUS ASYNCHRONOUS

The hatch of chicks in bird species that produce a clutch size greater than one egg can be synchronous, with all the eggs of a nest hatching within 24 hours of one another, or it can be asynchronous, with hatch being extend over a greater-than-24-hour period and can often involve several days between the first hatched and last hatched individual. Thus, asynchronous hatches typically result in a natural

FIGURE 7.26   Precocial chicks, such as the domestic chicken shown here a few hours after hatch, have open eyes, full down feathers and are capable of walking and feeding themselves soon after hatching.

FIGURE 7.27   Altricial chicks, such as these Carolina Chickadees, are hatched naked, blind, and helpless.

size hierarchy of the hatchlings. Birds that produce precocious chicks tend to have synchronous hatches for the most part and leave the nest typically within a day of hatching. Even if incubation is initiated before the last couple of eggs are produced, a synchronous hatch can still be produced. Eggs that are touching one another in a nest can communicate with one another by producing clicking sounds during the last few days of incubation before hatching. Research indicates at least two to three days of hatching asynchrony can be abolished by embryo communication. The frequency of the clicking either retards or accelerates hatching (Ockleford and Vince, 1985; Persson and Andersson, 1999). Species differences exist in whether later developing embryos delay hatching in further developed clutch mates or if further developed embryos speed up development and hatching in embryos that have not been incubated as long. In addition to embryo communication, female birds can adjust egg size and egg composition to potentially influence hatching time to ensure synchrony. Wood ducks produce smaller eggs at the beginning and end of the clutch (Kennamer et al., 1997). Smaller eggs develop and hatch more quickly, so producing smaller eggs at the end of the clutch, when incubation has already commenced, makes biological sense. The small eggs at the beginning of the clutch seems counterintuitive; however, these eggs also contain more lipid, which suggests that small embryos in eggs packed with lipid could have the energy resources to delay their hatch.

Species that produce clutches of altricial chicks generally have asynchronous hatches. This results in hatchlings of different sizes, and death of the later-hatched, smaller chicks due to lack of food, trampling, and siblicide is common. This seemingly wasteful incubation strategy is the most common in bird species and must have evolved as an adaptation. Many theories have been proposed for the evolution of this incubation strategy, and an excellent review of the topic exists (Stoleson and Beissinger, 1995). Lack (1947) suggested that an asynchronous hatch was an adaptive function for birds based on unpredictable food resources at the time of egg production. According to this theory, parents should lay an optimistic clutch at the time of egg laying, hoping there will be enough food to feed all offspring in the future. If, after incubation, food resources are scarce in the brooding period, an asynchronous hatch has resulted in a natural size hierarchy. The youngest nestlings would die by starvation or could be killed, allowing the parents to easily reduce their brood to fit available food supplies. In some years, enough food would be available so that all offspring could survive, thereby greatly enhancing the lifetime reproductive success of the parents. While evidence supports this original hypothesis, other hypotheses have been proposed and gained experimental support, some of which will be briefly discussed.

The demand of providing food to fast-growing, altricial nestlings consumes a great deal of energy for parents. Even with both parents working tirelessly, many chicks die of starvation. By having an asynchronous hatch, parent birds can spread the food demand out over time to maximize parental efficiency. This can be visualized by thinking in human terms. The total amount of food needed to be gathered and delivered at one time can be reduced if offspring are spread out between a newborn, a toddler and a teenager, when compared to the effort needed if three teenagers of all the same age were being fed at the same time. In addition, in some bird species, newborn chicks receive very specialized diets, but as they get older, they can tolerate a wider variety of food. Again, in this situation, not having all the chicks hatching at the same time will make this task easier. Further, having a natural size hierarchy based on an asynchronous hatch also establishes a stable dominance hierarchy and avoids sibling fighting, which wastes valuable metabolic energy that can be used for growth.

Having an asynchronous hatch can also be utilized as a reproductive insurance policy. For example, Hooded Grebe parents abandon the second of two eggs if the first egg hatches successfully; but if the first egg does not hatch, incubation continues until the second egg hatches. Asynchronous hatches may also result based on parents commencing incubation on the first egg of the clutch if they are protecting a nest site from other competitors when suitable nest sites are limited. Similarly, if the threat of brood parasitism or predation is prevalent, the parents may start incubation with the first egg of the clutch to continuously protect the nest from these threats.

Brood reduction is common when food resources become limited, with the later-hatched offspring being killed by parents or older siblings. Cannibalism of the killed offspring is rare. However, in the American Kestrel and Black Kite, the consumption of killed younger siblings by older siblings has been documented (Bortolotti, 1991; Viñuela, 2000), which has given rise to the hypothesis that hatching asynchrony provides larder for the first hatched in limited bird species and situations. Overall, hatching asynchrony has likely evolved for many reasons in different species of birds. Although it is associated with high death rates in later-hatched siblings, there is clearly an adaptive value that outweighs this cost.

EMBRYOLOGY BASICS

Upon the union of the genetic material from the female and male gametes after fertilization, a new embryo starts to develop. Because fertilization occurs shortly after the egg ovulates, the new embryo is a mass of several thousands of cells by the time the rest of the egg is formed and laid. Once the egg is laid, further development of these cells is arrested. Based on research with domesticated birds, development of these cells is arrested if the temperature of the egg is less than about 75 degrees F (23.9 degrees C). Once incubation commences, cellular division and growth begins again.

Cleavage refers to the mitotic cell divisions that occur in the embryo after the union of the genetic material from both gametes. During cleavage, cell number is increasing more than cell mass. Cleavage comes to an end when the mass of cells in the developing embryo undergo extensive migrations and rearrange themselves into three primary germ layers. The germ layers are called ectoderm, mesoderm, and endoderm, respectively, and the formation of these germ layers is referred to as gastrulation. The cells in the individual germ layers are now on programmed developmental tracts that will lead to the different parts of the complete new individual. For example, the ectoderm will form such things as the feathers, scales, and nervous system, while the mesoderm will form tissues such as the muscles, kidney, skeleton, and reproductive tract, and the endoderm will form the epithelial lining of organs such as the lungs, liver, and pancreas. Based on research with domestic species of birds, when an egg is laid, the embryo is at or in the gastrulation phase.

With gastrulation, the cell mass is becoming large enough that a complex support system, the extraembryonic membranes, must start developing from the germ layers to deliver nutrients and oxygen to the developing embryo, while transporting metabolic wastes (carbon dioxide and uric acid) away from the embryo. The first extraembryonic membrane formed is the yolk sac, which, over time, envelops the yolk and eventually forms a connection with the albumen (Figure 7.28). The yolk sac membrane is critical for initial oxygen delivery. It metabolizes the protein and lipid contained in the yolk and delivers it to the embryo and sends protein and water from the albumen to the embryo.

The next extraembryonic membranes formed are the amnion and chorion, which are formed from the same membrane. The amnion is the inner membrane; it contains the amniotic fluid in which the embryo floats and moves. Thus, the amniotic fluid contained in the amnion cushions the developing embryo from mechanical shock if the egg is jostled. It provides a liquid environment, allowing movement of developing limbs for proper formation. The amniotic fluid will be swallowed by the chick just prior to hatch. The chorion is the outer membrane in contact with the inner shell membrane, but it is avascular and has no function on its own.

Day 5

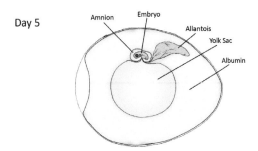

Day 10

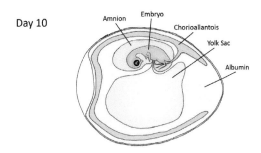

Day 15

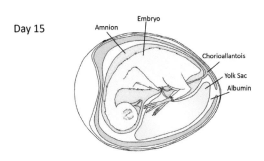

Day 20

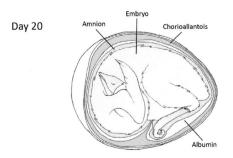

FIGURE 7.28 Embryo development in the domestic chicken, which has a 21-day incubation period.

The allantois is the final extraembryonic membrane to form. Depending on the species and the incubation duration of its eggs, all of the extraembryonic membranes are formed within the first days of incubation, with the allantois forming on day 3 of a 21-day incubation period in chickens. The allantois is highly vascular and fuses with the chorion to form the chorioallantois. Once formed, the chorioallantois provides respiration for the developing embryo, transporting carbon dioxide away from the embryo to the shell membranes and transporting oxygen back to the embryo. The oxygen and carbon dioxide diffuse freely through the pores of the shell and through the shell membranes. The chorioallantois also takes uric acid—the nitrogen excretory product of birds—and deposits it at the inner shell membrane away from the embryo. As the only source of calcium to form bones in the embryo is from the shell, calcium crystals are transported back to the embryo by the chorioallantois. Finally, the chorioallantois absorbs some of the albumen content for delivery back to the embryo.

As in other developing embryos that are supported by a placenta, most of the growth of the embryo in an egg occurs in the last third of the incubation period (Figure 7.28). Although embryonic death can occur at any point during incubation, there are two peak periods when embryos can fail during development. The first peak in mortality is early in incubation, typically due to circulatory failure. The heart forms early in incubation, and in the chicken embryo, the heart is beating by the 30th hour of incubation (Table 7.1). During the first day of incubation, clusters of mesoderm cells form away from the embryo to form blood islands where erythrocytes (red blood cells) proliferate. The heart then starts forming the major arteries and veins, which radiate out from the heart. At the same time, the blood island locations are forming and radiating outward the small arteries and veins. These networks must meet and fuse to form a vascular circuit that connects the embryo and the yolk sac membrane; once they do fuse, the heart starts to circulate red blood cells. Failure of these networks to fuse leads to embryonic death.

The other peak period of embryonic death is at the time of hatching when the embryo must transition from respiration by the chorioallantois to the developed lung. This transition starts once the chick initiates hatching by puncturing the air cell and continues over the next 24 hours or so, as the lung takes over more respiratory responsibility and blood flow is lessened to the chorioallantois. Hatching typically takes about 48 hours to complete and involves several steps in addition to the respiration change. The remaining yolk is drawn into the abdominal cavity, where it will serve as a nutrient and water reservoir via its connection to the small intestine for the first hours to days after hatch. All amniotic fluid will be consumed, and residual liquid in the airways will be absorbed. The hatching muscle in the neck of the embryo has reached maximum size, and the egg tooth, a small knob on the tip of the upper beak, will be fully formed. Using its hatching muscle, the chick will move its head and beak so the egg tooth pips the shell of the egg. Then, over the next day or more, the embryo will break the shell laterally in a ring that goes around the egg until the fully developed embryo pushes and separates the upper one third of the shell from the rest of the shell and is free of the egg.

TABLE 7.1 ONTOGENETIC DEVELOPMENT PATTERNS IN CHICKENS

Day of Incubation	Notable Embryo Developments
1	Blood islands forming, foregut formation
2	Heart formation and beating by 30 hours, forming of eyes, ear pits, and tail bud; amnion begins to develop
3	Limb buds formed, allantois beginning to form from hind gut, esophagus started
5	Proventriculus and gizzard formed
6	Voluntary movement, main divisions of legs and wings, duodenal loop formed
7	Allantois and chorion fuse and lie against shell membranes, indications of digits
8	Eyes prominent, feather genesis in tracts
9	Allantois nearly surrounds embryo, amnion, and yolk; body contour appears birdlike
10	Forelimb appears like wing and digits of feet completely separated
13	Scales and nails appear; down feathers over body
16	Albumen nearly gone, and yolk becomes increasingly important as source of nutrients
17	Amniotic fluid decreasing as embryo prepares to hatch
19	Yolk sac starts to enter body through umbilicus, beak pierces air sac, and lungs start to function
20	Pulmonary respiration becomes more dominant, while allantoic circulation and respiration ceases and allantois begins to dry up
21	Hatching

SUMMARY

Efficient reproduction is necessary for the continuation of a species. All bird species reproduce by producing an encased egg(s) that develops outside of the mother's body. With nearly 10,000 species of birds, it is not surprising that there is incredible variation in the composition of produced eggs, methods of incubation, synchrony of hatch, parental care after hatch, and survival after hatch. For most species of birds, the female is the one that makes the mate choice, often based on males making displays targeted to her most highly developed senses of vision and hearing. Most bird species form monogamous relationships, as it requires the dedication of both parents working tirelessly for the successful rearing of any offspring. Finally, the females in many—and potentially all—species have the ability to manipulate the sex ratio of produced offspring, as well as the ability to provision specific eggs with factors that will influence the future growth and health of the embryo in a given egg.

REFERENCES

Alonso-Alvarez, C. 2006. Manipulation of primary sex-ratio: An updated review. *Avian and Poultry Biology Reviews* **17**:1–20.

Anderson, D. J., J. Reeve, and D. M. Bird. 1997. Sexually dimorphic eggs, nestling growth and sibling competition in American Kestrels Falco sparverius. *Functional Ecology* **11**:331–335.

Angelier, F. and O. Chastel. 2009. Stress, prolactin and parental investment in birds: A review. *General and Comparative Endocrinology* **163**:142–148.

Bakst, M. R. 1988. Duration of fertility of turkeys inseminated at different times after the onset of photostimulation. *Journal of Reproduction and Fertility* **84**:531–537.

Bakst, M. R., G. Wishart, and J. P. Brillard. 1994. Oviducal sperm selection, transport, and storage in poultry. *Poultry Science Reviews* **5**:117–143.

Bearden, H. J. and J. W. Fuquay. 1984. *Applied Animal Reproduction, Second Edition*. Reston Publishing Company, Inc., Reston, VA.

Bortolotti, G. R. 1991. Cannibalism of nestling American Kestrels by their parents and siblings. *Canadian Journal of Zoology* **69**:1447–1453.

Brennan, P. L. R., R. O. Prum, K. G. McCracken, M. D. Sorenson, R. E. Wilson, and T. R. Birkhead. 2007. Coevolution of Male and Female Genital Morphology in Waterfowl. *PLoS ONE* **2**:e418.

Briskie, J. V. and R. Montgomerie. 1997. Sexual Selection and the Intromittent Organ of Birds. *Journal of Avian Biology* **28**:73–86.

Briskie, J. V. and R. Montgomerie. 2001. Efficient copulation and the evolutionary loss of the avian intromittent organ. *Journal of Avian Biology* **32**:184–187.

Cruz, A. and J. W. Wiley. 1989. The Decline of an Adaptation in the Absence of a Presumed Selection Pressure. *Evolution* **43**:55–62.

Davies, N. B. 1983. Polyandry, cloaca-pecking and sperm competition in dunnocks. *Nature* **302**:334–336.

de Riviers, M. 1968. Détermination de la durée des procussus spermatogénetiques chez le coq. *Proceedings of the 6th International Congress of Animal Reproduction and Artificial Insemination* **1**:183–185.

Etches, R. J. 1996. *Reproduction in Poultry*. Pages 106–124 Photoperiodism. CAB International, Cambridge, UK.

Frances, P. and S. Larter. 2011. *Illustrated Encyclopedia of Birds*. BirdLife International. Dorling Kindersley Limited, London.

Ghalambor, C. K. and T. E. Martin. 2001. Fecundity-Survival Trade-Offs and Parental Risk-Taking in Birds. *Science* **292**:494–497.

Göth, A. and D. T. Booth. 2005. Temperature-dependent sex ratio in a bird. *Biology Letters* **1**:31–33.

Groscolas, R. and J.-P. Robin. 2001. Long-term fasting and re-feeding in penguins. *Comparative Biochemistry and Physiology—Part A: Molecular & Integrative Physiology* **128**:643–653.

Hatch, S. A. 1983. Mechanism and Ecological Significance of Sperm Storage in the Northern Fulmar with Reference to Its Occurrence in Other Birds. *Auk* **100**:593–600.

Heinsohn, R., Naomi E. Langmore, A. Cockburn, and H. Kokko. 2011. Adaptive Secondary Sex Ratio Adjustments via Sex-Specific Infanticide in a Bird. *Current Biology* **21**:1744–1747.

Howarth, B. 1990. Fertility Following Intrauterine Insemination Near the Time of Oviposition. *Poultry Science* **69**:138–141.

Howarth, B. 1995. Physiology of reproduction: The male. Pages 243–270 *in* P. Hunton, editor. *World Animal Science: Poultry Production*, Elsevier, Amsterdam.

Jetz, W., C. H. Sekercioglu, and K. Böhning-Gaese. 2008. The Worldwide Variation in Avian Clutch Size across Species and Space. *PLoS Biology* **6**:2650–2657.

Jiang, N., H. Wu, X. M. Xang, Y. Y. An, and C. Y. Liu. 1999. Effect of heat stress on body temperature of high and low heat tolerant layers. *Journal of China Agricultural University* **4**:102–106.

Karaca, A. G., H. M. Parker, and C. D. McDaniel. 2002. Elevated body temperature directly contributes to heat stress infertility of broiler breeder males. *Poultry Science* **81**:1892–1897.

Kennamer, R. A., S. K. Alsum, and S. V. Colwell. 1997. Composition of Wood Duck Eggs in Relation to Egg Size, Laying Sequence, and Skipped Days of Laying. *Auk* **114**:479–487.

Komdeur, J., S. Daan, J. Tinbergen, and C. Mateman. 1997. Extreme adaptive modification in sex ratio of the Seychelles Warbler's eggs. *Nature* **385**:522–525.

Komdeur, J., M. J. L. Magrath, and S. Krackow. 2002. Pre-ovulation control of hatchling sex ratio in the Seychelles Warbler. *Proceedings of the Royal Society of London. Series B: Biological Sciences* **269**:1067–1072.

Lack, D. 1947. The significance of clutch size. *Ibis* **89**:302–352.

Lahti, D. C. and A. R. Lahti. 2002. How precise is egg discrimination in weaverbirds? *Animal Behaviour* **63**:1135–1142.

Lormée, H., P. Jouventin, O. Chastel, and R. Mauget. 1999. Endocrine Correlates of Parental Care in an Antarctic Winter Breeding Seabird, the Emperor Penguin, Aptenodytes forsteri. *Hormones and Behavior* **35**:9–17.

McCracken, K. G. 2000. The 20-cm Spiny Penis of the Argentine Lake Duck (Oxyura vittata). *Auk* **117**:820–825.

McCracken, K. G., R. E. Wilson, P. J. McCracken, and K. P. Johnson. 2001. Are ducks impressed by drakes' display? *Nature* **413**:128.

McDaniel, C. D., R. K. Bramwell, and B. Howarth. 1996. The male contribution to broiler breeder heat-induced infertility as determined by sperm-egg penetration and sperm storage within the hen's oviduct. *Poultry Science* **75**:1546–1554.

McDaniel, C. D., R. K. Bramwell, J. L. Wilson, and B. Howarth. 1995. Fertility of the male and female broiler breeders following exposure to an elevated temperature environment. *Poultry Science Reviews* **74**:1029–1038.

Moskat, C. 2005. Common Cuckoo parasitism in Europe: Behavioural adaptations, arms race and the role of metapopulations. *Ornithological Science* **4**:3–15.

Müller, W., C. M. Eising, C. Dijkstra, and T. G. G. Groothuis. 2002. Sex differences in yolk hormones depend on maternal social status in Leghorn chickens (Gallus gallus domesticus). *Proceedings of the Royal Society of London. Series B: Biological Sciences* **269**:2249–2255.

Nager, R. G., P. Monaghan, R. Griffiths, D. C. Houston, and R. Dawson. 1999. Experimental demonstration that offspring sex ratio varies with maternal condition. *Proceedings of the National Academy of Sciences* **96**:570–573.

Navara, K., G. Hill, and M. Mendonça. 2006. Yolk androgen deposition as a compensatory strategy. *Behavioral Ecology and Sociobiology* **60**:392–398.

Ockleford, E. M. and M. A. Vince. 1985. Acceleration of hatching in fowl and quail: Relationship between artificial and natural stimulus amplitude. *British Poultry Science* **26**:57–63.

Perrins, C. 2009. *The Princeton Encyclopedia of Birds*. Princeton University Press, Princeton, New Jersey.

Persson, I. and G. Andersson. 1999. Intraclutch Hatch Synchronization in Pheasants and Mallard Ducks. *Ethology* **105**:1087–1096.

Pike, T. W. 2005. Sex ratio manipulation in response to maternal condition in pigeons: Evidence for pre-ovulatory follicle selection. *Behavioral Ecology and Sociobiology* **58**:407–413.

Pike, T. W. and M. Petrie. 2003. Potential mechanisms of avian sex manipulation. *Biological Reviews* **78**:553–574.

Pizzari, T. and T. R. Birkhead. 2000. Female feral fowl eject sperm of subdominant males. *Nature* **405**:787–789.

Robin, J.-P., L. Boucontet, P. Chillet, and R. Groscolas. 1998. Behavioral changes in fasting emperor penguins: Evidence for a "refeeding signal" linked to a metabolic shift. *American Journal of Physiology—Regulatory, Integrative and Comparative Physiology* **274**:R746–R753.

Rutkowska, J. and A. V. Badyaev. 2008. Meiotic drive and sex determination: Molecular and cytological mechanisms of sex ratio adjustment in birds. *Philosophical Transactions of the Royal Society B: Biological Sciences* **363**:1675-–1686.

Sheldon, B. C., S. Andersson, S. C. Griffith, J. Ornborg, and J. Sendecka. 1999. Ultraviolet colour variation influences Blue Tit sex ratios. *Nature* **402**:874–877.

Stoleson, S. H. and S. R. Beissinger. 1995. Hatching asynchrony and the onset of incubation in birds revisited: When is the critical period?

Sutherland, W. J. 2002. Conservation biology: Science, sex and the Kakapo. *Nature* **419**:265–266.

Takeda, A. 1969. Labeling of cock spermatozoa with radioactive phosphorus. *Japan Journal of Zootechnological Science* **40**:412.

Tazawa, H. and G. C. Whittow. 2000. Incubation Physiology. *In* G. C. Whittow, editor. *Sturkie's Avian Physiology, 5th edition*. Academic Press, San Diego, CA.

Trivers, R. L. and D. E. Williard. 1973. Natural selection of parental ability to vary the sex ratio of offspring. *Science* **179**:90–92.

Viñuela, J. 2000. Opposing selective pressures on hatching asynchrony: Egg viability, brood reduction, and nestling growth. *Behavioral Ecology and Sociobiology* **48**:333–343.

Walton, A. and E. O. Whetham. 1933. The survival of the spermatozoon in the domestic fowl. Journal of Experimental *Biology* **10**:204.

Wesotowski, T. 1999. Reduction of Phallus in Birds: An Avian Way to Safe Sex? *Journal of Avian Biology* **30**:483–485.

Winterbottom, M., T. Burke, and T. R. Birkhead. 1999. A stimulatory phalloid organ in a weaver bird. *Nature* **399**:28–28.

Yom-Tov, Y. 2001. An updated list and some comments on the occurrence of intraspecific nest parasitism in birds. *Ibis* **143**:133–143.

VIII PARROTS

In the wild, parrots have a distribution in the Southern hemisphere and tropics, with most being found in South America and Australia. No species of parrot naturally occurs in Europe or Russia. Despite being thought of as exclusively tropical, parrot species are found in temperate and cold mountain elevations within New Zealand and the Indian subcontinent. Parrots are typically found in lowland tropical forests, open forests, and savanna ecosystems. The extinct Carolina Parakeet (Figure 8.1), which had a range across the eastern half of the United States, from as far north as New York and south through Florida, had the distinction of having the most northern latitude range of any parrot. The last reliable record for Carolina Parakeets existing in the wild occurred in 1904 (Fuller, 1987) and the last captive Carolina Parakeet—the only indigenous parrot of the United States—died in the Cincinnati Zoo in 1918. Ironically, the last Passenger Pigeon (see Chapter 10) died at the same location in 1914. The decline of the Carolina Parakeet from widespread and abundant to extinct in a 100-year period remains a bit of a mystery. Habitat destruction was a contributor to its decline, as forests were cleared for agricultural purposes. As agriculture increased, the Carolina Parakeet changed its habitats to take advantage of agricultural crops as a food source. Because they were highly social and often formed large flocks, they could quickly decimate fruit and grain crops. The Carolina Parakeet began to be persecuted heavily as an agricultural pest to protect crops, while at the same time it was also being killed for food and for the collection of its feathers for the fashion industry. Their highly social flock behavior made killing them in large numbers relatively easy, especially because of their propensity not to leave fallen comrades that had already been shot (Fuller, 1987). The toll of this heavy hunting may have been enough to cause their extinction.

The Pygmy Parrot species is one of the few parrot species never successfully maintained in captivity. They are the smallest parrots, with a length of about 3.5 inches, while the large macaw species are the largest parrots at over 3 feet in length. The Buff-faced

FIGURE 8.1   Now extinct, this Carolina Parakeet specimen is on display at the Harvard Natural History Museum.

FIGURE 8.2   The distinctive bill of a parrot as seen in this African Grey parrot.

Pygmy Parrot weighs about 12 to 12.5 grams, in contrast to the largest parrot, the Kakapo of New Zealand, which can weigh 3 to 4 kilograms (**Box 8.1**). Overall, parrots tend to have short necks which add to their overall plump appearance. Their most distinguishable anatomical features are their bills and feet. Parrots have a relatively large downward-curved upper mandible that ends at a point and an upward curving lower mandible positioned so that the upper mandible closes over the lower mandible (Figure 8.2), creating the appearance of a significant overbite. The bill is used by many species like a third foot that assists them in climbing about the canopy of trees. The prominent bill of many parrot species is capable of generating a great deal of force in cracking very hard-shelled nuts and other seeds. Parrots are zygodactyl, meaning that their first and fourth toes of their foot point backwards, while the middle two digits point forward. This allows for a powerful grasp and facilitates in many parrot species the use of their feet as hands. The dexterity of these "hands" is highly accomplished and allows parrots to hold and manipulate food or objects close to the bill (Figure 8.3).

Flight ability varies considerably across parrots, with the small parrots typically being fast, efficient fliers, while the larger species typically have a slower flight speed. The parrot with the largest body mass, the Kakapo, is flightless. Tail feathers vary widely in parrot species and range from the long and pointed tails of parakeet and macaw species to the short and square tails found in lovebird and hanging parrot species. The well-known large macaws are some of the most colorful birds in existence in the bird world. This, combined with their size and intelligence, has made them highly desirable in the pet trade. However, as a whole, the predominant feather color of parrot species is green. In most parrot species, males and females are typically indistinguishable from one another. Juveniles are simply dull versions of their eventual mature plumage coloration.

Parrot diets tend to consist of seeds, fruits, buds, and small insects. They are often agricultural pests because they eat grain and fruit crops. However, there are exceptions to the typical seed and/or fruit diet found in many parrots. The Kea parrot of New Zealand is a true omnivore whose diet also includes meat. Lories and lorikeets have diets consisting primarily of pollen and nectar, supplemented with fruits (Figure 8.4). Many parrot species also participate in geophagy—consuming soil—and in particular for parrot species, clay soil. This behavior has been documented in parrots from South America, Africa, and Papua New Guinea. The basis for this behavior has not definitively been concluded. But it may be related to neutralizing the toxins ingested with their food (Diamond et al., 1999; Gilardi et al., 1999). Many of the seed kernels that parrots eat contain alkaloid toxins such as strychnine and quinine placed in seeds by the plants that produce them to inhibit their consumption. Clay particles are negatively charged and bind to the positively charged alkaloids, preventing their absorption from the intestine, thus potentially protecting the bird's health. Other research suggests that, at least in South America, the consumption of clay may also be a source for sodium that would otherwise be deficient in parrots without the consumption of very specific clay rich in sodium (Brightsmith and Muñoz-Najar, 2004; Brightsmith et al., 2008; Powell et al., 2009).

Behaviorally, parrots tend to stay in small flocks (and in some species, very large flocks) or family groups. They are highly social, except during the breeding season, when pairs in most species will isolate themselves somewhat. Parrots are very loud and noisy and their calls tend to be harsh squawks and screams intermixed with some chattering. Most species are monogamous and pair for life, forming very strong pair bonds. However, the Kea and the highly endangered Kakapo are exceptions, as they are both polygamous. Golden Conures are a communal nesting species of parrot, while Monk Parrots will nest in a large communal twig nest that can be as large as a small car, but each pair will have its own nest chamber compartment within the communal nest. Eclectus and Vasa Parrots are both cooperative breeders, with females mating with multiple males that provide food to the female. Most parrot species are tree cavity nesters. Suitable nesting cavities are often scarce, as they are not created by the parrots themselves, but by other animals. A shortage of nest cavities is especially likely in locations where selective harvesting of older large trees has occurred. In almost all species, the female incubates the eggs, while the male supplies food. Fledging occurs in three to four weeks in species like the budgerigar, while large macaws do not fledge for three to four months after hatching.

Predators to full grown parrots include man and birds of prey, while monkeys and other tree-dwelling animals take eggs and nestlings. Man's predation includes killing for food, crop protection, and trapping birds for the pet trade. In the year 2000, it was estimated that between 186,000 and 297,000 Amazon and macaw parrots were killed and eaten each year in Brazilian Amazonia (Peres, 2000). The exploitation of parrots for the pet trade has been profound, as discussed in Chapter 3. But in Africa alone, conservative estimates and actual data indicate that 8 million parrots have been removed from the wild since 1975 (Boyes, 2011). In Central and South America, the wild populations of many of the large macaw species have been decimated, in part by illegal trapping for the pet trade (**Box 8.2**).

CURRENT POPULATION STATUS OF WILD PARROTS

BirdLife International (BirdLife International, 2012) lists 374 species of parrots. Of this total, 19, 15, 34, 48, 42, and 216 species are listed as extinct, critically endangered, endangered, vulnerable, near threatened, and least concern, respectively. Thus, 97 out of the 355 extant species are threatened. Of the 19 extinct parrots, all but one—the Carolina Parakeet of North America—was endemic to islands. For the critically endangered parrot species, the Spix's

FIGURE 8.3 Parrots use their feet like hands to grasp food.

FIGURE 8.4 Rainbow Lorikeets are parrots that consume a diet primarily of nectar and pollen.

Macaw is considered possibly extinct in the wild (limited population in captivity), and the New Caledonian Lorikeet, Red-throated Lorikeet, and Glaucous Macaw have not been recorded in the wild (and do not exist in captivity) since 1913, 1993, and the 1960s, respectively. Of the 15 species listed as critical, 13 of them have a population of less than 250 individuals; 10 of the 15 are endemic to islands.

Many of the other threatened parrots have limited ranges, with many species restricted to islands which, as discussed in Chapter 2, make them especially sensitive to invasive species, storms, and human encroachment. Particularly hard hit have been parrot species located on the Caribbean Islands, where several of the extinctions have occurred. As the threat from the pet trade diminishes due to enforcement of laws protecting parrots, the most serious threat to parrots is the continued loss of habitat, as a result of forest clearing, particularly in the tropics for wood harvesting, agricultural activities, and urbanization. Without aggressive protection of habitat and the continued intervention through captive breeding programs, several of the critically endangered and endangered parrot species will be lost in the next 50 years.

PARROTS AS PETS

Parrots can make wonderful pets and have been used for pet purposes for thousands of years. An early written account of a parrot as a pet was penned by a Greek physician who wrote about his Plum-headed Parakeet in about 400 BC, because he was captivated by the bird's ability to learn the Greek language as well as mimic words from the language of its original homeland, modern-day India (Perrins, 2009). Exotic parrots were a long-standing status symbol for the ruling classes of the Greek, Roman, and Egyptian empires, followed by the ruling class of Europe. As new lands were discovered—such as the Americas, Southeast Asia, and Australia—parrots from these regions became treasured gifts by explorers to their sponsors in Europe. Interestingly, despite the long history of parrots as pets, only the budgerigar (Figure 8.5) and possibly the cockatiel can really be considered domesticated. Instead, harvesting wild populations of parrots was the constant source for bird influx into the pet trade, and that trend continued until the last 20 to 25 years, when severe restrictions began to be implemented to protect the dwindling populations of wild parrots.

When thinking about getting a pet parrot, there are many things to consider before buying a bird. A key factor to establishing a lasting positive relationship with a parrot as a pet is to consider what type of bird you are looking for as a companion. Pet parrots come in a huge array of sizes, from macaws to parrotlets (Figure 8.6). If you are intimidated by a large bird, this should be the last type of parrot for you to get, as that intimidation will get in the way of establishing a trusting and rewarding relationship with the bird. Some parrot species—such as many cockatoos—are attention seekers that want to be petted and cuddled, while others, like Eclectus Parrots, are content to be around their owner, but do not seek a lot of physical contact. Finally, some species such as Rosella Parrots do not want much human contact, but are absolutely ideal for the person who wants to watch a strikingly colorful bird (Figure 8.7) in a flighted aviary that is undemanding for attention and physical contact. You should choose a species that fits the physical contact level you want to give.

FIGURE 8.5   Budgerigar

The next critical factor to consider is your commitment duration. Large parrots such as the large macaws may live in captivity to 80 to 90 years of age, while medium-sized parrots such as Amazon and African Grey Parrots have captive life spans more typically in the range of 30 to 60 years. Several of the small parrot species, on the other hand, such as budgerigars and cockatiels, have life spans in the 10- to 20-year range. If you are not ready to commit or not settled in your future life endeavors, a medium or large parrot should be potentially avoided until your life is more settled. Your living arrangements should also factor into your decision. Parrots can be very loud—typically, the larger the bird, the greater the capability of producing loud noises. So if you live in an apartment complex, a loud parrot should be avoided and as apartments can be small, a parrot that is relatively small in size and does not require a large cage (such as a budgerigar) may be the best choice. Many people discover that they can be allergic to parrots or at least certain kinds of parrots that produce a lot of feather dander. Potential parrot owners need to spend time around the species of their choice to make sure that this will not be a problem.

Costs also need to be factored into the purchasing decision equation, and that includes both direct and indirect costs. Usually, the larger and less available parrot species cost thousands of dollars; a hand-fed Hyacinth Macaw can easily cost $10,000. On the other hand, budgerigars and cockatiels can often be obtained for less than $25. Indirect costs normally also increase with the size of the bird. The larger the bird, the larger the cage it requires, and cage prices increase with size and durability, as will be discussed shortly. Large birds can generate tremendous force with their beaks, which increases wear and tear on cages, making cage replacement more likely in a few years. With small parrot species, one cage will typically last for the bird's entire life. Food and toy costs also increase with bird size. Finally, a large parrot left unattended and free in a household—even for a short period of time—can easily damage household wooden furniture and other objects that are easy to chew and destroy with their powerful beaks.

FIGURE 8.6 Parrotlets are some of the smallest parrots species.

FIGURE 8.7 The Eastern Rosella is one of the more colorful parrots kept as pets.

SOURCES FOR PET BIRDS

Parrots are typically purchased directly from breeders or obtained from pet stores. More widely available breeds of parrots such as cockatiels, lovebirds, African Greys, and some Amazons are fairly common in pet stores. Specialized bird pet shops have an even greater selection, including a variety of macaws, Amazons, and large cockatoos, but bird-themed pet shops are relatively rare. Bird breeders that sell to the general public are the most numerous and widespread sources of parrots and the source of common and pet-trade rare species of parrots as well. Locating parrot breeders with Internet searches is very easy, and shipment of birds throughout the

United States is common. With pet stores and bird breeders, it is always good to get references from other people who have dealt with them. Ideally, either source should be willing to provide a health guarantee, provided you get a complete veterinary check of the bird within two to five days of purchase. Finally, new parrot owners often have many questions and concerns that arise after purchase of the bird, and the seller should be willing to provide further contact as a source of information. Sellers who are concerned for birds and ask many questions and actually interview prospective owners of their birds are what you are looking for as a buyer.

It is always important to remember that flea markets, bird marts, and newspaper ads are all used by smugglers and bird thieves to dispose of their birds. Typically, the old adage "you get what you pay for" applies—and if the deal seems to be too good to be true, there is probably something wrong. Of course, there are breeders who simply enjoy breeding birds and are not breeding parrots for profit. Such breeders will look for good homes for their birds and often charge nominal fees for their birds.

LEG BANDS

Leg bands can assist you in gaining valuable information about a parrot that you may purchase. Seamless or closed metal leg bands (Figure 8.8) are slid over the toes of young parrots, typically when they are 10 to 20 days of age. A closed leg band is an almost 100 percent indicator that the parrot was born in captivity. However, babies stolen from nests in the wild can have closed bands placed on them. The band is slipped over the three longest toes (2 front and one back) held together and then moved over the foot. Finally, it is slid up over the short rear toe, which is being held next to the shaft of the leg. Once beyond this final toe, the bird's foot is released and the bird is banded. The band will only fit over the foot and not come off for the short window of age described above. Closed bands that are small enough to remain on the leg cannot be fitted on a bird after about two to three weeks of age. Closed bands help in bird identification and record keeping. There are no universal rules on the information placed on closed bands, but often a year of birth and a breeder identification are included. Bands can be purchased from several sources, and there is a growing trend for registry databanks being maintained by issuers of bands, especially those bands issued by bird associations.

Imported birds are given open bands (Figure 8.9) when they are placed in quarantine stations. These are metal bands that are bent into the form of a circle around the bird's leg with a band applicator. These bands are engraved with an identifying number and a specific code for the quarantine station that banded the birds on arrival. More information can be obtained on import bands from your local United States Department of Fish and Wildlife Service. Although

FIGURE 8.8   Closed leg bands are placed on captive-bred parrots while they are young, and indicate the bird was born and raised in captivity.

FIGURE 8.9   Open leg bands have been used on wild-caught parrots.

open bands typically indicate wild-caught imported birds, they are sometimes used on captive-bred birds that were not banded at a young age.

Parrots may not have leg bands. This can result for a few reasons. Many people who obtain imported birds remove the open leg bands for the bird's protection, as it could get caught on cage wires or toys, leading to serious injury or death on very rare occasions. Additionally, some individual parrots of large species such as macaws will, on occasion, break their bands or damage their closed bands, so that it impairs blood circulation and thus has to be removed. Finally, some breeders simply do not band their babies.

PURCHASE OF A PARROT

Once you have selected the type of bird you desire and have identified sources for your specific bird species, you then have to focus on the compatibility of a specific bird and you. This is especially true for the larger-sized parrots which could be lifetime companions. Never be hasty in the decision, and only purchase when you are absolutely confident in your choice. Make sure the bird is tame enough for you from the start, and do not assume that it will become tamer as you spend more time with it. There needs to be a connection between you and the bird that is not forced. A really good approach is to let the bird pick you by it coming over to interact with you freely. Individual parrots often show a male or female preference in people. Similarly, if the bird is going to be a family pet, it is imperative to bring all the members of the family when selecting the bird. A bird may like you, but not be so keen on other family members. Birds liking one family member but not others may cause problems, which will ultimately lead to the bird having to be placed in another home or a sanctuary, as discussed later.

Never buy an unweaned baby, as hand-feeding a parrot is not something for the novice to attempt, as will be discussed in a later section of this chapter. The bird will still bond to you strongly if you do not hand-feed it, despite what an eager seller may tell you. Buying a recently weaned baby is a bit like getting a puppy, as you are going to have to provide all of the training for the bird. Older birds that are trained are at times available and can make wonderful pets. However, it is always imperative to be cautious with older birds and to investigate thoroughly why the bird is being sold. Some unscrupulous people will try to sell birds with behavioral problems simply to recoup their money or it might be a retired breeder bird that should never be sold as a pet. Spend time with the bird before purchase to make sure there are no problems. Older parrots will bond with new owners and can make just as wonderful a pet companion as a recently weaned bird.

CAGES

Parrot cages come in a plethora of styles and construction material (Figure 8.10). The most common construction materials are stainless steel, wrought iron, and heavy-gauge wire. Medical surgical grade stainless steel is the most expensive, with medium-sized cages costing over a thousand dollars and large (macaw) cages costing over $2,000. Although the initial cost is expensive, these cages do not rust and last many years to a lifetime if constructed well. They are easy to wipe clean and maintain. Wrought iron cages are durable for a few years for most birds. When manufactured, these cages are finished with non-toxic paint or a powder coat finish. The paint and powder coating will be chipped and flaked off over time by most medium- to large-sized parrots. Exposed wrought iron will rust and parrot droppings are very effective in causing rust and degradation of exposed wrought iron. Thus, while wrought iron cages cost typically from $200 to $800, they may

FIGURE 8.10   Cages come in a variety of styles and shapes.

FIGURE 8.11   It is important to have a large cage door on the cage so it is easy to remove and return your bird from its cage.

need replacement or refurbishing in just a few years when housing a medium- to large-sized parrot. Cages constructed from heavy-gauge wire are the cheapest. However, they can be easily destroyed by large parrots with powerful beaks and are typically only suitable for small to medium parrots. Of course, large macaws will eventually destroy the welds holding the bars of any cage. They are the most difficult and expensive birds to house.

When cages are manufactured, it is cheaper to construct them as one solid unit versus in separate parts that are then put together. While the price of a solid unit cage may be attractive, for convenience a knock-down (a cage that can be assembled and disassembled) cage is worth the extra money. Consider the fact that the doors in most homes are often less than 32 inches wide, which means that many large-sized, solid cages are ordered and delivered, but never make it into the home simply because they will not fit through the door. You may move to a new house in the future, and moving a cage that will disassemble and lie flat is a lot less hassle. When buying a cage, always get the largest cage you can afford, but at a minimum, a good rule is that the cage must be big enough that the bird can easily flap its wings without hitting any part of the cage or cage accessories, such as toys and feeders. If your bird is going to be spending a lot of time out of his cage in your home, the cage can be a bit smaller. Always make sure the cage door is very large (Figure 8.11) so it is easy to remove and put back your parrot. The more complicated the locks of the cage doors the better, as parrots are very adept at getting simple catch latches/locks open. Make sure there is a floor grate and that it is well away from the tray collecting waste. The bird should not have access to dropped items that have fallen through the grate to be contaminated by old food and feces at the bottom of the cage because if accessed after being contaminated, it could cause health problems.

Bar spacing should be small enough that the bird's head cannot fit through the bars. As parrots will climb about their cage a great deal using their beak like a hand, it is better to have horizontal bars on two sides of the cage and vertical bars on the other two sides. Ideally, the horizontal bar spacing will be such that the bridge of the upper beak will not make contact with the upper bar above the one grasped (Figure 8.12), but this is impossible for large-beaked parrots (Figure 8.12). So for these birds, having vertical bars on two sides will alleviate constant stress on the bridge of the upper beak that an all-horizontal barred cage would cause as the bird climbs about the cage. However, an all vertical bar cage is not favored, since these bars are harder to grasp with the feet.

It is better to purchase cages that have simple square edges and avoid the cages with bars arranged like spokes that are wide at the top and come to a point (Figure 8.13) and cages with ornate intricate scroll work. Parrots will spend much of their day climbing around the cage—the last thing you want is to come home and find your parrot hanging by his head in the vise-like grip of two spoke bars, or dangling by a leg caught in intricate scroll work.

FIGURE 8.12 Bar spacing is important. The top of your bird's bill should not hit the bars, as shown here (a). With horizontal barring, this is difficult to avoid for larger parrots, so vertical bars are recommended on two sides of the cage for such species (b).

FIGURE 8.13   A cage containing some of its cage bars in a spoke arrangement. If a parrot can fit its head through the wide end of the adjacent spokes, it may slide its head down and become stuck as the bar spacing narrows.

Cage location should always be approached from the bird's point of view. Generally, avoid high traffic areas in the house, as this can stress the bird as it reacts to all the coming and goings. Avoid windows if there is a lot of activity outside for the same reason. Never place the cage directly in front of a window if the entire cage would be illuminated entirely by sun shining through the window, as the bird would have no place to escape the glare and radiant heat. Be conscious of the potential of car headlights shining through a window, preventing restful sleep if your home is near a highway. In the end, cage placement should provide a place where the bird feels secure and provides an escape. If the cage is placed in a highly active area of the house, you should block off part of the cage where the bird can retreat if it desires some alone time. It is better to use play gyms to place the bird in a highly active area with the family for part of the day.

PERCHES

A variety of perch sizes and textures should be placed in the cage since it will better represent the choices in nature. Your goal is to make sure your bird's feet remain comfortable and do not develop pink pressure sores from providing perching that is all of one size and texture. Allowing the feet to grasp a variety of perch diameters will make your bird happy and comfortable. Wood perches are ideal, as they are used naturally in the wild and they naturally vary in diameter if actual branches are used instead of wood dowels. Parrots can chew on wood perches, which helps maintain beak health and provides activity. The downside of wood perches is that they have to be replaced and are hard to clean and disinfect. Typically, many owners will provide some soft wood perches such as apple and then some hard durable wood perches, such as oak or manzanita.

Plastic perches can be easy to clean, fairly durable, but slippery unless textured, which then makes them harder to clean. Cement/conditioning perches (Figure 8.14) are good as one perch in the cage. If a conditioning perch is the correct diameter for your bird so the toenails naturally grasp it as the bird is perched, then it will wear the nails down so that they do not need clipping. Conditioning perches will also be used by the bird to naturally file or wear down its beak. Conditioning perches should never be the only perch provided, as overuse would lead to sore, irritated feet. Electric heated thermo perches are a good option to provide if the bird is housed in a cool location so that the bird can receive supplemental heat through its feet through contact with the perch. Rope perches (Figure 8.15) are vine-like, soft textured, and swing. However, as soon as they start to fray they should be discarded. Frayed rope material will often be ingested by parrots as they work to tear up and destroy the rope. Rope strands are indigestible and can collect in the upper portions of the digestive tract and block/impact the digestive tract from normal function. Surgery would have to be performed to remove the rope strands.

FIGURE 8.14   A colorful array of conditioning perches.

FEED AND WATER DISHES

Water and feed dishes come in a huge variety of shapes and sizes. They are typically constructed of stainless steel (Figure 8.16 a) or durable plastic (Figure 8.16 b). Ideally, they should be easy to access, with swing-out cage doors for feed and water bowl access being ideal (Figure 8.17). The bowls also should be locked or held in place (Figure 8.18) so they cannot be picked up and tossed about—a favorite pastime of many parrots if they can do it. Open bowls can mean a lot of tossed and wasted food, so specialized feeders exist that try to limit the bird's ability to toss its food while eating (Figure 8.19). Water bowls and feed bowls should be separated as much as possible, as this will discourage food being placed in the water bowl. Once food contaminates the water bowl, there is increased risk of bacterial proliferation in the water, which could lead to sickness. Water bottles placed on the outside of the cage with the tip pointing into the cage are ideal, as the water will not be soiled with food or fecal material. Parrots readily learn to drink from water bottles. But individual birds will often crush the metal tip, destroying this type of watering system.

PLAY GYMS AND TOYS

All pet parrots should be taken out of their cage on a regular basis, ideally on a daily basis. Some large cages will have play areas built on

FIGURE 8.15   Rope perches.

FIGURE 8.16   Food and water bowls should be durable and either made of stainless steel (a) or thick plastic (b).

FIGURE 8.17   It is convenient to be able to access bowls with swing-out holders.

top of them and this is convenient. However, as mentioned previously in the cage section, it is often better to have the cage located away from the central family area and then have a play gym in the family area that the bird can be brought to for interaction with the family. Play gyms are large wooden or plastic stands (Figure 8.20) equipped with perches and a place to attach a variety of toys. They often have a spot for a water and/or feed bowl. After playtime and interaction, the bird can be returned to its cage.

Toys should be provided in the cage, as well as on play gyms. Toys provide the bird with mental stimulation and physical activity when owners are away at work or school. They are key ways to prevent behavioral issues related to boredom that will be discussed below. A variety of toys should be provided, and they should be of different colors and shapes and textures to provide maximum stimulation and activity (Figure 8.21). Rotating non-destructible toys is also recommended to prevent disinterest in playing with them. Toys can be as simple as pine cones to elaborately made gadgets. At least some of the toys should be highly destructible, as parrots derive great joy from destroying objects. Destructible toys (Figure 8.22) are typically soft wood, leather or even ink free paper. Hard plastic toys that are hard to destroy can also be part of the mix. Being imaginative and constructing your own toys is recommended, as this will add variety. Make sure the toys are free of lead and zinc if they contain metal parts. For medium- or larger-sized parrots, it is often advisable to remove the clapper that is found on the bells that are often included on manufactured toys. These larger birds will remove the clapper themselves and may swallow it and it could remain in the gizzard for some time, slowly leaching out toxic levels of heavy metals. As previously mentioned, any frayed rope material should be removed and avoided if your bird shows a propensity to ingest frayed fibers.

BEHAVIOR AS PETS

Many parrot owners run into problems with behavioral issues with their pet parrots, in part because they are very different from training dogs or a similar pet animal that people have prior experience in training. Dogs are typically eager to please their owner, and training based on reward and punishment is effective. In parrots, the overwhelming demand is not pleasing the owner per se, but is instead the desire to get attention and be part of the flock that includes the humans of the household. It is also always important to keep in mind that typically, once you move beyond budgerigars and cockatiels, the larger parrots available for purchase are still the descendants of parents or grandparents that were wild, free-living birds before they were caught and placed into the pet trade. So you are dealing with a pet that is still a wild animal which has not been bred domestically for many generations with extensive genetic selection for pet qualities as many of our cats and dog breeds have been. However, parrots are highly intelligent and trainable. Their intelligence and mentality are very similar to a human three- or four-year-old. An owner of a parrot should start with verbal commands while using a firm tone and direct eye contact. The best commands to start with are "up" and "down" so you can teach your bird to get on and off your hand or arm. The direct eye contact helps establish dominance, and the firm tone coveys a seriousness they perceive.

Beyond simple commands, the approach to training parrots always needs to focus on the positive and the redirection of negative behaviors through the use of distractions. Above all, be fair and consistent. Parrots are attention sponges and when they want interaction from their human flock, they prefer positive interactions, but will settle for negative—and even seek negative interactions. So behavior modification cannot successfully involve punishment, as that provides attention and although negative, if that is the only attention the bird can get, it will seek it out. Instead, praise and reward positive behaviors to encourage their continuation and use distractions such as providing a toy or a new activity to redirect negative behaviors. Although difficult, it is imperative not to react to negative behaviors by yelling, getting agitated, or punishing the bird, as this provides stimulation, attention, and drama rewards to the bird. Typically, simply telling the bird no firmly or making direct eye contact with a stare will convey the message and correct the behavior as it is happening. It is all right to ignore a negative behavior if it seems to be a one-time event, but correct it if it continues to happen. With regard to being fair, if a behavior was acceptable or even rewarded several times, an owner cannot suddenly decide it is unacceptable and expect the bird to understand this. Furthermore, do not correct a behavior one day and not the next: You must be consistent. Also, do not correct for an incident well after it happened. For example, if you come home from work and find a mess created by your parrot, it may have happened ten minutes after you left. Therefore, expecting your bird to figure out why you might be attempting to do a corrective behavior once you got home would be unfair. In addition, always consider the possibility that the bird might be acting up simply to get your attention if you have been busy and not provided the level of interaction that you normally do with your bird.

BITING

Parrots have large, powerful beaks and can cause serious permanent injuries with their beaks. Biting can be broken up into two categories: biting by young birds and biting by mature birds. In young birds that were recently weaned, exploring their environment by "mouthing and tonguing" is common. Parrots are very tactile, and they use their tongues to touch and feel objects. They also use their beaks to explore and to chew on things, similar in some regards to the way puppies chew on objects. When this mouthing and tonguing activity

FIGURE 8.18 As parrots love to tip over everything for fun, bowls that lock in place are ideal.

FIGURE 8.19 A variety of specialized feeders are available, like this reduced-waste feeder that catches much of the food that would have been thrown on the bottom of the cage.

FIGURE 8.20   Play gyms are large, wooden or plastic stands that allow a pet bird to play with toys or interact with people.

FIGURE 8.21   Parrots need lots of stimulation through a variety of toys.

focuses on the parrot owner, it is fine to let them do this if you are prepared. If the bird starts to tighten its beak grip and pinching flesh, it is critical for the owner not to jerk back or pull away, as this just stimulates the bird to grab on hard. Often, the bird simply moves on and the pinch never becomes serious. If the pinching starts to hurt, the bird should be told "no" firmly and given a toy to chew. It is imperative not to yell or get excited, as this will just stimulate the bird and encourage the biting behavior. Also, don't return the bird to its cage as punishment, since this teaches the young bird that if it wants to return to its cage all it has to do is bite. Similarly, if the biting occurs while meeting a new person, taking the bird from that person also conveys to the bird if it does not want to interact with a person all it has to do is bite.

In mature, well-trained parrots, biting is unusual, but it can happen for a few reasons. Mature parrots can bite because something is wrong, such as they are sick, have been startled, or they are frightened. In addition, adult parrots that have reached sexual maturity may bite due to elevated sex hormones and sexual behavior. The alert owner will be in tune to these changes, and even inexperienced owners will detect sexual behavior when the parrot arches its neck and fans its tail or attempts to regurgitate food to the owner. When birds are sexually active, owners need to be alert for the potential to bite. As pets are not in a breeding situation, this behavior will typically pass fairly quickly. Finally, pet parrots may bite when feeling dominant. It is always best for the owner to be the dominant member of the flock and the parrot to be subordinate. However, new owners will often allow their parrot to be in a dominant position—the bird's head above the owner's head. In the wild, dominant birds seem to perch higher than subordinates. When a parrot is feeling dominant to an owner and the owner does not recognize this and tries to move the parrot, the parrot may bite defensively to maintain its position. Whatever the cause is for biting in a parrot, is important not to overreact to a single bite, as this can turn it into a major event which promotes habit formation. Overall, parrots are rarely serious bitters. Considering the power they can generate with their bills, if it was in their desire or nature to cause serious injuries and maim, they easily could do so. However, owners should always be aware of this potential and act accordingly.

PHOBIC BIRDS

There are times when a parrot is encountered that is very scared and "shell-shocked." In these cases, giving the bird confidence so you can work with it is critical. This situation is often encountered when parrots are rescued from bad conditions or abuse. It is not unusual for these birds to be shaking with fear. In this situation, it is critical to be submissive by approaching the bird with your head down while making no direct eye contact with the bird. Stay calm, relaxed, and take it slow—let the bird dictate events. As the bird gains confidence, you will be able to work with it.

TALKING

One of the primary reasons that people purchase larger parrot species for pets is because of their ability for communicative speech. However, the use of words in a meaningful context is not a given just because it is a parrot. Many species of parrots, and quite likely individuals, in all parrot species are capable of human speech. Parrots known for their talking ability are African Greys, Amazons, Eclectus Macaws, and cockatoos, but not all individual birds even within these types of parrots will learn to speak. Within the parrots known for their talking ability, the African Greys and Eclectus are usually unsurpassed in their ability to mimic the nuances of the human voice, such that they can easily be mistaken by people as other humans talking (**Box 8.3**). It is not unusual for family members in households with these birds to respond to the bird, thinking it was another family member. Cats and dogs in these households can also be fooled and can respond to a calling bird rather than its human owner. Macaws, cockatoos, and Amazons often speak very well, but typically there is no question that it is a bird doing the talking. Besides talking, several species of Amazons are well known for their ability to learn to mimic human singing.

There is no magical universal method for teaching a bird to talk. Teaching birds to talk involves speaking clearly and a lot of repetition. Birds learn to talk by observing someone else learn. It is much easier to teach a bird to talk if there is already another bird in the house that talks or a young child learning to speak. This is the basis of the model/rival method of training popularized by Irene Pepperberg and the African Grey, Alex (Pepperberg, 2006). With this method, there is

FIGURE 8.22   Parrots enjoy destroying toys, so providing some toys that are meant to be destructed, such as the ones pictured, are ideal.

the bird being taught, the trainer, and a rival, which can be another bird or person. The trainer will work with the rival, and when the rival says the word, it is rewarded with praise, or a treat such as a toy. The bird being taught now has a model to emulate and the motivation because it wants the positive reinforcement in the form of praise and a treat. Whenever possible, try to provide a reference or meaning to the word or a contextual application. This is why birds will often learn the word hello because they may observe the following: the phone rings, the owner gets up and answers the phone, and says hello. In the future when the phone rings, the bird will say hello. For bird owners who may also own a dog or a cat, the bird may observe and hear you call the cat or dog to come inside or to come get food. The bird sees the cat or dog respond and will start mimicking the owner by calling the cat or dog.

Although it is always important to remember each bird within a species is an individual and may not learn to talk, a non-talking bird may be a closet talker. Numerous bird owners have discovered when instructed to place a recording device in the presence of their bird when it is alone while they are gone, that their bird talks up a storm in their absence. This really tends to happen, mostly to people who have put in a lot of effort in teaching their parrots to speak. It may well be that the parrot is smart enough to enjoy all of the attention lavished by the owner in attempting to teach it to talk. But more importantly, with a highly interactive owner, the bird may be so occupied in the owner's presence that it simply does not speak.

ELIMINATING FOUL LANGUAGE AND NUISANCE SOUNDS

The propensity to learn by example and context is why foul language and nuisance sounds can be a problem in parrots that talk. It becomes a habit because they have been shown what to do (modeling), have done the behavior (enactment), and then been rewarded for the enactment (reinforcement). So mimicking a car alarm, a microwave oven beep, or answering machine beep are all common because the bird has typically witnessed these noises getting a reaction from their human companion(s). In addition, with foul language, such words are normally spoken in a different pitch and louder—which immediately catches the bird's attention and adds drama to the situation. Regretfully, when a bird mimics a car alarm the first time or drops the f-word, we may laugh or even reward the behavior, which is all the more likely to make the new sound or word a habit for the bird as it tries to get the same reaction for subsequent repetitions.

The solution to eliminating such sounds or language is to ignore it, meaning no negative or positive reaction once it is done. This will prevent the reward. At the same time, focus on new words or sounds that are more pleasing. Not only does this provide a distraction to the bird, but if new sounds or words are accomplished and rewarded, they will become the new focus and the annoying sounds and words will become a distant memory. They still will be uttered with decreasing frequency and may remain in the memory bank, but if the bird is never rewarded for them they will be rarely uttered. Having said that, certain sounds such as answering machines and car alarms are nearly impossible to eliminate as the operation of these devices provide constant reminders to the bird.

SCREAMING

In the wild, parrots often live in large, gregarious groups for at least part of the year when they are not raising offspring. Parrots have some of the loudest, harshest, and unmelodic calls of any birds. Contact calls, alarm calls, ritual greetings, and farewell calls are all part of these social birds' vocal repertoire. Thus, screaming is part of their natural flock behavior, and almost all pet parrots are only one or two generations removed from the wild. But you can use this knowledge to your advantage in limiting such vocalizations. In a home situation, the human occupants are viewed by the bird as its flock mates. So it is always important to greet the bird when you arrive and when leaving to say good-bye and let it know you will be back. This gives the bird a sense of flock security and prevents it from initiating contact and farewell calls to reestablish the flock dynamic. Birds that are startled or see a strange or unfamiliar animal or person approaching their visual view will let out alarm calls just as a dog would bark. Anticipate other situations that will cause loud vocalizations and prevent when possible. For example, if the bird is in the dining room or has a view of the dining room and the rest of its human flock is eating a meal and the bird is not getting to take part, you can be assured the parrot is going to make some noise. Similarly, if you have more than one bird and they are near each other and you give one a treat and not the other, the one missing out will vocalize. As stated earlier, a parrot in the household is like having the equivalent of a three- to four-year-old child. Finally, birds will vocalize in the morning around sunrise and in the evening around sunset. It will typically only last 10 to 20 minutes and will include both natural calls, but will also incorporate mimicked language. If this daily noise is going to be a problem, you should not get a bird.

With screaming, the best option is to anticipate it and prevent it before it happens, followed by redirecting the parrot's focus on something else, such as a toy or acceptable activity. There are several things not to do, as quick fixes treat the symptom and do not work in the long run. It is common to see owners or have them report the following actions to stop screaming birds: squirting the bird with water, tapping or grabbing the beak, or walking over to the bird's cage yelling at the bird. All of these provide drama reward, which will only encourage the bird to repeat the behavior at a future time to get the drama attention. Squirting the bird with water is similar to misting the bird with a water bottle, which should be done regularly for feather and skin care. Furthermore, it simply teaches the bird if it wants water for a bath, all it needs to do is scream. Wild parrots often grab each other's beaks and it seems to be a game akin to arm wrestling in humans. Thus, grabbing the beak is often viewed as a game by a parrot. Finally, walking over to the cage and yelling at the bird accomplishes two things. If the scream was a contact call, you have just rewarded the bird by coming over and making contact with it; yelling is topping it off with a drama reward—a sure recipe for continued screaming.

TOWELING A BIRD

If your bird needs to be immobilized for routine nail or feather care or for a visit to the veterinary clinic, toweling your bird protects the bird and you. In this procedure, take a folded-over towel (the size of the towel varies with bird size) and hold it in both hands. Approach the bird from the back and place your hands holding the towel over both wings (Figure 8.23 a & b). It is essential to immobilize the wings to prevent flapping, as the wings are very delicate and can easily be broken. Once the bird is immobilized in the towel, it can be laid on its back so that its feet or wings can be accessed (Figure 8.23 c). Obviously, it is best if your bird has been accustomed to this procedure from an early age so that it is not fearful of it.

BEAK AND NAIL CARE

Often, the nails of a bird's feet do not need to be clipped if they are provided with proper perches of the correct size. In particular, if a bird makes use of a rough textured cement perch, it will wear down its nails naturally. However, not all birds will make use of such perches, and so from time to time its nails will have to be clipped. Procedurally, it is no different than clipping your dog's or cat's nails if you own one of these pets. Just like your fingernails, the tips of a bird's nails are dead but the rest of the nail is live tissue. Therefore, you will only cut or file the end of the nail the same as you would your own fingernail. If you cut too far back the nail will bleed, but the bleeding can be stopped using commercially available Kwik-Stop or by applying flour to the end of the nail.

Beak overgrowth is a more serious problem and needs a trained professional such as a veterinarian to file it down if it is overgrown. Beaks continually grow, and the lower beak is ground down by the upper beak. The upper beak, especially in parrots, which have a natural overbite, can become overgrown if the bird does not actively wear it down by chewing on perches or toys (Figure 8.24). The tips

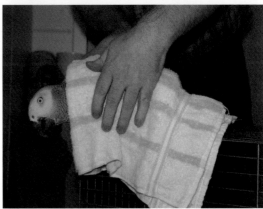

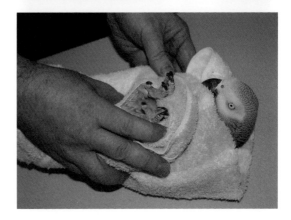

FIGURE 8.23   To immobilize a bird for nail or feather care, first take a folded-over towel and approach the bird from the back (a). Place hands holding the towel over both wings (b). Once the bird cannot move its wings, it can be laid on its back to gain access to the wing feathers or the feet (c).

FIGURE 8.24   The bird on the left has a normal-length beak. The upper beak on the bird on the right has become overgrown and may soon require filing by a professional.

of the bill should never be cut as the pointed, tapered shape of the upper beak must be maintained for normal function. Thus, it will need to be filed down in a manner that maintains the overall shape of the upper beak. It is not unusual for birds to be sedated during this procedure.

CLIPPING PRIMARY WING FEATHERS

Clipping primary flight feathers so that your pet bird is not flighted is essential if your bird is going to be outside of its cage for extended periods of time, which is recommended to provide activity for your bird. If the bird is flighted and free in your house, it is just a matter of time before an open window is forgotten or a door is opened accidentally so that your bird escapes. In addition, if your bird is not flighted, it will also reduce the risk of it flying into a window in your house, which can cause serious injury or death. The most logical and safest method of preventing flight in a pet bird is to clip the seven primary flight feathers on each wing. Using sharp scissors to make a clean cut, you will cut the primary flight feathers about two inches from where they meet the tips of the primary coverts (Figure 8.25). This clip will prevent flight in even lightweight excellent fliers, such as cockatiels and parakeets. It will also provide protection to new primary flight feathers that replace molted feathers (Figure 8.25). It is important to always clip both wings, as clipping only one wing will allow the bird to launch into the air, but it will quickly spiral down to the floor uncontrollably as both wings are not providing lift. When the bird hits the floor, the force of the crash landing can cause injury such as bruising to the flight muscles or even rupture of the skin covering the bird's keel. Some people will pluck the entire flight feathers rather than clipping them. While a fully grown feather is dead, pulling the feather will induce the growth of new feathers, which will make the bird obtain flight capabilities that much quicker. A clipped feather will fall out in its normal molting sequence and then be replaced. When the flight feathers are replaced, they will have to be clipped again, but for many parrot species the flight feathers may only be molted once or twice a year. Never pull out or cut the portion contained in the outer shaft, a growing flight feather. Flight feathers that are still actively growing have a rich blood supply as discussed in Chapter 4, and pulling the live growing feather or clipping it near its base would not only cause severe pain, but it would cause severe bleeding that could even lead to death.

NUTRITION IN PET PARROTS

Tremendous advances have been made in understanding the nutrition of parrots kept in captivity, but further advances are needed to
optimize their well-being in captivity. Part of the problem is that there
are well over 100 different species of parrots kept in the pet trade,
and each has different natural dietary habitats in the wild that ideally
should be replicated in captivity. The idea that one diet is adequate
for all parrots in captivity has been abandoned, and commercial diets
that are tailored to specific types of parrots commonly kept as pets
are becoming more available.

The goal is to provide a nutritious and balanced diet for your
bird. There is a long-standing tradition and intuitive idea in the
general public that parrots eat seeds, and that is what they should
be fed. Although some parrots are seed-eaters, others eat such things
as fruit, buds, and nectar and providing a seed-only diet is a death
sentence to them. Even for seed-eaters, providing an exclusively seed-
based diet in captivity is problematic. Seed diets can be excessive in
fat, low in fiber, and low in sodium, calcium, and other vitamins and
minerals. In order to sell them as complete diets meeting all the daily
nutrient requirements of the standard parrot, the manufacturers
of these parrot seed mixes will add minerals and vitamins on the
hulls of the seeds (Figure 8.26) and add pellets, dried fruits, and
vegetables to the seeds. The hulls of the seed, along with their coat
of added supplements, will be at the bottom of the cage, as only the
kernel of the seed is eaten by the bird. The pellets and hard dried
fruits and vegetables will be ignored as the bird picks out its favorite
high-fat seeds, such as sunflowers. It is basically no different than
putting candy bars and desserts on a tray with carrots, celery, and
broccoli and giving it to children, with the expectation that they will
eat the vegetables over the other stuff.

Pelleted diets offer the advantage in manufacturing in that all the
ingredients are ground to make the diet, mixed, and then cast into
uniform pellets. Think of it as making a cake: You take all the individual ingredients and combine and mix them into a uniform batter
that is then baked to form a uniform cake. The pellets are uniform
in composition, all consumable, and ideally provide a complete and
balanced diet. However, just because it is a pelleted diet does not
mean it is nutritionally complete. You can pellet anything, including
dirt, and sell it as long as you do not falsify what it contains and
the nutrients available from its consumption. Thus, the savvy parrot
food shopper (as the shopper for any pet food) has to read labels
and make sure the diet is providing for 100 percent of all nutritional
requirements. For parrot owners, the latter gets very complicated, as
the nutritional requirements for some parrot species are not known
and the nutrient requirements of parrots varies considerably across
species, as will be discussed shortly.

Typically there has been and is still some consumer resistance
to pelleted parrot diets. The arguments range from, "they eat seeds
in the wild," which is not altogether true for many species, to the

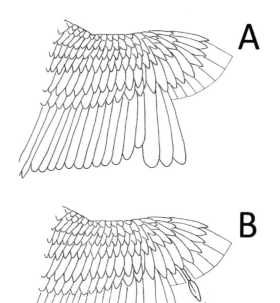

FIGURE 8.25 The safest method of preventing flight in a pet bird is
to clip the 7 primary flight feathers on each wing (a). Be aware and
avoid clipping new, developing feathers that are still receiving a
blood supply (b). Clipping one of these feathers can lead to serious
bleeding.

FIGURE 8.26 Manufacturers will often add minerals and vitamins
mixed with dyes to the hulls of seeds. The hulls end up at the
bottom of the cage, after the parrot has shelled and eaten the
internal portion of the seed.

FIGURE 8.27   Pellets often come in a mixture of colors and sizes.

FIGURE 8.28   All-natural pellets are becoming more popular in the U.S.

preference of providing different sizes, shapes, and colors associated with seed mixes, as people think this alleviates potential food boredom with their birds. To combat this, pellet manufacturers of parrot diets often make the pellets a mixture of sizes, shapes, colors, and even flavors (Figure 8.27). The dyes associated with these colors are not harmful to the birds, but may cause the droppings to be colored and the consumption of water to increase slightly as the dyes are flushed out in urine. Interestingly, with the organic all-natural movement gaining ground in the United States, many parrot owners are opting for plain colored, all organic pellets (Figure 8.28).

On a daily basis, a parrot owner should strive to have 80 to 85 percent of the bird's caloric intake be from appropriate pellets, with the other 15 to 20 percent made up of fruits, vegetables, nuts, or other human food. Although species-specific pelleted diets are becoming widely available for such species as African Greys and Eclectus, most species do not have specific manufactured diets available. However, different base diets are manufactured that have different levels of protein, fat, and fiber in them. Choose the closest pelleted diet available that matches the dietary needs of your species of parrot, and then choose supplements of fruits, nuts, vegetables, and human foods to make a complete diet. For example, the large macaws require a high-fat diet, as some of the palm nuts they consume naturally have a fat content over 50 percent. Therefore, it is essential for large macaw owners—especially those owning a Hyacinth Macaw—to choose the highest fat pelleted diet available and then supplement these pellets with high-fat foods such as macadamia and Brazil nuts.

The supplemental fruits and vegetables that parrots often enjoy are those that you eat, but in particular broccoli, apple, pear, cauliflower, berries, corn, peas, and melon are typically favored. Keep away from highly processed and fatty foods and instead go with pasta, cooked lean meat, and plain whole grain cereal. Parrots like fatty foods and junk food just like humans and will beg for it if they see you eating it, but these should be avoided or offered very sparingly. When sharing your food, keep the portions small as birds weigh very little so a little goes a long way. One piece of cooked macaroni to a budgie is like a whole heaping plate of it to you. When soft human foods are offered to your bird they should only be given for an hour or so before being removed. At room temperature bacteria will start growing on these soft, wet foods very easily. Their removal after a short time will prevent your bird from ingesting bacteria-laden soft food that has sat out for hours. Many owners offer soft foods in the early evening when they are home to remove it after a short while and because this often ensures that the birds have eaten pellets during the day and are not eating too much soft supplemental foods.

Parrots fed based on the above guidelines should not need vitamin and mineral supplements, as they should be provided with 100 percent of their dietary requirement in the pellets. Additionally, birds fed under the above guidelines will not need grit, as the pellets and soft human foods are highly digestible and do not need excessive mechanical breakdown. Finally, parrots fed on the above guidelines will not need sunlight or exposure to ultraviolet light to synthesize vitamin D, as again, the bird's vitamin D requirement will be met by consuming the fortified pelleted diet.

Converting seed-eating parrots to a pelleted diet can be a challenge. The process needs to be slow (several weeks), as you should never radically change any diet. Often, the best method is to slowly decrease the percent of the diet derived from seeds while making pellets available all day. Seed-eaters will typically resist and test whether their owner will give in and return the seeds as the owner becomes convinced the parrot is starving to death. Do not give in to the bird unless it has lost body weight. To enhance the conversion to pellets, you can add a bit of fruit juice to them to entice your bird to try them. However, the pellets that have added fruit juice should be removed within a couple of hours, as they are a great substrate for bacteria and mold growth.

Introducing new human foods can also be a challenge. Usually, any food offered the first time will be refused and likely flung on the floor. It is important to keep offering the food. To enhance its acceptance, you can mix it with one of the bird's favorite foods. But more importantly, if the bird sees you eat the food item, it is more likely to try it. This is taking advantage of flock behavior, as you are part of the bird's flock. Your acceptance and excitement for the food item will go a long way in getting the bird to eat it.

Several food items should be avoided such as chocolate and avocado, both of which are toxic. Milk should also be avoided, as birds are lactose intolerant. The seeds of such fruits as apples, pears, cherries, plums, apricots, and peaches should be avoided as well. They contain toxic compounds which wild parrots would neutralize with the ingestion of clay or other substances, but in captivity they do not have access to natural antidotes.

Amazons (**Box 8.4**) are prone to obesity in captivity, as are cockatiels and some budgies. Avoid feeding Amazons fatty foods; monitor weight in Amazons to make sure they are not becoming overweight. For most parrots, pelleted diets can be offered freely throughout the day—the parrots will only eat to meet their energy needs. However, with Amazons, the usual practice of making pellets freely available at all times may not be possible, since individual Amazons will overeat and become obese under these conditions.

FEATHER PICKING

Parrots pulling out their feathers (Figure 8.29) or mutilating their feathers (Figure 8.30) is probably the biggest problem encountered by owners of larger parrot species. Feather picking and destruction can be self-inflicted, mate-inflicted, or a combination of both. If the bird is housed with a mate and the mate is picking the feathers, then the feathers from the head of the affected bird will be plucked. If the head of the plucked bird is fine, this is a sure sign that the feather damage or plucking is self-inflicted.

BEHAVIORAL FEATHER PICKING

The causes of feather picking are not fully understood, but the causes seem to fall into three broad categories: behavioral, environmental, and medical. Behavioral feather picking can be thought of like humans smoking or biting their fingernails—it is a habit. Once a bird forms a

FIGURE 8.29 Feather picking can be a common problem in larger parrot species. Due to stress factors, this Blue-and-Gold Macaw has plucked all of its breast and abdominal feathers out.

FIGURE 8.30 Feather shredding is also a self-inflicted problem in large parrot species, such as this male Eclectus. Also, note that the length of the bill is quite long and needs to be filed down by a professional.

FIGURE 8.31 Eclectus parrots are highly prone to feather picking and shredding.

feather-picking habit, it is very difficult for them to stop it, just as it is for humans to stop their behavioral habits. What starts the habit can be more difficult to pinpoint, but boredom is a key ingredient. In the wild, parrots are busy foraging, interacting with a mate or flock mates, and can engage in other activities, such as play and exploration. Pet birds, on the other hand, are provided with food and are confined to a restricted area, typically a cage. They have less environmental stimulation. Usually, when new owners obtain a parrot, they lavish attention on the bird, but as time goes on, the attention paid by the owner may wane. If the bird does not have ample toys, activity, and/or mental stimulation to make up for the lost attention, it can start plucking its feathers out of boredom. Regretfully, many owners who may come home from work, for example, to find their bird missing a lot of feathers overreact and may perpetuate the problem. As the owner is asking the bird what is wrong and showing great concern for the bird, the bird is learning "all I have to do to get attention is pull some feathers," and a vicious habit is initiated.

Other reasons that may instigate the habit include a continuation of nesting behavior or a bad wing-clipping job. As discussed in the previous chapter, birds will pluck the feathers on their lower chest and upper abdomen in forming a brood patch for the efficient transfer of heat from the parent's body to eggs during incubation. It is not uncommon for parrots that are breeding repeatedly to continue to pluck these feathers and expand to feathers located elsewhere on the body, even when not breeding. This behavior is commonly seen, for example, in female Eclectus parrots (Figure 8.31). If the wing feathers were clipped poorly, the ragged ends of the feathers may irritate the parrot and cause plucking of the offending feathers; that spreads to plucking other feathers as the habit takes hold.

Breaking the habit of feather plucking out of boredom can be achieved, especially if intervention occurs early. Redirecting the bird's attention away from the habit by providing ample stimulation is key. Providing toys, increasing activity through playtime, or making the bird actually forage for food through the use of specialized feeders can all help. Providing the bird more attention is also good, but the attention level needs to be constant and not decrease significantly in the future or the impetus for the problem could be recreated.

ENVIRONMENTAL FEATHER PICKING

Behavioral feather picking is the most common cause of parrots plucking their feathers, followed by environmental perturbations. Dry air, allergens, and new environmental stimuli are all causes of environmental feather picking. Parrots can suffer from dry skin the same as humans, especially in the winter months when the humidity in homes may be low, as most home heating systems dry out the air. Unlike humans, birds have contour and down feathers, preventing direct contact of their skin with their feet or bills. To gain access to dry, itchy skin, birds may pluck their feathers. To help prevent this feather picking, it is important to mist your bird with water using a spray bottle on at least an every-other-day basis and provide a complete bathing opportunity at least weekly.

As discussed previously, birds have an extensive respiratory system with the air sacs having contact with most of the internal viscera. Allergens and inhaled irritants thus can be distributed extensively. Cigarette smoke, room deodorizers, cleaning product fumes, etc.—all can cause respiratory irritation, which can lead to feather plucking. The pattern of this plucking is more likely to be just the feathers of the chest and abdomen—the surface areas that lie above the internal air sacs. It is always important to access the possibility of exposure to a new inhaled irritant if a parrot starts picking its feathers.

Anxiety caused by an abrupt environmental change can also cause feather picking. Examples of this would include changing a bird's cage location or new noises associated with construction of a house next door or the road in front of the owner's house. These events are normally short lived or correctable, so that the anxiety the bird feels will be alleviated and the bird's normal routine and sense of security returned, which typically halts the feather picking before a chronic behavioral feather-picking problem develops.

MEDICAL FEATHER PICKING

There are many medically related causes or associated risk factors with feather picking. Medically induced feather picking is the least common. But birds are sensitive to metal toxicosis, with lead and zinc toxicity the most common, and this condition may be associated with feather picking. Skin infections, vitamin A deficiency, impacted feathers, thyroid problems, and obesity have also been suggested as contributors to feather picking. Some of these factors have direct links to normal feather growth and skin health. Thyroid hormones stimulate feather growth and are associated with the molting process. Vitamin A acts in birds as it does in humans in maintaining skin health. Impacted feathers are feathers that do not rupture out of the feather follicle and can cause irritation as do skin infections. Therefore, a bird may pluck its feathers to access the irritated skin. These medical factors can be treated. Consequently, the feather picking should be temporary unless it turns into a chronic habit.

Feather picking is a huge source of frustration to pet parrot owners and ultimately one of the leading reasons for parrots to be placed in rescue/sanctuary facilities (Figure 8.32). The owner feels responsible for the feather picking, and seeing and interacting with a severe feather picker that may have no feathers left on its body just further upsets the owner, until parting with the bird becomes seemingly the only option. If a complete medical check has indicated that the bird is healthy and the feather picking is simply the result of an uncontrollable habit, it is important to realize the pet bird could be relatively happy. As indicated before, chronic behavioral feather picking is no different from uncontrollable human habits, such as smoking, nail biting, etc. Just as you would not send away a child who is a chronic nail biter, sending a feather-picking bird to a parrot rescue or sanctuary is not necessary. As long as the plucked bird's environment is maintained at a warm temperature (typically about 72 degrees F because of the loss of feather insulation), the bird can still be a wonderful companion. It is also becoming more common for veterinarians to try and treat chronic behavioral feather picking with psychotropic drug therapy, but the effectiveness seems mixed.

HOUSEHOLD HAZARDS

Certain areas of a house pose more threat than others, but standing water is a threat wherever it is found in the house. Open toilets, sinks with water, pools, and bathtubs can all become death traps

FIGURE 8.32   Several rescued macaws at Feathered Friends Forever rescue facility in Harlem, Georgia.

for parrots. Parrots like to bathe and play in water, and this can attract them to standing water. However, while they may get into any of the above-described containers of water, they typically cannot get out of them once their feathers are wet—thus, they drown. In the wild, they walk into water and choose shallow pools of water from which they can easily extract themselves. Lead paint also poses a serious risk to parrots wherever it is found in the house. Parrots like to chew and explore with their tongue, so it is very easy for them to ingest the lead from paint, which can cause lead toxicity and death. Because lead is a serious threat to human health, especially for children, lead-based paints have been replaced. As a result, this problem is diminishing but can still be a worry in old houses, where the lead paint may have simply been covered up with a fresh coat of non-lead-based paint.

It is best to avoid the kitchen altogether with parrots. The typical kitchen is full of appliances with plugged in electrical cords. The parrots will simply view the electrical cords as something new to chew. Parrots have good appetites and enjoy human food but do not have a well-developed sense of what is hot because that is not something they experience in the wild. The bubbling pot of spaghetti sauce may look appetizing enough that a parrot gets on the pot and burns it feet, or parrots may simply dig into hot food and burn their tongues. In addition, the fumes generated from overheated non-stick cookware made from polytetrafluoroethylene (PTFE) are deadly to birds, while not killing other household pets.

Bedrooms are another source for problems. Parrots should not be allowed to be free in bedrooms while humans are sleeping. When the human is sleeping, the parrot may decide that it wants to be with its owner and it snuggles up on top or next to its owner. Unfortunately, the bird may start resting as well and become less alert, and when the person rolls over, the parrot is crushed, causing broken bones or death.

SICKNESS

Typically, parrots—as most pet birds—are incredibly healthy and disease free. This is very fortunate, as detecting sickness in pet birds is very difficult until they are very sick. In the wild, birds are prey animals and exhibiting signs of sickness alerts predators that this is the bird they should pursue, as it is in a weakened, less alert state. Thus, birds will hide being sick up until the point that they are so sick that they can no longer keep up the charade. When you notice your pet bird with ruffled feathers and sleeping excessively, he is very likely already extremely sick. Therefore, it is important to monitor on a daily basis food consumption and feces appearance. Food consumption varies some from day to day and less pellets may be eaten on a given day, if, for example, the day before more of a treat or of favorite fruits and vegetables were eaten. So, a decrease in food intake is an alert for you to watch your bird for other signs of sickness such as sneezing, runny nares, eye discharge, weight loss, and increased sleeping. If other signs of sickness are present, consult a veterinarian.

Observing your bird's feces can also alert you to potential sickness problems. As discussed previously in the nutrition chapter, birds void both feces and urine together out the vent of the cloaca. Normal bird dropping will consist of liquid, feces, and a white pasty material—uric acid/urates. Uric acid is the nitrogen waste product of birds that results from the digestion and metabolism of proteins, as discussed in Chapter 6. Feces, primarily undigested food, are usually brown in color, especially for birds fed pellet diets and more dark green in color for seed-eaters. The color of feces can vary, as the consumption of pellets containing dyes to make the pellets colorful will be present in the feces and often give the feces more of a red color. Similarly, if colorful fruit/berries were ingested, the feces will take on those colors as well. Birds that are not eating will have very little feces, and the fecal portion of the droppings become very dark green, almost black in appearance, and is very sticky. The feces portion should be the major component of the bird's droppings and it should be well formed in most parrot species, except for lories that consume mostly nectar and pollen and produce very liquid feces. If the feces portion is not formed, the bird has diarrhea. It is not diarrhea if the bird is voiding more water and has a very wet dropping with the fecal portion still formed, but just associated with excess relatively clear fluid. If the dropping has no formed fecal material and is a liquid mix of feces and water, then the bird has diarrhea—an indication that the bird is sick.

The white pasty urates should not be the major portion of the bird's dropping. The urates can have an off-white, creamy, slightly yellowish tint to them and still be normal. If the urate portion becomes stained green or yellow, this should be brought to the attention of your veterinarian, as it is likely a sign of illness. The final portion of the bird's dropping is the liquid urine portion. The amount produced varies widely, depending on water consumption. Often, this water consumption is in the form of fruits and vegetables, which have high water contents. For example, if your bird consumed watermelon as a treat, expect the urine volume to increase; this is not diarrhea. With a lot of fluid consumption, it is not unusual for birds to pass just urine and urates with no fecal material.

Potential health problems tend to be scrapes and bruises obtained from minor accidents. Respiratory problems are also common, and range from life-threatening diseases to minor sniffles and allergies. Endoparasites, especially intestinal worms, can occur in birds that have access to the outside, but for the typical bird maintained exclusively inside, this is not a source of concern. Ectoparasites are again relatively rare in parrots and more common in other pet bird species, but sometimes mite infestation can occur. Liver disease caused by fatty liver syndrome or hepatitis also occurs in parrots.

Avian veterinarians can be difficult to locate, and one should be identified long before the need arises, since the nearest competent avian veterinary service may be several hours away from your home location. Ideally, your veterinarian will be an avian specialist who sees many bird cases on a routine basis and has familiarity with your type of parrot. Because owners often do not discover their parrot is sick until it is seriously ill, it is best that your veterinarian has immediate access to laboratory testing facilities, as the quick results from diagnostic testing could be critical in proper diagnosis—and the difference between life and death.

COMMON PROBLEMS ENCOUNTERED

Parrots can be messy. They will often dump feed and water bowls unless they are anchored. Flinging food can be a favorite pastime, as is splashing water. But beyond the messiness, the ability to escape if the flight feathers are not clipped and their noise, some other serious problems can occur. Boredom is typically the number one issue and the root of the some of the problems just mentioned, as well as feather picking. Parrots are highly intelligent, interactive creatures. Being locked in a cage all day with nothing to do is mistreating them. Parrots should have a wide array of toys in their cages, with different toys being rotated in and out over time to provide further stimulation. Some of the toys should be wood and destructible to provide normal beak wear and entertainment. Ideally, the parrot should get playtime outside of the cage on a daily basis and interaction from its owner for stimulation.

Frequently, people who get one parrot get another one, sometimes as a source of companionship for the first parrot. Multiple parrot households present their own unique problems. The interaction of the two birds will need to be monitored closely. In some sense, it is like having two human siblings competing for their parent's attention. The new bird is viewed as an interloper and it is not unusual for the dominant bird to cause physical damage (bitten toes, for example) to the other bird. This competition does not always happen, and two birds that are the same species or close in size may form a friendship, but never assume this is going to happen, especially if you and the first bird are highly bonded. Additionally, parrots vary a lot in personality: macaws are loud and somewhat rambunctious, while Eclectus tend to be more sedate and quiet; mixing them closely together will bring stress to the Eclectus, so housing them far apart is recommended.

Parrots like a lot of sleep. In the wild, they often get 12 hours or more of sleep. In our homes, with work schedules, it is not unusual for pet birds to only get around 8 hours of sleep, which is not enough to support happy, healthy birds. Additionally, it is not uncommon for bird owners to think they are providing enough sleep to their birds because they cover their cages with a cage cover to block the light. This is not enough, as light will still filter in through the cover or under the cover, so while this may provide a restful environment, it is not a sleep environment. If at all possible, your pet bird ideally should receive about 12–14 hours of total dark for sleep time. Erring on the upper end toward 14 hours of total darkness will also have the added benefit of repressing reproductive activity to some extent. Providing 14 hours of darkness per night typically solves the problem of a pet bird that is a chronic egg layer or constantly displaying sexually.

Night frights are also a common problem. Birds are prey animals and are always conscious of activity around them when they are sleeping, and they can easily be startled by such things as strange noises, vibrations, and shining lights. The natural response to this in the wild is for the bird to fly off its perch, but when this happens in a cage, it is going to fly into the cage wall and fall down to the cage bottom. Hitting the cage bars and falling just traumatizes the bird more and may cause injury. Cockatiels and African Greys seem especially prone to this behavior. To minimize its occurrence, make sure the bird cage is located in a place that minimizes disturbances that could occur in the night.

RESCUE/SANCTUARY FACILITIES

In part because of the public's high regard for birds, pet birds are rarely euthanized. Instead, they are placed in rescue and sanctuary facilities either temporarily or permanently. Feathered Friends Forever is one of the largest pet bird rescues in the United States and is located not that far from our base at the University of Georgia. However, such bird sanctuaries exist all over the United States, as well as internationally. Birds are placed into sanctuaries for many reasons. Feathered Friends Forever accepts birds and maintains birds in residence for owners that are no longer or temporarily unable to care for their birds due to things like military service, health reasons, old age, or moving from a house to an apartment. Additionally, birds are often placed in sanctuaries because of life event changes such as the death of an owner, loss of a job, a marriage, or birth of a child. Sometimes, large parrots that are especially bonded to one person will not be compatible or may even be aggressive toward an owner's new spouse, or parents may be worried about the safety of a toddler with a parrot. But most often, parrots, especially cockatoos (**Box 8.5**), end up in rescues because of behavioral problems such as chronic feather picking or screaming or increasingly as a disposal ground for breeder parrots that are no longer productive, but may live for another decade or two. Finally, many small parrot species such as lovebirds (Figure 8.33), budgerigars, and cockatiels are considered disposable by many people. Because these birds are cheap, individuals buy them on impulse, often as gifts for holidays; after a few weeks, they end up in rescues. Common species of finch such as Zebra or Society Finches (**Box 8.6**), which are also inexpensive to purchase, often face the same fate.

As the number of pet birds increases, the demand for sanctuaries continues to grow. Many birds that end up in refuges are exceptional birds, that if adopted, would make excellent companions for owners. If you are interested in birds and gaining experience with them, many sanctuaries accept volunteer help and adopt birds.

CAPTIVE BREEDING OF PARROTS

Breeding large parrots is not easy—even successful aviculturalists often can have difficulty in successfully obtaining offspring. Additionally, the initial investment can be substantial, as many of the large macaws and cockatoos do not reach sexual maturity until they are 6 to 10 years of age, which is a long time to wait for a potential return on an investment. Even medium-sized parrots typically take three to five years to reach sexual maturity after hatch.

SEXING PARROTS

When setting up breeding pairs of parrots, for many species the first order of business is determining the sex of potential breeding birds as the majority of parrot species are not sexually dimorphic. Bird sexing can be accomplished by DNA sexing, in which a genetic analysis is performed using a blood sample to detect the presence of a sex-specific gene. This method is advantageous as it is non-invasive and relatively cheap. The disadvantage of this method is that only the sex of the bird is determined, and no assessment of the actual reproductive capability of the bird is made. With laparoscopic surgery, a small incision is made so a laparoscope can be inserted into the body

FIGURE 8.33   Lovebirds are often considered disposable by their owners in the pet trade and commonly end up in rescue facilities by the hundreds.

cavity on the left side of the bird to determine if an ovary or testes is present. The advantage of this method is that, in addition to determining if the bird is male or female, an assessment of the bird's reproductive maturity is made and anatomical structural defects in the reproductive tract may be detected. The disadvantage of this surgical method is the cost and the risk associated with anesthesia.

ACHIEVING BONDED PAIRS

The types of birds used for breeding is also important. Many imported wild-caught birds still remain in the United States. Many of these birds never adapted to captivity and have often been shunted from location to location because of their breeding inadequacy. Parrots that were hand fed and became pets are not ideal either. Although they may become successful breeders and are easy to work with because they are not afraid of humans, more often than not they are more bonded to humans and view humans as potential mates rather than a bird of the opposite sex from its species. The ideal breeding stock is parent-raised domestically born birds. These parrots are used to people and captivity, but have learned from their parents and are not bonded to humans. Finding these birds can be difficult, since they are not often produced because hand-fed babies are worth more in the pet trade. Additionally, having parents raise their offspring until they are weaned will put them out of production for a longer period of time. Thus, the short-term financial incentive is simply not there for the production of parent-raised offspring for future breeding success, and with bills to pay, it is often easy for breeders to ignore the long-term gain.

Once appropriate males and females have been identified, breeding pairs have to be set up for reproduction. Regretfully, this typically means the breeder takes an appropriate male and an appropriate female and puts them together in a breeding cage. The expense of breeder birds for medium- and large-sized parrots can easily be from $1000 to over $10,000 per pair, depending on the species. This expense typically precludes the best method of setting up pairs, in which several appropriate males and females are put in a large aviary and allowed to choose their own mates. This method is superior because parrots are highly intelligent social birds that typically pair with a mate for life. Just as humans like to make mate choices based on mutual compatibility, so do parrots.

A successful pairing will result in strongly pair-bonded birds. Pair-bonded birds feed together, with the male feeding the female during the breeding season, they preen one another, roost together, and defend their territory together. Non-bonded pairs will show no togetherness. Partially bonded pairs are very common and the toughest to diagnose. Partially bonded birds will show togetherness but do not exhibit all characteristics of a fully bonded pair. They often produce infertile eggs or will hatch babies, but will not feed them—or will even kill them.

MATE TRAUMA

In confined areas associated with captivity and without the normal daily activities associated with survival in the wild, mate trauma can occur in breeding pairs of captive parrots. This trauma is associated with bite wounds to the beak, feet, eyes, wing and/or tail. If the birds are not separated, death often occurs. In Eclectus and Vasa Parrots, the female is dominant, while in cockatoos, the male is dominant. Male cockatoos (excluding cockatiels) are notorious for killing female mates in captive breeding situations. In other species, the two sexes tend to be more balanced, but individual problems within a given pair can occur.

The key to preventing mate trauma is vigilant observation. This means looking for injuries, but for many breeders it involves monitoring breeding areas with video feeds so that the birds can be observed without disturbing them for signs of problems. If mate trauma is occurring, the flight feathers of the aggressor can be clipped. More importantly—especially for cockatoos—escape nest boxes are highly recommended. These nest boxes are designed with double entrance/exit holes (Figure 8.34 b) so that as the aggressor comes into the nest box through one hole, the mate can leave through the other hole, preventing it from being trapped and potentially killed.

NEST BOXES

Nest boxes are typically made out of wood, plastic, or metal. Wood is ideal, as most parrot species are cavity nesters in trees. Wood nest boxes also can be chewed by the parrots and this activity helps to stimulate reproduction. The disadvantage of wood is that it is hard to clean and disinfect; this, combined with damage from chewing activity, results in the wood boxes needing to be replaced, as much as every breeding season for some species. Metal and durable plastic nest boxes have the

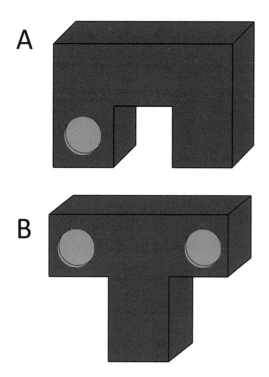

FIGURE 8.34   Two types of nest boxes. Depending on the species, the nesting pair may require a dark, secure box with a single opening (a), or a box with two openings to offer an escape route to help prevent mate trauma (b).

advantage of being easy to clean and disinfect. Large macaws can even destroy metal nest boxes in one breeding season, but for most species, they are highly durable and can be used year after year. With metal and plastic nest boxes, it is more important that the nesting material be shavings that include larger pieces of wood that can turn into shavings, thereby satisfying the reproductive need to chew wood.

Commercially available nest boxes come in all sizes and configurations. Do not be afraid to experiment with different styles of nest boxes until success occurs. If the breeding cage has ample room, allowing the pair of parrots a choice of a couple of different nest boxes is a good option. Ideally, nest boxes should be constructed to make the female or both the female and male feel secure, which often means a configuration that limits light exposure (Figure 8.34a) and fits the incubating parent's body size. The nest box also must be functional for the caretaker to clean and be equipped with inspection door(s) so fertility of eggs and health of the babies can be assessed. Often, nest boxes are constructed so that miniature cameras can be placed in them. In this way, the bird breeder can monitor nesting progress without disturbing the parents.

When locating nest boxes in a breeding cage, the goal is for the birds to feel their nest location is secure. Thus, place the entrance hole of the nest box away from disturbances and typically as far away as possible from the feeding and watering location, which the caretaker accesses on a daily basis. The nest box entrance hole should be above the caretaker's head height, which will also provide a sense of security for the pair of parrots. If several pairs of birds are being bred at a location, it is often necessary to provide solid partitions between breeding cages so individual pairs cannot see one another. In addition to the proper location of the nest box, it is important to enhance copulation success with proper perches. Providing double perches—two separate perches at the same level spaced close together—allows the female to stand on one perch, where she can lean forward and balance herself by placing her beak on the other perch, while the male is standing on her back for copulation. Species of macaws breed side to side without the male standing on the female's back. Perches need to be well secured so that copulation is not interrupted by perches moving. Finally, the perches should be rough and the correct diameter so that the female can get a secure grip during copulation.

BREEDING DIETS

Providing a nutrient-dense diet is important to help stimulate and allow successful reproduction, as discussed in the previous chapter. Diets for breeding need to provide more calcium for egg shell formation. As there is massive growth of the testes, ovary, and oviduct, a higher dietary protein level is needed to support this tissue growth. Additionally, the female has increased dietary energy and protein requirements for egg synthesis, and this is typically met with increased dietary fat and protein concentrations. The increased dietary protein and energy levels also support the growth of chicks once they hatch. There is a variety of commercially available breeder diets; most offer the needed increase in dietary protein, but the degree to which dietary fat is increased in the breeder diets is highly variable.

INFERTILE EGGS AND EGG BREAKAGE

Even if a pair of parrots proceeds to the production of eggs, getting fertile eggs in many captive-bred parrot species—especially medium- and large-sized parrot species—is a real challenge. The causes for infertility are varied but may include the birds being the same sex, the male being reproductively immature, or the pair not being pair bonded. Additional causes could be improper perches, health problems—especially with overweight males, as this reduces fertility—and environmental stress, which may prevent the pair from copulating, while not preventing the female from laying eggs.

It is not unusual for parrot pairs in captivity to purposefully and chronically break eggs or to even stop incubating at some point during the incubation period. This may be due to lack of pair bonding or environmental stress. In this situation, the eggs need to be taken from the parents for artificial incubation. Eggs are also removed from parents for artificial incubation to induce them to produce a second or even third clutch of eggs and thus increase offspring production.

HAND-FEEDING

As hand-feeding baby parrots is labor intensive and challenging, most breeders will allow parents to raise their chicks for the first 10 to 14 days before they remove the chicks and hand-feed them, which still results in ideal pet parrots (Figure 8.35). However, babies that result from artificial incubation will have to be hand fed a few hours after hatch. Hatchlings may be removed prior to 10 to 14 days from the parents because the parents refuse to feed their offspring or because they actually kill their babies. This behavior again results from the pair not being pair bonded or from environmental stress. If the clutch has an asynchronous hatch, some of the older chicks may also be removed prior to 10 to 14 days, to allow the last chicks that hatched a better chance of survival with less competition from older siblings.

Hand-fed babies are typically kept in brooders that provide heat and humidity. The brooder is maintained at about 95–98 degrees F for just-hatched chicks through two days of age, and then the temperature is decreased about half a degree every 24 hours. Be observant and adjust the temperature if babies are panting or if a group of babies is not staying together and avoiding contact and each other's heat. In contrast, if the babies are shivering, huddled tightly together, and food digestion is slow, then the babies are too cold. Brooders are maintained relatively dark to simulate the natural conditions of most nest cavities. As parrots are altricial chicks, their eyes are not developed fully at hatch and will not open for several days to a couple of weeks, depending on the species. Within brooders, babies are typically kept in small containers lined with soft padding that also allows for them to prop their heads up. The soft lining material will be changed often to maintain a clean environment free of bacterial growth. Healthy and happy babies sleep most of the day and wake up to be fed, only to go back to sleep once feeding is accomplished.

A variety of commercial hand-feeding formulas are available for purchase. The nutritional composition of these formulas varies widely, and an appropriate one needs to be purchased based on the species of parrots being fed. For example, large macaws need high-fat formulas. The protein content needs to be high (22–26 percent) in species that grow and fledge very quickly, while the protein level can be slightly lower in species that grow slower and don't fledge for months. The formula will be mixed with water following the manufacturer's guidelines, but in general hatchlings are fed about one part formula and eight parts water for the first 24 hours after feeding commences—about 12 hours after hatch. Baby birds should not be fed immediately after hatch; they

FIGURE 8.35 Hand-fed Blue-fronted Amazon babies.

have the retained yolk sac with yolk (Chapter 7) that provides nutrients in the period after hatch. The formula is thickened slowly, so that the ratio is about 1 to 2 by 14 days of age. As the bird gets older, the formula can be thickened to a ratio of 1 to 1.5.

Formula will be fed at temperatures from 98 to 108 degrees F. Most birds seem to prefer 102 to 105 degrees F, but individual preferences slightly outside this range are seen. It is imperative for the heated formula to be well mixed so it is a uniform temperature and for an accurate thermometer to be used. Formula fed too hot will burn a hole through the crop, while formula fed too cold is likely not to leave the crop for digestion. The formula will typically be fed with a syringe or pipette. When hand-feeding the baby bird, you will pick the bird up, support its head with one hand, and touch-stimulate the bird if it is already not opening its mouth, begging for food. Once the mouth is open, food will be given, and the bird will normally grab on to the tip of the syringe or pipette with it mouth and bob/pump its head as it swallows the food you are giving it (Figure 8.36). It is critical to just fill the crop and not overfeed the bird. If too much is fed, the bird will start to regurgitate the food and often then will aspirate on the food and die. After feeding the bird, any excess formula around the mouth or dripped onto the bird's chest or head is wiped away to prevent a place for potential bacteria colonization. Hand-feeding the bird will occur every couple of hours to start with, but as the bird gets older, feeding will be spaced four or more hours apart (Table 8.1).

TABLE 8.I. AN AVERAGE HAND-FEEDING SCHEDULE FOR AN AFRICAN GREY

Day of age	Feeding frequency	Number of feedings per day
1–4	every 2 hours	10
5–10	every 3 hours	7
11–14	every 4 hours	5
15–40	every 5 hours	4
41–65	every 6 hours	3
66–weaning	up to 2 feedings, for about 5 days, then one feeding at night while the bird learns to eat on its own	

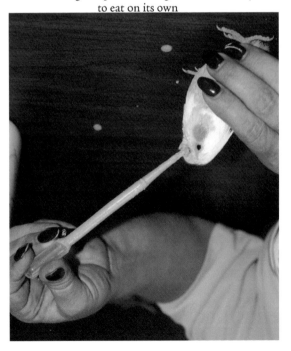

FIGURE 8.36   Hand-fed parrots are often hand-fed using a large syringe or pipette to deliver the formula as seen here when hand-feeding this young Cockatiel.

The baby bird should be hand-fed only when the crop is empty or almost empty. Avoid topping off with new food before the old has passed out of the crop, as this can lead to food not leaving the crop and bacterial growth in the crop. The crop should be allowed to completely empty at least once a day in older birds, once or twice a day in birds less than two weeks of age. If food is not passing from the crop into the proventriculus, the formula may have been under-hydrated and the crop is now compacted. The food may have been too cold when fed or the brooder is too cold. Finally, the baby may have a bacterial infection. If the crop does not empty and the brooder temperature is correct, a small amount of warm water

(102–105 degrees F) can be fed, after which the crop can very, very gently be massaged—this will help if the original formula was fed under-hydrated. Also, check the vent area to make sure it is not blocked with dried fecal material. It is better to err on the formula being a little too watery when fed, as this will simply result in you having to feed the bird more often, but will not cause crop stasis, as feeding formula too thick will. Always make sure feeding utensils are sterile to help prevent bacterial infections of the crop, which are typically deadly. Finally, it is not uncommon for air to be inflating the crop some after hand-feeding, as the bird typically swallows air along with food. Leave the air alone, it will dissipate on its own.

Weaning occurs over time, and every bird is different. As the birds become fully feathered and start to perch, start offering soft foods and pellets to the bird. Typically, their natural curiosity will cause them to investigate and even consume the food. As the bird transitions from hand-feeding to eating on its own, it will become disinterested in being fed by hand. Encourage them to eat on their own by only feeding them at the end of the day before their bedtime. Weaning babies will lose weight; this is natural and actually good, as hand-fed babies are typically slightly overweight before weaning anyhow. Generally, for birds that do not wean, it is the hand-feeder that is the cause of the problem and their unwillingness to allow the bird to become independent.

It should be apparent from the foregoing that hand-feeding birds is a labor-intensive process, where many problems can occur that lead to the death of the bird. It is not something for a novice to attempt. Some breeders will sell at a discounted price birds that are not weaned, as it will save them a lot of work. Do not be tempted if you do not have hand-feeding experience—it is typically a recipe for disaster.

FURTHER INFORMATION

There is a plethora of further information available on parrot-related topics. A very good general website for parrot information with extensive links to more specific information can be found at http://www.birdchannel.com/. Many species associations and societies exist such as the National Cockatiel Society (http://www.cockatiels.org/main/), the American Budgerigar Society (http://www.abs1.org/), and African Lovebird Society (http://www.africanlovebirdsociety.com/). There are magazine sources of information, including Bird Talk and the AFA Watchbird, with the latter publication complimentary with membership to the American Federation of Aviculture (http://www.afabirds.org/). There are also a host of organizations that support parrot conservation such as the World Parrot Trust (http://www.parrots.org/), Loro Parque Foundation (http://www.loroparque-fundacion.org/), and Parrots International (http://www.parrotsinternational.org/).

SUMMARY

Parrots are highly intelligent and social birds that have been maintained as pets and thrilling their owners for thousands of years. Parrots can be challenging pets, as their behaviors, training, and life spans are very different from the commonly kept pets—dogs and cats. Because of their pet potential, many parrot species have been relentlessly trapped from the wild. At least 19 species of parrots are already extinct and another 97 species of parrots are currently threatened with extinction. It is imperative for the demand for pet parrots to be met through the reproduction of domesticated birds so that the illegal smuggling of wild-caught birds ceases entirely.

BOX 8.1 KAKAPO

The Kakapo is the heaviest parrot, with males weighing up to 4 kilograms (Clout and Merton, 1998) with a more typical average weight of 2.2 kilograms (Kakapo Recovery, 2012). Females weigh 30 to 40 percent less than males, with a typical weight of about 1.4 kilograms (Kakapo Recovery, 2012). Adult weights fluctuate by as much as 100 percent or more (Clout and Merton, 1998) based on food availability. Both males and females can add about a kilogram of fat reserves prior to the breeding season (Kakapo Recovery, 2012). Despite having large wings, the Kakapo Parrot is flightless. This herbivore species of parrot walks through its forest and scrubland range feeding on fruits, seeds, buds, leaves, and roots of a wide variety of plant species. It is a very good climber and will climb trees for food. It is also nocturnal, and it appears more like a large owl than a typical parrot. Similar to an owl, it has very soft feathers, which are green mottled with flecks of brownish gold and black (Box Image 8.1). These parrots have been described as having a strong musty, distinctive smell that actually alerts introduced predators to the presence of the bird, which was a primary cause of its rapid population decline (Kakapo Recovery, 2012). Vocally, the Kakapo has a wide range of sounds beyond the usual squawk typical of large parrots. Its other calls could be mistaken for a braying donkey, a grunting or squealing pig, or a booming bittern (Kakapo Recovery, 2012). It also produces metallic-sounding noises called "chinging." As with other large parrots, it is estimated that Kakapo can live up to 90 years of age.

BOX IMAGE 8.1   The critically endangered Kakapo parrot.

The reproductive characteristics of Kakapo are also highly unusual for parrot species, as they are the only known lekking species of parrot. Males do not start breeding until they are about four years old, while females do not start breeding until they are six years old. Reproduction in sexually mature adults does not occur every year. Kakapo Parrots are opportunistic breeders that will breed when there is episodic mass fruiting of podocarp trees, which happens in intervals from two to five years. In particular, Kakapo very much prefer the rimu fruit of the rimu tree species of the podocarp family. If fruit production is heavy and the birds have gained the body condition necessary for reproduction, the males will display vocally at night to attract females. Breeding activity normally starts in earnest in December when males start booming from a series of excavated bowls linked by tracks that are kept clear and defended by each male. From his bowl, a male will fill his thoracic air sacs and then emit a low-sounding boom. This boom will be followed by 20 to 30 more booms before they make a high-pitched nasal metallic call, or "ching." A male may produce as many as 1000 booms in a night and because the cleared bowls for lekking will be found on high ridges or hilltops with low-growing vegetation, the boom produced by the male can be heard up to 5 km away (Shewokis, 2011). Lekking behavior can last from two to three months. Females attracted by the booming select and mate with the competing males. The female then lays one to four eggs in the nest she has made. Incubation lasts for about 30 days, and because the male does not participate in the reproduction beyond copulation, the female has to leave the nest during incubation and brooding to find food, which puts the eggs and chicks at high risk for predation. Chicks typically fledge in about ten weeks, but mothers will often continue to feed chicks up to six months of age.

It was easy for the predecessors of today's Kakapo to give up flight in favor of being able to add extra weight, because prior to Polynesian settlement (about 1000 years ago), there were no land-based mammals and only three species of small bats in New Zealand (Clout and Merton, 1998; Kakapo Recovery, 2012). With the Polynesian settlers came their dogs and rats, which preyed upon the Kakapo and their eggs. In addition, the Polynesian settlers also found the Kakapo easy to catch, and its meat was considered a delicacy. By the time the Europeans arrived in the early 1800s, the number of Kakapo had already declined and was not found in many parts of New Zealand. Their decline was only hastened by the European settlers who cleared forests and brought with them new predators such as cats, stoats, and more rat species, as well as food competitors such as possums, deer, and domesticated sheep. Charlie Douglas, a Westland explorer, wrote of Kakapo in 1899, "they could be caught in the moonlight, when on the low scrub, by simply shaking the tree or bush until they tumbled on the ground, something like shaking down apples. I have seen as many as half a dozen kakapos shaken off one tutu bush this way," (Kakapo Recovery, 2012). In fact, the vulnerability of Kakapo to predation by introduced mammals is singularly unique compared to all other terrestrial birds, given its flightlessness, nocturnal behavior, ground nesting, and rearing of altricial young only by the female (Merton, 1976; Best and Powlesland, 1985; Merton, 1994; Clout and Merton, 1998).

By the 20th century, Kakapo sightings were very rare. From the late 1940s to the late 1970s, the wildlife service made over 60 expeditions to find Kakapo, with little success. By 1977, 18 males were known to exist in Fiordland, but no females were known to exist—the species was considered to be doomed for extinction. However, later that year a population of about 200 Kakapo Parrots was found in southern Stewart Island, and this population contained females. This population was in rapid decline due to feral cats. Thus, in 1987 the decision was made to move all remaining Kakapo to offshore island sanctuaries. Today, Kakapo Parrots are kept on two islands, Codfish and Anchor. Breeding success was initially poor on these islands due in part to continued predation of chicks by rats; by 1995, only 3 of at least 12 chicks had survived. This led to a reevaluation of the recovery program and the formation of a National Kakapo Team and Kakapo Recovery Program. In 1998, rats were eradicated on Codfish Island, and in 2001, stoats were eradicated on Anchor island, thereby making both islands suitable as long-term sanctuaries for the Kakapo (Kakapo Recovery, 2012).

During the recovery program, another unexpected problem arose which threatened the success of the program. As discussed earlier, Kakapo are opportunistic breeders that breed in synchrony with the fruiting of podocarp trees, in particular rimu fruit. To ensure that females were in good enough breeding condition to breed more often, and that enough food was available to prevent chicks from starving, a supplementary feeding program was initiated, in which feed dispensers were placed in the home range of individual female Kakapo. This program was successful in increasing the number of females with a body condition to support a reproductive attempt, the number of eggs produced per clutch, and preventing starvation of chicks if the rimu crop failed to ripen. However, an unexpected side effect of the supplemental feeding was a skew in the sex ratio of produced offspring toward the more expensive sex, which is the larger and faster-growing male. Clout et al. (2002) reported that, in 18 clutches produced from 1978, 13 males and 5 females were produced in supplemented clutches, while 4 male and 11 female offspring were produced by non-supplement-fed females. The male bias is as expected, given the original hypothesis that females should manipulate the sex ratio of offspring toward the more costly sex when resources are abundant. But given that the original population of Kakapo moved to the sanctuary islands were already heavily male-biased, the supplementary feeding program was making the shortage of female Kakapo even direr. Subsequently, the supplementary feeding program was modified in the winter of 2001. With the new feeding regimen, supplemental food was only offered ad libitum in the months prior to mating in mid-January to females predicted to have a weight below 1.5 kilograms in December. Females with a weight predicted to be above 1.5 kilograms were only minimally provisioned at their feeders to maintain their interest in the feeder. After mating, all females were provided supplemental feed ad libitum. In 2002, all adult females but one produced eggs, and there was no sex bias in either those fed ad libitum or minimally provisioned females (Robertson et al., 2006).

From a low total population of about 50 individuals in 1995, the population had risen to a high of 131 individuals in 2011. Over half of these birds are in the young breeder stage (Kakapo Recovery, 2012; Shewokis, 2011). Subsequent deaths due to age and accidents have lowered the current population to 127 individuals as of early 2012. With the kinks worked out of the recovery program, there is increasing optimism for the survival of the Kakapo. With the anticipated continued success of the recovery program, the next hurdle facing the Kakapo is similar to that of the flightless Kiwi discussed in the ratite section, in that there needs to be large predator-free islands established that could hold Kakapo populations greater than the 100-bird capacity of the current sanctuary islands (Kakapo Recovery, 2012).

BOX 8.2 MACAWS

The macaws show a wide variety of sizes from the largest Hyacinth Macaw (Box Image 8.2.1), which can measure almost 3.5 feet, to the Red-shouldered Macaw (Box Image 8.2.2), which at 12 to 14 inches in length is the smallest macaw. All macaws are characterized by having long tail feathers, large beaks, and facial skin patches that may or may not have tiny feather tracts in them, depending on the species. Many of the macaws—especially the larger species—have strikingly beautiful colored plumage. They are native formally to the Caribbean and found today in Mexico and Central and South America. Depending on the species, they are found in tropical forests or open forests associated with savannas.

BOX IMAGE 8.2.1 The Hyacinth Macaw is the largest macaw species.

BOX IMAGE 8.2.2 The Red-shoudered Macaw is the smallest macaw species.

Because of their bold appearance, intelligence, and friendliness, the macaws have been highly desired as pets. Several of the large macaws are common pets such as the Red and Green (green-wing), Blue and Yellow (Gold), Scarlet, and Military macaws (Box Image 8.2.3). In addition, because of their size, some of the large macaws weigh over 3 pounds. They have also been hunted and eaten by humans. The combination of man's persecution of macaws for the pet trade and food, combined with habitat loss and restricted ranges for many macaw species, has led to a high rate of extinction and endangerment. BirdLife International (BirdLife International, 2012) lists 22 macaw species; of these, the population status of 5, 3, 4, 2, 1, and 7 are considered extinct, critically endangered, endangered, vulnerable, near threatened, and least concern, respectively. Of the three critically endangered species, the Glaucous Macaw is likely extinct, as there is no documented observation of this species since the 1960s; the Spix's Macaw is likely extinct in the wild, with less than 100 existing in captivity; and the Blue-throated Macaw, which has between 200 and 500 individuals left in the wild—but many more than these exist in captivity, as they breed well in captivity and are even available in the pet trade in the United States. The Spix's Macaw is successfully breeding in captivity, especially at the Al Wabra Wildlife Preservation in Qatar, where over half of the roughly 100 existing birds of this species are maintained. Loro Parque Foundation of the Canary Islands is also successfully breeding the Spix's Macaw.

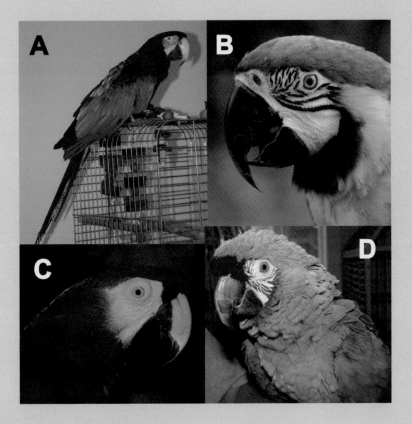

BOX IMAGE 8.2.3 Various macaws: Green-wing (a), Blue and Yellow/Gold (b), Scarlet (c), and Military (d).

In addition to the successful breeding of the Spix's Macaw, both Loro Parque and Al Wabra Wildlife Preservation are successfully breeding the Lear's Macaw, which prior to the past couple of years had only bred successfully in captivity once, at Busch Gardens, Florida. The wild population of the Lear's Macaw has also increased from a low of about 60 individuals in the late 1980s to about 1000 today. This has resulted in its movement from critically endangered to just endangered. The success of the Lear's Macaw recovery through habitat protection and guarding nest sites from poachers provides hope that no more extant macaws will be lost to extinction. There is also a pay-back program to local farmers that pays them more if the macaws eat their corn than they would make on the common market; this stops them from killing Lear's Macaws,

As pets, macaws can make excellent life-long companions. The macaws tend to be very mouth- and beak-tactile and explore with their mouths and tongues. So, if you will be intimidated by a large bird exploring your arms and fingers, etc., with a large beak, a macaw is not the right bird for you. They are playful, incredibly loyal, adaptable, highly trainable, and like a fair amount of physical contact. They can get wound up and overexcited—a clear warning of this will be eye blazing, in which the pupils of the eyes constrict to reveal greater iris area, only to rapidly dilate and constrict repeatedly.

Macaws can generate very loud vocal noises so close neighbors are not recommended. With strangers, they love to lunge like they are going to bite only to pull back. The large macaws eat palm nuts which can require over 1000 pounds of force to open, so macaw cages must be very strong, preferably with the bars placed through drilled holes of crossbar holders, since the welds of welded cages are typically broken. Finally, it is essential to provide macaws with a high-fat diet.

Regretfully, because of the popularity of macaws as pets and the desire to create different plumage colorations, some captive macaw breeders have chosen to hybridize the large macaws. This practice is shameful, given the limited genetics for these species in captivity and for some in overall existence. An example of a hybrid is the Catalina Macaw (Box Image 8.2.4), obtained from breeding a Blue and Yellow Macaw with a Scarlet Macaw. At this point, even the hybrids are, in turn, being crossed with pure macaws to generate interesting colored hybrids, but again at a cost of further contaminating the original wild species genetics.

BOX IMAGE 8.2.4   The Catalina Macaw is a hybrid between a Blue and Yellow Macaw and a Scarlet Macaw.

BOX 8.3 AFRICAN GREYS AND ECLECTUS

The African Grey Parrot is found in the wild in Western Central Africa. It consists of two subspecies, the Congo and the Timneh. The Timneh subspecies has darker colored gray plumage and maroon-colored tail feathers (Box Image 8.3.1). It is also considerably smaller (300 grams) than the larger (475 grams), lighter-gray-colored Congo African Grey (Box Image 8.3.2). The Congo African Grey also has bright red tail feathers. The African Grey is one of the most common mid-sized pet parrots in America. They are also popular worldwide and are still exported internationally both legally (CITES regulated) and illegally from Africa. African Greys make wonderful pets, and both species are equally adept at talking, but both subspecies can take a little longer to start talking (over a year) than other parrot species that can be less than half a year old when they commence talking. African Greys use language for meaningful communication that is contextually relevant (Pepperberg, 2006; Colbert-White et al., 2011). They enjoy human physical contact and are highly empathic and sense and respond to their owner's moods and possibly their thoughts (Sheldrake and Morgana, 2003). They are fairly adaptable, with possibly the Timneh subspecies being slightly more easygoing and adaptable. Socialization at a young age—by exposing them to as many people and situations as possible—makes them better adjusted to handle change. Feather picking can be a problem in Greys. They can be prone to hypocalcaemia, and specialized African Grey diets are manufactured, commercially available, and recommended. When scared, African Greys can utter a very alarming and loud continuous growl.

BOX IMAGE 8.3.1   Timneh African Grey

BOX IMAGE 8.3.2   Congo African Grey

The Eclectus Parrot is found in the wild in the Solomon Islands, New Guinea, and associated islands, as well as in Northeastern Australia. These parrots are known for their dramatic reverse sexual dimorphism, in which the female is much more brilliantly colored (Box Image 8.3.3). However, the red and purple colors of the female make her nearly impossible to spot when she is nesting in hollowed-out tree cavities, while the green colors of the male allow him to blend into the tree canopy. Females are fed by the males while nesting and spend much of their adult life in a nesting situation and may be brought food by more than one male. In the wild, Eclectus eat fruits that are relatively low in protein, high in simple sugars and packed with antioxidants such as beta carotene and vitamin A. These fruits are also very high in fiber. In captivity, Eclectus are hearty eaters if provided with high-fiber fruit and vegetable options. Typically, they tend to like wet, mushy fruits such as figs. So while pellets can be fed to Eclectus, especially those that are specifically formulated for them, it is essential to provide them with bulk (fiber) with ample fruits and vegetables that have high water content. The supplemental fruit and vegetables should also provide the high levels of antioxidants that these birds are accustomed to in the wild.

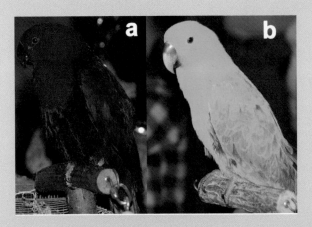

BOX IMAGE 8.3.3   Eclectus parrots exhibit reverse sexual dimorphism with the female (a) having more brightly colored plumage than the male (b).

As pets, Eclectus are somewhat more sedate and enjoy being near humans, sitting on a shoulder or beside a human, but they do not tend to prefer an abundant amount of physical contact, such as petting. There are at least seven subspecies of Eclectus in the wild that vary mostly on size with slight color modifications. The Grand, Vosmaeri, Solomon Island (Box Image 8.3.4) and Red-sided subspecies are all commonly found in the pet trade in the United States. Some breeders insist that the health of males can be assessed somewhat visually, as the upper beak should look like Halloween candy corn—that is, bright orange at the top followed by yellow color to the tip. If the beak is uniform yellow, that may be an indication of poor health. Eclectus Parrots are known for their hairlike feathers but they are also prone to feather pick in captivity. This especially seems to be the case in females and may be related to nesting behavior.

BOX IMAGE 8.3.4   Solomon Island subspecies of Eclectus.

BOX 8.4 AMAZONS

Amazon Parrots are very common and popular in the United States as a mid-sized pet parrot. There are just over 30 species of Amazon Parrots in the wild. They can be found in the wild from Mexico down through Central and South America, as well as on several Caribbean islands. Although CITES-listed, because of their proximity and good pet characteristics, they are still illegally and commonly smuggled into the United States. Two species of Amazons are classified as extinct—the Martinique Amazon and the Guadeloupe Amazon. The Puerto Rican Amazon is critically endangered, and an active captive breeding program is ongoing in an attempt to prevent the extinction of this species. The Puerto Rican Amazon population has rebounded from less than 20 to over 200 individuals. Amazons are predominantly green in plumage color, short tailed, and identified from one another at the species level in part based on head, neck, and wing colors.

As pets, they often exhibit excellent human speech and singing abilities. They are outgoing, loyal, curious, excitable, and playful. This good outgoing nature makes them more adaptable and less prone to behavioral issues, compared to several other parrot species. They enjoy toys, especially ones that can be chewed and destroyed. As discussed earlier, they are prone to obesity more than other parrot species in captivity and body weight needs to be monitored. When sexually mature, they can react more strongly to seasonal hormone changes than other parrots. During this time, they are more prone to be a bit nippy and when they bite, they tend to hold on and not pinch and let go like macaws and cockatoos. Common species in the pet trade include the Blue-fronted, Yellow-naped, Orange-winged, and Yellow-headed Amazons (Box Image 8.4.1). Domestically raised hand-fed Amazons from these four species have good temperament, excellent talking capability, and playful personalities (Box Image 8.4.2). Several species of Amazons such as Red-crowned, Lilac-crowned, and Red-lored that have escaped captivity in California have established feral populations, some of which are successfully breeding.

BOX IMAGE 8.4.I   (a) Yellow-headed Amazon, (b) Blue-fronted Amazon, (c) Yellow-naped Amazon, (d) Lilac-crowned Amazon

BOX IMAGE 8.4.2   Amazons raised in captivity, like this Yellow-headed Amazon, can be quite playful and even enjoy riding remote-controlled cars.

BOX 8.5 COCKATOOS

Native to Australasia, the cockatoos vary in size from the very large Palm Cockatoo (Box Image 8.5.1) to the very small cockatiel (Box Image 8.5.2), one of the most commonly kept parrots in captivity. If the cockatiel is excluded, all the other cockatoos are medium- to large-sized parrots. There are just over 20 species of cockatoos and while the Philippine Cockatoo and Yellow-crested Cockatoo are critically endangered, over half of the species are classified as least concern for extinction by BirdLife International. Some species are considered agricultural pests and persecuted as such. Known for their striking feathered crests, most cockatoos are either white or black, along with a couple of species that have pink and/or gray plumage coloration, with the Major Mitchell's (Box Image 8.5.3) and Galah (Box Image 8.5.4) being incredibly beautiful birds. Many of the species, especially the black cockatoos like the Palm Cockatoo (Box Image 8.5.1), are exceptionally rare in aviculture in the United States. However, several of the light-colored cockatoos—including the White or Umbrella Cockatoo (Box Image 8.5.5), Salmon-crested or Moluccan Cockatoo (Box Image 8.5.6), and Tanimbar or Goffin Cockatoo (Box Image 8.5.7)—are fairly widely available. As pets, the large cockatoos can be very demanding. They love attention and especially like to be held and petted. They also can bond very strongly to one individual and be protective of that individual. This also can make re-homing large cockatoos very difficult. With cockatoos, it is best to heavily socialize them while they are young and to establish a regulated and constant level of attention to them. Cockatoos that become accustomed to high levels of attention can develop behavioral issues such as feather picking and constant repetitive movements or noises if this level of attention disappears. However, a well-socialized and trained large cockatoo like a Moluccan or an Umbrella is probably the best pet parrot for someone looking for a hands-on, affectionate, and playful pet bird. Furthermore, the cockatiel is an ideal starter bird. They possess the wonderful characteristics of the larger cockatoos, but are more adaptable, inexpensive, and easy to maintain in a typical household. Before purchasing a cockatoo or cockatiel, a prospective owner should spend time with these birds, as they have powder feathers and produce lots of dander on a constant basis, which can cause an allergic response in some people.

BOX IMAGE 8.5.1   Palm Cockatoo

BOX IMAGE 8.5.2   Cockatiel

BOX IMAGE 8.5.3   Major Mitchell's Cockatoo

BOX IMAGE 8.5.4   Galah or Rose-breasted Cockatoo

BOX IMAGE 8.5.5   White Cockatoo

BOX IMAGE 8.5.6   Salmon-crested or Moluccan Cockatoo

BOX IMAGE 8.5.7   Goffin or Tanimbar Cockatoo

BOX 8.6 SOFTBILLS AND FINCHES

The term softbill was developed in part to provide a name to a collection of birds that were not parrots, but kept by humans as caged-bird pets. They do not have soft bills: the name was originally coined as more of a reflection of the soft foods—such as fruits, insects, and leaves—that many of the species clumped into the softbill category consumed. Originally, the birds lumped into this category included toucans, mynahs (mynas), starlings, turacos, and hornbills, but it has expanded over time to include other birds, such as tanagers, jays, and thrushes (Box Image 8.6.1).

BOX IMAGE 8.6.1 Softbills have expanded to include a variety of colorful birds. From top left, clockwise: White-naped Brush-Finch, White-throated Magpie-Jay, Blue-gray Tanager, Scarlet-thighed Dacnis, Golden-hooded Tanager, Passerini's Tanager, Green Honeycreeper, Silver-throated Tanager.

The term finch also had a broad definition in aviculture to include small- and medium-sized birds that possess strong, sharp, relatively stout beaks designed for holding and cracking seeds. This definition includes a great number of passerine bird species that often fall into one of the following families: Fringillidae (the true finches), Emberizidae (American sparrows, seedeaters, and allies), Estrildidae (waxbills, grass finches, and munias), and Viduidae (whydahs). There is overlap between species considered finches and softbills, and some aviculturalists will lump finches into the softbill category. Many of the softbill and finch species—especially those from South and Central America—are still routinely imported to the United States.

Toucans, mynahs, and starlings are commonly kept softbills. The toucans belong to the family Ramphastidae and actually are broken into three separate categories, roughly based on size. The toucans are the largest (Box Image 8.6.2 a & b), toucanets (Box Image 8.6.2 d) are medium sized, and the aracari (Box Image 8.6.2 c) are the smallest. As impressive as the bills are on these birds they are actually incredibly lightweight, as internally they are hollow and honeycombed. Toucans, toucanets, and aracari use these long bills to reach the fruit of trees suspended at the ends of branches. Because of their weight, these birds cannot perch at the ends of branches without the branches bending and breaking. Additionally, these birds also consume the nestlings of other birds (Box Image 8.6.3), and the long beaks help in extracting their victims from their nests. Finally, it may also serve in thermoregulation, allowing the bird to lose excess heat.

BOX IMAGE 8.6.2   Keel-billed Toucan (a), Chestnut-madibled Toucan (b), Collared Aracari (c), and Emerald Toucanet (d) in Costa Rica.

BOX IMAGE 8.6.3   Toucans are opportunistic and will often consume the nestlings from other birds' nests for extra protein nutrition.

With starlings, we normally think of the invasive European Starling, but the Sturnidae family—which includes starlings, mynahs, and two species of oxpeckers—has over 100 species. Many of the starling species such as the Violet-backed (Amethyst) Starling and Emerald Starling are two of the most striking bird species (Box Image 8.6.4). The mynahs are well known for their vocal mimicry, and the Hill Mynah can mimic human voices more clearly than even parrots renowned for this ability, such as African Greys. The beautiful Bali Mynah (Box Image 8.6.5) is critically endangered, with less than 100 mature adults in the wild because of illegal poaching for the pet trade (BirdLife International, 2012).

BOX IMAGE 8.6.4   Violet-backed Starling.

BOX IMAGE 8.6.5   Bali Mynah in captivity.

While toucans, toucanets, acacari, mynahs, and starlings all make wonderful pets, it is a challenge to provide an optimum diet. They have a highly mixed diet in the wild and in captivity are prone to hemochromatosis, or iron storage disease. With this disease, too much iron accumulates primarily in the liver but in other tissues as well, such as the heart and spleen. The iron accumulation ultimately leads to oxidative damage to cells and cell death and cumulative loss of function in these vital organs (Sheppard and Dierenfeld, 2002). To avoid hemochromatosis, it is critical to keep dietary iron at a minimum, which means using distilled water, as tap water can have high levels of iron. In addition, when feeding susceptible softbills, a low-iron pelleted diet should be used that is specifically manufactured for softbills. Ideal softbill diets consist of about 40 percent low-iron softbill pellets, 45 percent fruit, 10 percent live food (worms, crickets, etc.) and 5 percent greens. For birds, the most susceptible to iron storage disease, choose fruits and greens with low iron and limit fruits high in vitamin C, which promotes iron absorption.

Finches have been maintained and bred in captivity for centuries. In Asia, the maintenance of finches as pets has occurred for thousands of years. In fact, the Society or Bengalese Finch has been maintained in domestication for so long that its exact origin is unclear. It has no counterpart in the wild and is likely a product of domestic breeding and never existed in the wild. Its appearance suggests that is related to members of the manikin finch family of Asia. Society Finches make wonderful foster parents and are often used to incubate the eggs and brood the young of the many finch species that do not breed as well in captivity.

Finches come in a wide array of colors, sizes, and singing ability. The vocals of male canaries, the long tails of whydahs and the striking colors of Gouldian or Cordon Bleu Finches are all reasons that finches are kept as pets (Box Image 8.6.6). Zebra Finches have become a common research specimen, and their entire genome has been sequenced to aid research. Finches are very active birds that are entertaining and enjoyable to watch. They are not demanding for attention like parrots and are content going about their daily routines while humans watch. Finches are often sexually dimorphic with the males having brighter colors than females. Finches in captivity do well on seed-based diets containing a mix of seeds, such as millet and canary, nyjer, and rape seeds. Based on the individual species, this will need to be supplemented with insects, larvae, egg food, and finely chopped leaf vegetables and fruits. Many of the bright colors associated with finch plumage result from the ingestion of carotenoid pigments, so providing colorful fruits or leafy material helps ensure these vivid colors. In addition, supplements are also sold that contain carotenoids.

BOX IMAGE 8.6.6   Gouldian Finches

When housing finches and other softbills, it is imperative to provide a large cage or aviary. All of these birds are not like parrots that spend much of their time climbing in their cages using their beaks and legs—finches and softbills need room to fly from location to location in order to maintain good physical strength and health. Therefore, the length of the cage with these birds is more important than height and to some extent width. The large toucans and hornbills really need a walk-in aviary or to be allowed to fly in a room of their owner's house. The smaller softbills such as tanagers, starlings, and the finches also need the largest possible cage so that flight is readily allowed.

REFERENCES

Best, H. A. and R. G. Powlesland. 1985. *Kakapo*. J. McIndoe and New Zealand Wildlife Service, Dunedin.

BirdLife International. 2012. "Datazone species search." Accessed 04/29/12: http://www.birdlife. org/datazone/species/search

Boyes, S. 2011. "Wildlife trade and uncontrolled deforestation threaten Africa's parrots." *Explorer's Journal, National Geographic.* Accessed 04/29/12: http://newswatch.national-geographic.com/2011/12/19/wildlife-trade-and-uncontrolled-deforestation-threaten-africa%E2%80%99s-parrots%E2%80%A6/

Brightsmith, D. J. and R. A. Muñoz-Najar. 2004. Avian Geophagy and Soil Characteristics in Southeastern Peru. *Biotropica* **36**:534–543.

Brightsmith, D. J., J. Taylor, and T. D. Phillips. 2008. The Roles of Soil Characteristics and Toxin Adsorption in Avian Geophagy. *Biotropica* **40**:766–774.

Clout, M. N., G. P. Elliott, and B. C. Robertson. 2002. Effects of supplementary feeding on the offspring sex ratio of Kakapo: A dilemma for the conservation of a polygynous parrot. *Biological Conservation* **107**:13–18.

Clout, M. N. and D. V. Merton. 1998. Saving the Kakapo: The conservation of the world's most peculiar parrot. *Bird Conservation International* **8**:281–296.

Colbert-White, E. N., M. A. Covington, and D. M. Fragaszy. 2011. Social context influences the vocalizations of a home-raised African Grey Parrot (Psittacus erithacus erithacus). *Journal of Comparative Psychology* **125**:175–184.

Diamond, J., K. D. Bishop, and J. D. Gilardi. 1999. Geophagy in New Guinea birds. *Ibis* **141**:181–193.

Fuller, E. 1987. *Extinct Birds*. Facts On File Publications, New York.

Gilardi, J. D., S. S. Duffey, C. A. Munn, and L. A. Tell. 1999. Biochemical Functions of Geophagy in Parrots: Detoxification of Dietary Toxins and Cytoprotective Effects. *Journal of Chemical Ecology* **25**:897–922.

Kakapo Recovery. 2012. "Kakapo Recovery." Department of Conservation. Accessed 04/29/12: www.kakaporecovery.org.nz

Merton, D. V. 1976. Conservation of the Kakapo: A progress report. In *Proceedings of Seminar on Science in National Parks*. National Parks Authority, Wellington, New Zealand.

Merton, D. V. 1994. Saving the Kakapo: A case of intervention, or extinction. Pages 145–155 in *Proceedings of III International Parrot Convention*.

Pepperberg, I. M. 2006. Cognitive and communicative abilities of Grey Parrots. **100**:77–86.

Peres, C. A. 2000. Effects of Subsistence Hunting on Vertebrate Community Structure in Amazonian Forests (Efectos de la Cacería de Subsistencia sobre la Estructura de la Comunidad de Vertebrados en Bosques Amazónicos). *Conservation Biology* **14**:240–253.

Perrins, C. 2009. *The Princeton Encyclopedia of Birds*. Princeton University Press, Princeton, NJ.

Powell, L. L., T. U. Powell, G. V. N. Powell, and D. J. Brightsmith. 2009. Parrots Take It with a Grain of Salt: Available Sodium Content May Drive Collpa (Clay Lick) Selection in Southeastern Peru. *Biotropica* **41**:279–282.

Robertson, B. C., G. P. Elliott, D. K. Eason, M. N. Clout, and N. J. Gemmell. 2006. Sex allocation theory aids species conservation. *Biology Letters* **2**:229–231.

Sheldrake, R. and A. Morgana. 2003. Testing a language-using parrot for telepathy. *Journal of Scientific Exploration* **17**:601–615.

Sheppard, C. and E. Dierenfeld. 2002. Iron Storage Disease in Birds: Speculation on Etiology and Implications for Captive Husbandry. *Journal of Avian Medicine and Surgery* **16**:192–197.

Shewokis, R. 2011. AFA My Fascinating Journey with the Kakapo. *Watchbird* 38(3).

IX   RAPTORS

Often referred to as "birds of prey," raptors commonly represent notions of wilderness and power, as these birds are at the top of the food chain. The word "raptor" even means "one who seizes by force." There are over 300 species of raptors ranging throughout the world, with the exception of Antarctica and a few isolated oceanic islands. Raptors' numbers as a whole are becoming more of a concern, as 53 species—about 17 percent—are vulnerable, endangered, or critically endangered, with another roughly 12 percent listed as near threatened (BirdLife International, 2012). Those threatened species of raptors often require large, contiguous territory and large, older trees for nesting, though with habitat fragmentation, these birds are losing valuable foraging areas. With less suitable habitat, fewer territories can exist. For example, the Philippine Monkey-eating Eagle (*Pithecophaga jefferyi*) is a large powerful raptor with a wingspan of 7 feet. These birds need 100 mi^2 (258 km^2) per breeding pair, which is becoming more difficult to find, classifying the Monkey-eating Eagle as critically endangered. In addition, reproduction is very slow, with these eagles typically only laying one egg every two years, making small contributions to an already dwindling population (Birdlife International, 2009). The Guadalupe Caracara (*Polyborus lutosus*) and the Reunion Kestrel (*Falco buboisi*) are the only two known extinct species of raptors (BirdLife International, 2012). Both of these species were isolated to island populations and therefore were susceptible to extinction with human persecution and depredations of habitat. The Guadalupe Caracara was once native to Guadalupe Island, off of Baja California. The population was decimated due to human deforestation and hunting practices, with the last few shot down by a field collector in 1900 (Abbott, 1933).

In North America, 34 species of raptors are regularly found. Raptors range in size dramatically, with the California Condor (Figure 9.1) having a wingspan of nearly 10 feet and weighing over 20 pounds, while the Sharp-shinned Hawk (Figure 9.2) weighs only 3–7 ounces and has a 20-inch wingspan (Cornell Lab of Ornithology, 2011). Similarly,

FIGURE 9.1   The California Condor has almost a 10-foot wingspan.

FIGURE 9.2   Sharp-shinned hawks are some of the smaller hawks, with only 20-inch wingspans.

FIGURE 9.3   As formidable predators, Gold Eagles are capable of killing large prey such as deer and wolves.

raptors prey on animals of various sizes, with the larger eagles, such as the Golden Eagle (Figure 9.3), capable of taking prey as large as a coyote or pronghorn antelope. Smaller raptors, like the American Kestrel (Figure 9.4), feed on small prey like grasshoppers and mice.

Raptors are reverse sexually dimorphic. Though their plumage is generally similar between the sexes, the females are generally 50–70 percent larger than the males (Figure 9.5), with a few exceptions. Mortality is high in young raptors, with only 10 percent surviving to adulthood (Boughman, 2003). Since the female is larger, she will prey on larger food than the male, reducing competition, and allowing for a more diverse food supply for the young. Another unique characteristic of raptors is the fact that many females have both ovaries (depending on the species), while most birds have only the left. It is unknown why raptors have this distinction.

RAPTOR ORDERS AND FAMILIES

There is much discrepancy among taxonomists regarding the raptor orders and families. Now with new molecular and DNA research, taxonomy is changing regularly. For the purposes of this book, raptor taxonomy will be based on BirdLife International's species listings. However, this book will still retain the order Accipitriformes, as opposed to considering all raptors to be in Falconiformes. Additionally, though they are often referred to as raptors, this chapter will not cover owls, as they belong to their own order, Strigiformes.

ACCIPITRIFORMES

ACCIPITRIDAE

The Accipitridae family is a very diverse family, including Osprey, Secretary Birds, kites, harriers, hawks, eagles, and Old World vultures. The American Ornithologists' Union places the Osprey into its own family, Pandionidae, but BirdLife International (2012) considers it a member of Accipitridae. Found throughout much of the world, the Osprey prefers lakes, rivers, and coastal habitat. Osprey feed almost exclusively on fish and will often hover above the water before diving feet first to make a catch. They will then use their strong feet with barbed pads on the soles to assist in carrying the slippery fish (Figure 9.6). As an additional adaptation for handling fish, osprey are able to reverse their outer toe allowing two toes to face forward and two backward. This adaptation is unique and puts the Osprey in a family of its own. When flying with a fish, Osprey will orient the fish head first so that it is more aerodynamic and easier to maneuver.

The Secretary Bird (Figure 9.7) was once in its own family, Sagittariidae, but has been reclassified to be included in Accipitridae (BirdLife International, 2012). It is native to Africa, south of the Sahara. The Secretary Bird populations have recently been decreasing, and therefore the species has recently been uplisted to vulnerable due to habitat degradation, disturbance, hunting, and capture for trade (BirdLife International, 2012). It has long legs and short toes adapted for walking, so it cannot carry prey with its feet. It kills its prey, typically snakes, by stomping and crushing it. Consequently, it has adapted thick scales on its long legs for protection. The females tend to be smaller than males, which is unusual for raptors.

Kites are a diverse group of medium-sized hawks. A unique characteristic that sets them apart from the rest of the raptors is their lack of a supraorbital ridge. The Swallow-tailed (Figure 9.8) and Mississippi Kites belong in this family. The Accipiters, or forest hawks, have short, rounded wings convenient for their dash-and-grab hunting style. They vary in size, with the largest about crow-sized. The Sharp-shinned Hawk, Cooper's Hawk, and Northern Goshawk (Figure 9.9) are a few examples of Accipiters. Buteos include large, wide-winged, short-tailed hawks that prefer forest with open areas for soaring. Red-tailed Hawks (Figure 9.10) and Harris's Hawks fall into this category. Harriers are medium-sized hawks with long wings and tails. They often hunt by slowly soaring low, searching grasslands and marshes. Harriers have soft feathers and fly smoothly and silently, similar to owls. The Northern Harrier (Figure 9.11) is an example of this group.

The eagles are also found in the Accipitridae family. Eagles such as Bald Eagles (Figure 9.12 a) and Golden Eagles (Figure 9.12 b) are the largest hawks, with heavy bodies and large, powerful feet. They

FIGURE 9.4 Smaller raptors, like this American Kestrel, hunt insects and small rodents.

FIGURE 9.5 Reverse sexual dimorphism in Harris's Hawks. The female (left) is much larger than the male (right).

FIGURE 9.6   Osprey have specialized tuber cells on their feet that allow them to grip slippery fish. Once in the air with their prey, osprey will face the fish head first to reduce air drag.

FIGURE 9.7   Secretary Birds have very long legs for walking great distances, searching for food. With weak feet and talons, they use their long legs to stomp their favorite prey: snakes.

tend to have a varied diet, with Bald Eagles eating anything from fish to large mammals. Very opportunistic, this powerful predator will often intimidate smaller raptors and steal their food. They are also not too proud to eat trash or carrion. Bald Eagles were once threatened with extinction due to the use of the chemical DDT, but protection under the Endangered Species Act, in combination with reintroduction programs, increased populations significantly. The eagles were removed from the endangered list in 1999 and later removed from the threatened list altogether in 2007 and presently sit at "least concern," a true conservational success (Cornell Lab of Ornithology, 2011). While the Bald Eagle is the national symbol of the United States, the Golden Eagle is the national emblem of Mexico. The Golden Eagle—slightly larger than the Bald Eagle, with a wingspan of over 7 feet—is common to western North America. Though capable of hunting large prey such as deer, the Golden Eagle usually hunts smaller prey such as rabbits, ground squirrels, and prairie dogs.

The Old World vultures are also found in the Accipitridae family. Though often misunderstood, vultures play a vital role in the ecosystem by cleaning up rotting flesh and preventing the spread of animal diseases (Koenig, 2006). From 1992–2007, populations of three vulture species, the White-rumped (*Gyps bengalensis*) (Figure 9.13), Indian (*Gyps indicus*), and Slender-billed Vultures (*Gyps tenuirostris*) in South Asia (specifically India, Pakistan, and Nepal) fell by more than 95 percent, prompting the IUCN to classify their status as critically endangered. This decline was due to secondary exposure to diclofenac, an anti-inflammatory drug given to cattle, a main source of food for the local vultures. After the vultures consumed dead cattle that had been treated with this drug, they became ill and died from renal failure. The environment also began to show the repercussions of using this drug. With fewer vultures, the presence of carrion increased. With the plentiful food supply, rats and feral dog and cat populations increased, leading to a rabies outbreak that later became a human health concern (Markandya et al., 2008). India, specifically, has the highest rate of human rabies infection in the world, and dog bites are the main source (APCRI, 2004). Vultures also help control livestock diseases such as brucellosis, tuberculosis, and anthrax by disposing of infected carcasses (Swan et al., 2006). This example shows the ecological importance that vultures play. Fortunately, in this case, diclofenac has been banned in India, Nepal, and Pakistan, but there are still other drugs being used that may be detrimental to these already threatened species. Studies are being conducted to determine what is suitable and safe to use in the environment.

Old World vultures are also found to be quite intelligent. Some vultures crack open eggs by dropping them onto rocks (van Lawick-Goodall and van Lawick, 1966). Moreover, one species of vulture has been observed using tools: Egyptian Vultures fly over Ostrich nests carrying stones and dropping them to break the eggs, allowing them to reach the normally inaccessible contents (Thouless et al., 1987).

CATHARTIDAE

The Cathartidae family includes New World vultures, though DNA evidence does predict that they are more closely related to storks than raptors. New World vultures are also genetically distinct from Old World vultures, yet evolved to fill the same niche of eating dead meat through convergent evolution. Both classes of vultures have large, broad wings used for soaring and weak feet with talons. They consume carrion and therefore have no need for the powerful talons of other raptors. They have featherless necks and heads that allow them to reach into a carcass cavity without dirtying their feathers. They have a perforated nostril, with no septum (Figure 9.14). In the U.S., populations of Turkey and Black Vultures, both New World vultures, have exploded in the past 20 years into Canada due to an explosion in deer populations, and therefore road-kill frequency." Turkey Vultures (Figure 9.15) use their keen sense of smell to detect food from miles away. Black Vultures (Figure 9.16), however, have a poor sense of smell and use their sight to seek out food or to follow Turkey Vultures.

FALCONIFORMES

FALCONIDAE

The Falconidae family includes falcons and caracaras. Falcons have long, narrow, pointed wings, and long, narrow toes with bumps for holding prey. They have a very pronounced mandibular notch (Figure 9.17) on their bill, used for breaking the necks or spines of prey, though this is not the primary killing method. Falcons are excellent fliers and fly leisurely at about 40 miles per hour, but some falcons such as the Peregrine Falcon (Figure 9.18) can make quick dives reaching speeds between 100 and 200 miles per hour. Falcons tend to exhibit extreme sexual dimorphism, with the female much larger than the male. Falcons generally prefer open areas and avoid forests, with the exception of five species of forest falcons found in the tropics. Prairie falcons, Gyrfalcons, American Kestrels, and Merlins are also classified in this group. The American Kestrel is one of the most abundant and smallest falcons, weighing about half a pound, hunting bats and small mammals and birds. Though common, their numbers are declining due to rodent population control.

Caracaras usually walk while scavenging or searching for food. These falcons have a narrow face and a large beak without a mandibular notch. They live in tropical climates of the Western Hemisphere and are the only falcons to build stick nests. The Crested Caracara (Figure 9.19) is found from the southwestern United States and Florida into Central and South America, often walking in open country and pastureland.

FIGURE 9.8 Swallow-tailed Kites lack a supraorbital ridge. They are often seen soaring on thermals.

FIGURE 9.9 The Northern Goshawk is a powerful accipiter, known for its fearless demeaner.

FIGURE 9.10   Red-tailed Hawk.

FIGURE 9.11   The Northern Harrier has a disc-shaped face to funnel sound to its ears, similarly to owls.

RAPTOR REPRODUCTION

Female raptors tend to choose the male, called a tiercel, based on fitness, and this fitness is sometimes tested through elaborate courtship displays. These displays (Figure 9.20) vary greatly among raptor species and may include high-flying undulations, figure eights, talon presentations, and aerial food exchanges. Male and female Bald Eagles will lock their talons and engage in a cartwheel fall. All of these displays require vigor and endurance, and since the female desires a fit male to sire her offspring, this courtship assists in her selection process.

Raptors typically pair with a mate for the breeding season, yet some species such as the Red-tailed Hawk pair-bond for years, sometimes lasting their lifetimes. Other raptors such as Harris's Hawks can be monogamous but often practice polyandry, or mating with more than one male. After the female has paired with two males, both of the males will continue to care for and feed the young equally. It is believed that this increases the young's chances of survival with the increased food collection. Other raptors, like the Harris's Hawk, are polygamous and the males mate with two to three females.

Presumably in order to reduce their weight for flight, most female birds have adapted to having a single left ovary with its associated oviduct. Several raptor species are exceptions to this rule, having both the right and left ovaries. Both ovaries are functional and it is not understood why these species still maintain both ovaries, while the vast majority of birds only have the left side.

Many raptors build large, platform nests (Figure 9.21), in trees, on cliffs, or on the ground. They often use the same nest year after year, repairing it as needed and piling new sticks on top of the old nest. Sometimes they will decorate the nest with greenery such as pine needles to possibly cover the foul scent that lingers from repeated prey consumption in the nest. The greenery may also be used to repel insects that may linger, drawn to the smell of the nest.

Many raptors have more than one brood per season, or "double clutch." They are also indeterminate layers so, with breeding programs, the eggs can be collected, the young can be raised in the protection of captivity, and the parents will lay more eggs. This practice was successfully utilized for threatened species like the Peregrine Falcon and California Condor, as mentioned in Chapter 2. A concern of the captive breeding program is the possibility of the chicks imprinting on humans and depending on them for food, therefore not being able to feed themselves as adults. To avoid this, breeding centers often use puppets to mimic the chick's natural parents, or they use blinds so the chicks cannot see the handlers. Raptor chicks are altricial, or featherless and helpless, at hatch. Most raptors have asynchronous hatches, producing two, three, four, seven, or eight eggs. The asynchronous hatch leads to a chick hierarchy, with the early-hatching chicks being larger. In many raptor species, when food is scarce, the young will undergo siblicide, with the older chicks pushing the smaller chicks out of the nest. Often, only a single chick survives. While the nestlings are growing, parents bring them, pieces of dead prey first, then disabled prey that the chicks may practice killing within the nest. After the young fledge the nest, they follow the parents for several months to learn how to hunt.

THREATS TO RAPTORS

Raptors as a whole are threatened by several human-related factors. The shooting of raptors is strictly prohibited and one can receive jail time as a result— regardless, thousands are shot every year. Habitat fragmentation is threatening many raptor species. For breeding pairs, the carrying capacity of a habitat determines the survivability of the young. Among many limiting factors, two basic requirements must be present for a successful brood: nest sites and abundant food. Raptors that nest in large trees are impacted greatly in landscapes that have been deforested or fragmented. Even forest hawks have difficulty finding large trees, since older-growth forests are rare, with most forests comprised of only young trees. In some highly popu-lated areas, people have built platforms for raptors such as Ospreys to build their nests, and it has helped increase populations. European raptor populations are in serious trouble, however, since the land is so fragmented and overpopulated (Stroud, 2003). The second limiting factor is food availability. Large raptors sometimes struggle to find food in suburban areas where rodent pest populations are controlled. Eagles tend to need very large territories, sometimes over 100 square miles, to sustain themselves with enough food supply. Small, generalist raptors tend to do better since they can adapt and hunt the available prey, including insects and small birds.

Toxic chemical contamination has also taken its toll on raptor populations. Pesticides such as organochlorines are extremely stable and easily dispersed by water and dissolve in fat, giving them the ability to accumulate in the body, referred to as bioaccumulation. If the chemicals are not at lethal levels, at the very least, reproduction will be disrupted. DDT, or dichloro-diphenyl-trichloroethanal, was developed in 1939 as a miracle drug used to kill lice, flies, and mosquitoes in the 1940s, 1950s, and 1960s. DDT itself is not toxic to birds, but the principal breakdown product is DDE, which causes a thinning of the egg shellss of some bird species. This thinning leads to the parents crushing the eggs when they are incubating. Songbirds and gamebirds did not seem to be affected by the use of DDT, and in fact, several studies had fed DDT and DDE to chickens and Japanese quail with no detrimental effects (Cecil et al., 1971; Chang and Stokstad, 1975; Scott et al., 1975; Robson et al., 1976). The use of the pesticide did, however, lead to drastic population declines in raptors and fish-eating birds during the decades of its use in the mid 20th century. Peregrine Falcons, Sharp-shinned Hawks, Coopers Hawks, Osprey, and Bald Eagles were swiftly declining. Rachel Carson's book, *Silent Spring*, was one of the first wake-up calls to

FIGURE 9.12 Bald Eagle (a) and Golden Eagle (b).

FIGURE 9.13 The White-rumped Vulture is critically endangered due to a drug used to treat cattle, a favorite food of these vultures.

FIGURE 9.14 New World vultures, such as this Black Vulture, have perforated nostrils which allow one to see through their nose.

FIGURE 9.15 Turkey Vultures use their powerful sense of smell to find food.

officials and the public of the harm being caused by the use of DDT. The uproar against DDT led to quite a debate: On the one hand, millions of people around the world could be saved from malaria by wiping out mosquitoes, but on the other hand, entire species of birds could be sacrificed in order to do this. DDT was made illegal in 1972 in the United States, yet its use in other countries continues to be controversial.

Raptors are at the top of the food chain in the bird world, but they are still susceptible to accidents with cars or power lines. These two events alone account for millions of bird deaths per year, many of them raptors (Sibley, 2010). Certain raptor species are especially susceptible to car collisions because they often swoop down to capture the rodents that forage on the litter from passing cars. Regarding natural causes of mortality, raptors tend to be resistant to many diseases that can affect other avian species. Vultures and other carrion eaters, in particular, are resistant to anthrax, botulism toxin, and Newcastle virus, to name a few (Jones, 2006). Raptor mortality overall from infectious disease is relatively low, less than 10 percent (Wendell et al., 2002), though they can contract bacterial, viral, fungal, or parasitic illnesses. Some raptor species are more susceptible than others. For example, the Gyrfalcon lives in arctic climates where few bacteria are able to thrive, so these falcons have less need for a resistance to bacteria. If these birds are brought to warmer climates, they often contract a bacterial illness and die.

In general, the larger the raptor is, the longer its lifespan. Bald Eagles live 20 years in the wild and as long as 40 years in captivity. Medium-sized raptors like Red-tailed and Harris's Hawks live from 11 to 18 years; and small raptors like American Kestrels live two to four years. But there is a basic tenet that, in the wild, nothing dies of old age. Most raptors do not survive their first year (Beebe, 1999). Starvation is also a common cause of death in adults and especially young raptors. In one study with Common Kestrels in Britain, 35 percent of the birds studied were killed by collisions (cars, windows, other trauma), 11 percent were killed by other human-related causes (poisoning, shooting, electrocution, drowning), 46 percent died from natural causes (starvation, disease, predation), and 8 percent died from unknown causes. Interestingly, the numbers for Eurasian Sparrowhawks from the same study were quite different, with 65 percent of deaths resulting from collisions, 7 percent from other human-related causes, 22 percent natural causes, and 6 percent unknown causes (Newton et al., 1999). The most striking difference between the two species is the frequency of collisions, with 30 percent more collisions by sparrowhawks than kestrels. These results imply that individual species behavior is an important factor to consider in management, as some species are more vulnerable to human-related mortality.

HUNTING

Raptor hunting techniques are diverse across the raptor family. Forest hawks (Sharp-shinned Hawk, Cooper's Hawk, Goshawk) use thick cover for concealment and then they quickly dash and grab, using the element of surprise or ambush technique. This fast, surprise attack requires high-energy expenditure. Species like the Red-tailed Hawk and American Kestrel utilize perches to view a large area, allowing them to save energy sitting and waiting for their prey to come by. Many raptors soar to cover a great deal of territory at a relatively small energy cost. Buteos such as the Red-tailed Hawk often use this method to search for prey and then stoop, or dive rapidly, to kill on the ground. Vultures will also use the soaring technique, riding thermals to search for food while using little energy. Kites and American Kestrels often face a headwind and hover or kite, flying into the wing, remaining in the same spot, expending little energy. While kiting—similar to perch hunting from a still vantage point—the bird can detect movement, or urine from prey can be seen with their UV vision. Some falcons such as the Peregrine Falcon, are raptors that excel in flying and use aerial pursuit to capture prey. After scanning and waiting for prey by soaring, the falcon will stoop and kill prey, often other birds, in mid-air. Kites will use similar methods for killing insects, though the flight pursuit is slower. Plunge diving is also used by birds such as the Osprey and the Bald Eagle, where the bird will soar, hover, and then dive feet first into water to catch fish. Raptors using this method must have strong legs and feet to endure the impact of the water.

Nearly every raptor is opportunistic and will take advantage of a chance for easy prey. Larger raptors often steal from smaller raptors. To prevent this theft from larger raptors, after a kill, raptors will often mantle, or spread its wings and tail, to conceal their food from larger raptors. In the grasslands of the southwestern United States, where wildfires are prevalent, birds of prey such as the Swainson's Hawk will soar and search for smoke, then position themselves ahead of the fire. Taking advantage of the opportunity, they will then capture prey by air or ground escaping from the fire. White-tailed Hawks will behave the same way in Texas. Some raptors use cooperative hunting in either pairs (Red-tailed Hawk) or in groups (Harris's Hawks) to hunt prey. One bird will flush the prey and the other bird(s) will ambush it. Raptors will always utilize an opportunity or hunting technique to capture prey at a lower energy cost.

In addition to efficient hunting methods, raptors have a specialized anatomy that assists in hunting and killing prey. Their lower bill is flat and spoonlike, while their top bill is hooked and contains a mandibular notch (Figure 9.17), used for snapping spines. Some mandibular notches are more pronounced than others, depending on the species, and this groove is only used as a secondary method of killing, as a bird would rather not put its face near a biting, clawing squirrel. The true weapons are the raptor's huge, powerful feet and talons (Figure 9.21). As the primary method of killing, these

FIGURE 9.16 Black vultures have a relatively poor sense of smell and use sight to find their food or rely on Turkey Vultures to find it for them.

FIGURE 9.17 (a) Falcons have a pronounced mandibular notch in their bill for snapping the spinal cords of prey. (b) Peregrine Falcon

FIGURE 9.18   Crested Caracara, a member of the falcon familiy.

FIGURE 9.19   Red-tailed Hawks in courtship flight.

FIGURE 9.20   Bald Eagle nest or eerie with nestling.

crushing feet are used for collapsing diaphragms and causing the prey to suffocate, while the razor-sharp talons cause internal bleeding. Most raptors have a varied diet that requires these strong weapons, but the Everglade Kite feeds almost exclusively on the apple snail, which is only found in the Everglades. Due to this highly specialized diet on delicate snails, the Everglade Kite does not require strong, powerful talons like many raptors; consequently, it has a smaller bill and smaller feet comparatively (Figure 9.22). Raptors have excellent binocular vision, ranking eight to ten times better than human vision. Like all birds, they have a nictitating membrane (Figure 9.23) that covers and protects their eyes during flight or during an attack, acting like a windshield. Many raptors also have a supraorbital ridge (Figure 9.23), a bony protuberance above the eye. It is unknown for sure why they have this, but researchers theorize that it could protect their eyes from branches when flying in the forest. This theory holds for forest raptors, but most raptors have this ridge above their eyes, regardless of their habitat. A second theory hypothesizes that this ridge provides shade, acting like sunglasses, while the bird soars in open skies.

After a raptor captures and kills its prey, it will often mantle (Figure 9.24), or spread its wings and tail to conceal its food from larger raptors so they do not steal it. Some birds of prey will remove the prey's feathers or fur and cache their food for later. Raptors will often not eat the digestive tract, as it often carries harmful bacteria. Occasionally, if the bird is hungry enough, raptors other than vultures will eat carrion. Only vultures specialize in carrion, with some vultures eating the meat itself, others scraping the meat off of the bones, and still other species consuming the bone marrow.

FALCONRY

HISTORY

Falconry, or hawking, is the act of training raptors to hunt small game, gamebirds, or waterfowl in partnership with man. People do this by utilizing the raptor's natural instinct to hunt and combine it with training so they capture game and turn it over for a reward. It is unknown exactly when falconry originated. Some hypothesize that it developed in China over 4000 years ago, but those records only state that falcons were among presents given to Chinese princes during the Hia Dynasty (supposed to have begun in 2205 BC), but there is no record that these birds were used for hunting. It is presumed that falconry first developed as an efficient means of catching food by 1700 BC, supported by a bas-relief sculpture depicting a falconer, found in the ruins of Khorsabad in Mesopotamia (Glasier, 1998). Written evidence also shows that falconry was practiced around 400 BC in Central Asia. Falconry later spread to the Middle East, reaching

Europe in the Middle Ages, between 500 and 800 AD. Though the sport is often considered to belong only to the nobility, clergy, and popes of Europe, it is probably likely that many commoners also practiced falconry, flying goshawks and sparrowhawks (considered less desirable species at the time) in order to catch food. Since records were not well kept for the poorer classes, the history of falconry is better chronicled among the nobility and royalty (Figure 9.25). There were, however, certain species that were only allowed to be flown by the correctly titled man, with earls flying Peregrine Falcons, kings flying Gyrfalcons, and emperors flying Eagles, as explained by *The Boke of St. Albans*, written in 1486. The sport lost some popularity between 1200 and 1300 due to the development of firearms. There is little record of falconry existing in North America before the 1920s, when an article in *National Geographic* magazine (Fuertes, 1920) aroused interest in the practice. Of all sports in the United States, it is the only sport to utilize a trained wild animal. Presently, falconry has become popular as a hobby throughout much of the world.

BECOMING A FALCONER

Falconry is a very demanding endeavor and requires serious dedication and time from the falconer, yet it can be a rewarding sport. There are three levels of falconry licenses. To become a falconer, one must meet the minimum requirements: You must be 12 to 14 years of age, depending on the state, be patient, enjoy working with animals and hunting/working outdoors, be able to dedicate the time to tend to the bird's needs, be willing to dedicate years to the sport, etc. Once these criteria are met, the individual may contact his or her state or provincial wildlife agency (Department of Fish and Wildlife or Department of Natural Resources, etc.) for an information packet.

There are three levels of falconers: Apprentices, General Falconers, and Master Falconers. A General Falconer has at least two years of experience after completing the federal exam and meeting requirements. One becomes a Master Falconer after five years of experience. The initial stage is called Apprentice. Apprentices are trained by the two higher levels of falconer for two to five years. To become an Apprentice, one must first have a sponsor (a General or Master Falconer) agree to training, and with this signature, the future Apprentice may apply through the state or provincial wildlife agency. Once approved, an appointment may be made to take the first falconry exam. After completing the exam, another appointment will be made to have the facilities and equipment approved through the wildlife agency. He or she must build a suitable hawk house or mew (Figure 9.26) and outdoor flight pen, have acquired equipment, and must withstand an official state inspection. If all is approved, a permit to capture or possess a live raptor (select species) is granted. A separate hunting license is also required to hunt with raptors. Then, it is time to think about the type of bird the Apprentice wants to fly.

FIGURE 9.21   Many raptors have very strong feet and talons for killing prey.

FIGURE 9.22   Snail Kites have more delicate bills and feet because they are specialists, preferring to eat apple snails as their primary food.

FIGURE 9.23   The nictitating membrane is a second eyelid that acts as a windsheild to protect the eye.

FIGURE 9.24   Raptors will mantle by spreading their wings and tail feathers over their kill. This posture helps conceal the catch to prevent theft by larger raptors.

At one time, depending on the state, Apprentices had the choice of flying only a Red-tailed Hawk or an American Kestrel. In October 2008, the U.S. Fish and Wildlife Service finalized changes to the federal regulations governing falconry. Now according to federal law, Apprentices are able to fly a variety of wild-caught or captive-bred species, with the exception of eagles, Swallow-tail Kites, Swainson's and Ferruginous Hawks, Prairie and Peregrine Falcons, Northern Harrier, and several species of small owls. However, individual state laws may still restrict Apprentice species. General Falconers are allowed to fly all Strigiformes and Falconiformes except eagles; Master Falconers may fly all species including Golden Eagles. Bald Eagles are not legally used in falconry in the United States (USFWS, 2008).

ACQUIRING A RAPTOR FROM THE WILD

First, be aware that there are only certain times of the year when trapping raptors is allowed. There are several ways to acquire a raptor. A nestling, removed from the nest and raised in captivity, is called an "eyess." These birds are considered the most tame and will imprint on humans. "Passage hawks" or "passagers" are yearlings caught during their first fall migration, or "in passage." A "haggard" is a mature adult with complete adult plumage captured from the wild. When a mature adult is caught, it is tradition in falconry to release it, since it is actively reproductive, due to conservation implications.

There are several traps for catching young raptors, and one must have a permit to own any of these traps. The Bal-Chatri trap (Figure 9.27) is a cage externally covered in monofilament loops. A live bird, such as a pigeon or dove, is placed inside the protection of the

FIGURE 9.25 Falconry is relatively well-documented among the nobility of Europe, though commoners likely practiced as well.

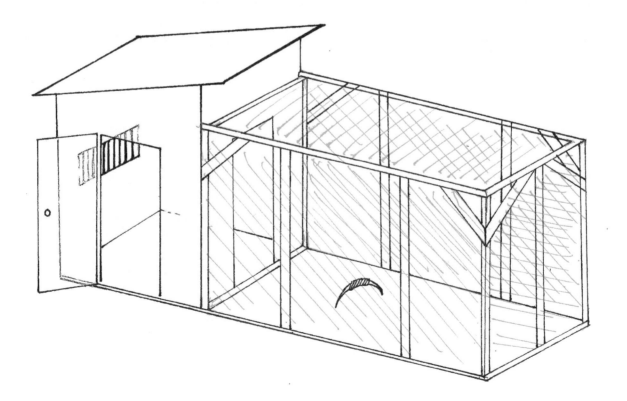

FIGURE 9.26 The raptor house, or mew, must include an indoor and outdoor area.

FIGURE 9.27   The Bal-chatri trap is externally covered in monofilament loops and the bait is contained within. When a raptor attacks the cage, its talons become tangled in the loops.

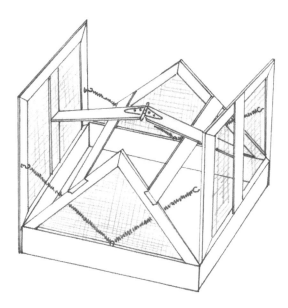

FIGURE 9.28   The Swedish Goshawk trap is a cage with a trap door. Once the raptor attacks the bait and knocks the door props down, the doors close behind it.

trap as bait. When the raptor tries to attack the bait, the filament loops become tangled in its feet and the falconer may come claim their catch. A Swedish Goshawk trap (Figure 9.28) is similar to the Bal-Chatri, with live bait in a bottom compartment to attract the raptor. A single, thin stick brace holds the two doors open, and when the raptor comes down onto the pigeon, the stick is knocked down, closing the top doors shut and trapping the raptor. The pigeon harness (Figure 9.29) is also a common piece of equipment used to capture a bird of prey. The pigeon is tethered to the ground on a leash so that is may fly until it reaches the end of the leash and then flutters down to the ground, attracting raptor predators. The harness has exposed microfilament loops coming out of the back that become tangled in the raptor's feet after an attack.

FALCONERS VERSUS PIGEON RACERS

There is a long-standing conflict between falconers and pigeon enthusiasts due to the natural tendencies of falcons and hawks to prey on pigeons. Also, falconers sometimes use live pigeons as bait to trap and lure falcons and hawks. Some traps allow the pigeon to remain safely behind cage bars such as the Bal-Chatri and Swedish goshawk traps mentioned above, but others—such as the pigeon harness—may result in the pigeon's injury or death in the process of the raptor's capture. Pigeon enthusiasts often think of this practice as cruel and unnecessary. With the negative sentiments towards falconers' capture techniques, combined with the raptor's natural instinct to kill pigeons, pigeon racers and enthusiasts occasionally make news headlines believing they are defending their pigeons by killing federally protected raptors (Mrozek, 2007; The Peregrine Fund, 2011; Williams, 2008).

CAPTIVE BREEDING AND HYBRIDS

If a falconer does not wish to capture a bird from the wild, he or she may buy a bird from a breeder. This route is becoming increasingly popular, especially for rare or difficult-to-capture breeds such as Harris's Hawks, which may cost upwards of $500 each. Before the 1970s, most falconry birds were first-year migrants trapped in the wild, often by professional trappers (Beebe, 1999). Since the 1960s and 1970s, the captive breeding of birds for falconry has become more prevalent, with the success exceeding expectations. In most of Europe, only captive-bred raptors are flown; in the United States, the use of captive-bred birds is now greater than the use of wild-caught birds. There is now a high demand for captive-bred birds, especially hybrids, in the Middle East. Since some of these birds can be sold for hefty prices, an opportunistic domestic trade has resulted in parts of the Middle East (FALCO, 2010). On the other hand, the benefits of successful captive breeding have led to the reintroduction of birds to supplement rare or endangered wild raptor populations throughout the world. In addition to the well-known Peregrine Falcon, at least 25 other raptor species worldwide have benefited from captive breeding programs since the 1970s (FALCO, 2010).

The hybridization of various species and subspecies of falcons and hawks has become popular over the past several decades—as well as controversial. The North American Falconry Association (NAFA) supports the use of non-native (exotic) raptors and hybrids in the practice of falconry in North America, though counsels against any deliberate release into the wild of such raptors (NAFA 2009). The USFWS requires that all hybrid raptors flown for falconry wear two separate radio transmitters to prevent the loss of the bird, as the intentional permanent release of hybrids into the wild is prohibited (USFWS, 2008). Some believe that the inevitably released or lost hybrid raptors may dilute or out-compete pure populations. Others consider hybridization a natural phenomenon, with some wild species such as Peregrine and Prairie Falcons inhabiting overlapping ranges and hybridizing naturally. Many ducks, especially the widespread Mallard, hybridize with many other duck species readily. Bred hybrids (Figure 9.30) come in countless combinations, from crosses between Gyrfalcons, Peregrines, and Prairie Falcons to crosses between Red-tailed, Ferruginous, and Harris's Hawks. There are falcon breeders that specialize in the raising of hybrids, and some falconers believe that they are the most vigorous—often termed "hybrid vigor"—and most desirable of falconry birds. Others are traditionalists and would never hunt with a bird that was not "pure."

ILLEGAL COLLECTION AND TRADE

Illegal trade of wildlife is covered in Chapter 3, yet it is worth mentioning the specifics of the falcon and hawk trade, since raptors are often the target of illegal bird trade. Certain species of raptors are legally allowed to be imported and exported through the U.S. borders, as long as proper methods are pursued through the Migratory Bird Treaty Act and the Convention on International Trade in Endangered Species of Wild Fauna and Flora (CITES).

Illegal harvesting of raptors involves the eggs of falcons and hawks being removed from nests in the wild or birds being trapped without authorization. These eggs and birds are then smuggled into countries where falconry is historically and culturally significant, where these specimens can be sold for tens of thousands of dollars. To help counteract this illegal trade, CITES has developed a guide, *CITES Guide to Falconry Species*, that will help customs and police officers monitor and control the cross-border movement of falcons. The guide comes in two editions: one for the public that includes an identification key and description for the six falcon and one hawk species most commonly traded for falconry purposes; and a restricted edition for law enforcement only. The restricted version

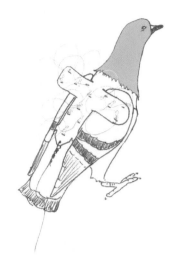

FIGURE 9.29   The pigeon harness is strapped onto the pigeon like a backpack. The harness is covered in monofilament loops that become tangled in the raptor's talons after it goes for the bait.

FIGURE 9.30   Hybrid raptors are becoming increasingly more desirable in the world of falconry. This is a hybrid between a Gyrfalcon and a Saker Falcon.

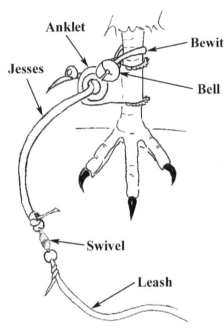

FIGURE 9.31   A common arrangement of falconry equipment on the legs of the bird. The equipment includes the anklets, jesses, bells, bewit, swivel, and leash. There are also other varieties and adaptations of this design.

FIGURE 9.32   A raptor wears a hood during transport or otherwise in order to keep it calm. The falconers glove is another necessary and basic piece of equipment.

includes the identification section, but also includes information on the identification of juvenile falcons and falcon hybrids.

FALCONRY EQUIPMENT

There are several pieces of necessary falconry equipment, or furniture, as it is called. Bells are often worn around one or both of the bird's ankles to help the falconer find the raptor throughout the hunt. The bells are strapped on with a soft leather strap called a bewit. A second soft leather strap called a jess on one of the raptor's legs is connected to a swivel that, in turn, connects to a leash (Figure 9.31). With this leash, the falconer may hold the bird in hand or tie the bird to a perch. In addition to this leg equipment, the raptor may wear a leather hood (Figure 9.32) that covers its eyes in order to keep the bird calm during transport. The hood has a draw string at the base that can be tightened to secure and generally comes with a leather tuft at the crown of the hood to assist with its removal.

The raptor will also require a training perch, which is staked into the ground outside of its mew. The goal here is safety and comfort. The perch must also be easily cleaned, which is a concern when feeding it raw flesh. Block perches (Figure 9.33) are typically made of wood or cement covered in Astroturf, which is easy to clean and offers a little padding for the bird's talons, as they need to be kept sharp. Block perches are commonly used for falcons for their comfort with their foot structure, long toes, and long tail. All other birds are typically given a bow or ring perch (Figure 9.34), which are handy and easy to make. They consist of a metal ring of various designs wrapped in rope for comfort padding. The bird can be tied to this perch, but one must be careful to make the leash short enough so the bird cannot walk through the ring of the perch and become tangled. Perches within the bird's mew are often made of rope or branches. A mew, or hawk house, must also be provided and inspected. Several requirements must be met, including the presence of at least one window, the ability to lock and secure the bird, and it must include a weathering area for outdoor activity. The mew itself must be large enough for activity. These standards are regulated by the federal government.

In addition to perches, a falconer will also need an accurate scale (Figure 9.35). Keeping an accurate record of the raptor's weight is absolutely essential for keeping it healthy and hunting. A leather glove (Figure 9.32) for holding the bird is also necessary. If the falconer is right-handed, the glove will be worn on the left hand so that the right hand is free to handle the lure. The lure (Figure 9.36), a piece of leather decorated to make it look like the particular game to be hunted, is also an important tool. The lure is swung around in the air to train the bird, condition the bird and increase its endurance, and can also be used to recover the bird from the hunt. To entice the bird to the lure, one may "garnish the lure" by attaching meat bits to it. The falconer also has a lure bag for holding food or treats, a scale for game weight, and sometimes even a live pigeon. The live pigeon is used as a last ditch effort to lure back a difficult raptor.

TRAINING THE RAPTOR

The training varies widely, depending on whether the falconer acquires a young hatchling or an adult bird. A young bird taken from the nest as an eyess or bought from a breeder will imprint upon the trainer and become tame, making handling slightly easier. The wild-caught passager will never be tamed and will only become tolerant of its trainer, at best. The time involved in training varies, also. An eyess requires a great deal of training because it needs to be taught how to hunt—unlike a passager, who knows how to hunt, but only needs to be accustomed to humans for a few weeks. Adult birds caught from the wild also come with prey size limitations. As experienced hunters, passagers will not go after larger prey if they have failed hunting them before. Eyesses, on the other hand, know no limits, and one can train them to go after much larger prey. Another concern with capturing an adult bird is its increased chance of flying away. Unlike eyesses, which are bonded and much less likely to fly off, passagers are wild animals and will likely fly away eventually.

When training a raptor, in addition to the age of the bird, the species must be taken into account. Each hawk or falcon has strengths and weaknesses, and when training, the falconer must be aware of these and not expect the bird to perform outside of its ability. For example, eagles are capable of being trained to capture very large prey such as wolves, but Red-tailed Hawks should not be expected to do the same. When training any type of raptor, encouraging the best field performance of which the species is capable will yield the most success. Another consideration to remember is that, with raptors, reward is the key to success. Punishment does not work because raptors are independent, solitary birds, and therefore dominance or submissiveness that would be found in a flock does not apply to them. The best method of training utilizes repetition and reward. There are several stages to the training process that can vary, depending on the protocol. For the purposes of this book, the following steps have been simplified and are not meant to act as instructions for training. The subsequent stages are outlined for an adult passager, caught from the wild.

STAGE I FIRST FEEDING AND MANNING THE BIRD

After capture, it is vital to record an initial weight. This weight will roughly be the weight needed during hunting because the bird was fit enough to hunt, yet desperate enough to go for the bait in the trap. Next, the acclimation to the equipment and the falconer begins. "Manning the bird" refers to making the bird tame or tolerant of humans. Soon after capture, the raptor may be given some food, but

FIGURE 9.33 Block perches are commonly used for falcons to accomodate their long tails and toes. They are often covered in astro turf to allow them to be cleaned easily.

FIGURE 9.34 Bow or ring perches are commonly used for hawks.

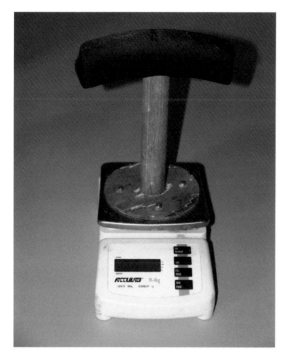

FIGURE 9.35   The scale is a vital piece of equipment that helps a falconer maintain the raptor's weight accordingly.

always in the falconer's presence. The next food offering incorporates an opportunity to feed from the glove. This progression moves from allowing the bird to feed on the ground in the falconer's presence, to gradually moving closer during feeding, to taking food from the glove, and finally being able to slip a food-bearing, gloved hand under the bird while it is feeding. The goal is achieved when the bird can comfortably feed on the glove without hesitation or suspicion of the falconer. This stage requires patience and may last anywhere from two to three days to as long as several weeks, depending on the individual and the species.

STAGE 2 FLYING TO THE FIST OR CREANCE TRAINING

The next step is to persuade the raptor to fly to the glove for food. The bird is useless on the hunt if it does not come to you. Initially, this stage can be done in enclosed areas or flight pens where the bird cannot fly away. The falconer may choose to begin this stage outdoors, which requires the use of a long leash, or "creance," attached to the bird that allows for longer flight, but not escape. For one adaptation of a creance leash, the raptor is attached to a shorter leash, attached by a ring to a long rope suspended above the ground, as illustrated by Figure 9.37. The ring on the leash allows it to move along the suspended rope as the bird flies. Beginning at close distances, the bird is encouraged to fly from its perch to the glove, enticed with meat treats. This distance of flight between perch and glove is steadily increased. Falconers may choose to cue the bird with a whistle or a sound, but some choose to silently rely on the bird's sight alone. This procedure must be performed each day at the same time for between 5 days and 2 weeks, depending on the species. The next stage can begin once (1) the bird comes reliably and without hesitation three or four times in succession at the desired distance, which varies for different species; and (2) the bird will reliably feed on the glove, unconcerned, without frequent "bating" (the falconer's term for trying to fly away).

STAGE 3 LURE TRAINING

Lure training involves training the bird to attack the lure, and then give up the lure in exchange for a treat. This portion of the training builds determination and endurance. Initially, this stage of training is also conducted with the bird on a leash and creance. Since the raptor has become accustomed to coming to the falconer for a piece of meat, the first few times the lure is introduced, it should resemble what the raptor is used to eating, having bits of meat attached to it, called "garnishing the lure." Later, the lure should resemble the target prey with feathers and wings for avian prey and fur for mammalian prey. While the bird is on its training perch, the lure is tossed to one side of the falconer, where it can be seen. Raptors may not go to the

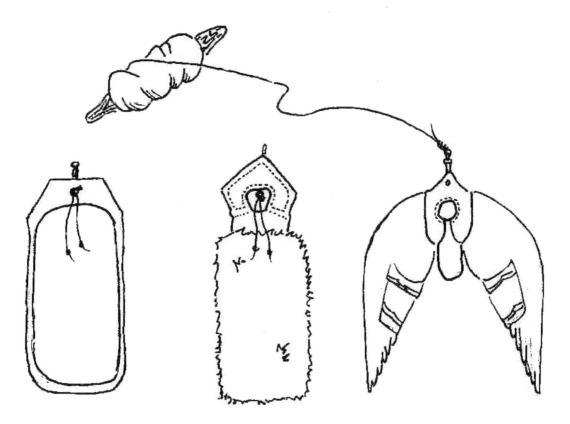

FIGURE 9.36 Falconers make lures with leather covered in fur or feathers to resemble the target prey.

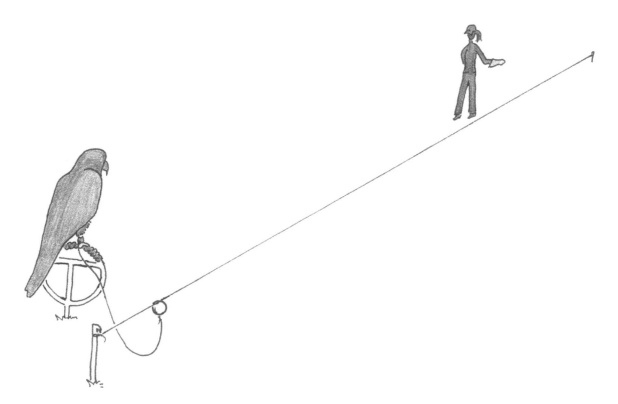

FIGURE 9.37 Creance training is meant to teach the raptor to fly to the glove for food, yet still be tethered so as not to fly away.

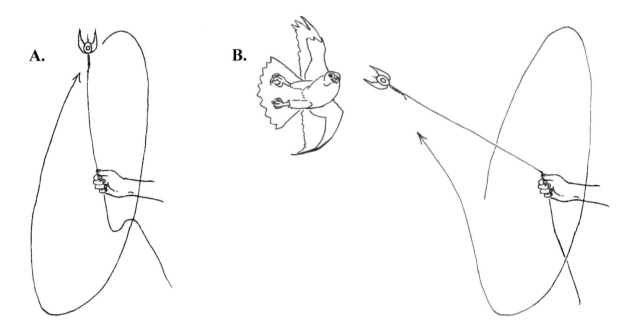

FIGURE 9.38   Lure training involves swinging the lure in a circle to capture the raptor's attention (a), and then releasing the slack in the line so the bird can attack it in the air (b) or on the ground. Lure training is an excellent form of exercise and helps build endurance in the bird.

lure the first time, but once they realize that the lure is baited with food, the process will get easier. After lunging for the lure on the ground, the bird may begin to feed from the attached bits of meat. At this point, the falconer may slowly walk over to the bird and offer a piece of meat from the glove, a situation the bird is comfortable with at this point. Gradually, the exchange can be developed where the raptor accepts food from the glove in trade for the captured prey. Once this exchange is taught and the bird has graduated into the free-flight stage, the lure may become an excellent tool for building and maintaining endurance, allowing the bird to acquire exercise when it is not out on an official hunt (Figure 9.38).

STAGE 4 ENTERING

When the bird will reliably fly to the glove, it may be let off of the leash to enter the next stage of training, which is "entering" the raptor to free flights at quarry. In the wild, the first kill is very important because it becomes the primary prey item for the rest of the bird's life. The falconer will simulate this in training by making the bird hungry, but not unhealthy, and using live, but compromised, prey of choice. By compromising (tethering, etc.) the prey, the successfulness is ensured so that the bird gains confidence. After the raptor has made the kill, it is allowed to eat its prey to drive home the success. This process is especially important for birds caught as eyesses, but can also be done with older birds.

Monitoring the bird's weight is essential for successful hunting and recovery. There is a fine balance that needs to be maintained. If the bird is slightly underfed, the bird is hungry, and therefore keen to hunt. This hunger is the goal, since the same hunger drives the raptor to hunt in the wild. If the bird is too light, however, due to prolonged underfeeding, there may be a loss of endurance and performance. If the bird is too heavy or overfed, there is no interest in hunting. In addition, if the bird is well fed when released on a hunt, there is no incentive to return to the handler for food. A successful raptor is a healthy raptor in the art and sport of falconry, so it is in the best interest of the falconer to maintain the bird at a healthy weight and condition.

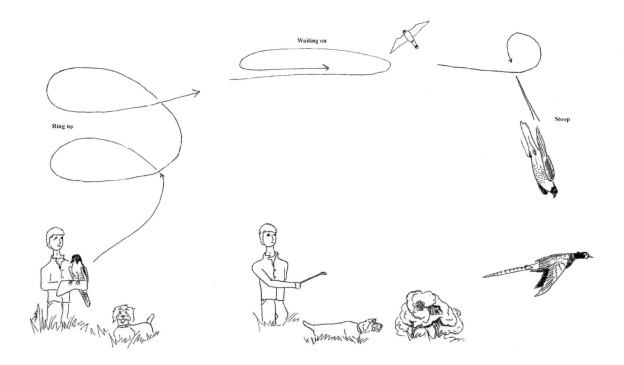

FIGURE 9.39 Referred to as gamehawking, a falconer will use the falcon to hunt gamebirds. The falcon will be released and will first gain altitude, called "ring up." Next, the falcon will "wait on" while the falconer, and possibly a hunting dog, flushes the gamebirds into the air. Finally, the falcon will "stoop" in a deep dive to attack the flushed prey in the air. After both birds have come to the ground, the falconer may run to the falcon and exchange a treat for the prey.

GAME HAWKING

When falconers use their raptors, specifically large falcons, to hunt gamebirds such as pheasants, quail, pigeons, or ducks, it is called game hawking. Falcons are most often used for this sport, since they are agile enough to catch other birds in flight. As Figure 9.39 illustrates, the bird will "ring up" to a suitable height and then "wait on," soaring and waiting for the flushing of the prey. Once the prey is flushed by either the falconer or the falconer's dogs, the raptor will "stoop," making a steep dive to kill the prey. The falconer will then run to the downed prey and exchange the prey for a treat with the raptor.

FLYING FROM THE FIST

Sometimes referred to as "drive-by falconry," flying from the fist is a type of hunting where the falconer will drive up close to the prey in a vehicle, roll down the window, and let his raptor go. This method is often used for kestrels hunting starlings. It is also used in "Crow Hawking," one of the most difficult and challenging types of falconry hunting due to the inherent danger of injuring the raptor. Crow hawking is risky for several reasons: (1) Crows are large prey and can gang up and injure a raptor; (2) Crows are always in a group, and there is always a spotter crow that sounds an alarm when the raptor is spotted; and (3) Crows are smart and live in family groups, meaning that they will mob a raptor and can kill it if left alone too long. It is important for the falconer to rescue their bird and fend off the other crows. With this said, the falconer must be physically fit, as well.

FIGURE 9.40   Gyrfalcon.

COMMON SPECIES USED IN FALCONRY IN NORTH AMERICA

PEREGRINE FALCON

The Peregrine Falcon is the most widely spread true falcon found throughout much of the world. At least one of the 18 subspecies of Peregrine Falcon is found on every continent, with the exception of Antarctica—therefore, it is a very common bird to hunt with. The Peregrine was listed as internationally endangered in the 1970s due to the use of DDT, but with the elimination of DDT in many countries, the introduction of intensive management practices, and active breeding programs, the Peregrine is now listed as of least concern, and with proper permitting, passage (first-year) Peregrines have been legal to take from the wild since 2009 in the United States (FALCO, 2010). The Peregrine is superior to other falcons in its ability to be trained to "wait on," where the falcon flies high above the falconer and waits for prey to be flushed from below. They also tend to be easy to train and have reliable temperaments (Beebem 1999).

AMERICAN KESTREL AND MERLIN

About the size of a Mourning Dove, the American Kestrel, or "Sparrow Hawk," in older bird books, is the smallest of North American falcons. It can be found year-round in most of the continental U.S. states and much of Central and South America. Both the male and female are close in size and are red-brown colored with black barring, while the mature male has slate-blue wings. Both sexes have pairs of black vertical stripes on the sides of their faces, called a "mustache" and a "sideburn." Kestrels tend to hunt primarily insects in the summer and mice and small birds in the winter. In falconry, kestrels are used to hunt sparrows and starlings, though some tamed birds will not hunt, due to their individualized nature (Beebe, 1999). As previously mentioned, kestrels are especially talented at facing a headwind and hovering to better spot prey on the ground. For this behavior, they are sometimes referred to as "hover hawks," though they are not technically hawks. They are very capable fliers and have been observed capturing prey such as blackbirds, robins, and mourning doves, sometimes as large as themselves (Beebe and Webster 2000).

The Merlin also belongs to the falcon family and measures about the same size as a kestrel; however, it generally weighs one third heavier. Merlins are listed as Least Concern and are more migratory than the American Kestrel, migrating between their summer range in Canada and Alaska and their winter range in the western United States, Mexico, Central America, and the northernmost part of South America. The Merlin is brown in coloration, with brown streaking on the chest and belly. Both sexes have a faint mustache mark on the face. They are excellent at maneuvering in flight, since their primary food is passerine, or perching, birds. Merlins train to the lure very well and are often used in falconry for hunting various small birds.

GYRFALCON

The largest falcon in the world, the Gyrfalcon (Figure 9.40) inhabits the arctic and subarctic regions of the Northern Hemisphere. It is broad-chested in appearance with long, pointed wings, and ranges in color from dark gray or black to pure white. Gyrfalcons typically pursue large birds such as Ptarmigan (grouse), ducks, geese, as well as songbirds. They have also been known to take hawks and owls. Gyrfalcons are some of the few raptors that store or cache prey during the breeding season and have been known to retrieve it mid-winter for much-needed nutrition. This species was very well known and highly regarded by medieval falconers, as only a king could hunt with a Gyrfalcon. It presently remains very desirable in the falconry arena (Beebe and Webster, 2000).

NORTHERN GOSHAWK

The largest of the North American hawks, the Northern Goshawk is a powerful raptor, able to capture a variety of prey from squirrels to snowshoe hare. The name "goshawk" comes from the Old English words *gos*, meaning goose, and *hafac*, meaning hawk. It is pronounced as if the words are still separate, without a "sh" sound (Cornell Lab of Ornithology, 2011). The species is found across northern America and Eurasia. Some populations of these large birds spend year-round in parts of the western United States and Canada, while some will winter in Midwestern states, flying back to northern areas of Canada to nest. Visually, they have long tails, broad, rounded wings, a gray belly and blue-gray back, and a distinctive dark cap and dark stripe through the eye with a white eyebrow stripe (Figure 9.41). Goshawks hunt mainly medium-sized mammals and birds by traveling forest edges from a hidden perch or patrol flights. In falconry, Goshawks tend to vary in their training, with some individuals being temperamental and others taming easily, yet they can become formidable hunters. They are highly desirable falconry birds due to their incredible speed and reactions, versatility to terrain and climate, and fearless demeanor in the field.

HARRIS'S HAWK

Harris's Hawks are year-round residents to a few southwestern U.S. states, but mostly Mexico and parts of South America. They are dark, medium-sized to large hawks with white rumps and undertail

FIGURE 9.41   Northern Goshawk.

FIGURE 9.42   Harris's Hawk.

(Figure 9.42). Their thighs and shoulders are chestnut red with legs and bare face skin yellow. Harris's Hawks often cooperatively hunt in the wild and are more successful when hunting in pairs or trios compared to individuals, with groups of five hawks being the most successful (Cornell Lab of Ornithology, 2011). Harris's may be allowed to hunt in this manner as falconry birds, as well. Working together, the hawks surround their quarry and one bird flushes the prey out so another can catch it, or they will take turns chasing it. Harris's Hawks can be trained to hunt either mammals or birds successfully, though females tend to make better rabbit hunters, while the tiercels are better bird hunters (Beebe, 1999).

RED-TAILED HAWK

Red-tailed Hawks are large, abundant, and easily seen among the larger North American raptors. As the name implies, most adults have brick-red colored tails and brown bodies, often with streaked breasts. There are at least 14 different subspecies of Red-tail that vary in size and coloration, each of which is specific to a geographic area, making identification in different parts of the continent challenging. Red-tails spend much of their time soaring or perching on high exposed poles or trees, adding to their conspicuous nature. Even without the practice of concealment, they seem to capture sufficient meals and thrive well with this lifestyle, indicated by their abundance. The majority of the Red-tail's diet consists of small rodents such as voles or rabbits. They have only been used in falconry since the 1970s and almost exclusively in North America. The Red-tail is one of the more easily trained and tamable of the larger hawks and therefore is a good fit for a novice falconer. However, since they can form such a strong bond with the trainer and they are so long-lived (more than 20 years), it can be difficult to become free of one. Often, beginner falconers become comfortable with the Red-tail's limited hunting techniques, and as they evolve to be a more experienced falconer, they desire a more challenging species. If released into the wild, Red-tails will likely return to their "home," and they hold little value to zoos or animal parks (Beebe, 1999). It is important to take this into consideration if one is planning on acquiring a Red-tail.

GOLDEN EAGLE

In the United States, Bald Eagles are not used for falconry; only Golden Eagles may be possessed for falconry and one must be a Master Falconer to qualify. Some states used to require a Federal Eagle Falconry Permit to possess and transport eagles for falconry purposes. Since the USFWS (2008) amendments, a federal permit is no longer required for a Master Falconer to possess eagles and they are treated similarly to other raptors. Nevertheless, in the United States, eagles are relatively tightly monitored. No permit authorizes the sale, purchase, trade, importation, or exportation of eagles and their parts or feathers (USFWS, 2008). While Golden Eagles naturally prefer small- to medium-sized mammals, as a bird of immense courage and strength, they can be trained to hunt much larger prey such as deer, antelope, or coyote. The Golden Eagle is found worldwide throughout much of the Northern Hemisphere. For centuries in Central Asia, falconry has remained very important in various cultures, with native tribesmen using Golden Eagles to hunt fox and wolf, a fine display of the power these birds have (Watson, 2010).

SUMMARY

Birds of prey inspire us with their beauty, grace, and power. They are able to soar unbridled to great heights in the sky and make dramatic dives at speeds considered extreme in the animal world. With over 300 species currently recognized, raptors are a diverse group in size and coloration, as well as behavior and adaptability, claiming nearly every continent. Often conspicuous, raptors are a constant reminder of our fascination with unknown wilderness and the predator-prey relationships that must exist in the natural world. The art and sport of falconry offer us an opportunity to play a part in this balance and experience nature's strength through the eyes of a formidable predator.

REFERENCES

Abbott, C. G. 1933. Closing history of the Guadalupe Caracara. *The Condor* **35**:10–14.

APCRI (Association for Prevention and Control of Rabies in India). Assessing burden of rabies in India. *Report of the National Multi-Centric Rabies Survey*, May 2004, Bangalore, India.

Beebe, F. L. and H. M. Webster. 2000. *North American Falconry and Hunting Hawks*. North American Falconry and Hunting Hawks, Fort Benton, Montana.

BirdLife International. 2009. "Pithecophaga jefferyi." In IUCN 2011. IUCN Red List of Threatened Species. Version 2011.2. ww.iucnredlist.org. Downloaded on 25 March 2012.

BirdLife International. 2012. "IUCN Red List for birds." Downloaded from http://www.birdlife.org on 27/03/2012.

Beebe, F. L. 1999. *A Falconry Manual*. Hancock House Publishers, Blaine, WA.

Boughman, M. 2003. *Reference Atlas to the Birds of North America*. National Geographic, Washington, DC.

Cecil, H. C., J. Bitman, and S. J. Harris. 1971. Effects of Dietary p,p'-DDT and p,p'-DDE on Egg Production and Egg Shell Characteristics of Japanese Quail Receiving an Adequate Calcium Diet. *Poultry Science* **50**:657–659.

Chang, E. S. and E. L. R. Stokstad. 1975. Effect of Chlorinated Hydrocarbons on Shell Gland Carbonic Anhydrase and Egg Shell Thickness in Japanese Quail. *Poultry Science* **54**:3–10.

Cornell Lab of Ornithology. 2011a. "All About Birds." Accessed 3/24/2012: http://www.allaboutbirds.org/guide/

FALCO. 2010. *The Newsletter of the Middle East Falcon Research Group*. Editors: A. Dixon and T. Bailey. Issue 36.

Fuertes, L. A. 1920. *Falconry: The sport of kings*. National Geographic Society, Washington, DC.

Glasier, P. 1998. *Falconry and Hawking, 3rd Edition*. Batsford, London.

Jones, M. P. 2006. Selected Infectious Diseases of Birds of Prey. *Journal of Exotic Pet Medicine* **15**:5–17.

Koenig, R. 2006. Vulture research soars as the scavengers' numbers decline. *Science* **312**:1591–1592.

Markandya, A., T. Taylor, A. Longo, M. N. Murty, S. Murty, and K. Dhavala. 2008. Counting the cost of vulture decline: An appraisal of the human health and other benefits of vultures in India. *Ecological Economics* **67**:194–204.

Mrozek, T. 2007. "Seven 'Roller Pigeon' enthusiasts charged with killing, or helping to kill, protected hawks and falcons." Accessed 03/03/2012: http://www.justice.gov/usao/cac/Pressroom/pr2007/2070.html. Department of Justice. United States Attorney's Office, Central District of California.

NAFA (North American Falconers Association). 2009. Accessed 03/22/2012: http://www.n-a-f-a.com/Ethics.htm

Newton, I., I. Wyllie, and L. Dale. 1999. Trends in the numbers and mortality patterns of sparrowhawks (Accipiter nisus) and kestrels (Falco tinnunculus) in Britain, as revealed by carcass analyses. *Journal of Zoology* **248**:139–147.

The Peregrine Fund. 2011. "Recent Raptor News." Accessed 03/03/2012: http://www.globalraptors.org/grin/SiteNews.asp?lNewsType=1

Robson, W. A., G. H. Arscott, and I. J. Tinsley. 1976. Effect of DDE, DDT and Calcium on the Performance of Adult Japanese Quail (Coturnix coturnix japonica). *Poultry Science* **55**:2222–2227.

Scott, M. L., J. R. Zimmermann, S. Marinsky, P. A. Mullenhoff, G. L. Rumsey, and R. W. Rice. 1975. Effects of PCBs, DDT, and Mercury Compounds upon Egg Production, Hatchability and Shell Quality in Chickens and Japanese Quail. *Poultry Science* **54**:350–368.

Sibley, D. 2010. "Sibley Guides: Causes of Bird Mortality." Accessed 03/27/12: http://www.sibleyguides.com/conservation/causes-of-bird-mortality/

Stroud, D. A. 2003. The status and legislative protection of birds of prey and their habitats in Europe. Pages 51–84 *in* D. B. A. Thompson, editor. *Birds of Prey in a Changing Environment*. The Stationery Office, Edinburgh.

Swan, G., V. Naidoo, R. Cuthbert, R. E. Green, D. J. Pain, D. Swarup, V. Prakash, M. Taggart, L. Bekker, D. Das, J. Diekmann, M. Diekmann, E. Killian, A. Meharg, R. C. Patra, M. Saini, and K. Wolter. 2006. Removing the Threat of Diclofenac to Critically Endangered Asian Vultures. *PLoS Biol* **4**:e66.

Thouless, C. R., J. H. Fanshawe, and C. R. Bertram. 1987. Egyptian vultures Neophron percnopterus and Ostrich Struthio camelus eggs: The origins of stone-throwing behaviour. *Ibis* **131**:9–15.

van Lawick-Goodall, J. and H. van Lawick. 1966. Use of tools by the Egyptian vulture, Neophrons percnopterus. *Nature* **212**:1468–1469.

USFWS (U.S. Fish and Wildlife Service). 2008. *Federal Register: Migratory Bird Permits; Changes in the Regulations Governing Falconry*. Vol. 73. Department of the Interior. National Archives and Records Administration.

Watson, J. 2010. *The Golden Eagle, 2nd Edition*. T & A D Poyser, London.

Wendell, M., J. Sleeman, and G. Kratz. 2002. Retrospective study of morbidity and mortality of raptors admitted to Colorado State University Veterinary Teaching Hospital during 1995 to 1998. *Journal of Wildlife Diseases* **38**:101–106.

Williams, T. 2008. Incite: Fowl Play. *Audubon Magazine*: May–June.

X PIGEONS AND DOVES

Pigeons and doves belong to the family Columbidae and the order Columbiformes. The terms dove and pigeon can be used interchangeably—there is no scientific taxonomic basis for distinguishing between the two. However, in common practice for ornithologists, the term dove is typically applied to smaller species, while pigeon is used to refer to the larger species of Columbidae. The terms dove and pigeon will be used interchangeably in this chapter. Young doves and pigeons are called squabs.

Pigeons have spread throughout the world on their own accord, based on their strong flight ability. They are found in almost all terrestrial habitats and have a worldwide distribution, except for Antarctica and a few isolated islands, including the Hawaiian Islands. They also are not resident in the northern latitudes of the Arctic and in the driest areas of deserts. The common Rock Pigeon (*Columba livia*), originally native to cliff areas from western Europe through eastern Europe, northern Africa, central Asia to China and Mongolia, has readily adapted to using ledges of buildings in cities all over the world for roosting and nesting. Doves and pigeons are known for their soft calls and coos. They are, for the most part, stocky birds with short necks and very well-developed breast muscles for strong, fast flight. The descendants of the common Rock Pigeon that have been selected for pigeon racing can fly at 60 miles per hour (97 kilometers/hour). The size range of dove species is fairly dramatic, from about 30 grams for small ground doves (Figure 10.1, Inca Dove) to about 2.5 kilograms for the crowned pigeons such as the Victoria Crowned Pigeon (Figure 10.2). Although many temperate pigeons are more sedate in coloring with shades of gray and brown, many of the tropical fruit-eating doves are very colorful (Figure 10.3 a & b).

Diets for pigeons and doves typically consist of fruit, seeds, or fresh green leaves. However, species tend to specialize, with many being seed-eaters, while others are almost exclusively fruit eaters. The grain (seed) eaters tend to be ground feeders, and they have very strong gizzards. The fruit-eating (frugivorous) pigeons have weaker gizzards and feed

FIGURE 10.1   The Inca Dove is one of the smaller members of the pigeon and dove order. It has a unique color pattern with dark brown at the feather edging, giving it a scaled appearance.

FIGURE 10.2   The Victoria Crowned Pigeon is the largest pigeon species with an adult weight of about 2.4 kg or 5 pounds. It is found on a few islands of Indonesia and on Papua New Guinea. The wild population is estimated at less than 10,000 adults and the population is declining due to hunting for meat and feathers and habitat loss (BirdLife International).

in trees. Only a few bird families are capable of drinking water by sucking water up in one continuous draft, and pigeons and doves are included (Figure 10.4). In contrast, most birds drink by sipping or scooping water up and then letting gravity pull the water down the gastrointestinal tract by raising their heads. While many pigeons and doves do demonstrate this suction method of drinking, as reviewed by Zweers (1982), apparently not all pigeons and doves utilize this method; several other species of birds drink in a similar manner. Subsequently, other birds have been identified that drink by a suction method (Moermond, 1983). It is also a common misconception that all species of pigeons and doves lack a gallbladder. While some species of doves and pigeons do not have a gallbladder, many species do possess one (Hagey et al., 1994).

BREEDING AND CROP MILK

Doves tend to build flimsy nests made mostly from twigs and other short pieces of vegetative material. Nests are typically found in trees, on ledges, on the ground or in ground burrows, depending on the species of pigeon. Pigeons are monogamous and pair for the breeding season or for life, depending on the species. Females lay one or two white eggs, with the females from most species producing two eggs. Tropical fruit doves and the largest species of pigeons generally lay only one egg. As a whole, pigeons produce very small eggs relative to adult body size. When this attribute is combined with the small clutch size, it means that pigeons have the smallest total clutch weights in relation to adult body weight of all the families of nest-reared, terrestrial birds (Perrins, 2009). However, several pigeon species produce several broods per year, because pigeon egg incubation periods are relatively short and fledging times are relatively fast compared to birds of similar size. The rapid development of the very altricial chicks is a result of both parents producing crop milk to feed their offspring.

In birds, milk is produced in the crop and/or esophagus by male and female pigeons/doves, male Emperor Penguins and male and female flamingos. In pigeons and doves, crop milk is fed exclusively to the developing chick(s) for the first few days. Thereafter, the total level of crop milk fed stays the same, but since the chick is continuing to get larger, its total intake of food is increasing, and this increase is made up of solid foods consumed by and regurgitated by the parents to their young. Pigeon crop milk is highly nutritious, with greater levels of fat and protein than human or cow milk (Table 10.1). The composition of flamingo milk and Emperor Penguin milk is also nutrient-dense. Flamingo milk is 83–89% water, 8–9% protein, 15% fat, 0.2% carbohydrate (Fisher, 1972' Ward et al., 2001; Perrins, 2009). Emperor Penguin milk on a dry matter basis is about 29% lipid, 59% protein, and 5.5% carbohydrate (Fisher, 1972).

TABLE 10.1 COMPOSITION OF PIGEON, COW, AND HUMAN MILK (IN PERCENT)

Species	Water	Protein	Fat	Carbohydrate	Ash
Pigeon[1]	65–81	13–19	7–13	Minimal[2]	1–2
Cow[3]	87–88	3.3	3.4	4.9	0.7
Human[4]	87–88	0.8–1	4.5	7.1	0.2

[1] PIGEON (CARR AND JAMES, 1931; REED ET AL., 1932; DAVIES, 1939; DESMETH AND VANDEPUTTE-POMA, 1980; PERRINS, 2009).

[2] PIGEON MILK CONTAINS NO LACTOSE AND MINIMAL (0.05%) FREE SUGARS (CARBOHYDRATES), BUT IT DOES CONTAIN SUGAR CARBOHYDRATES LINKED TO OTHER MOLECULES SUCH AS PROTEIN AND LIPIDS, GIVING IT ABOUT 1% CARBOHYDRATE CONTENT OVERALL (SHETTY ET AL., 1994).

[3] (MEIGS AND MARSH, 1913; JENSEN, 1995; CORNELL UNIVERSITY, 2012).

[4] (MEIGS AND MARSH, 1913; JENSEN, 1995; BELITZ ET AL., 2009).

Pigeon crop milk is not a secreted solution like milk produced from other species, such as humans and bovines. However, its production is controlled by the hormone prolactin which controls milk synthesis in other species. During incubation of the eggs, prolactin stimulates the hypertrophy of the epithelium cells lining the crop. The crop is lined with a proliferating basal zone of epithelium (Horseman and Buntin, 1995). As epithelial cells produced by this basal zone are replaced by new cells, they move away from the basal zone toward the lumen of the crop. As they move toward the lumen, the cells differentiate, and under the influence of prolactin, acquire large amounts of lipid and protein. Eventually, these epithelial cells are sloughed off into the lumen of the crop, much like you replenish and slough off skin cells. When prolactin is present, the cells that slough off into the crop are engorged with lipid and protein, and masses of these cells have a cottage-cheese-like texture when mixed with water. This mixture of water and cells is then fed by the parents to their chick(s). As the chicks get closer to fledging, the levels of prolactin start to decrease, and the production of crop milk begins to wane until it ceases entirely.

THE CURRENT STATE OF PIGEON SPECIES WORLDWIDE

BirdLife International lists 305 species of extant pigeons (BirdLife International, 2012). Of these species, 60, or 19.67 percent, are considered threatened. Of the threatened species, the Socorro Dove—named after Socorro Island, one of the Revillagigedo Islands of Mexico—is extinct in the wild. The last known sighting in the wild was in 1972. The species is maintained by aviculturalists in Europe and the Unites States, although much of the stock in the United

FIGURE 10.3   Rose-crowned Fruit-Doves and Pink-headed Fruit-Doves are some of the more colorful individuals in the pigeon family.

FIGURE 10.4   Pigeons and doves are some of the few birds that can siphon water through the bill in one continuous draft.

States is no longer pure due to cross breeding with the Mourning Dove. Ultimately, it is hoped that the Socorro Dove will be reintroduced to Socorro Island using birds from the pure European lines. Initial steps have been taken on Socorro to ensure that reintroduced doves survive.

Nine species of pigeons or doves are listed as critically endangered. Two of these, the Negros Fruit-dove and Sulu Bleeding-heart, have not been recorded in the wild since 1953 and 1891, respectively (BirdLife International, 2012). As discussed in Chapter 2, many threatened and vulnerable species are restricted to islands. Of the nine critically endangered pigeons and doves, seven are found only on isolated islands. As expected, habitat loss, invasive species, and significant weather events such as hurricanes have played roles in the decline of these seven island endemic species.

BirdLife International lists 12 species of doves and pigeons as extinct. A nice review of almost all of these species is presented in Errol Fuller's book *Extinct Birds*. The Fuller compilation also includes two species of Dodo Birds and the Rodrigues Solitaire as part of the pigeon family. Since the mid 1800s, morphological studies have linked the extinct Dodo and Rodrigues Solitaire, and it was widely assumed by taxonomists that both species had evolved from a common pigeon-like ancestor in Southeast Asia. BirdLife International classifies the extinct Dodo and Rodrigues Solitaire as the only members of the family Raphidae, which is placed within the order Columbiformes. However, recent molecular data indicates that the Dodo and Solitaire are part of the Columbidae family and most closely related to the extant Nicobar Pigeon (Shapiro et al., 2002; Fulton et al., 2012), thus increasing the number of extinct pigeon species.

PASSENGER PIGEON EXTINCTION

Without a doubt, based on the rapidity of the population decline and the sheer number of birds involved, the extinction of the Passenger Pigeon (Figure 10.5) is the most noteworthy bird extinction that exists. Passenger Pigeons were likely the most abundant bird species ever to exist, with a population estimate of 3 to 5 *billion* birds at the time of European settlement of North America (Encyclopedia Smithsonian, 2012). This number would have constituted 25 to 40 percent of the total bird population of North America at that time (Schorger, 1973). Despite this huge population, the last Passenger Pigeon died in 1914 in the Cincinnati Zoological Gardens. The last substantiated record of a wild individual was in 1900 in Ohio. The American Ornithologists' Union offered $1,500 to anyone finding a nest or nesting colony of Passenger Pigeons from 1909 to 1912, to no avail. The cause for this dramatic decline in population was caused principally by overhunting, followed by the bird's inability to prosper outside of the colony dynamic.

Excellent reviews on the Passenger Pigeon extinction exist (Schorger, 1973; Halliday, 1980; Blockstein and Tordoff, 1985; Fuller, 1987; Encyclopedia Smithsonian, 2012) and are in large part the basis for the following brief summary. Passenger Pigeons formed large, gregarious flocks, and this social structure appears to have been essential for their survival and the root of their extinction. The range of the Passenger Pigeon extended from central Ontario, Quebec, and Nova Scotia south to the uplands of Texas, Louisiana, Alabama, Georgia, and Florida. The western edge of the range in the United States was Texas and Oklahoma up through the Dakotas. The Passenger Pigeon fed primarily on beechnuts, acorns, chestnuts, seeds, and berries. In the winter months, the birds formed roosting sites in their southern territory. These roosting sites often contained birds so densely packed on one another that large limbs would snap from their weight, and even large

FIGURE 10.5   A rendition of the now extinct Passenger Pigeon.

trees would be toppled over by the weight of the birds. During the day, the birds would leave the roosting site to find food and then return at night. Once local food sources had been depleted at a given roosting site, the pigeons would move the communal roost to a new site.

In the spring, there was a massive migration of the pigeons in only a few immense flocks from the southern reaches of their territory to its more northern reaches for breeding. Breeding grounds would be selected based on the presence of large crops of nuts from the preceding fall still being present on the ground. In the 1830s, bird naturalist John James Audubon wrote about a Passenger Pigeon migration by stating "the air was literally filled with pigeons; the light of noonday was obscured as by an eclipse: dung fell in spots, not unlike melting snow … pigeons were still passing in undiminished numbers, and continued to do so for three days in succession." In most years, at least one massive colony nested in the forests of New York or Pennsylvania, while another massive colony nested in Michigan or Wisconsin. The largest nesting ever recorded was in Wisconsin—it covered 850 square miles and contained at least 135 million adult birds. Hundreds of nests could be counted in a single tree. After breeding, the large flocks dispersed into smaller flocks (still typically in the hundreds of thousands to millions) to forage for food across their entire northern range.

Food availability and the resulting devastation of the ecosystem brought on by the pigeons forced them to move their roosts and breeding grounds from year to year. Locations where the pigeons gathered en masse would be described as having the appearance of having suffered a tornado or hurricane. Extensive tree damage occurred, the feces under the trees was so think that it smothered the growth of vegetation, and there was such a complete depletion of seeds, nuts, and fruits that other resident animals starved. Thus, it was not unusual for locals to indicate that the colonies of pigeons only occurred in a given area every decade or so.

As settlers cleared forests and planted crops, the pigeons began utilizing farmers' grain fields for food, but the loss of forest and killing of pigeons by farmers to protect their crops did not noticeably diminish numbers or lead to their extinction. Even though deforestation was occurring and reducing Passenger Pigeon habitat and potentially pigeon numbers, the massive deforestation that occurred in the eastern and Midwestern forests of the United States did not occur until after the Passenger population had already crashed in the 1880s. However, what did take a massive toll on the Passenger Pigeon population were professional market hunters. These hunters took advantage of the Passenger Pigeon's communal nature and used techniques such as baited net traps and placing pots of burning sulfur under roosting trees so the fumes would daze the birds and cause them to drop to the ground. Squabs were simply poked out of nests with long sticks. One of the last large (nearly 250 square miles) colony nest sites to be discovered was in Petoskey, Michigan, in 1878, where 50,000 birds per day were killed. Incredibly, this rate of slaughter occurred at this location non-stop for nearly five months.

Market hunting of Passenger Pigeons had really taken hold by the 1840s, when it became a major industry that continued to prosper until about 1880. The advancement of rail and telegraph networks during this time spurred the growth of the industry. By the time of the Civil War, there were railroad and telegraph networks throughout almost all of the United States east of the Mississippi River. The railroad allowed transport of pigeons to the markets in the cities and the transport of professional hunters to wherever the pigeons were attempting to nest or roost. Telegraph communication allowed the hunters to be alerted as to where the pigeon colonies where located.

The squabs were the most desirable for the meat market in cities. But adults were also slaughtered for consumption and sold for as little as 50 cents per dozen. Live adult birds were also shipped to major cities, where they were used for live targets for trap shooting. Birds were also used to feed domesticated pigs.

As a result of market hunting, the population of Passenger Pigeons was only in the hundreds of millions by the early 1870s. Subsequently, by the 1880s they were scarce, and by the 1890s they were extremely rare. During the height of the decline in the Passenger Pigeon population during the 1870s and even into the 1880s, adult birds were harassed to such an extent by hunting activities that colony nesting attempts failed to produce offspring in any significant number to replenish those that had been slaughtered and the remaining aging population. The last known attempt at colonial nesting was in 1887 in Wisconsin, and the birds left about two weeks after starting to nest.

Natural predators were actually attracted to the immense colonies of birds at nesting sites. However, the massive number of birds provided overall security simply by satiating all the predators. With such large numbers, the losses to non-human predators were inconsequential to the overall population. This colonial lifestyle undoubtedly led Passenger Pigeons to become less predator-savvy over time, which made them more vulnerable once the numbers of birds became severely diminished. Similarly, their reproductive behavior was suited for a large colony situation with regard to predators. Nests in the colony were packed closely together and were conspicuous. After hatching, parents took care of their chicks for about two weeks before they left, with all the other adults leaving the chicks on their own in the nests. Although weighing more than adult birds at this time, the chicks did not have skilled flight capability for several more days, which put them at high risk for predation. But there were millions of such babies at a nesting site, so losing a small percentage to satiate all predators was again no big deal until flocks became small. Passenger Pigeons were capable of nesting in captivity in pairs and in small groups in the wild. So, while the colony was not needed for successful production of individual offspring, it did play a vital role in the successful overall survival of offspring and helps explain why the remaining small flocks of birds that had been spared during the hunting onslaught failed to sustain or reestablish the population.

Legislation by states to ban hunting and protect nesting sites of Passenger Pigeons began from 1862 onward, but the bans were widely ignored (Schorger, 1973). This legislation was some of the earliest conservation legislation in the United States. Its failure to save the Passenger Pigeon is ultimately credited for paving the way for future conservation awareness, legislation, and enforcement, which have occurred in this country since the early 1900s. It is credited with saving other species from going extinct.

PIGEONS IN NORTH AMERICA

In North America, BirdLife International lists 26 species of native pigeons and doves (BirdLife International, 2012). Of these 26 species, 13 of them can be seen in the United States, with most of the species occurring in the southern reaches of the United States (Table 10.2). In addition to these native species, there are four introduced species of wild doves (Table 10.2).

TABLE 10.2 NATIVE AND INTRODUCED SPECIES OF WILD PIGEONS AND DOVES IN THE UNITED STATES

Common name	Scientific name	Range[1]	Native or introduced
Mourning Dove	*Zenaida macroura*	Continental U.S.	Native
Inca Dove	*Columbina inca*	LA, TX, AZ, NM, NV, and CA	Native
Common Ground-Dove	*Columbina passerina*	South GA, FL to TX along the gulf coast, and South AZ, and CA	Native
Ruddy Ground-Dove	*Columbina talpacoti*	South TX to South CA	Native
White-tipped Dove	*Leptotila verreauxi*	South TX	Native
Band-tailed Pigeon	*Patagioenas fasciata*	West coast, AZ, NV, UT, and NM	Native
Red-billed Pigeon	*Patagioenas flavirostris*	South TX	Native
White-crowned Pigeon	*Patagioenas leucocephala*	South Florida and Keys	Native
White-winged Dove	*Zenaida asiatica*	From FL to LA along the Gulf Coast, TX and South CA, NV, AZ, and NM (range is expanding)	Native
Zenaida Dove	*Zenaida aurita*	FL keys and south FL (but rarely seen)	Native
Key West Quail-dove	*Geotrygon chrysia*	FL keys and South FL (but rarely seen)	Native
Ruddy Quail-dove	*Geotrygon montana*	South TX (but rarely seen)	Native
Rock Pigeon	*Columba livia*	Continental U.S.	Introduced
Eurasian Collared-Dove	*Streptopelia decaocto*	Continental U.S., but less prevalent in Northeast	Introduced
African Collared-Dove	*Streptopelia roseogrisea*	Isolated populations, especially in the Southern tier of the U.S.	Introduced
Spotted Dove	*Stigmatopelia chinensis*	California	Introduced
Passenger Pigeon	*Ectopistes migratorius*	extinct	Native

[1]RANGE DATA EBIRD (http://ebird.org/ebird/map)

FIGURE 10.6   Mourning Dove, a widespread and resilient native to the U.S. and much of the Western Hemisphere.

FIGURE 10.7   Originally native to Europe, the adaptable Rock Dove is now common throughout the world.

MOURNING DOVE

The most widespread native species is the Mourning Dove (Figure 10.6), which can be found across the entire contiguous 48 states of the United States. It is a year-round resident in most of the country and can be found in almost all terrestrial ecosystems, with the exception of deep forested areas. They are commonly seen perched on fences or transmission wires and feeding on the ground in open fields or yards. Mourning doves can be found in Canada during the spring/summer breeding season and in Mexico and Central America as a winter, non-breeding resident. As a migratory bird, the Migratory Bird Treaty Act of 1918 offers protection to the Mourning Dove, and its management is controlled by the Department of the Interior's U.S. Fish and Wildlife Service. Hunting of the Mourning Dove is allowed by the federal government, and it is one of the leading gamebirds shot in the United States each year, with over 17 million killed in 2010 (Seamans et al., 2011). However, in some states, especially in the northeastern United States, the Mourning Dove is classified as a songbird and hunting of it is not allowed. Recently, the Mourning Dove population in the United States was estimated at 350 million (Otis et al., 2008). Their high reproductive success rate has allowed the population to remain relatively stable despite being a leading gamebird shot each year in the United States.

INTRODUCED SPECIES OF DOVES

ROCK DOVE

Of the introduced species the common Rock Pigeon or Rock Dove (Figure 10.7) has been in the Unites States the longest, as it was introduced by European settlers in the early 1600s. Today, the Rock Pigeon is found from the tip of South America all the way up through to southern Alaska and southern Canada. The Rock Pigeon has readily adapted to survive in rural and urban areas of the United States and across the world. In large cities such as New York City, it uses tall buildings for perching and nesting and commonly can be seen eating scraps of food discarded by humans.

EURASIAN COLLARED-DOVE

The Eurasian Collared-Dove (Figure 10.8) is a commonly kept pet species that has escaped captivity and established feral populations in much of the world. The Eurasian Collared-Dove was brought to the Bahamas in the early 1970s by a bird breeder. In December of 1974, the aviary in which they were kept was burglarized and several birds escaped, which subsequently led the breeder to release the remaining birds, for a total release of what is believed to be less than 50 birds (Green, 1977; Smith, 1987). The birds quickly spread through the Bahamas and were confirmed in Florida in 1986 (Smith and Kale, 1986). The dove's arrival in Florida was probably earlier than 1986 (Smith, 1987), but it was mistakenly identified as the similar African Collared-Dove, another feral species existing in Florida (to be discussed next). Eurasian Collared-Doves quickly spread throughout Florida over the next decade (Romagosa and Labisky, 2000). This Florida population is the assumed source for the rapid expansion of the species across the continental United States, a progression that has been well documented through annual Christmas Bird Counts that are organized and reported by the National Audubon Society and research reports (Romagosa and McEneaney, 1999; Fujisaki et al., 2010).

The Eurasian Collared-Dove is found in open urban and agricultural habitats, where it forges for the grains that make up the majority of its diet. Thus, it is found in the same rural and suburban areas as the native Mourning Dove. In the field, the Eurasian Collared-Dove and the Mourning Dove are hard to distinguish based on a quick observation. However, closer inspection allows them to be readily told apart, as the Eurasian Collared-Dove is significantly larger than a Mourning Dove, and Mourning Doves lack the black colored half-collar found on the neck of Collared-Doves.

FIGURE 10.8 Eurasian Collared-Dove

As the Eurasian Collared-Dove is still rapidly spreading its territory and increasing its density across the United States and Canada, the extent of its final range and impact on native birds is still an evolving story. One of the biggest worries is its potential competition with the native Mourning Dove, because they share the same habitats as well as dietary and nesting requirements. However, given the larger size of the Eurasian Collared-Dove compared to the Mourning Dove, it may become the favored hunted dove, alleviating that pressure on the Mourning Dove population.

AFRICAN COLLARED-DOVE

The African Collared-Dove, often called the Ringed Turtle-Dove, is commonly kept as a pet bird in the United States and throughout the world. Some of these birds have escaped from captivity and have established feral populations in several areas of the United States, especially in the south, northeast, and areas near Chicago and Saint Louis (eBird maps). Their distribution has been limited and very slow, compared to the explosive spread of the Eurasian Collared-Dove. A population of African Collared-Doves in Southern California has existed since the late 1920s (Hardy 1973), and a population was established in St. Petersburg, Florida, in 1953 (Pranty, 2007). Both populations have shown limited expansion, and the St. Petersburg population disappeared within 13 years of the appearance of the Eurasian Collared-Dove (Pranty, 2007). The African and Eurasian Collared-Doves will breed with each other and produce hybrids (Smith, 1987; DeBenedictis, 1994; Bohlen, 1998; Pranty, 2007), and this hybridization with the Eurasian Collared-Dove is thought to be responsible for the disappearance of the African Collared-Dove population in St. Petersburg (Pranty 2007). It is very difficult to distinguish the African Collared-Dove from the Eurasian Collared-Dove. The Eurasian Collared-Dove is slightly darker in color and slightly larger than the African Collared-Dove. Hybrids of the two make identification even tougher.

SPOTTED DOVE

Originally native to southeastern Asia, the Spotted Dove has spread throughout much of the world and now has a feral population within California. This population is derived from domesticated stock that was apparently intentionally released in 1917 in Hollywood, California (Hardy, 1973). Despite thriving in Southern California for many years, it has not expanded beyond California (http://ebird.org/ebird/map).

PIGEONS AND DOVES THROUGHOUT HISTORY

Every year, the hundreds of students enrolled in our introductory avian biology class are asked at the start of the pigeon section about their perception of pigeons. Invariably, the answers always include comments like "rats with wings," "disease ridden," "dirty birds," and "city inhabitants." The perceptions are based almost entirely on the feral populations of Rock Doves, and very few realize that there are over 300 species of doves. Despite the common perception today, the historical record of pigeons is long and storied, as reviewed by Levi (1941) and Blechman (2007). Historical records with pigeons date back to at least 3000 BC. Egyptian archaeological records are full of pigeon depictions, indicating their domestication, use in messaging, and ceremonies, including tomb burial.

PIGEONS IN MYTHOLOGY AND RELIGION

Ishtar, the famous Babylonian goddess of love, was often represented by a white dove. Astarte, the Phoenician goddess of love, was represented by a white dove, and this was assimilated into Greek culture, with the subsequent naming of Aphrodite as the Greek goddess of love, who was also represented by a white dove. Venus, the Roman goddess of love, is often depicted in a chariot drawn by a pair of doves, and she was also often represented by doves. In Hindu mythology, Kamadeva, the god of love, is represented with a dove as his steed.

Several Greek writers note that, in the period from 455–19 BC, Assyrians (Syrians) hold pigeons and doves in high regard and abstain from harming them. In the early Hebrew culture, sacrifices of pigeons and doves were common, and the Old Testament makes many references to this use of doves. Doves were typically a sacrificial animal used by the masses, who could not afford more significant offerings such as goats or heifers. The Old Testament also makes mention of the dove as symbols of peace, love, and purity. In addition, the Hebrew version of Noah and the flood has the dove returning to Noah with an olive leaf, signifying that the flood had abated. Interestingly, the Arabian version and Acadian version of this event also had a dove playing a prominent role in determining the receding flood. In the Christian religion, as depicted in the New Testament, the dove is also used for sacrificial purposes, and the dove even becomes emblematic of the Holy Spirit. Doves are often portrayed in Christian art, from paintings to stained-glass windows. Pigeons and doves are also held in high regard in Islam.

Today, doves are almost universally viewed as symbols of peace, love, and purity and are commonly represented in funeral floral arrangements. They are often released at wedding and peace ceremonies.

USE OF PIGEONS TO SERVE MANKIND

Historical records and literature also give a good indication of the importance and use of the pigeon for communication, food, and entertainment. Pigeons were used by both the Greeks and Romans as messengers to share news and even the results from sporting events such as the Olympics. Both the Greeks and Romans used pigeons as a food source. The Romans maintained lofts containing thousands of pigeons and even selected traits for breeding to establish pigeon breeds that produced more meat. Pigeon references are numerous and often very detailed in both Greek and Roman literature, produced by such writers, scientists, and philosophers as Homer, Socrates, Aristotle, Virgil, and Pliny.

Rulers in the Middle East and Africa also used pigeons to communicate with distant parts of their kingdoms. Furthermore, historical records indicate that pigeon racing, including the placement of bets on the outcome of the races, was well established in Palestine by 200–220 AD. In the 12th century, Genghis Khan set up a system of pigeon posts in order to maintain quick and efficient communication throughout his vast empire, which stretched from China to the Black Sea. Finally, William Shakespeare's literature contains numerous pigeon references, and their detail indicates that either he was a pigeon breeder or that he was closely associated with pigeon breeders.

Pigeons have played vital communication roles during wars. Ancient commanders of fighters in war had limited means of communication. Foot couriers and men on horseback were slow compared to pigeons. As reviewed by Levi (1941), detailed written records of their use in war does not occur until the Roman Empire, but thereafter many accounts of their use in war communications are recorded. A few important examples are highlighted. Records from the Roman Empire indicate that Julius Caesar used pigeons as messengers during his conquest of Gaul, and that Hertius and Brutus used pigeons in 43 BC to communicate during the battle for Mutina (later spelled Modena). Pigeons were also used for communication during the Crusades of the Middle Ages. In 1574, pigeons provided news of relief to the citizens of Leyden (Leiden) during the six-month siege of this city by the Spanish during the War of Independence (Eighty Years' War) in Holland. During the Franco-Prussian War, Paris was under siege from late 1870 until falling to the enemy in early 1871. During the siege, balloons carrying pigeons were released from the city. The pigeons were then taken to other cities in France and to London, England. Subsequently, the pigeons would be released and returned back to Paris carrying messages. During the siege, 150,000 official and 1,000,000 private communications were carried back to Paris by pigeons. This success of communicating by pigeon spurred the Germans, Russians, Italians, and French to establish government-operated pigeon lofts. Germany became one of the first nations to establish military pigeon lofts, with several existing by 1887.

PIGEONS AND THE WORLD WARS

Although telephone and telegraph communication existed during World War I, it was not reliable in battle situations, as the wires could be cut or tapped by enemy forces. The use of pigeons as messengers allowed radio silence for surprise attacks—therefore, pigeons played vital roles in wartime communication. The importance of pigeons is easily seen by the fact that, as soon as German forces occupied French and Belgian territory, they ordered all pigeons to be destroyed. As a result, anyone found in possession of pigeons was punished for possessing contraband of war.

Great Britain did not realize the importance of pigeons until after the war had started, but subsequently, an emergency pigeon service was established, and the first pigeons were used on the front lines in 1916. Similarly, when the United States entered the war, they had no organized pigeon force. Wendell Levi, an infantry first lieutenant, was ordered to study the use of pigeons in

FIGURE I0.9   A mobile pigeon loft in Northern France during WWI.

FIGURE I0.I0a   A PG-67 message holder used in WWII.

FIGURE I0.I0b   A message would be placed in the holder and then the holder would be attached to a homing pigeons' leg. The pigeon would be released from the battlefield to deliver the message back to its home loft.

war, especially their training in mobile lofts (Figure 10.9). He and his men discovered that pigeons would recognize a distinctive marking on the roof of their loft even if they had been moved some distance. He trained 65 men on the care and use of the racing homing pigeons; thus, the United States Military Pigeon Service was established.

During World War II, pigeons played an important role, not only for battlefield communication, but also for espionage. Both the German and Allied forces used pigeons for communication (Figure 10.10 a & b), as radio communication often failed in the field. Additionally, pigeons were an ideal form of communication when radio silence was desired, such as for the beach landing in Normandy on D-day. Pigeons were used by spies that were in enemy territory to relay messages back to their governments (Figure 10.11). Additionally, undercover pigeons were used. For example, the British forged their own lower-quality homing pigeons to appear as if they were German pigeons based on identification marking, and equipped them with forged German message holders. These pigeons were then dropped in Germany, and because they did not have excellent homing ability, they would join (infiltrate) the local German Pigeon Corps. However, if these pigeons were subsequently used by undercover German agents in Britain or released in occupied territory closer to Britain, these pigeons would fly back to their original home loft in Britain, with the information intended for the German command.

So important was the use of pigeons in communication and espionage that both the Allies and Germans had marksmen trained to shoot pigeons seen heading away from their respective territories. Additionally, the Germans started breeding and releasing Peregrine Falcons—naturally highly efficient predators of pigeons—to kill enemy pigeons. Britain had an active program exterminating Peregrine Falcons near the coast of the English Channel, so that they would not kill British pigeons delivering messages back to Britain from occupied Europe. Of course, eliminating the Peregrine Falcons along the coast made it easier for German pigeons with intelligence messages to leave Britain and return to their lofts in German-held territory.

There are countless heroic pigeons from both World Wars that could be covered in this book. However, coverage will be limited to two of the most famous war pigeons. Cher Ami served in World War I. Cher Ami was assigned to the 77th Infantry Division, commanded by Major Charles Whittlesey. On October 2, 1918, the 77th Division, along with French forces and other American units, attacked German forces in the Argonne Forest. Regretfully, only the 77th Division broke through enemy lines, which led to them being isolated and surrounded by the Germans. The 77th Brigade became known as the Lost Battalion. The 500-plus men of the 77th Division took up a defensive position and tried to get communication about their precarious position out to their commanders, using foot couriers and pigeons. By the afternoon of October 4th, Major Whittlesey only had one pigeon, Cher Ami, left. By this point, the lost battalion was under fire from shelling by American artillery. The following message was placed in Cher Ami's message canister: "We are along the roads parallel to 276.4. Our own artillery is dropping a barrage directly on us. For heaven's sake, stop it." Cher Ami successfully delivered the message, and the surviving 194 men of the Lost Battalion were rescued.

On Cher Ami's last mission, he was badly wounded (Harry Farrington, 1926), but Cher Ami still made it back to the loft, and the soldier alerted to Cher Ami's return found the bird lying on his back, covered in blood. Cher Ami had been blinded in one eye, had a quarter-sized hole through his breast and the leg carrying the message canister was hanging by only a few threads of tissue. It is interesting to note that, over time, the stories of Cher Ami's Lost Battalion heroics and the injuries sustained during Cher Ami's last flight are typically combined into one dramatic story that indicates Cher Ami was injured during the flight that delivered the message that saved the Lost Battalion.

Medics saved Cher Ami, but not his leg. Cher Ami was sent to the United States and died in June of 1919 as a result of his multiple war wounds. For his bravery, the French government awarded Cher Ami the *Croix de Guerre*, or Cross of War, with palm, which represents one of France's highest honors. Cher Ami is now displayed with the award in the National Museum of American History in the Smithsonian (Figure 10.12).

G.I. Joe served in World War II and is credited with saving the lives of at least 1,000 British troops. The British 56th Brigade easily entered the Italian city of Colvi Vecchia on October 18, 1943. Taking the city was supposed to be a stiff battle, but the Germans had retreated prior to the arrival of the 56th Brigade. Because taking Colvi Vecchia was anticipated to be difficult, the United States Air Support Command was scheduled to bomb the city to soften German resistance. However, because the British troops had already entered the city, the planned bombing campaign would have resulted in many casualties for these troops. All attempts to cancel the bombing raid through radio contact failed, so G.I. Joe was released by a communications officer of the 56th Brigade with a message to cancel the bombing. G.I. Joe flew the 20 miles back to the U.S. Air Support Command base in 20 minutes and arrived as the planes were warming up to take off. G.I. Joe was subsequently awarded the Dickin Medal for Bravery by the Lord Mayor of London. Though several other pigeons from a variety of countries have been given this honor, G.I. Joe is the only bird or animal from the United States to be given this high award. After his death in 1961, G.I. Joe became an exhibit at the Army's Historical Center at Fort Monmouth, New Jersey.

As modern electronic communication technology advanced, the use of pigeons in war waned, especially for the highly industrialized nations. But even in modern warfare, pigeons are still being used. Saddam Hussein was said to communicate in Iraq with homing pigeons during the first Gulf War (Blechman, 2007). Currently, with

FIGURE 10.11   Spy pigeons in World War II.

FIGURE 10.12   A great war hero, Cher Ami is now preserved at the National Museum of American History in the Smithsonian.

the uprising in Syria, residents from the besieged city of Homs are communicating with each other by use of homing pigeons (Zablit, 2012).

PROJECT SEA HUNT

A more recent use of the pigeon by the United States government occurred in the late 1970s and early 1980s. Based on previous research that indicated pigeons could be trained to pick out colors and shapes in exchange for a food reward, the U.S. Coast Guard initiated Project Sea Hunt. During this project, pigeons were conditioned by U.S. Navy scientists to conduct search-and-rescue actions from Coast Guard helicopters. Utilizing an observation bubble on the underside of rescue helicopters, three pigeons were positioned 120 degrees from each other, so that a full 360 degrees would be scanned from underneath the helicopter. When the pigeons recognized a target, they would be able to peck a key to alert the flight crew. In a series of trials, the pigeons were 93 percent accurate in locating objects in the water, with an extremely low false positive rate, while human flight crews were only successful with location 38 percent of the time (U.S. Coast Guard, 2012). Despite these successful results, the program was ended in 1983 due to federal budget cuts before it could be implemented beyond the trial phase.

PIGEONS AND POLLUTION MONITORING

Pigeons are also receiving attention for their potential role in pollution monitoring. In 2006, it was demonstrated that homing pigeons outfitted with GPS units, real-time air pollution sensors, and cell phone transmitters could provide location specific air quality measurements in real time (Pigeon Blog, 2012). Additionally, feral pigeons and homing pigeons have been shown to be effective biomonitors of environmental pollution, especially in China (Hutton and Goodman, 1980; Schilderman et al., 1997; Nam et al., 2004; Nam and Lee, 2005, 2006; Liu et al., 2010). Because the pigeons live in large cities, they are exposed to the same air as the human population, and tissue samples from them can potentially reflect human exposure to pollutants such as heavy metals and organic hydrocarbons.

HOMING ABILITY

Many birds display an ability to find their way home from distant sites. This ability is seen with migrating birds, which move between broad geographic locations—more specifically in philopatric species, like many duck species, which migrate to their specific birth areas for their own reproductive efforts. What allows birds to effectively navigate has been studied extensively and most thoroughly in homing pigeons. But, a complete understanding of all the mechanisms and details involved in the homing ability has not been achieved, in large part because a great deal of biological redundancy exists in homing ability. Having multiple biological mechanisms to ensure the ability to home makes sense, given the importance of the task. However, experimentally, the redundancy creates problems for testing a specific hypothesis and can lead to conflicting results, as will be detailed in the section on factors used for homing.

As reviewed by Walcott (1996), homing pigeons seem to adopt a home location at about six weeks of age. Prior to this time, a pigeon is willing to adopt any location as home. After this point, training pigeons to adopt a new home location is very difficult, and once a location is adopted, it lasts throughout the bird's life. Adoption of a location is enhanced by a young bird's ability to fly around the location, but adoption of a location will still occur, even if the young pigeon is not given outside access to the location (Walcott, 1996).

FACTORS USED IN HOMING

SUN COMPASS

Homing pigeons possess a time-compensated sun compass, which allows them to take into consideration the movement of the sun across the sky during the day and calculate a correct orientation toward home (Schmidt-Koenig, 1990; Walcott, 1996; Wiltschko et al., 2000). A given position of the earth relative to the position of the sun changes continuously during the day by 15 degrees per hour. Classic experiments have been conducted, in which homing pigeons are tricked with artificial lights into thinking it is a certain time, while in reality, it is another. Pigeons that have been clock-shifted by six hours and released while it is sunny will fly off toward home in a direction that is 90 degrees in error, depending on the direction of the shift (Schmidt-Koenig, 1990; Schmidt-Koenig et al., 1991). It is important to note that clock-shift experiments indicate that the compass sense is affected, but not their overall sense of home, since they still head off in the direction of home, just on a shifted course.

SENSITIVITY TO THE EARTH'S MAGNETIC FIELD

Interestingly, if six-hour clock-shifted pigeons are released on overcast days such that the sun never appeared, they orient and home, which suggests another biological system can provide for homing ability orientation (Keeton, 1969). Pigeons are sensitive to the earth's magnetic field and use this sensitivity to return home, as reviewed by Walcott (1996). Pigeons wearing magnets on their head, which interfere with this sensitivity, could not orient and return home properly on cloudy days, but they could do so if released on sunny days. Control pigeons wearing brass bars instead of magnets could return home on both overcast and sunny days. The data indicates that the sun compass and sensitivity to the earth's magnetic field can each be used by homing pigeons in returning home, with the sun compass taking priority on sunny days and sensitivity to the earth's magnetic field taking precedence when the sun is not available for orientation. Magnetic sensitivity appears to provide both orientation and navigation information to homing pigeons and may be detected by magnetoreceptors located both in the eye and in the beak (Wiltschko and Wiltschko, 2007; Stapput et al., 2010; Wiltschko et al., 2010).

VISION AND MEMORY

Pigeons have excellent eyesight and can search and scan the terrain and their surroundings very efficiently. More importantly, they can combine this visual acuity with an excellent memory. Thus, homing pigeons are able to form a mental map of landmarks and the terrain around their home location and use that to assist in their return to this location (Braithwaite and Newman, 1994). Pigeons that have been outfitted with frosted lenses, depriving them of visual landmarks, still orient but have difficulty finding/returning to their home location, as reviewed by Walcott (1996).

Although birds have visual sensitivity to polarized light (Muheim, 2011) and ultraviolet (Bennett and Cuthill, 1994) light, there is no convincing evidence as of yet that these two factors play any definitive role in homing ability.

OLFACTORY CUES

Olfactory information also appears to play a role in homing ability. Olfactory navigation was first proposed by Floriano Papi in the early 1970s. Since that time, evidence has accumulated to support this hypothesis (as reviewed by Papi, 1989; Walcott, 1996; Wallraff, 2005). Experienced homing pigeons made unable to smell by olfactory nerve section were unable to home well when released at unfamiliar sites, but homed normally when released at familiar sites (Streng and Wallraff, 1992). Pigeons transported long distances orient well if allowed to breathe the air along the journey, while birds provided filtered air do not orient well (Wallraff and Foa, 1981). Evidence suggests that pigeons develop a map of the area around their home based on olfactory cues, and that changes in the odor gradient are then used in order to help them home. Recent data indicates that the right-side olfactory system may be more important than the left in processing olfactory information for navigation (Gagliardo et al., 2011). Further research is needed to determine the exact roles that smell has in pigeon homing ability.

OTHER

Acoustic information does not appear to play a role in homing ability (Walcott, 1996). Pigeons can be disoriented by unusual magnetic anomalies at given locations (Walcott, 1996). Pigeon racers avoid releasing birds in areas with a high concentration of electromagnetic waves associated with data transmission (television, cell phone, radio, etc.) cell towers, because they feel they can confuse/disrupt the homing ability.

In research trials, there is also a difference in results between young and inexperienced pigeons and older, experienced ones released at unfamiliar sites to return home. Young, inexperienced birds take longer to home because they appear to be taking time to explore and obtain new information to further refine their maps (Schiffner et al., 2011). Homing ability in racing homing pigeons improves with training and experience and with genetic selection, as will be discussed in the upcoming section on Racing Pigeons.

OVERALL

Simplifying homing ability into two phases: Orientation and navigation allows a summary of the cues used in homing. When pigeons are released at a new distant location, they will first orient and head off in the general direction of home, using the sun compass and sensitivity of the earth's magnetic field (Figure 10.13). Navigating toward home may use magnoreception to detect shifts in intensity gradients, as well as odor gradients. As the birds get closer to their home location, eyesight and memory come into play as they start recognizing landmarks and specific terrain, which allow them to navigate very quickly and specifically home.

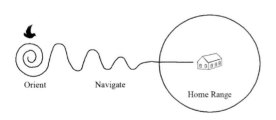

FIGURE 10.13   The stages of pigeon homing. The pigeon will first fly upward in circular movements, orienting itself. Once oriented to the general direction, the pigeon will navigate in a meandering path towards the loft. As it gets closer to home, it will begin to recognize its home range and can then fly straight back to the loft.

RACING HOMING PIGEONS

Racing Pigeons became widely popular in the last half of the 19th century as the sport spread from France, Belgium, the Netherlands, Germany, Britain, and to the United States. In the 1860s, racing homing pigeons were imported to the United States from Europe, and by 1872 the first racing club was formed to conduct races (American Racing Pigeon Union, 2012). In 1880, the precursor organization to the present-day American Racing Pigeon Union and the International Federation of American Homing Pigeon Fanciers developed.

Internationally, the Belgians popularized pigeon racing, as well as gambling on the results. At its peak after World War II, a quarter million Belgians—roughly one in nine families—raced pigeons and had a backyard loft (Blechman, 2007). It became the national sport of Belgium. But as the populations of western Europe and the United States became more affluent, electronic diversions and a busy lifestyle caused the hobby of pigeon racing to dwindle through attrition. In the past 20 years, there has been a resurgence in homing pigeon racing, fueled by a gain in popularity in eastern Europe and an explosion of popularity in Asia, especially in Taiwan and China. In Taiwan, the sport is now associated with professional pigeon trainers, investor owners, and million-dollar winnings, similar to horse racing in the United States.

PIGEON LOFTS

Racing homing pigeons are kept in structures called lofts (Figure 10.14). Lofts can be very basic, consisting of a floor, four walls, and a roof, but tend to get more elaborate as the owner has greater racing success. The loft has to be equipped with a landing board for returning pigeons to land and enter the loft through a trap (located near the center of the landing board). The trap (Figure 10.15) allows entry into the loft but does not allow exit from the loft. Lofts are also equipped with an aviary, which provides the bird a chance to go outside to enjoy the elements if it desires to do so. As aviaries consist of wiring or wooden slats to provide exposure to the environment, it is important to keep the wire or wood slat spacing small enough not to allow in predators or small birds like House Sparrows to reduce disease exposure. Overall, the loft must be designed to keep intruders such as mice, rats, snakes, cats, dogs, raccoons, possums, weasels, and other birds out. The loft needs to be dry, clean, well illuminated, and well ventilated but not drafty. Vents (Figure 10.16) are typically placed at the bottom of the loft structure for air intake and also near the top of the loft for air escape.

Lofts should be located in an open area away from trees, wires, and other buildings. Trees and wires provide perching areas that may delay birds from landing on the landing board and trapping. In addition, birds can injure themselves if they hit hard-to-see wires. Placing the loft away from neighbors will minimize any potential complaints. It is important to have major openings to the loft, such as the aviary, facing away from the direction of bad weather. Lofts are recommended to be elevated 12–18 inches off the ground so air can circulate underneath, to keep the floor dry, and to prevent rodents from taking up residence. Often, the roof edge of the loft will have a small picket fence to discourage landing, so they go straight to the landing board.

Homing pigeons do not require a great deal of space, but at least 1 cubic foot per bird should be provided. Internally, the loft must have feed, water, and grit containers, as well as perches and nest boxes. Many more perches than birds should be provided, and they should be placed as high as possible, as pigeons tend to prefer high, flat perches. Remember—the goal is a peaceful loft with not a lot of fighting or flight that could lead to damaged flight feathers. Inside, the loft should be easy to clean and easy to access.

FIGURE 10.14   Variations of pigeon lofts.

FIGURE 10.15   The one-way trap door of a loft allows pigeons to enter the loft, but not leave. Photo by Roger Wyatt.

Typically, a serious pigeon racer will have multiple lofts or one large loft split into sections for breeders, young birds, and old birds (the old bird section often is further separated so cocks and hens can be kept apart). There is typically a storage area for supplies and an infirmary for sick birds in the large, well-equipped loft.

FEEDING HOMING RACING PIGEONS

Pigeons can only live for a few days without water. Therefore, it is essential to always have fresh, clean water available. As the pigeon will completely immerse its beak when drinking, water containers need to be 1.5 to 2 inches deep. Water consumption increases during hot weather, when parent birds are feeding young and when pigeons are training or racing.

Racing Pigeons were genetically selected from the common Rock Dove, which is a seed-eater. Thus, while Racing Pigeons will eat pellets, they prefer a diet of whole grains (Figure 10.17) that can consist of such things as millet, popcorn, peas, milo, buckwheat, rice, safflower, and oat groats. As seed-based diets can be low in essential minerals and vitamins, it is essential to provide these nutrients.

Typically, the minerals and vitamins are provided with the grit as a mixture (Figure 10.18). The grit is often crushed/ground granite that aids the gizzard in the mechanical digestion of the ingested seeds. Homing pigeons can be prone to eating too much and become overweight, so it is typical to feed them twice a day as much as they will eat in 10 minutes, in the morning and in the evening. Diets for pigeons are formulated to meet their nutrient requirements for their physiological needs, which differ for growth, racing, breeding, and feeding offspring. Feed, water, and grit should be presented in a way to avoid fecal contamination. With this, along with keeping a dry, well-ventilated, clean loft and aviary will be key in preventing illness/disease.

BREEDING RACING PIGEONS

Nest boxes are often used for breeding and are generally 16 inches deep, 16 inches high, and 30 inches wide and equipped with two nesting bowls (Figure 10.19). Two nesting bowls are often provided, as the hen will lay a second clutch before the first clutch is fully weaned. Nest materials such as pine straw, alfalfa straw, and small tree twigs can be placed on the floor. The cock (male pigeon) will bring material to the hen (female pigeon) who builds the nest. The hen will produce two white-colored eggs, with the second egg laid 48 hours after the first. Incubation will commence with the laying of the second egg. The cock incubates the eggs during the day, while the hen incubates them at night. The eggs hatch 17 days after incubation onset. Babies are altricial and are fed pigeon milk exclusively for about 10 days; thereafter, grains provided by the parents make up an ever increasing amount of their diet until they wean/fledge at about 27 days. Homing pigeons will mate for life unless the pigeon fancier changes their mates, and this often occurs for genetic selection purposes. Hens can easily handle two to three clutches per breeding season but should not exceed four clutches in a year, as recommended by the American Racing Pigeon Union, Inc. Finally, it is essential for breeders that have been brought from other locations to remain confined to the breeding loft. If granted flight access outside the loft, they will try to return home.

Baby homing pigeons are banded with a unique, seamless, and permanent identification band (Figure 10.20) at five to seven days of age. Banding is accomplished by placing the three forward-facing toes of the right foot through the band, with the fourth toe bent gently backward against the leg and then gently pulling the band over them onto the leg. Once the band is slid past the back toe, this toe will return to its normal position, leaving the band permanently around the pigeon's leg. The banded baby should be checked in a couple of days to ensure that the band has remained on the leg, as it is possible for the band to slide back over the toes and come off if the bird is banded too early or is small in size.

FIGURE 10.16 Vents are necessary in the loft to allow for ventilation. Photo by Roger Wyatt.

FIGURE 10.17 Racing pigeons are fed a diet of whole seeds.

FIGURE 10.18   Grit is given to racing pigeons to aid digestion and provide minerals and vitamins.

FIGURE 10.19   A nest box inside the loft. Photo by Roger Wyatt.

FIGURE 10.20   Each racing pigeon is given its own unique leg band for identification. Photo by Roger Wyatt.

TRAINING RACING PIGEONS

Squabs that are going to be raced are typically weaned early from their parents at 23 to 25 days of age because many pigeon racers feel that this makes them more independent. At about 40 days of age, the young pigeons are taught how to trap, and they are imprinting on the home loft. The pigeons are placed in a cage on the landing board so they can see their surroundings, but they cannot fly off, and have to use the trap to get back into the loft to obtain food, water, and shelter (Figure 10.21). After one or two weeks of this training, the birds are allowed to come out of the loft unrestricted. Ideally, the birds will have been fed a half ration in the morning and placed outside on a sunny evening with no wind about two hours before sundown (pigeons have a strong desire to be in the protected loft and roosted by nightfall). By following this methodology, the pigeons will be eager to return home, should they start venturing off on short flights. Initial forays may typically be no further than the roof of the loft, followed by surrounding trees or fences. With confidence and memorization of the surrounding areas, the youngsters will fly off together in formation for short forays that build to an hour at around 70 to 75 days of age. Once they have done this and are trapping quickly on return, they can be flown in the mornings. Morning flights will often involve the birds being gone for one to four hours as they refine their sun compass and sensitivity to the earth's magnetic field while memorizing local landmarks and terrain. This training phase is called ranging and starts when the birds are around 90 days old. During this phase, it is essential that the birds know they will be fed once they return so that they trap quickly—which is essential for racing. It also prevents their desire to forage for food outside.

Road training starts at about 120 days of age. For this phase of the training, the birds will be placed in a basket (Figure 10.22), driven to a remote location, and tossed (liberated). Road training will allow physical conditioning and builds homing experience, such that the bird could eventually fly 12–15 hours non-stop from a remote release site to home. This repeated physical training typically starts with evening tosses so that the motivation for food and loft safety is strong. Initial tosses start 5 miles from the loft (by air, not by road) and are repeated at this distance a minimum of two times, or until the released pigeons are returning within 1.5 to 2 minutes per flying mile (10 minutes or less for 5 miles). Once the distance has been repeated twice and the birds are returning to the loft in the expected time, 5-mile increments are added and repeated, following the same protocol. As the birds gain experience, morning tosses are utilized, as races commence in the early morning. Once 20 miles is reached, the increment is increased by 10 miles, until 60 miles or 70 miles is reached. At least five to six tosses at the 60-mile range are necessary before short races are started. Races typically start at the 100-mile range and then increase by 50 miles each weekend for young birds, until a distance of 300 miles is reached. For older, experienced birds typically raced in the spring, the increments increase by 100 miles each weekend, until 600 miles is reached. Older birds fly faster to get home, based on experience and the stronger desire to get home to their mates, nest, and eggs/babies. During racing season, training tosses are made two times a week at the 60-mile range to maintain stamina and cultivate the homing instinct.

LOCAL CLUB RACING

With about 700 clubs affiliated with the American Racing Pigeon Union alone, pigeon racing at the local level is found across the United States. These local club races involve a social aspect, the thrill of competition, and a sense of individualism because each club member has trained his or her own birds. For these local club races, a club member selects the birds that he or she will race. The club member then fills out an entry sheet that lists each bird's permanent band information, the bird's color, and sex. The club member will then transport the birds to a designated meeting place for race preparation by all of the participating racers. Typically, this meeting will be in the evening (essential for long races) prior to race day. The pigeon racer will turn his or her race entrants over to the race secretary and his or her assistant, and they will read each bird's permanent band number and place an elastic race band called a countermark (Figure 10.23) on the bird's leg. The countermark number is recorded by the course secretary, and each bird is placed in a sex-specific crate for transport to the race start point by the liberator. The liberator is a paid individual not affiliated with any of the racers, who transports the birds to the designated race starting point and releases them at the designated time.

Before leaving the meeting place, all of the pigeon racers will synchronize their individual race clocks (Figure 10.24). Each clock will be sealed with a tape signed by the race secretary and the clock's owner to ensure it is not opened prior to the "opening of the clocks" after the race is completed. (If the seal is broken, the racer is disqualified.) On race day, the pigeon racer will go to his or her loft prior to the birds' expected return. Once a bird returns and traps, the countermark is removed and placed into a capsule in the first opening of the clock. The clock's crank is turned until it records the official time of the bird on the paper tape and opens the next slot for placement of the countermark of the next returning bird. After the birds have been clocked, the pigeon racers return to the designated meeting spot to open the clocks. The seals of the clock are checked, the clocks are again synchronized. Each clock is opened by the race secretary, who records the countermarks and stamped times. A computer program is then used that calculates the speed in yards per minute for all the pigeons in the race. The bird with the fastest average speed in yards per minute is the winner. Since the mid 1990s, electronic timing systems (Figure 10.25) are available and often used by pigeon racers. It utilizes microchips embedded in

FIGURE 10.21 When training racing pigeons, young pigeons are taught how to use the trap door and are encouraged to imprint on their home loft. This is done by placing them in a cage surrounding the landing board so they can see their surroundings, but cannot fly away. The young birds become accustomed to using the trap door to obtain food and water. Photo by Roger Wyatt.

FIGURE 10.22 A pigeon basket is used to transport racing pigeons.

FIGURE 10.23   In addition to their permanent leg bands, racing pigeons are banded with a countermark for each race. Photo by Roger Wyatt.

FIGURE 10.24   An official race clock. Photo by Roger Wyatt.

special leg bands and a reading unit installed in the loft entry point (trap), so that returning pigeons are automatically clocked as they cross through the trap. This system does not require the pigeon racer to be in the loft when the pigeons return.

With local club racing, the race participants' lofts are all different distances from the release point (Figure 10.26). It is often incorrectly assumed by casual race observers that the loft that is the shortest distance away from the release site would have an advantage in having the winning pigeon. Actually, the advantage is for the loft that is farthest away. Remember, homing pigeons fly the fastest and most direct route once they recognize local terrain and landmarks. Thus, the pigeons flying to the farthest loft will fly at this fastest speed for the longest period of time—thereby increasing their overall average speed—making them more likely to win. For this reason, the release points for local races are rotated in direction each week. It also becomes apparent in local races that attention to training pays dividends. The trainer that has allowed his birds to memorize a greater circumference around his loft would have an advantage and may win the race, even though his bird is not genetically the best racer.

ONE LOFT RACES

While local club races are still the most common throughout the world, over the last 15 to 20 years, one loft races have become increasingly popular and have revitalized pigeon racing. In one loft races, pigeon breeders enter their best genetic stock into the one loft race. The selected pigeons are shipped as squabs to the race loft, prior to imprinting on their home loft. The squabs will imprint/home to the race loft. All the entrants will be trained using the same protocol and training staff of the race loft. After the birds have been trained, they will be raced, and in this case, since all the pigeons are returning to the same loft, it is the first bird back to the loft that is the winner. The appeal of these races is that all the nuances that can affect local club racing are eliminated, so that it becomes a true test of the participants' genetically derived abilities. Additionally, the purses for these races are substantial. They are often large social events. One of the most well-known one loft races is the Sun City Million Dollar Race held in South Africa (Sun City Million Dollar, 2012).

Typically, the day after the conclusion of a major one loft race, there is an auction in which the top finishing pigeons are sold, with the sale proceeds distributed equally between the race administration and the person who entered the pigeon in the race. Prices for winning pigeons at auction can be in the hundreds of thousands of dollars, with purchasers assuming that the winning birds will pass on their superior homing and flying capabilities to offspring.

DRUGS IN PIGEON RACING

As with so many other sports, performance-enhancing drugs have made their way into pigeon racing. Attention to the problem of performance-enhancing drugs in pigeon racing began in Belgium, when many pigeons tested positive for steroids after drug testing started in 1995, with subsequent police raids of breeders, pigeon feed, and medicine suppliers only worsening the scandal (Carreyrou, 2004). Throughout the world, policies on regulating and detecting performance-enhancing drug use vary, based on the racing association. Large associations that have significant prize purses have had to address the issue to a greater degree than smaller, more localized associations. As an example, the policies of the Royal Pigeon Racing Association, representing the sport of pigeon racing in England, Scotland, Wales, Ireland, the Channel Islands, and Gibraltar will be examined. This association has established guidelines for performance-enhancing drugs, which it includes in the official rules of the association (Royal Pigeon Racing Association, 2011). The Royal Pigeon Racing Association bans the use of anabolic steroids, beta-agonists, corticosteroids, anti-inflammatory non-steroids, opiates, analgesics, performance-enhancing stimulants, synthetic hormones, any drug found to be performance enhancing, and any substance which may be used in an attempt to mask the above drugs. In general, this list of banned drugs is used either to enhance flight muscle mass, increase respiratory efficiency to delay fatigue, reduce pain to increase endurance, or stimulate the birds. To detect the use of the banned drugs, the Royal Pigeon Racing Association is authorized to take samples (typically feces rather than blood) before, during, and after a race from the lofts or pigeons of its members, as well as the containers used to transport the pigeons to race preparation facility. As with drug testing in other sports, at least two samples will be taken. One will be sent for testing, while the second will be utilized for confirmation of positive tests. Members found guilty of giving birds performance-enhancing drugs are suspended from the association for a minimum of three years, and any prize won in the race preceding the tests will be forfeited.

HOMING PIGEONS AND ILLEGAL ACTIVITY

Homing pigeons have long been used in illicit activities. As chronicled by Blechman (2007), homing pigeons are often used for smuggling drugs. Additionally, miners for precious gems such as diamonds, have smuggled homing pigeons into mines. Then, when the worker has found precious gems, , they are placed on the pigeon, which smuggles it back to the miner's home. Recently, there have been several instances worldwide where prisoners have tamed wild pigeons living on prison grounds. The pigeons were then smuggled

FIGURE 10.25   Some modern races utilize electronic timing systems, which note the time the bird enters the loft by automatically reading the microchip contained in the racing leg band attached to the bird prior to the race. Photo by Roger Wyatt.

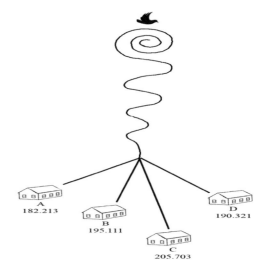

FIGURE 10.26   A simple illustration of a 200-mile race involving four racing lofts. Each loft is a surveyed point, as is the release site, so distances can be calculated to the thousandths of a mile. During the return home, the pigeons from the different lofts will often fly together, but as they get closer to home the birds from individual lofts will break away from the group as they start to recognize local terrain and landmarks. From this breakpoint, the birds will make a direct flight to home at their fastest speed.

FIGURE 10.27a   Galati Roller Pigeon

FIGURE 10.27b   English Long-faced Mufffed Tumbler (black)

out in the clothes of visiting relatives and then fly back to the prisoners with smuggled contraband.

FANCY PIGEON BREEDS

In addition to homing Racing Pigeons, people raise all kinds of fancy pigeons, which are also descendants from the Rock Pigeon. Through selective breeding efforts, several hundred breeds and varieties have been developed from the Rock Pigeon. The breeds are often named to reflect the way the birds fly or the way they look. Rollers and Tumblers (Figure 10.27 a & b) are known for flying to elevation (500–600 feet) and then somersaulting over and over in a descent, until they pull out of the descent to simply repeat the process. Birds are judged on the number and quality of the somersaults (rolls) and the depth of the rolling (how far they perform). Parlor Rollers (Figure 10.28) cannot fly and have instead been bred to roll (somersault) on the ground. Tipplers have been bred for endurance flying that involves obtaining a very high elevation (barely visible without binoculars) and then sustaining a roughly circular flight pattern that can last nearly 24 hours. Fantails, Frills, and Frillbacks (Figure 10.29) are three of the many breeds that have been developed with unique feathering characteristics. The Pouter and Cropper Pigeons are known for their prominent spherical inflatable crops that are possessed by long, thin-bodied birds (Figure 10.30). Many pigeon breeds have also been developed based on color and color pattern. Fancy pigeons are exhibited and judged in shows around the United States, and local clubs for these pigeons exist across the nation. In his book, *Extraordinary Pigeons*, Stephen Green-Armytage captures the beauty of fancy pigeon breeds from around the world with stunning photographs.

Utility pigeon breeds have been developed for food purposes, but they are also shown at exhibitions. As the name implies, these pigeons have been developed for size, rapid growth, and meat yield. Pigeons, especially squabs, are considered a delicacy that is highly prized by many individuals. Squabs have not exercised their flight muscles and they are plump. Not surprisingly, squab meat is often described as tender, moist, and delicate. As mentioned previously, many doves and pigeons are still hunted for food purposes, and production of domestic birds for eating can help alleviate the demand for wild birds.

HOUSEHOLD PET PIGEONS AND DOVES

In addition to the various selectively bred breeds of Rock Pigeons kept by pigeon racers and fanciers, many other species of pigeon are kept as pet birds around the world, as well as the United States.

The Diamond Dove (Figure 10.31) is the smallest member of the pigeon family, weighing about 30 grams. This native to Australia and Indonesia is found in open areas, and its diet consists primarily of grains. It is very commonly kept as a pet bird. The already-discussed Eurasian Collared- and African Collared-Doves are also very commonly kept birds, and many different color mutations of each species have been selectively bred in captivity. In the pet trade, the Collared-Doves are often referred to as Ring-necked Doves, Ringed Doves, or even Ringed Turtle-Doves.

Pigeons and doves kept in captivity can easily live 12 to 20 years. Small doves like Diamond Doves can be kept in 24-inch square cages, especially if allowed out each day. Larger doves, such as the African and Eurasian Collared-Doves, need larger cages that have widths and lengths from 3 to 4 feet. Cage length is the most important component when keeping doves in captivity, so they have the opportunity to fly from perch to perch in the cage, because unlike parrot species, they do not climb about in their cages. As with all pigeons, flat perches are typically preferred by these species, but as discussed in the parrot chapter, providing a variety of perching sizes and shapes is preferred, especially until observation has determined their preferences.

It is important to provide adequate food types for each captive species. The most commonly kept pet pigeon species are seed-eaters, and these species should be provided with seeds, grit, and offerings of greens. As an all-seed diet can be low in essential minerals and vitamins, grit should be supplemented with the seed, as it is for homing pigeons. Species such as the Diamond Dove and the Collared-Dove like to feed on the ground of the cage or aviary. In fact, many people will keep them in large, mixed-species aviaries to have ground feeders that complement non-aggressive species of parrots such as cockatiels or other pet birds like finches that feed in elevated positions. Although much rarer in aviculture, species of Fruit Doves will need to be fed a diet that is fruit based.

Doves are often preferred as pet birds because they are docile and quieter compared to other species of birds such as parrots, and they enjoy human interaction. Doves, especially Collared-Doves, can be finger trained. But even if not finger trained, many people find the calm presence and cooing voices of doves very relaxing. Pigeons and doves are not known for playing with toys like parrots, but providing a couple of simple toys for interaction is recommended. Doves sometimes enjoy arranging small sticks, and some individuals also seem to enjoy swings and mirrors in the cage. As pigeons do not climb around in their cages, toys should be placed near perches or at the bottom of the cage. Because interaction with toys is limited, daily human enrichment is critical—if it cannot be consistently provided, one should strongly consider keeping doves and pigeons in groups of two or with other types of non-aggressive pet birds to provide enrichment. When keeping more than one dove or pigeon, it is important to keep in mind that two males paired together will tend to squabble with each other, so pairing two females or a male

FIGURE 10.28   Parlour Tumbler (black tigered)

FIGURE 10.29a   Chinese Owl Frill

FIGURE 10.29b   A pigeon with a neck frill

FIGURE 10.29c   Frillback

FIGURE 10.29d   Fantail

and female together is better. It is never recommended to keep odd numbers of males and female doves as pairs, because it will often lead to excluding one bird, which can lead to scuffles.

DOVE RELEASES AT SPECIAL OCCASIONS

As religious symbols and as universal symbols of peace and love, white doves or pigeons (Figure 10.32) are often released to celebrate or commemorate special events, such as weddings, funerals, and opening ceremonies. The birds used for these ceremonies should be white-colored homing pigeons rather than white-colored doves like the African Collared-Dove. Homing pigeons have been selected and bred for their ability to return home, while domesticated doves such as the Eurasian and African Collared-Doves have not. Thus, only white homing pigeons should be released at these special events, as they will return to their home lofts, while any other white doves released at such occasions will not be able to return home and will quickly become prey for predators.

HOW TO READ A PIGEON BAND

The information on a pigeon's permanent band typically follows a general format that provides information to help you return a lost pigeon to its owner. Bands contain a series of letters and numbers that are unique to each bird. As an example, here is the information from a band: AU 09 ATH 3002, which conforms to the band format of the American Racing Pigeon Union.

The "AU" is the abbreviation for the American Racing Pigeon Union and indicates that this organization issued the band and has a registry for the band. The band could also have other abbreviations instead of AU, such as IF, CU, NPA, NBRC, or ADA. These are the abbreviations for the International Federation of American Homing Pigeon Fanciers, the Canadian Racing Pigeon Union, National Pigeon Association, National Birmingham Roller Club, and the American Dove Association, respectively. Some individuals purchase personalized bands that will have the owner's name and contact information.

The "09" indicates the year the pigeon was hatched and banded. In this example, the pigeon was born in 2009. Sometimes the entire year will be printed on the band.

The "ATH" represents the local pigeon club where the band is registered, and no two clubs have the same designation letters. Club designations can be one, two, or three letters.

The "3002" represents the specific number of the bird having this band. No other band will have this same number from the same national organization in this specific year and with this club's specific identifying letters.

GETTING A LOST BANDED PIGEON HOME

Often, Racing Pigeons may get disoriented or harassed by raptors and fail to return home. Additionally, fancy pigeons or pet doves may also escape. While these birds may fall victim to predators, they are often found by the members of the public because they are domesticated and not afraid of human contact. If you found the pigeon with the band from the above example, you could log on to the American Racing Pigeon Union's website at http://www.pigeon.org/ and then click on the "lost bird" icon. Then, you would be able to do a search to determine the local club that the owner belonged to and telephone contact information for this club. The club would then provide contact to the owner, so that he or she could retrieve the bird. The American Racing Pigeon Union's website also has web links to the other major associations that issue bands, so you would be able to contact the owners of bands issued through those organizations as well. In addition, the American Racing Pigeon Union website provides instructions on caring for a found pigeon.

RAPTORS AND PIGEONS

A conflict occurs between raptors and pigeons in nature and between pigeon fanciers and falconers. As discussed earlier in this chapter, Peregrine Falcons were raised by the German military to combat the success of the Allied homing pigeons. Additionally, as discussed in Chapter 9, falconers often use pigeons as live bait to trap and lure falcons and hawks. In the wild, pigeons and doves are highly prized prey animals by raptors that hunt other birds. Pigeons have well-developed breast muscle and thus are a high-yield prey. Therefore, it is not uncommon for raptors such as Goshawks, Cooper's Hawks, Red-tailed Hawks, and Peregrine Falcons to prey upon racing and show pigeons, especially rollers that attract attention with their aerial performances. Because of this, there have been high-profile cases of pigeon enthusiasts killing federally protected raptors in the United States and in other parts of the world (Mrozek, 2007; the Peregrine Fund, 2011; Williams, 2008).

FIGURE 10.30a   Norwich Cropper

FIGURE 10.30b   English Pouter

FIGURE 10.31   Diamond Doves

FIGURE 10.32 White pigeons and doves are often released at special events as symbols of peace and love.

ADDITIONAL PIGEON AND DOVE INFORMATION

Further information about pigeons and doves can easily be found through publications and the websites of such organizations as the American Dove Association (http://www.dovline.com/), American Racing Pigeon Union (http://www.pigeon.org/), National Pigeon Association (http://www.npausa.com/), National Birmingham Roller Club (http://www.nbrconline.com/), and the International Federation of American Homing Pigeon Fanciers (http://www.ifpigeon.com/).

SUMMARY

Pigeons and doves make up one of the larger orders of birds, the Columbiformes. Their strong flight has allowed them to colonize much of the world. Despite this success, pigeons and doves have been persecuted heavily in the past, with many species becoming extinct. Presently, nearly 20 percent of the remaining species are listed as threatened with extinction.

Pigeons were one of the first birds to be domesticated. Their service to man for communication, food, entertainment, and companionship has been remarkable throughout history. Today, pigeons are still utilized for food, sport, and pet purposes. They are also used for scientific research.

FURTHER READING

Green-Armytage, S. 2003. *Extraordinary Pigeons*. Harry N. Abrams, New York. 112 pages.

REFERENCES

American Racing Pigeon Union. 2012. "Introduction to the AU: The origin and history of the American Racing Pigeon Union." Accessed 03/06/2012: http://www.pigeon.org/history.htm

Belitz, H.-D., W. Grosch, and P. Schieberle. 2009. *Food Chemistry, fourth revised and extended edition*. Springer-Verlag, Berlin, Heidelberg.

Bennett, A. T. D. and I. C. Cuthill. 1994. Ultraviolet vision in birds: What is its function? *Vision Research* **34**:1471–1478.

BirdLife International. 2012. "IUCN Red List for Birds." Downloaded from http://www.birdlife.org on 1/31/2012.

Blechman, A. D. 2007. *Pigeons*. Grove Press, New York.

Blockstein, D. E. and H. B. Tordoff. 1985. Gone forever: A contemporary look at the extinction of the Passenger Pigeon. *American Birds* **39**:845–851.

Bohlen, H. D. 1998. A new dove colonizinig Illinois. *Living Museum* **59**:6–7.

Braithwaite, V. A. and J. A. Newman. 1994. Exposure to familiar visual landmarks allows pigeons to home faster. *Animal Behavior* **48**:1482–1484.

Carr, R. H. and C. M. James. 1931. Synthesis of adequate protein in the glands of the pigeon crop. *American Journal of Physiology—Legacy Content* **97**:227–231.

Carreyrou, J. 2004. Doping scandal hits pigeon racing. *Wall Street Journal.*

Cornell University. 2012. "Milk Composition." Accessed 02/15/2012: http://www.milkfacts.info/ Milk Composition/Milk Composition Page.htm

Davies, W. L. 1939. The composition of the crop milk of pigeons. *Biochemical Journal* **33**:898–901.

DeBenedictis, P. 1994. Ringed Turtle-Dove vs. Eurasian Collared-Dove: Answers. *Birding* **26**:133.

Desmeth, M. and J. Vandeputte-Poma. 1980. Lipid composition of pigeon cropmilk—I. Total lipids and lipid classes. *Comparative Biochemistry and Physiology Part B: Comparative Biochemistry* **66**:129–133.

Encyclopedia Smithsonian. 2012. "The Passenger Pigeon." Accessed 03/06/2012: http://www. si.edu/encyclopedia_Si/nmnh/passpig.htm

Farrington, H. W. 1926. *Cher Ami.* Rough and Brown Press, New York.

Fisher, H. 1972. The Nutrition of Birds. Pages 431–469 *in* D. S. Farner, J. R. King, and K. C. Parkes, editors. *Avian Biology.* Academic Press, New York.

Fujisaki, I., E. V. Pearlstine, and F. J. Mazzotti. 2010. The rapid spread of invasive Eurasian Collared-Doves Streptopelia decaocto in the continental USA follows human-altered habitats. *Ibis* **152**:622–632.

Fuller, E. 1987. *Extinct Birds.* Facts On File Publications, New York.

Fulton, T. L., S. M. Wagner, C. Fisher, and B. Shapiro. 2012. Nuclear DNA from the extinct Passenger Pigeon (Ectopistes migratorius) confirms a single origin of New World pigeons. *Annals of Anatomy—Anatomischer Anzeiger* **194**:52–57.

Gagliardo, A., T. Pecchia, M. Savini, F. Odetti, P. Ioalè, and G. Vallortigara. 2011. Olfactory lateralization in homing pigeons: Initial orientation of birds receiving a unilateral olfactory input. *European Journal of Neuroscience* **25**:1511–1516.

Green, C. 1977. The exotic birds of New Providence. *The Bahamas Naturalist* **2**(2): 11–16..

Hagey, L. R., C. D. Schteingart, H. T. Ton-Nu, and A. F. Hofmann. 1994. Biliary bile acids of fruit pigeons and doves (Columbiformes): Presence of 1-beta-hydroxychenodeoxycholic acid and conjugation with glycine as well as taurine. *Journal of Lipid Research* **35**:2041–2048.

Halliday, T. R. 1980. The extinction of the Passenger Pigeon ectopistes migratorius and its relevance to contemporary conservation. *Biological Conservation* **17**:157–162.

Hardy, J. W. 1973. Feral Exotic Birds in Southern California. *Wilson Bulletin* **85**:506–512.

Horseman, N. D. and J. D. Buntin. 1995. Regulation of pigeon crop milk secretion and parental behaviors by prolactin. *Annual Review of Nutrition* **15**:213–238.

Hutton, M. and G. T. Goodman. 1980. Metal contamination of feral pigeons Columba livia from the London area: Part 1—Tissue accumulation of lead, cadmium and zinc. *Environmental Pollution Series A, Ecological and Biological* **22**:207–217.

Jensen, R. G. 1995. Miscellaneous factors affecting composition and volume of human and bovine milks. Pages 237–267 *in* R. G. Jensen, editor. *Handbook of Milk Composition*. Academic Press, Inc.

Keeton, W. T. 1969. Orientation by pigeons: Is the sun necessary? *Science* **165**:922–928.

Levi, W. M. 1941. *The Pigeon*. The R. L. Bryan Company, Columbia, SC.

Liu, W., X. Ling, R. Halbrook, D. Martineau, H. Dou, X. Liu, G. Zhang, and S. Tao. 2010. Preliminary evaluation on the use of homing pigeons as a biomonitor in urban areas. *Ecotoxicology* **19**:295–305.

Meigs, E. B. and H. L. Marsh. 1913. The comparative composition of human milk and cow's milk. *Journal of Biological Chemistry* **16**:147–168.

Moermond, T. C. 1983. Suction-drinking in tanagers Thraupidae and its relation to frugivory. *Ibis* **125**:545–549.

Mrozek, T. 2007. "'Seven 'Roller Pigeon' enthusiastis charged with killing, or helping to kill, protected hawks and falcons." Page http://www.justice.gov/usao/cac/Pressroom/pr2007/2070. html. Department of Justice. United States Attorney's Office, Central District of California.

Muheim, R. 2011. Behavioural and physiological mechanisms of polarized light sensitivity in birds. *Philosophical Transactions of the Royal Society B* **366**:763–771.

Nam, D.-H. and D.-P. Lee. 2005. Possible routes for lead accumulation in feral pigeons (*Columba Livia*). *Environmental Monitoring and Assessment* **121**:353-359.

Nam, D.-H. and D.-P. Lee. 2006. Monitoring for Pb and Cd pollution using feral pigeons in rural, urban, and industrial environments of Korea. *Science of the Total Environment* **357**:288–295.

Nam, D.-H., D.-P. Lee, and T.-H. Koo. 2004. Factors causing variations of lead and cadmium accumulation of feral pigeons (Columba livia). *Environmental Monitoring and Assessment* **95**:23–35.

Otis, D. L., J. H. Schulz, D. A. Miller, R. Mirarchi, and T. Baskett. 2008. Mourning Dove (Zenaida macroura). In A. Poole and F. Gill, editors. *The Birds of North America, No. 117*. Philadelphia: Academy of Natural Sciences, Washington, DC.

Papi, F. 1989. Pigeons use olfactory cues to navigate. *Ethology Ecology and Evolution* **1**.

Perrins, C. 2009. *The Princeton Encyclopedia of Birds*. Princeton University Press, Princeton, NJ.

The Peregrine Fund. 2011. "Recent Raptor News." Accessed 03/03/2012: http://www.globalraptors.org/grin/SiteNews.asp?lNewsType=1

Pigeon Blog. 2012. "Pigeon Blog." Accessed 03/06/2012: http://www.pigeonblog.mapyourcity. net

Pranty, B. 2007. The Ringed Turtle-Dove on Christmas Bird Counts in Florida: Cases of "Boom and Bust" and mistaken identity. *107th Christmas Bird Count*. National Audubon Society, New York.

Reed, L. L., L. B. Mendel, and H. B. Vickery. 1932. The nutritive properties of the "crop-milk" of pigeons. *American Journal of Physiology—Legacy Content* **102**:285–292.

Romagosa, C. M. and R. F. Labisky. 2000. Establishment and dispersal of the Eurasian Collared-Dove in Florida. *Journal of Field Ornithology* **71**:159–166.

Romagosa, C. M. and T. McEneaney. 1999. Eurasian Collared-Dove in North America and the Caribbean. *North American Birds* **53**:348–353.

The Royal Pigeon Racing Association. 2011. "RPRA Official Rule Book 2011." Accessed March 2, 2012: http://www.rpra.org/MemberSupport/RuleBook/tabid/88/Default.aspx

Schiffner, I., T. Pavkovic, B. Siegmund, and R. Wiltschko. 2011. Strategies of Young Pigeons during "Map" Learning. *Journal of Navigation* **64**:431–448.

Schilderman, P. A., J. A. Hoogewerff, F. J. van Schooten, L. M. Maas, E. J. Moonen, B. J. van Os, J. H. van Wijnen, and J. C. Kleinjans. 1997. Possible relevance of pigeons as an indicator species for monitoring air pollution. *Environmental Health Perspectives* **105**:322–330.

Schmidt-Koenig, K. 1990. The sun compass. *Experientia* **16**:336–342.

Schmidt-Koenig, K., J. U. Ganzhorn, and R. Ranvaud. 1991. The sun compass. Pages 1–15 *in* P. Berthold, editor. *Orientation in Birds*. Birkhauser Verlag, Basel.

Schorger, A. W. 1973. *The Passenger Pigeon: Its Natural History and Extinction*. University of Oklahoma Press, Norman.

Seamans, M. E., K. Parker, and T. A. Sanders. 2011. *Mourning Dove population status, 2011*. U.S. Department of the Interior, Fish and Wildlife Service, Division of Migratory Bird Management, Washington, DC.

Shapiro, B., D. Sibthorpe, A. Rambaut, J. Austin, G. M. Wragg, O. R. P. Bininda-Emonds, P. L. M. Lee, and A. Cooper. 2002. Flight of the Dodo. *Science* **295**:1683.

Shetty, S., P. V. Salimath, and S. N. Hegde. 1994. Carbohydrates of pigeon milk and their changes in the first week of secretion. *Archives of Physiology and Biochemistry* **102**:277–280.

Smith, P. W. 1987. The Eurasian Collared-Dove arrives in the Americas. *American Birds* **41**: 1370–1379.

Smith, P. W. and H. W. Kale. 1986. Eurasian Collared-Doves collected in Florida. Florida *Field Naturalist* **14**:104–107.

Stapput, K., O. Güntürkün, K.-P. Hoffmann, R. Wiltschko, and W. Wiltschko. 2010. Magnetoreception of Directional Information in Birds Requires Nondegraded Vision. *Current Biology* **20**:1259–1262.

Streng, A. and H. G. Wallraff. 1992. Attempts to determine the roles of visual and olfactory inputs in initial orientation and homing of pigeons over familiar terrain. *Ethology* **91**:203–219.

Sun City Million Dollar. 2012. "The Sun City Million Dollar Pigeon Race." Accessed 03/06/2012: http://info.scmdpr.com/index/home.php

U.S. Coast Guard. 2012. "Pigeon Search and Rescue Project (Project Sea Hunt)." U.S. Department of Homeland Security. Accessed 03/06/2012: http://www.uscg.mil/history/articles/PigeonSARProject.asp

Walcott, C. 1996. Pigeon homing: Observations, experiments and confusions. *Journal of Experimental Biology* **199**:21–27.

Wallraff, H. G. 2005. *Avian Navigation: Pigeon Homing as a Paradigm*. Springer-Verlag, Berlin.

Wallraff, H. G. and A. Foa. 1981. Pigeon navigation: Charcoal filter removes relevant information from environmental air. *Behavioral Ecology and Sociobiology* **9**:67–77.

Ward, A. M., A. Hunt, M. Maslanka, and C. Brown. 2001. Nutrient Composition of American Flamingo Crop Milk. *Proceedings of the American Zoo and Aquarium Association Nutrition Advisory Group*:187–193.

Williams, T. 2008. Incite: Fowl Play. *Audubon Magazine*: May–June.

Wiltschko, R., I. Schiffner, P. Fuhrmann, and W. Wiltschko. 2010. The Role of the Magnetite-Based Receptors in the Beak in Pigeon Homing. *Current Biology* **20**:1534–1538.

Wiltschko, R., M. Walker, and W. Wiltschko. 2000. Sun-compass orientation in homing pigeons: Compensation for different rates of change in azimuth? *Journal of Experimental Biology* **203**:889–894.

Wiltschko, W. and R. Wiltschko. 2007. Magnetoreception in birds: Two receptors for two different tasks. *Journal of Ornithology* **148**:61–76.

Zablit, J. 2012. "Syrian activists resort to pigeons to communicate." Agence France-Presse (AFP). Accessed February 18, 2012: http://ca.news.yahoo.com/syrian-activists-resort-pigeons-communicate-161355893.html.

Zweers, G. A. 1982. Drinking of the Pigeon (Columba livia L.). *Behaviour* **80**:274–317.

XI RATITES

DE-EVOLUTION OF FLIGHT

Ratites are a group of flightless birds divided into four orders and five families: Ostriches, Rheas, Emu, Cassowaries, and Kiwis. Research has shown that all ratites evolved from a common flighted ancestor, yet recent DNA evidence links Emu, Cassowaries, and Kiwis to flighted, present-day tinamous in South America. It also indicates that during evolutionary phases, these birds lost their ability to fly (Harshman et al., 2008). Why would a bird de-evolve flight? If there are no predators, there would be no need to fly. Instead of continuing to invest in high-energy flight, ratites could invest in size or behavior. Their muscle mass could be reduced, allowing their basal metabolic rate to lower, requiring less energy (Calder and Dawson, 1978; McNab, 1996; Maloney, 2008). Ratites are not the only flightless birds. All penguins and rails are flightless, while some herons and pigeons are flightless. Because flight generates a tremendous stress on the skeleton, the muscles required for flight must be solidly attached to the skeleton. An enlarged sternum, or keel, allows for such musculoskeletal attachment (Figure 11.1 a). The sternum is unkeeled, or flat, in certain flightless birds, such as the ratites (Figure 11.1 b). The word "ratite" originates from the Latin word *rata*, meaning raft, referring to the flat sternum. Scientists believe that in the ratites, the keeled form of the sternum has been lost as a result of the birds having adopted a flightless lifestyle. Along with the loss of flight, ratites have developed strong legs and feet, adapted for running and used in defense against predators (Harris, 2009). The majority of bird species have four toes, yet most ratites have three (Figure 11.2 a), and Ostriches have only two toes on each foot (Figure 11.2 b). The general anatomy of the digestive tract is comparable to other avian species, except that ratites do not have crops (Sales, 2006).

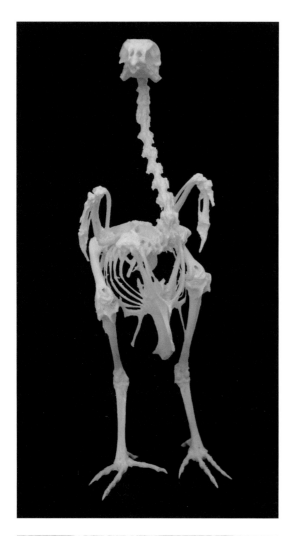

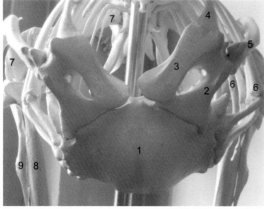

FIGURE 11.1 The first skeleton of a flighted bird (a) shows a keeled sternum where the flight muscles attach, while the second image (b) shows a flat, unkeeled Ostrich sternum.

CASSOWARIES

Cassowaries live deep in the rain forests of New Guinea and surrounding islands as well as northeastern Australia and are rarely seen. They consist of three species: Southern/Double-wattled Cassowary (Figure 11.3), Dwarf Cassowary, and the Northern Cassowary. These birds have several unique physical characteristics. Their casque (Figure 11.4), a relatively soft, foam-like helmet structure, is unknown in function, but may assist in turning over soil or rocks, and could protect the head through dense underbrush. It is also believed that the casque may be used in communication as sound reception in dense rain forests, since females have larger casques—possibly for hearing and locating males in the breeding season. Cassowaries produce a very low frequency call which lies on the edge of human hearing, but travels well in dense underbrush. These birds have five or six spike-like wing quills on each wing that they use in fighting and defense. New Guinea tribesmen use these quills as adornment in noses and headdresses. In addition to the wing quills, cassowaries also have a claw or major digit on their wings. This is a primitive, reptilian characteristic, and its use is unknown. They will eat fungi, snails, insects, frogs, and snakes and other small animals, but they mainly eat fruit. Therefore, they need a diverse forest that produces a variety of fruit year-round. As a large-bodied frugivore, their role in seed dispersal has been found to be very important to forest success, with seeds distributed over distances greater than a kilometer. In some plant species, germination rates are higher after passing through the Cassowary gut (Bradford and Westcott, 2010, 2011).

Cassowaries stand between 3.8 to 5.8 feet (1.16–1.77 meters) tall. Males and females are not distinguishable with regard to color, but the females are larger. Their juvenile brown or adult black plumage appears sleek yet fluffy due to their double-plumed feathers, caused by an enlarged afterfeather (Figure 11.5). These birds have no uropygial, or preen, gland, which means that their feathers cannot be waterproofed, leaving them with an especially fluffy appearance.

In the wild, Cassowaries are solitary except in the breeding season, when males and females will briefly tolerate each other and form pairs. Males attract females by making a very low frequency booming call that travels far through dense forest. Females lay clutches of four to five blue-green eggs, and the males exclusively incubate. Incubation lasts for 50 days, and then the male tends to the chicks for up to one year. Cassowaries have no serious natural predators besides humans. However, the Northern Cassowary population is threatened and the Southern Cassowary is endangered, with fewer than 1500 individuals. Threats to the population include habitat loss, habitat fragmentation, and human exposure (roads, dogs, etc.). Though Cassowary chicks are very tame and bond strongly to handlers, once the young reach maturity, they become extremely aggressive. With the difficulty of keeping Cassowaries in captivity, breeding programs are rare.

Cassowaries are shy and seldom seen in the wild. If confronted, they are likely to defend themselves by kicking with their powerful legs, using the sharp nails on their inner toes (Figure 11.6)—which can grow to 7 inches (18 cm) long—to rip flesh. They have been referred to as "velociraptors with feathers" because they are extremely aggressive and are capable of using these dagger toenails to attack and even kill humans. Despite long-term attempts to keep the birds tame, they are considered one of the most dangerous animals kept in zoos, based on the frequency and severity of injuries incurred by zookeepers.

FIGURE 11.2a   Most ratites have three toes.

KIWIS

Kiwis evolved in the absence of mammals on the island of New Zealand and are considered a national symbol. There are five species of Kiwis: The Northern Brown (*Apteryx mantelli*), Little Spotted (*Apteryx owenii*), Great Spotted (*Apteryx haastii*), Tokoeka or Southern Brown (*Apteryx australis*), and Okarito Brown or Rowi Kiwi (*Apteryx rowi*) (Burbidge et al., 2003; Sales, 2005). Kiwis are small compared to other ratites, about the size of a football. They are committed to flightlessness, with tiny vestigial wings buried in feathers. Kiwis have no visible tail externally. While the other ratites have reduced, unkeeled sternums, Kiwis have no breastbone at all (Figure 11.7). Most birds have hollow bones to reduce weight during flight, but Kiwi bones are comparatively denser and only partially hollow. They have an excellent sense of smell and perception of vibration and are able to detect worms, spiders, larvae, and beetles by shoving their long, thin bill just under the surface of the ground. They accumulate large fat deposits in order to withstand the long breeding season. Kiwis are monogamous for life, a characteristic unique among the ratites (Harris, 2009). Breeding occurs in New Zealand's spring, around August and September, and then the female invests enormous energy in one to three large eggs, rather than a clutch of many smaller eggs (Harris, 2009). The nutrient-rich egg comprises 25 percent of her body weight (Figure 11.8) (Perrins and Middleton, 1985); therefore, the eggs are laid individually with a gap of 14–30 days, depending on the species (Harris, 2009). Incubation duties vary among the different species of Kiwi. In the North Island Brown Kiwi and the Little Spotted Kiwi, the male does most of the incubation of the egg (Colbourne, 2002). In the Great Spotted, Tokoeka, and Okarito Brown Kiwi species, both the male and the female incubate the large eggs (Colbourne, 2002). Some Tokoeka Kiwi form family groups and share territories and incubation duties, with the eggs being incubated by non-breeding adult "helpers," as well as the parents (Colbourne, 2002). Kiwis have one of the longest avian incubation periods, lasting 74–84 days (Calder et al., 1978). Kiwi chicks do not have an egg tooth, so they break out of their shell using their feet and are then independent by

FIGURE 11.2b   Ostriches have only two toes.

FIGURE 11.3   Double-wattled Cassowary.

FIGURE 11.4   The casque of the Cassowary.

14 to 20 days after hatch (Harris, 2009). Kiwis do not reach sexual maturity until they are five years old and are capable of living 20 to 30 years; however, few have the means to achieve long life due to the many mammalian predators such as dogs, cats, weasels, and stoats that have been introduced to New Zealand. The Southern Brown and Great Spotted Kiwis are both classified as vulnerable on the IUCN Red List, while the Northern Brown is endangered; the Little Spotted Kiwi is near threatened (IUCN, 2011).

Many conservation programs have worked to promote awareness and protect the Kiwi. Operation Nest Egg is one organization that removes eggs from the wild, hatches them in the protection of captivity, and then releases the chicks back into the wild once they are able to defend themselves from predators. This process increases the survival rate from 5 to 60 percent, and the program successfully hatches about 150 eggs per year (Project Kiwi, 2011). The Little Spotted Kiwi once occurred throughout New Zealand, but the present population is now restricted to a few isolated predator-free islands. These islands require consistent monitoring to see that emerging predators are managed and Kiwi populations are maintained; however, through these efforts, the Little Spotted Kiwi population has been stable. The species has recently been downgraded from vulnerable to near threatened (Birdlife International, 2011). Despite the extraordinary conservation efforts of New Zealand's

FIGURE 11.5   Cassowaries appear fluffy because they are double-plumed with an elongated afterfeather.

national symbol, the populations of Kiwis are either growing very slowly or continuing to decline.

RHEAS

There are two species of Rhea, the Greater, or Common, Rhea (*Rhea Americana*) and the Lesser, or Darwin's, Rhea (*Rhea pennata*). The Greater Rhea (Figure 11.9) is larger at about 5 feet (1.5 meters) tall and is native to Brazil. The Lesser Rhea (Figure 11.10) is only about 3 feet (0.9 meters) tall and is native to Argentina, Chile, and Peru. Both species live in medium-sized flocks of five to 50 individuals. They feed mainly on vegetation, but will eat insects and small vertebrates when possible. Rheas are adapted for running as a means of escaping predation—they run very quickly, reaching speeds of 30–40 miles per hour (48–64 kilometers per hour). Their wings are proportionally larger than those of other ratites, and they use them to help gain speed and for stability during quick, sharp turns.

The Rhea's breeding season is from August to January, depending on the region. Males will court two to 12 females. The males will become territorial, evicting other males from the flock. Younger males leave the flock first, while the older males remain to fight using their heads and necks, until the dominant male emerges. The victorious male will choose territory near some water and scrub to make a nest. After mating, the females start depositing eggs in the male's nest. As soon as some eggs are laid, the male starts incubating them and becomes very broody and protective—sometimes to such an extent that females wishing to lay more eggs cannot get to the nest and must lay them nearby. Many eggs are lost this way. Once the male is firmly in place incubating 10 to 60 eggs, the females leave to mate with and lay eggs for another male. The eggs take 30–40 days to hatch, and again, like other ratites, the young are precocial and ready to leave the nest within hours. The males remain extremely protective of their chicks and will charge female Rheas or humans who come too close. They have even been known to attack small planes.

Rhea populations have declined considerably and are now considered to be near threatened on the IUCN Red List (IUCN, 2011). They are considered a pest to farmers, as they will eat nearly any type of agricultural crop. In 1980, over 50,000 skins were traded; however, a permit is now needed for their export and import. Commercially, Rheas are raised for eggs, feathers, meat, leather, and oil. The Rhea is at a disadvantage for widespread commercial development given its smaller size and aggressiveness compared to Emus and Ostriches.

FIGURE 11.6 Cassowaries have dagger-like toenails on their inner toes. These nails can reach 7 inches in length and can be formidable weapons.

FIGURE 11.7   Kiwis have no notable sternum or keel bone.

FIGURE 11.8   In the bird world, the Kiwi lays the largest egg relative to its body.

FIGURE 11.9   Greater Rhea

EMUS

Divided into three subspecies, a single species of Emu (*Dromaius novaehollandiae*) remains in Australia after the several other Emu species were hunted to extinction in the past 200 years (Boles, 2001). Emus (Figure 11.11) stand 5.7 feet (1.74 meters) tall and weigh about 110 pounds (50 kilograms), with females weighing up to 120 pounds (54 kilograms). They have three toes and shaggy, double-plumed feathers, like many ratites. Their wings are only 8 inches long, but are quite vascularized so that they can hold them away from their bodies to release heat. Emus are nomadic, following the regular pattern of rain in western Australia. They eat seeds, fruit, insects, and young green foliage, which is only available with rainfall. This annual migration of about 70,000 Emus has become a problem for the vast fields of cereal grains and other agriculture in southwest Australia; as a result, a 600-mile fence was erected to protect the crops.

Emus pair in December and January and defend a territory of about 30 km². The female lays her eggs in April, May, and June, and the male then takes full responsibility for the incubation and care of the offspring. He incubates 9–20 eggs for 56 days, with no eating, drinking, or defecating during this time, losing up to 20 percent of his body weight (Sales, 2007). Once the chicks hatch, the male becomes very aggressive, often driving away the female. Males stay with the young for five to seven months.

The Emu is raised commercially for several products. Emu meat is a low-fat (97 percent fat free), high-protein red meat similar in texture and taste to beef. One bird yields 25 to 40 pounds (11–18 kilograms) of meat, which is higher in vitamin C and iron than beef, and lower in cholesterol than chicken. The feathers and dark green egg shells from emus are also used for unique and creative jewelry accents and for craft goods. In addition, Emus are farmed for their skin, which is a soft, supple, quill-patterned leather used for clothing and fashion accessories. Emus are also raised for their oil, the most valuable part of the bird. Emu oil is rendered from the fat layer on the Emu's back when processing for meat. Harvested in the United States, the odorless and greaseless oil is sold at typical grocery stores. It claims to penetrate the skin quickly and deeply so that it is an excellent transdermal carrier for other moisturizers and therapeutics (Whitehouse et al., 1998). It is a proven anti-inflammatory (Yoganathan et al., 2003) and painkiller (comparable to ibuprofen), and also a bacteriostatic, preventing bacterial growth. Emu oil is also believed to have healing properties for arthritis, joint pain, muscle pain, etc. (Snowden and Whitehouse, 1997). It is hypoallergenic and is not known to have negative side effects. The oil contains vitamins E and A and is most commonly used in cosmetics for its penetrating abilities without clogging pores, and the fact that it contains oleic acid, an anti-wrinkling agent.

OSTRICHES

The Ostrich is native to Central and Southern Africa, inhabiting the savanna and desert environments. There is only one species of Ostrich remaining, with the extinction of the Saudi Arabian species in the 1940s. This single species is divided into four subspecies: North, South, Masai, and Somali. The Ostrich eats select high-quality grasses, seeds, flowers, and leaves. Females are brown, and the much larger males are black with white primaries and tail (Figure 11.12). Both males and females have bare necks and thighs. Their feathers are soft, lacking barbs, giving a fluffy appearance. Ostriches are preyed upon mostly by lions and sometimes leopards and cheetahs. The adult Ostrich kicks with its powerful legs, which can be formidable weapons, able to kill a potential predator as large as a lion. In addition, each two-toed foot has a long, sharp claw. Using their strong legs, a single stride can be between 10 and 16 feet (3–4.8 meters) wide, and they are able to reach speeds up to 45 miles per hour (72 kilometers per hour), using their wings as rudders to help them change direction quickly.

As the world's largest living bird, the male Ostrich stands between 7 and 9 feet (2.1–2.7 meters) tall and 220 to 287 pounds (100 to 130 kilograms), while the female is 5.7 to 6.2 feet (1.77–1.89 meters) tall and 200–242 pounds (90 to 110 kilograms). Ostriches become sexually mature at four to five years (Shanawany and Dingle, 1999) and live over 40 years (Perrins and Middleton, 1985). In breeding season, the male maintains a loose pair bond with a major hen and up to seven minor females (Cooper et al., 2010). After mating with the male, the major hen and minor hens deposit their eggs into the nest with the dominant hen's eggs in the center. The minor hens take no other part in raising young. For the next six weeks, the male and major hen will alternate incubation duties, with the female sitting during the daytime and the male incubating through the night. If the major hen finds that she has too many eggs to incubate, she will role the minor hens' eggs out to the edge of the nest, where they will not be incubated. The eggs at the edge of the nest are also more likely to be predated. After the chicks hatch, both parents raise and protect the young. Often, chicks from several parents are tended together. What are the benefits of being a minor hen? First, there are fewer males than females (1.4 females to every one male); thus, if the females are to reproduce, they must share the males. Second, there is safety in numbers: More eggs together increase the chances of survival. Fewer than 10 percent of nests survive three weeks of laying and six weeks of incubation due to predators, such as hyenas, jackals, and Egyptian Vultures. Only 15 percent of the chicks survive to be one year old, when they will be at full height (Perrins and Middleton, 1985).

Ostriches are presently farmed commercially around the world for feathers, leather, meat, and oil. Ostrich feathers were traditionally worn by Osiris, the god of the dead in ancient Egyptian mythology, as a sign of divinity and justice. In more recent times, these feathers have been prized by fashion designers for their robust beauty (Figure

FIGURE 11.10 Lesser Rhea

FIGURE 11.11 Emu

FIGURE 11.12   Male Ostriches are black with white primaries and tail feathers. Females have a dusty brown plumage.

FIGURE 11.13   The desire for Ostrich feathers in high fashion nearly led to the extinction of the species.

11.13). The demand for Ostrich feathers grew so high in the 18th century that the only remaining species was nearly eradicated. Fortunately, by the mid 19th century, the practice of Ostrich farming started to become more common, with over one million captive-bred individuals worldwide by 1913—allowing the bird to be domesticated and plucked, rather than hunted. With the onset of the First World War in 1914, the Ostrich industry crashed disastrously and remained in a slump until after the Second World War. The industry, nevertheless, did survive on a small scale, mainly in South Africa, by diversifying its products, and gradually becoming the larger, global industry that exists today (Shanawany and Dingle, 1999). In addition to feathers, the Ostrich had many commercial products to offer, such as meat and leather. Ostrich hide provides a soft, flexible, and durable leather that is distinguished by its tell-tale pattern of quill sockets and its suppleness. It is an ideal material for the manufacture of most leather goods, particularly boots, shoes and clothing, as well as wallets, briefcases, handbags, and other leather accessories. Ostrich meat is a healthy alternative for red meat lovers, with a similar color, flavor, and texture to beef, but with two thirds less fat. It has been served in the United States in fine restaurants since 1992. While Ostrich meat is new to the United States, it has long been commonly served in European gourmet restaurants. Demand for the meat is growing in the Pacific Rim and in the United States. However, it is illegal for ratite meat to contain curing agents (Hui, 2006), which are used to preserve and flavor beef and poultry. Without these preservation methods, the shelf life of ratite meat is shortened, inhibiting its export sales. Lastly, Ostriches are farmed for their oil. Ostrich oil has been used for skin care in Egyptian, Roman, and African cultures for over 3000 years. The refined oil has been used on lesions, burns, contact dermatitis, eczema, psoriasis, dry skin, dry hair conditions, bed sores, and many other ailments. Ostrich oil is commonly found in lotions, shampoos, creams, soaps, pain relief lotions, balms, and other cosmetics.

REFERENCES

BirdLife International. 2011. "IUCN Red List for Birds." Accessed 12/29//2011: http://www.birdlife.org

Boles, W. E. 2001. A new Emu (Dromaiinae) from the Late Oligocene Etadunna Formation. *Emu* **101**:317–321.

Bradford, M. G. and D. A. Westcott. 2010. Consequences of Southern Cassowary (Casuarius casuarius, L.) gut passage and deposition pattern on the germination of rain forest seeds. *Austral Ecology* **35**:325–333.

Bradford, M. G. and D. A. Westcott. 2011. Predation of Cassowary dispersed seeds: Is the Cassowary an effective disperser? *Integrative Zoology* **6**:168–177.

Burbidge, M. L., R. M. Colbourne, H. A. Robertson, and A. J. Baker. 2003. Molecular and other biological evidence supports the recognition of at least three species of Brown Kiwi. *Conservation Genetics* **4**:167–177.

Calder, W. A. and T. J. Dawson. 1978. Resting metabolic rates of ratite birds: The Kiwis and the Emu. *Comparative Biochemistry and Physiology a—Physiology* **60**:479–481.

Calder, W. A., C. R. Parr, and D. P. Karl. 1978. Energy content of eggs of Brown Kiwi *Apteryx australis*—extreme in avian evolution. *Comparative Biochemistry and Physiology a—Physiology* **60**:177–179.

Colbourne, R. 2002. Incubation behaviour and egg physiology of Kiwi (*Apteryx spp.*) in natural habitats. *New Zealand Journal of Ecology* **26**:129–138.

Cooper, R. G., J. O. Horbanczuk, R. Villegas-Vizcaino, S. K. Sebei, A. E. F. Mohammed, and K. M. A. Mahrose. 2010. Wild Ostrich (Struthio camelus) ecology and physiology. *Tropical Animal Health and Production* **42**:363–373.

Harris, T. 2009. *National Geographic Complete Birds of the World*. Brown Reference Group Ltd.

Harshman, J., E. L. Braun, M. J. Braun, C. J. Huddleston, R. C. K. Bowie, J. L. Chojnowski, S. J. Hackett, K. L. Han, R. T. Kimball, B. D. Marks, K. J. Miglia, W. S. Moore, S. Reddy, F. H. Sheldon, D. W. Steadman, S. J. Steppan, C. C. Witt, and T. Yuri. 2008. Phylogenomic evidence for multiple losses of flight in ratite birds. *Proceedings of the National Academy of Sciences of the United States of America* **105**:13462–13467.

Hui, Y. H. 2006. *Handbook of food science, technology, and engineering*. Taylor & Francis.

IUCN 2011. "IUCN Red List of Threatened Species. Version 2011.2." Accessed 12/29/2011: www.iucnredlist.org

Maloney, S. K. 2008. Thermoregulation in ratites: A review. *Australian Journal of Experimental Agriculture* **48**:1293–1301.

McNab, B. K. 1996. Metabolism and temperature regulation of Kiwis (Apterygidae). *Auk* **113**:687–692.

Perrins, C. M. and A. L. A. Middleton. 1985. The Encyclopedia of Birds. *Proceedings of the National Academy of Sciences of the United States of America*. Facts On File, Inc., New York.

Project Kiwi. 2011. "Operation Nest Egg." Accessed 03/30/2012: www.projectkiwi.org.nz

Sales, J. 2005. The endangered Kiwi: A review. *Folia Zoologica* **54**:1–20.

Sales, J. 2006. Digestive physiology and nutrition of ratites. *Avian and Poultry Biology Reviews* **17**:41–55.

Sales, J. 2007. The Emu (Dromaius novaehollandiae): A review of its biology and commercial products. *Avian and Poultry Biology Reviews* **18**:1–20.

Shanawany, M. M. and J. Dingle. 1999. Ostrich Production Systems. *FAO Animal Production Health Paper 144*, Rome, Italy, 1-14.

Snowden, J. M. and M. W. Whitehouse. 1997. Anti-inflammatory activity of Emu oils in rats. *Inflammopharmacology* **5**:127–132

Whitehouse, M., A. Turner, C. Davis, and M. Roberts. 1998. Emu oil(s): A source of nontoxic transdermal anti-inflammatory agents in aboriginal medicine. *Inflammopharmacology* **6**:1–8.

Yoganathan, S., R. Nicolosi, T. Wilson, G. Handelman, P. Scollin, R. Tao, P. Binford, and F. Orthoefer. 2003. Antagonism of croton oil inflammation by topical Emu oil in CD-1 mice. *Lipids* **38**:603–607.

XII GALLIFORMES

Galliformes is an order of ground-dwelling birds that are relatively heavy bodied, with well-developed flight muscles and short, rounded wings. This type of wing allows explosive takeoffs by these birds when threatened by danger. Their flights are typically short in distance, but some migratory species exist. All of the species produce precocial offspring, but their mating habits vary across the many Galliformes species. They are sometimes referred to as landfowl, gamefowl, or gamebirds. Landfowl is the more appropriate name, as the word game indicates any animal that is hunted for food. As previously discussed in other chapters, many birds—whether it be songbirds, doves, or parrots—are hunted for food, so giving this distinction to Galliformes is not appropriate. Galliformes include a wide array of species. For sheer beauty, it is hard to beat the iridescent plumage coloration of a Monal (Figure 12.1) or the wattle of a displaying male Satyr Tragopan (Figure 12.2). Other species belonging to this family are colorful pheasants and peacocks, as well as the wild species of the turkey and chicken from which the domesticated versions are descended. BirdLife International (2012) splits the Galliformes into the following families: Cracidae, Megapodiidae, Odontophoridae, Numididae, and Phasianidae.

CURASSOWS, GUANS, AND CHACHALACAS

The Cracidae family consists of the Guans, Curassows, and Chachalacas (Figure 12.3 a–c). These birds are found in South America, Central America, and Mexico. The Chachalacas are the smallest members of the family and can weigh under a pound (0.45 kilograms). Guans are larger, but not as large and heavy bodied as Curassows, which can weigh close to 10 pounds (4.5 kilograms). The larger species are ground feeders but as size decreases, feeding occurs on the ground and in trees. Diets consist mainly of fruits, buds, flowers,

FIGURE 12.1   The colorful iridescent plumage of the Monal Pheasant

FIGURE 12.2   The display wattle of a male Satyr Tragopan

FIGURE 12.3a   Great Currasow

and some seeds and insects. BirdLife International (2012) lists 51 species in this family. While there are no extinct species, the Alagoas Curassow is extinct in the wild. Eighteen of the 51 species, or 35 percent are threatened with extinction (one extinct in the wild, three critical, eight endangered, and six vulnerable), and another five are considered near threatened. These bird species are relatively tame and inquisitive in the wild. These characteristics, combined with being limited to slow, short flights, have resulted in them being heavily persecuted for food purposes. They are also suffering further declines due to habitat destruction.

MEGAPODES AND BRUSH TURKEYS

The Megapodiidae family was discussed previously in Chapter 7 because of its unusual egg incubation methods that can involve volcanic thermal vents and decaying vegetation. This family consists of Brush Turkey and megapode species. BirdLife International (2012) lists 21 species within this family. Although no members of this family are classified as extinct or critically endangered, four and six species are listed as endangered or vulnerable—meaning that about 48 percent of the species are threatened with extinction. However, archeological evidence suggests that up to 33 additional megapode species have become extinct in their current Australasian distribution in the last few thousand years (Perrins, 2009). The extant species within the Megapodiidae family are found in Australasia, with several of the species having very small ranges on islands which predisposes them to endangerment/extinction; their eggs have long been harvested by local people. They are dietary generalists, foraging on forest floors for insects, fruits, and roots. The megapode species tend to be monogamous for the most part, with both members of the pair involved in egg mound preparation, but some instances of polygyny are observed. The Brush Turkey species is not monogamous, with the male accepting any female willing to mate with him and deposit eggs within his incubation mound. Chicks for megapodes and Brush Turkeys are classified as highly precocial. Chicks have no or little contact with parents.

NEW WORLD QUAILS

The Odontophoridae family is made up of the New World Quail species, which are found from Canada southward through southern Brazil. BirdLife International (2012) lists 31 species in this family. Of these species, one is considered endangered, while five species are considered vulnerable to extinction. These six threatened species are all found in Central and South America and have limited natural ranges. Twenty-two species (70 percent) of this family are classified as least concern for endangerment. Three species, including the Northern Bobwhite, are classified as near threatened. The Northern

Bobwhite has a vast range that stretches over much of the eastern and central United States down through parts of Central America. It has undergone a rapid population decline for the last 40 years, with a 35 percent decline in numbers per decade associated with habitat loss for agriculture and hunting pressure, as up to 20 million are killed annually in the United States (BirdLife International, 2012).

The New World Quail are small landfowl that are named for their similar appearance and habits with the Old Word Quail, which are members of the Phasianidae family and are only very distantly related to the New World Quail. New World Quail are ground feeders that eat seeds, insects, and vegetation. They tend to run from danger, but as a last resort can use their explosive and strong flight capability for short distances. New World Quail exhibit sexual dichromism, with males having brighter plumage than females, but the differences in plumage are not as dramatic as seen in some of the members of the Phasianidae family we will discuss. They are generally monogamous, with males and females both involved in raising their offspring. It is common for some species of New World Quail such as the Northern Bobwhite Quail to be raised in captivity for release in the wild for hunting purposes.

GUINEAFOWL

The Numididae family consists of the Guineafowl native to Africa. They are noted for their noisy vocalizations and nearly featherless, but richly colored, skinned head. There are six species recognized by BirdLife International (2012). Five of the species have populations that warrant a least concern classification for extinction, while one species, the White-breasted Guineafowl, is considered vulnerable for extinction. Guineafowl are social birds that live in small (20–40 individuals) to medium-sized groups (2,000 individuals, and only Helmeted Guinea) in non-breeding periods. During the breeding season, stable pairs form, and while the male will wander as the female incubates, he returns before the chicks hatch to assist in their rearing. Helmeted and Vulturine Guineafowl can be found in fairly open savanna, sub-desert-type habitats, while the remaining species are found in more forested habitats. They eat seeds, insects, and tubers/roots.

Helmeted Guineafowl (Figure 12.4) have been domesticated and are found particularly in Europe, where they are commonly raised for human consumption. In the United States, they are typically kept for hobby purposes. They are effective in controlling insects in yards (especially ticks), and their loud distinctive call alerts owners to the arrival of any visitors.

FIGURE 12.3b   Crested Guan

FIGURE 12.3c   Grey-necked Chachalaca

FIGURE 12.4   Helmeted Guineafowl

PHEASANTS AND ALLIES

The Phasianidae family is the largest and most diverse of the Galliformes families. It consists of Pheasants, Tragopans, Monals, Peafowls, Junglefowls, Turkeys, Partridges, Francolins/Spurfowl, Grouse, Ptarmigans, Prairie Chickens, Capercaillies, and the Old World Quails. Phasianidae have ranges from the Arctic southward through Europe, Russia, Asia, North and Central America, Africa, Australia, and the upper half of South America. Males tend to be larger and more brightly colored than females. Diets tend to be varied but are heavily vegetarian (seeds, leaves, fruits, and roots), supplemented with insects and small grubs. BirdLife International (2012) lists 181 species in this family. Of these species, 2, 11, 26, 28, and 112 are considered to have total populations in the wild that are critically endangered, endangered, vulnerable, near threatened, and of least concern. One of the critically endangered species, the Himalayan Quail, has not been recorded since 1876, but persistent reports of occasional potential sightings keep hope alive that an extremely small number of these birds persists.

Two species of the Phasianidae family, the Double-banded Argus and the New Zealand Quail, are extinct. The Double-banded Argus is only known from a single portion of a primary feather from an 1871 shipment of other Argus feathers to London. This feather does not match the pattern of the other two Argus Pheasant species—the Crested Argus and the Great Argus. However, given that there are no other records of the Double-banded Argus, the feather specimen may be no more than one abhorrent feather in shape and color from an individual Great Argus bird (Parkes, 1992). The reasons for the extinction of the New Zealand Quail are not entirely understood. Although habitat loss and heavy persecution by introduced cats, dogs, and rats took a heavy toll, this species of quail was widespread and common on New Zealand until 1850. However, by 1875 it was extinct, and the rapidity of the decline may indicate that disease(s) from introduced gamebirds may have played a role (BirdLife International, 2012).

PHASIANIDAE IN CAPTIVITY

Several members of the Phasianidae family are kept by humans in captivity. This is especially the case in the United States, where over 50 million landfowl (New and Old World Quail, pheasants, partridges, and Wild Turkeys) are raised commercially (Food Safety and Inspection Service, 2011). The commercial birds are raised for sale to restaurants and to consumers directly as gourmet items. Commercially raised birds are also reared to be released on private or public hunting reserves to ensure that birds are available for prospective hunters. Private commercial hunting reserves are becoming more popular as an outlet for urban recreational hunting enthusiasts that would otherwise have a hard time accessing private lands for hunting. As the landfowl industry grows, commercial operations are becoming more specialized within specific facets of the industry. For example, some individuals have the breeding birds and produce hatchlings, which are then purchased by other individuals who grow them to market size and sell them. Besides commercial production, many hobbyists grow members of the Phasianidae family in small numbers for enjoyment, food purposes, and in some cases, preservation of threatened species. A few of the most common Phasianidae raised commercially or by hobbyists will be highlighted along with their natural history.

OLD WORLD QUAIL

Old World Quail are found throughout, Africa, Asia, Europe, and Australia. They inhabit grasslands and eat seeds, other plant foods, and insects. Like the New World Quails, they normally associate in a small family group called a covey. They are the smallest members of the Phasianidae family and are heavy, short-legged birds that are primarily terrestrial, as they feed and nest on the ground. However, some species such as the Common Quail (*Coturnix coturnix*) and Japanese Quail are migratory and fly long distances. Old World Quail, especially the Common Quail and the Japanese Quail, are raised by hobbyists around the world. Japanese Quail that have been genetically selected for greater size or egg production are raised for commercial meat and egg production. Japanese Quail are also used extensively for scientific research because of their small size and quick generation time.

PARTRIDGES

Overall, partridges are medium-sized birds that are larger than quail but typically smaller than pheasants. They are ground-nesting birds that primarily eat seeds. Partridges are found most commonly in open grassland, scrub, or semi-desert habitats, but a couple of forest and alpine species also exist. They are native to the Middle East, Asia, Africa, and Europe. The Chukar and Grey Partridges adapt well to agricultural habitats and have been introduced or escaped from captivity to establish feral populations in the United States. The Chukar Partridge is one the most commonly kept and bred members of the Phasianidae family as it is a hardy bird that naturally withstands cold and hot temperatures in its rocky, dry, open hillside habitat that stretches from Turkey through most of the Middle East to India and the Western Himalayas. In the United States, about 4 million Chukar Partridge are raised commercially (Food Safety and Inspection Service, 2011).

FIGURE 12.5 A male Golden Pheasant

FIGURE 12.6 A male Lady Amherst's Pheasant

FIGURE 12.7 A male Ring-necked Pheasant

PHEASANTS

Pheasants are native to Asia, with several species found in China. Pheasants exhibit strong sexual dimorphism, with males having vivid, bright colors, long tails and/or colorful wattles. Males also tend to be larger than the cryptic colored females. Male pheasants are some of the most colorful of all birds, and two especially stunning species are the Golden Pheasant (Figure 12.5) and Lady Amherst's Pheasant (Figure 12.6). Pheasants are generally forest birds, rarely seen in the wild, as they are shy birds. This skittishness and desire to flee human contact remains in most of the species kept in captivity. After mating, female pheasants produce their clutch of eggs. The male Common Pheasant is unusual in the pheasant world, as he collects/bonds with a group of females that he mates with and guards until they have laid their eggs. Confident in his paternity, he then allows the female to incubate the eggs and raise the resulting offspring by herself.

The Common Pheasant, often called the Ring-necked Pheasant (Figure 12.7) has been widely introduced and has established thriving populations in the United States, Canada, New Zealand, Australia, and throughout most of Europe. Estimates of its wild population go as high as 300 hundred million (BirdLife International, 2012). Over 30 different subspecies of the Common Pheasant are recognized. It was introduced in the United States in the late 1800s and is now widely distributed across this country, except in the southeast over through Texas. Despite being an introduced species, it is actually the state bird of South Dakota. In the United States, as it does in its other ranges, the Common Pheasant eats primarily seeds, fruit, leaves, and insects. It was introduced as a bird to be hunted and it fulfills that role as—in South Dakota alone, over a million of these birds have been killed each year for the past decade (South Dakota Game, Fish and Parks, 2012).

Pheasants are widely kept in captivity in the United States. Several of the more colorful and rare species are kept as exotic ornamental pets by hobbyists. But, Pheasants are also raised commercially for two different markets. The Common Pheasant is raised by individuals and then sold to hunting preserves. Genetically selected lines of the Common Pheasant are also widely produced for direct sale as a gourmet item to restaurants and to the public.

PEAFOWL

There are three species of the Peafowl, the Congo, Indian, and Green. The Congo Peafowl is native to the lowland river forests of eastern Democratic Republic of the Congo. Relatively little is known about this species that was recognized in the last 100 years and lives in a region marked by years of armed conflict. It is considered vulnerable, with a decreasing population that is probably less than 10,000 mature birds (BirdLife International, 2012).

The Indian and Green Peafowl of south and Southeast Asia are widely known, as they (especially the Indian species) are raised around the world for ornamental display purposes. Peafowl have been domesticated for centuries, as the sexually mature male's (peacock) fan of enlarged tail covert feathers is remarkably striking (Figure 12.8). In the Indian Peafowl, the peacock is mainly blue in color, while the female (peahen) is brown in color. In contrast, both the peacock and the peahen share the green overall plumage color in the Green Peafowl, but the female lacks the large fantail. In both species, the peacocks can weigh 10 to 12 pounds (4.5 to 5.4 kilograms); the peahens may weigh less than half that amount.

FIGURE 12.8 Male green peacock displaying

For most of the year, Indian Peafowl live in small groups, but when breeding season commences, adult males become aggressive loners that establish territories which they defend vigorously. The territories will have one to a few carefully selected display areas, and when females approach, the male quickly goes to the display area to start his courtship dance. If the female is impressed, she will mate with the male and then leave. The male will then wait for the arrival of the next female.

Due to declining numbers as a result of habitat loss and hunting, the Green Peafowl has been upgraded to endangered (BirdLife International, 2012). The Indian Peafowl, the national bird of India, is listed as least concern for the threat of extinction as the population is stable in its native range and in several introduced locations around the world. There are well-established feral populations of Indian Peafowl in California and Florida, and in both states the presence of these birds causes controversy. Peacocks like to roam and eat many ornamental plants. As large birds, they produce a good deal of droppings and they have very loud calls. Invariably, communities end up divided with some people wanting the peafowl eliminated, while others are thrilled to have them in the community and visiting their yards.

TURKEYS

There are two species of turkeys: the Wild Turkey and the Ocellated Turkey. The Ocellated Turkey is considerably smaller than the Wild Turkey, and it has a near threatened population status. Its population is declining due to hunting and habitat loss. It is endemic to the Yucatan peninsula of Mexico, Northern Guatemala, and parts of Belize.

The Wild Turkey is the largest member of the Phasianidae family, with males (also called a tom or gobbler) weighing 20 to 25 pounds (9.1 to 11.4 kilograms). Females (hens) weigh about half to a little over half this amount. Wild Turkeys are characterized by having a mostly featherless head and upper neck that has the following distinguishing features: snood, wattle, and caruncles (Figure 12.9). The turkey also has a unique tuft of bristle feathers called a beard protruding from the chest of adult males and some females. The beard of a female Wild Turkey is much smaller than what is found on a mature male. Females are also about 10 inches shorter in stature than males, are less colorful, and lack the display feathers of males.

A habitat that is a mix of mature forest and open agriculture areas is preferred by Wild Turkeys that roost in tall trees at night. Their diets consists of seeds, especially acorns, as well as berries, insects, snails, and plant shoots. Adult males and females form sex-specific groups for much of the year, but during the spring the adults intermix for reproduction. During courtship, males strut and gobble and often court in groups of males, but there is only one dominant male per group of males. Wild Turkeys are polygamous, with one male mating with several females. Once mating is complete, the female will select a suitable nest site and lay about 10 to 15 eggs. The

FIGURE 12.9 Wild Turkey. The mature male has several unique features to assist in attracting mates. Caruncles are the bumpy skin growths around the head and neck. The snood is a fleshy piece of skin that sits erect when relaxed and extends over the bill when the male displays for females. Wattles are extra flesh that hang under the throat. The beard is made of specialized bristle-like feathers that protrude out of the male's chest. When in full display, all of these accessories, along with a fanned-out tail, are desirable features used by females to assess fitness.

female incubates and cares for the hatchlings—called poults—with no assistance from the male. The female and her poults will merge back with the original female group. Juvenile males are called jakes, while the young female is called a jenny. Jennies will either stay with the female group containing their mother or they will join another female group. Jakes will separate from the female group and join male groups. Although sexual maturity is reached by one year of age, males rarely get to breed until they are older because they are outcompeted by stronger, more aggressive, older males.

The Wild Turkey has six subspecies: the Eastern, Osceola, Rio Grande, Merriam's, Gould's, and Mexican that are differentiated in large part by geographic range. The Eastern Wild Turkey is the most numerous and widespread, found from the East Coast through the Great Plains and from southern Canada to the Gulf Coast of the United States. The Mexican, or South Mexican, subspecies is the source of the domestic Turkey breeds found throughout the world. Currently, this subspecies is highly endangered or extinct (Lerich, 2012). The Aztecs are said to have domesticated this species, and Spanish explorers took this tamed species back to Spain and from there it spread in Europe. The colonists that came to America brought domesticated European Turkeys with them, apparently unaware that the Eastern Wild Turkey would be present. In fact, the Wild Turkey population was very abundant in the United States upon the arrival of the Europeans, who started hunting it for food. By the end of the 19th century, mass hunting and the clearing of forests were making extinction a real possibility in the wild, as the number of wild turkeys had plunged to about 30,000.

Extensive conservation efforts and highly successful trapping and relocation of wild birds to areas where the population had been eliminated previously has allowed the population to increase by over 240 percent for each of the last four decades. They are now classified as least concern for the threat of extinction (BirdLife International, 2012). The total Wild Turkey population in North America is over 7 million birds (NWTF, 2011). Funds generated from the Pittman Robertson Act of 1937—which allows the collection of an 11 percent excise tax on all gun and ammunition sales to support wildlife conservation in the United States—have been vital in the conservation of the Wild Turkey.

In a letter to his daughter, Benjamin Franklin made it clear he thought the Wild Turkey was the much better choice as the national bird of the United States rather than the Bald Eagle. However, it is unclear if he ever officially proposed the Wild Turkey as the national bird.

At least 200,000 Wild Turkeys are raised in captivity to provide meat to the gourmet specialty market in the United States (Food Safety and Inspection Service, 2011). In addition, domestic turkey production in the United States in 2011 was 248.5 million birds, which had a direct value of $5 billion (USDA, 2012).

JUNGLEFOWL

There are four junglefowl species native to Southeast Asia, and at least two of them have contributed to the genetics found in modern-day domesticated chickens. They exhibit strong sexual dimorphism with the males (cocks) being larger and more colorful than the cryptic colored females (hens). The males also have fleshy combs and wattles that are much more developed than in the females. They are medium-sized members of the Phasianidae family at weights of 1.5 to 2.7 pounds (0.7 to 1.2 kilograms), more similar to the pheasants and much smaller than peafowl and turkeys. Although listed as least concern for extinction (BirdLife International, 2012), there is growing concern—especially for the Red Junglefowl species (Peterson and Brisbin, 1998)—that genetic extinction of the species could be imminent due to their hybridization with feral or free-ranging domesticated chickens. Often what are claimed or assumed to be pure representatives of the four species of junglefowl are not. For example, true Red Junglefowl species should exhibit eclipse plumage during the months of June through September after the breeding season, in which some of the feathers of the male are less showy. Female Red Junglefowl should almost completely lack combs (Peterson and Brisbin, 1998). Finding such birds in the wild is increasingly difficult, as most no longer have eclipse plumage from June through September and many females have combs, indicating genetic contamination.

The Green Junglefowl (*Gallus varius*) is native to Java and a few small islands east of Java. They forage in open mangrove swamps, along beaches and cultivated areas for marine insects and terrestrial crustaceans, and then retreat to forested areas for cover. Most of the feathers on the male are black at their base and then transition from blue to green, except for the feathers on the mid to lower back, which are outlined in a gold color. The males possess only one wattle, which is multicolored (red, yellow, and blue). Their combs share the same colors as the wattle, but the comb is non-serrated (without indentations and points). The Green Junglefowl also has two additional tail feathers, compared to the other junglefowl. The Green Junglefowl is maintained in captivity by hobbyists due to the male's beauty, but morphologically it is the most distant from domesticated chickens and the other junglefowl, based on the extra feathers in the tail and an unusual comb and wattle structure.

The Sri Lanka Junglefowl (*Gallus lafayetii*) is endemic to Sri Lanka. They feed on small fruits and insects that are found on the forest floor. The female, as in the other junglefowl species, is mostly a brownish color. The male has a single upright red comb with a large yellow colored spot in its center. The blade of the comb is serrated. The male is very striking during the breeding season when it has golden-colored neck plumage. The feather color slowly transitions from orange/brown on the chest to black, with a blue sheen for the tail feathers. They are difficult to maintain in captivity and require diets that are similar to their natural ones for optimum survival in captivity.

The Grey Junglefowl (*Gallus sonneratii*) is native to southern, central, and western India. Associated with forests, the Grey Junglefowl eats fruit, seeds, and insects. The plumage on the cock's abdomen and lower body parts are gray in color, and the feathers of the head and neck are black with gray edging. The tail feathers are black, as are the primary wing feathers. Primary wing coverts and the feathers on the back leading to the tail are orange and golden with some red fringes. The cock's comb is a single upright serrated blade with a pair of wattles.

Red Junglefowl (*Gallus gallus*) have the widest natural range, as they are endemic to northeast India moving eastward across southwestern China and southward through Burma, Thailand, Cambodia, Vietnam, and into Malaysia and Indonesia. Unlike the other species of junglefowl that have no subspecies, there are five to six recognized subspecies of the Red Junglefowl, based primarily on geographic location. The Red Junglefowl's range in India borders with that of the Grey Junglefowl; hybridization has occurred. The female Red Junglefowl is a cryptic dull golden brown color, while the male has brighter golden brown and red neck feathers, red, brown, and orange body feathers, and a black metallic-colored tail feathers. The cock's comb is a single upright serrated blade with a pair of wattles, while the hen's comb is almost non-existent.

FROM JUNGLEFOWL TO THE MODERN CHICKEN INDUSTRY

The movement of domesticated chickens is used to help understand human movement and cultural influences throughout history. Chickens were small and easy to transport across land—but more importantly by boat—as people settled and moved to new areas. Tracing domestic chickens through history has depended traditionally on finding chicken bones in areas where chickens were not native and finding bones that were larger than those of the modern Junglefowl, and thus suggestive of selective breeding. More recently, genetic analyses from current domesticated chickens and from DNA extracted from bones are adding insight into the origin of domesticated chickens and their global movement. Many books and scholarly research articles have been written on the topic. The reader is encouraged to consult them if the brief overview provided here is not enough. Two suggested readings are a recent review by Boichard et al. (2011) or *The Chicken Book*, by Smith and Daniel (2000).

Traditionally the view has been that all domesticated chickens were derived from the Red Junglefowl, since morphologically they are the most similar—even plumage patterns are very similar to some of the oldest breeds of domestic chickens. Additionally, fertile offspring are easily produced from crosses of modern domesticated chickens with the Red Junglefowl. Such crosses with the other Junglefowl species yield very poor hatchability and chick survival.

Genetic analyses of chicken DNA are now providing insight into chicken domestication, both from an origin viewpoint and the movement of domesticated chicken lineages around the world. We will discuss this later in the section on the arrival of the chicken in the Americas. As for the origin of the domestic chicken, the idea that domestic chickens are derived exclusively from the Red Junglefowl has to be rethought. Genetic analysis has revealed that the yellow skin phenotypic trait common in many commercial lines of chickens originates not from the Red Junglefowl, but the Grey Junglefowl, suggesting a hybrid origin of the domestic chicken (Eriksson et al., 2008). In addition, genetic analyses indicate there may have been multiple origins of domestication in south and Southeast Asia, and that the expansion from these sites followed specific expansion routes (Liu et al., 2006; Kanginakudru et al., 2008; Berthouly-Salazar et al., 2010).

FIRST AREAS WITH KNOWN DOMESTIC CHICKENS

The Indus Valley Civilization, or the Harappan Civilization, was a large ancient civilization that spread over what is now Pakistan, eastern Afghanistan, and northwest India. Excavation of sites within this civilization has been ongoing almost constantly for the past 100 years. Among the findings have been chicken bones that are larger than those of wild junglefowl. These larger chicken bones indicate selective breeding. In addition, chicken figurines and figures of fighting cocks have been found. Taken together, these findings suggest that this civilization was keeping domestic chickens in the period around 2500 BC. The figures of cockfighting are appropriate, as it is believed that chickens were initially domesticated for the purpose of cockfighting, which became widespread and was one of the first spectator sports. Cockfighting still persists in many locations throughout the world and still illegally occurs in many other parts of the world, including the United States. In addition to cockfighting, the utility of the domestic chicken for egg and meat production was also recognized and utilized, as will be discussed later.

Another, even earlier, center of domestication was northern China—chicken bones have been found in several archaeological sites and dated toward 6000 BC (West and Zhou, 1988). These bones are larger than wild junglefowl bones, indicating potential selective breeding, and the bones are recovered from northern areas of China that would not have had a habitat (too cold) to support junglefowl in the wild. Thus, it is very likely these bones can only be explained by the presence of domestic chickens in this location. If they were already domesticated in northern China at about 6000 BC, this indicates that junglefowl had been domesticated elsewhere at an earlier time and brought to northern China. The most likely source is somewhere in Southeast Asia, such as present-day Thailand.

Although the exact location(s) for the domestication of the chicken is not known, there is a better understanding of its spread throughout the world due to written accounts from the Greek, Roman, and Egyptian civilizations. The Egyptians initially kept chickens as exotics for display purposes (Foster, 1999) starting around 1450 BC. Written references mention them through 1123 BC, followed by a period with little mention, until they come back abundantly by 650 BC, when a period of significant production and use commences (Macdonald and Blench, 2001). The Egyptians mastered mass production of chickens through large-scale incubation, using clay brick incubators kept warm by fires watched over by attendants using their skin as a thermometer, as noted by Greek written accounts. These incubators were capable of incubating thousands of eggs (indications of 10 to 15 thousand) at a time (Smith and Daniel, 2000) which was not accomplished in modern incubators until after 1900.

The Greeks were using chickens for cockfighting by 600 BC, and by 300 BC were using them for meat and eggs. They selected birds for all three purposes (Smith and Daniel, 2000). Based on Greek literature, the Greek Empire was exposed to chickens by both the Persian Empire and the Egyptian Empire. The Persian Empire encompassed the Indus Valley, which had been an early center of chicken domestication. The Persians are thought to be the ones who introduced the Greeks to cockfighting, while the influence from Egypt was more likely for food production, since the Egyptians were mass producing chickens (as noted earlier) by the time of Greek contact. The Greeks also used chickens to a limited extent as sacrificial animals. The Greek philosopher Aristotle performed and recorded results from embryology studies by observing chick embryos at each day of incubation.

The Greeks introduced the Romans to the chicken, and the Romans became completely enamored with it. Not only did the Romans use the chicken for entertainment and for food purposes, they also used it for divination. Most state business was based on auspices (observation of the flight and feeding of birds to discover omens). The domestic chicken was used heavily for this purpose. Even the army and navy carried with them cages of the sacred chicken. When a decision was needed to go into battle, the *pullarius* who cared for the chickens would open the door of their cage and crumble a soft cake in front of them. If the chickens stayed in their cage, flew off, or did not eat the food, that was a bad omen. If, on the other hand, the chickens ate hungrily, the omen was good. Roman literature is also full of basic husbandry guidelines for the breeding and production of chickens. Historical records from the Roman Empire also indicate that when the Romans conquered England, they found chickens were already present. It is believed the Celts had brought chickens to England prior to the Roman Conquest. The source of the Celtic chickens is typically believed to be from the Indus Valley.

DOMESTIC CHICKENS IN THE AMERICAS

Ultimately, as the European powers started to explore and settle other parts of the world, chickens were taken with them. The most commonly promoted idea is that European settlers are the source of the chicken on the east coast of the Americas. However, compelling evidence suggests that a west coast introduction by Polynesian settlers may have preceded the European introduction. Contact between the Americas and Polynesia has been suggested—and hotly debated—based on archaeological and linguistic evidence. Now the domestic chicken has entered into this debate, and has only added more fuel to the heated discussion.

OCEANIA AND SOUTH AMERICA

Discovery and settlement of the islands of Micronesia, Polynesia, and Eastern Melanesia by the Lapita culture started about 3,300 to 3,500 years ago and continued to about 700 to 800 years ago when New Zealand and Easter Island were colonized, respectively. Hawaii was colonized over 1,000 years ago by the Polynesians. Based on radiocarbon and DNA evidence, Storey et al. (2007, 2008) reported that domesticated chickens arrived on the west coast of South America prior to European contact. Using one of the chicken bones isolated from an archaeological site on the west coast of southern Chile, Storey and her colleagues radiocarbon-dated the bone to 1304 to 1424. DNA was extracted from the bone, and based on results from a mitochondrial DNA sequence, it appears this bone was from an individual chicken of Polynesian stock. Storey et al. (2007) also argue that if the chicken was introduced to the east coast (Brazil) of the New World by the Spanish or Portuguese in 1500—as accepted by most scholars—then it seems highly unlikely that when Pizarro arrived in what is today Peru in 1532, he would have found the chicken deeply integrated into the Inca culture. For this to have happened, once the chicken was introduced in 1500, it would have had to be rapidly dispersed across the continent through the Amazonian basin and be immediately accepted and incorporated into the Inca economy and culture.

There is also the presence of the Chilean breed of chicken called the Araucana, which produces blue/green-shelled eggs. The gene associated for this egg color is found in Chinese breeds, but not in European breeds (Tixier-Boichard et al., 2011). The source of the original Polynesian chickens was from Southeast Asia and possibly present-day China, and there is a clear genetic signature for these chickens that follows Polynesian settlement all the way to Easter Island. The Araucana was derived from breeds of chickens maintained by the Araucana Indians, a highly independent people who may have had some contact with poultry of European origin by the mid-sixteenth century, but maintained hostile relations with the immigrant communities until the 1870s. However, the Araucana breed itself was not developed until after 1900.

Gongora et al. (2008a, 2008b) question the Storey et al. results by suggesting that the radiocarbon dating was faulty, as it did not account for marine carbon input. If the chicken that produced the radiocarbon-dated bone consumed a diet that contained more than 20 percent of its dietary carbon intake from marine sources (marine shell grit, shellfish, etc.), then the bone date would be adjusted just into the post-Columbian time period. They argue that given the proximity of the Chilean archaeological site to the coast, the birds could have had a marine-based diet. Gongora et al. also analyzed mitochondrial DNA sequences from 41 modern native Chilean chickens. Their sequences aligned closely with those from Europe and the Indian subcontinent, which is consistent with a European genetic origin. However, the Araucana samples did have some linkage to an Asian genetic origin, but the authors argue that this is a recent introgression of Asian chicken DNA into modern Chilean chickens.

So who is right? The issue remains unresolved because there is research to support both the Polynesian and European hypotheses for the first introduction of domestic chickens into the Americas. There is no doubt that the European settlers brought with them chickens that ended up dominating the chicken population in the Americas. However, the Araucana—but more importantly, the genetic stocks from which it was derived—remains an interesting enigma. And as Gongora et al. (2008a) point out, there are some chickens kept by some indigenous communities in the Amazon forest that have not been genetically tested. These birds may turn out to have a non-European genetic signature. Furthermore, the DNA data sets are getting more extensive, which will ultimately mean major sweeping conclusions are not based on limited sequence data as they are now.

UNITED STATES

Chickens were brought over with the first settlers and provided a source of eggs and meat for these early American settlers. The settlers were also busy hunting native Wild Turkeys and quail as well as pigeons for meat, so chickens remained a backyard fixture, but not extensively bred selectively, especially for meat purposes. The appreciation of and interest in the chicken increased tremendously as the breeding and exhibition of chickens exploded in the mid 1840s. Queen Victoria of England was a poultry enthusiast and had a large poultry house. The Chinese had effectively shunned contact with the outside world and had strictly controlled trade from China. The Opium Wars, or the Anglo Chinese Wars (First Opium War, 1839–1842, Second Opium War, 1856–1860), lifted these restrictions. Queen Victoria was presented with Cochin Chickens from China in the early 1940s. When displayed to the public, these birds created an instant sensation, given their large size and appearance compared to European breeds (Figure 12.10). The breeding of ornamental chickens exploded in Britain and much of Europe among chicken fanciers, and the hobby spread, as it seemed everyone wanted to create a new ornamental/fancy breed of chicken—especially using the new genetics available from imported Asiatic breeds. Britain held the first poultry show in London in 1845, and this national show still occurs every year. Showing chickens in Britain spread after this first show, and poultry exhibits were promoted as a way for competition to occur in the poultry world once cockfighting was banned in Britain, about three years after the initial poultry show.

The ornamental chicken breeding craze and poultry shows spread from Europe to the United States. The first poultry show was held in Boston in 1849, and this show still occurs every year. The first Boston Poultry Show attracted over 10,000 spectators, but more importantly, this show was replicated in locations all over the United States. Due to the popularity of these shows and the hobby of breeding chickens, the American Poultry Association—the oldest poultry organization

FIGURE 12.10   In the mid 1800's Europeans were accustomed to chickens that were the size of the game hen on the left; so it is easy to see why large Cochin chickens like the hen on the right, created a public sensation when first displayed after their import from China.

in North America—was founded in 1873 in Buffalo, New York. This organization was established to provide standards for poultry breeds and regulations for judging. This goal remains today, along with its intent to promote both the standard-bred poultry industry and the exhibition poultry hobby. The American Poultry Association is also committed to using poultry shows as an educational tool for the public about poultry and a means of interesting youngsters in taking up poultry as an interest/hobby.

In 1874, the American Poultry Association published the Standard of Excellence, which is constantly updated and produced to this day. In 1905, the publication was renamed the American Standard of Perfection. This publication classifies and describes the standard physical appearance (with color illustrations), coloring, and temperament for all recognized breeds of poultry, including chickens, ducks, turkeys, and geese.

CLASSES, BREEDS, VARIETIES, AND BANTAMS

In general, the standard breeds of chickens can still be divided into four major classes based on the place of origin. The four classes are: American, Asiatic, English, and Mediterranean. The Asiatic class is characterized by feathered shanks; the Mediterranean class has white ear lobes; the English are white skinned, except for the Cornish, which has yellow skin; the American class is birds with yellow skin, non-feathered shanks, and red ear lobes. Each class is subdivided into breeds and

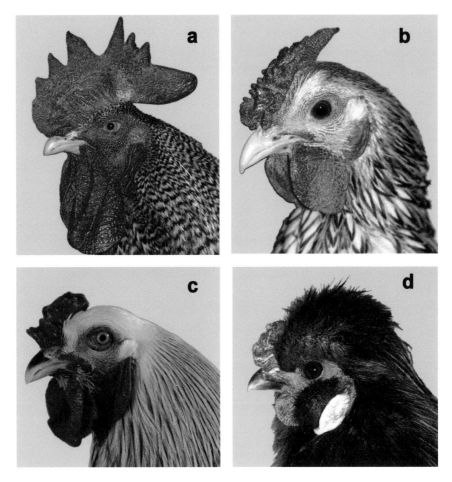

FIGURE 12.11 A few examples of the various comb types found in domestic chickens: single (a), rose (b), pea (c), and walnut (d).

varieties. Breeds are distinguished by such things as body size and shape, skin color, and shank color, while varieties are distinguished by plumage color and pattern, as well as comb type (Figure 12.11). Simplifying it even further, two broad classes can be made: Asiatic and European, with the Asian class consisting of birds with feathered shanks, red ear lobes, pea combs, and large/heavy bodies. The European chickens would have bare shanks, single combs, white ear lobes, and be light in weight and produce more eggs. Selection for increased mature body size and weight leads to a decrease in reproductive efficiency, so egg production is less in hens from these genetic lines.

In addition to standard breeds of chickens, bantam breeds have been developed, which are small versions of a standard breed. They are usually about one quarter the size of a standard breed, but other than size have all the standard breed's characteristics. There are some breeds of bantams that have no standard counterpart. These are often called true bantams, and they are naturally small. Bantams are very commonly kept by backyard hobbyists, as they eat less and require less room. They have also become popular pets that are even kept in their owners' homes.

Much of the genetic selection during the chicken breeding frenzy of the late 1800s and early 1900s was based on morphological features regarding comb size and shape, plumage color, and plumage distribution. Today, hundreds of chicken breeds are recognized, and the variation in appearance is striking (Figure 12.12). In addition, there was the development of breeds like the New Hampshire, Plymouth Rock Wyandotte, and Rhode Island Red, which were considered dual-purpose or utility-type birds (Figure 12.13). These chicken breeds were ideal for the backyard production flock, as they weighed more than Leghorn egg-type chicken breeds, but less than the large Cochin and Brahma breeds of chicken. Thus, dual-purpose chicken breeds produced a

FIGURE 12.12   Some representative chicken breeds: Polish (a), naked-neck (b), frizzle (c), naked (d), seabright (e).

FIGURE 12.13   Barred Plymouth Rock

good amount of eggs, but were also large enough to provide a good meat yield if slaughtered for that purpose.

Backyard flocks were the staple of chicken production in the United States from colonial times through the early 1900s. The hens of the home flock provided a steady supply of eggs for the family, while the young, nearly or full-sized juvenile males (cockerels) and old hens and roosters could be slaughtered for meat. Typically, a chicken dinner was reserved for special occasions. The birds were maintained as free-range birds or in large outdoor cages attached to the chicken house. Free-range chickens would be locked in the chicken house at night. Besides what they consumed outside on their own, chickens were also fed kitchen scraps and provided corn at times. The chicken operation was almost always maintained by the woman of the house. This is an important component of the history of women in the United States. Any extra eggs and especially cockerels would be sold to local hotels, restaurants, or general stores. This provided spending money—often called "egg money"—for the woman of the house. This money provided some independence and is often tied to the beginnings of the women's movement.

In the early 1900s, many agricultural leaders and investors did not promote poultry industry development because they did not see a potential in competing against the current system in which labor was free, feed was mostly free, and the wife of the house was counting on the chickens for her spending money. However, several key things were happening that would ultimately allow the rapid development of the industry. Commercial incubators had been developed, and commercial chicken hatcheries were established in several locations in the United States by 1900. But the real impetus for buying chickens from hatcheries started in 1918, when chicks were approved to be sent by parcel post by the United States Postal Service. Additionally, the causative agent—*Salmonella Pullorum*, for Bacillary White Diarrhea (also called pullorum disease), which caused significant mortality in baby chicks and inhibited the hatchery business—was identified in 1899 and was effectively eradicated by the mid 1920s. People moved to population centers for manufacturing jobs. The demand for food in these population centers was increasing, and transportation advances were allowing for it to be met, including the use of refrigerated box cars, which were common by 1900. Transportation advances also meant that feed ingredients and chicken feeds could be easily transported to distant locations.

The United States government also invested in agriculture by passing several acts. The Morrill Land-Grant Acts of 1862 and 1890 created in each state a land-grant college to teach agriculture. The Hatch Act of 1887 fostered the establishment of experimental stations for research and development in the land-grant colleges. It provides research funding for agriculture and veterinary research at these colleges. Finally, the Smith-Lever Act of 1914 established and provided funding for the Cooperative Extensive Service within the land-grant universities, which resulted in the dissemination of knowledge about current developments in agriculture and home economics to the public. Poultry Science Departments became common in land-grant institutions, starting at Cornell University in 1907 followed by several others, such as at the University of Missouri (1911), University of Georgia (1912), and Pennsylvania State University in 1920. Research at these schools and many others led to key discoveries that would ultimately lead to chickens being able to be maintained inside in large numbers with low mortality and high productivity.

INDUSTRY ESTABLISHMENT

While many people played key roles in the establishment of the poultry industry, Cecile Steele and Jesse Jewell played critical roles. Cecile was a housewife from Ocean View, Delaware, who ordered 50 chicks from a hatchery for delivery in the spring of 1923. When the delivery arrived, there were 500 chicks rather than 50. She decided to keep all of the chicks and quickly had a shed built to house them. About 18 weeks later, when the 387 surviving birds weighed about 2.5 pounds (1.1 kilograms) each, Steele sold them for 62 cents a pound—equivalent to almost seven dollars in today's terms (Horton, 2006: Brown, 2007: Plowman, 2012). Mrs. Steele ordered 1,000 chicks the next year; by 1926 the order was 10,000 chicks, and by 1927 the order was 25,000 birds. Mrs. Steele's neighbors took notice, and by 1928 there were 500 growers in the area. Soon, production was more than 1 million birds per year and the Delmarva broiler (chickens raised for meat) industry was founded.

Jesse Jewell started managing his family's feed, seed, and fertilizer business in 1930, in Gainesville, Georgia. The Great Depression had hit the region hard as had the crash of the cotton farming industry due to the boll weevil, an insect that devastates cotton production. In 1911, Georgia produced 2.8 million bales of cotton; the boll weevil arrived four years later, and by 1921 it destroyed 45 percent of the state's cotton crop. Cash-strapped farmers were not able to buy products from Jewell's store, so Jesse decided to buy baby chicks and supplied them, along with the required chicken feed, on credit to local farmers. Once the chickens were grown, he bought the chickens back from the farmers at a price that covered the credit the farmer owed for the feed and chicks, but also guaranteed the farmers a profit. Jewell then sold the chickens to make a profit for his company. Soon, many farmers were contracted to grow chickens for Jewell. In the early 1940s, Jewell opened his own chicken hatchery, and then in the early 1950s, he opened his own feed mill and processing plant. Thus, Jesse had pioneered the modern poultry business model, in which one company controls all the phases of production from raw materials, processing and distribution, and contracts with farmers to grow chickens for it. This model is called vertical integration, and Jewell's creation of this model has led to Gainesville, Georgia, being called the poultry capital of the world.

Spearheaded by Jewell's company, the growth of the north Georgia poultry industry was phenomenal. In 1940, broiler production in north Georgia doubled to 3.5 million birds; by 1945, the state was producing 29.5 million broilers. Production had reached 62.9 million by 1950, and the following year Georgia became the number one broiler-producing state in the United States (GPLN, 2012). Today, Georgia is still the number one broiler-producing state, with over 1.375 billion broilers produced in 2011—for a direct value of $3.46 billion (USDA, 2012). On an average day, Georgia produces 26 million pounds of chicken and 7.8 million hatching eggs (Georgia Poultry Federation, 2012).

The efficiency of the broiler industry has increased tremendously since the days of Cecile Steele and Jesse Jewell. Production gains have been a large part in achieving this efficiency. It took an average of 16, 10, and 7 weeks to grow birds to market weight in the years 1925, 1955, and 2010, respectively (Georgia Poultry Federation, 2012). The live weight of the bird produced in 1925, 1955, and 2010 has increased from 2.4, 3.1, and 6 pounds (1.1, 1.4, and 2.7 kilograms), respectively. The amount of feed fed to produce each pound of live chicken weight has decreased from 4.7, 3.0, and 1.8 pounds from 1925, 1955, and 2010, respectively. Finally, the percent mortality during broiler production has decreased from 18, 6.9, and 3.8 percent in 1925, 1955, and 2010, respectively. There have also been tremendous gains in the egg industry as well. In 1940, the average egg production per hen was 101 eggs per year. Today, it is about 300 eggs per hen, and the amount of feed needed to produce a dozen eggs has decreased from 8 to about 3 pounds (or 3.6 to 1.4 kilograms) in this period. In 2007, 90 million dozens of table eggs were produced in the United States (Food and Agriculture Organization of the United Nations, 2010).

Poultry production is a very efficient means to convert vegetable mass into high-quality meat protein. The 1.8 pound feed conversion efficiency for broiler chickens is very favorable to the 3.6 pounds of feed for every pound of gain in pigs and the 8 pounds of feed for every pound of gain in beef. However, the feed efficiency in beef is based in part on the ingestion of forage material as well as cereal grains—unlike poultry and swine, where the efficiency is based on highly digestible cereal grains and protein sources such as soybean meal. The gains in poultry production efficiency have come from scientific research conducted by university and poultry industry personnel. This research has yielded advancements in poultry breeding and genetics, nutrition, disease control, and management.

For about the last 60 years, the poultry industry has emphasized heavy genetic selection in their commercial lines of poultry, based on performance parameters. The advancements have been substantial because generation time is only one year in chickens. The genetic selection emphasis has been based on the two primary commercial components of the industry: table egg production, utilizing a laying hen, and the meat production, utilizing the broiler (Figure 12.14). Interestingly, the modern commercial strains used for poultry production have roots in some of the breeds developed during the breeding frenzy that occurred from the mid 1800s to the early 1900s. Major contributors to the commercial broiler strains of today were the Plymouth Rock, used for their body conformation, and the Cornish, developed from Asiatic stocks for large size. The major breed utilized for the white-colored table egg market is the White Leghorn (Mediterranean class) because of their high egg production, while commercial breeds for brown-colored table eggs come from crosses of dual-purpose breeds like New Hampshire, Plymouth Rock, and Rhode Island Reds. It is also important to keep in mind when we think about the incredible production traits of modern commercial lines, that these birds are derived from Junglefowl, which weigh less than 2.5 pounds (1.1 kilograms) and produce less than 50 eggs per year.

Advancements in poultry nutrition have also been tremendous. More is known about the nutritional requirements for chickens than any other animal, including humans. This allows poultry

FIGURE 12.14 Each of these birds has undergone genetic selection over many generations resulting in very different phenotypic characteristics. The bird on the left is a broiler chicken, selected for its fast growth for meat production. The bird on the right is a Leghorn, selected for its egg prodution.

producers to feed diets that match the requirements for growth and production on a weekly basis, thereby optimizing performance and minimizing wasted nutrients. Similarly, disease research allows baby chicks—as well as adults—to receive multiple vaccines to prevent a host of diseases. Disease prevention has also been enhanced by management and technological advancements that provide better environmental control in poultry farms and enhanced biosecurity control.

REDUCED PRICES AND CHICKEN CONSUMPTION

The advancement of the science of poultry production has allowed the birds to perform better and permitted the increase in size of poultry farms, thereby lowering production costs. Consequently, chicken today is less expensive than it has been in the past. Remember, the wholesale price adjusted for inflation for Cecile Steele's birds was about $7 per pound, while the wholesale price per pound in 2010 was 74 cents (USDA, 2011).

The cheapness of poultry meat relative to other meats, its healthiness, ease of preparation, versatility, and suitability as a fast food has made chicken the American public's favorite meat. Poultry consumption in the United States in 1960 was less than 30 pounds (13.6 kilograms) per person; in 2007, it was just below 90 pounds (40.9 kilograms) per person (Georgia Poultry Federation, 2012). Turkey consumption in 2007 was about 17 pounds (7.7 kilograms) per person. For comparison, beef and pork consumption in 2007 was about 66 and 50 pounds (30 and 22.7 kilograms), respectively.

Egg consumption in the United States in 2007 per person was 250 eggs including eggs in the shell and in products (Food and Agriculture Organization of the United Nations, 2010).

POULTRY RESEARCH BENEFITS MANKIND

The dramatic gains in poultry production efficiency and the success of the poultry industry in the United States are associated with a dramatic elimination rate for poultry science departments, whose research and scientific discovery helped pave the way for the success of this sector of agriculture. With dwindling resources and tight budgets, it has been easy to redirect focus to other emerging agricultural priorities and away from poultry research, especially as the poultry industry became heavily concentrated in the southeastern United States and dwindled in other regions. In 1960, there were 44 independent departments of poultry science in the United States (Cook, 1988). Today, there only six independent poultry science departments in the United States, and while they are located where the industry has become most concentrated, they too have shrunk in overall size and funding. This is a worrying trend, as research is just as important in maintaining the competitiveness of poultry production as it was in establishing it in the first place.

The loss of poultry departments is also of concern because throughout history, research with poultry has been vital to scientific discovery that has affected human well-being. This can be highlighted with just a few examples. Louis Pasteur was studying chicken cholera when he developed the first vaccine using attenuated forms of the causative agent of the disease, *Pasteurella multocida*, which causes chicken cholera (Plotkin, 2005). The Nobel Prize-winning concept of the immunological recognition of self and non-self, which was critical for tissue transplant, resulted in large part from research with chicken embryos (Burnet, 1960). B cells that produce antibodies were first defined in chicks and then subsequently in mammalian species (Glick et al., 1956). By using chickens, Peyton Rous described the first virus known to trigger cancer, and this research earned him a Nobel Prize. In 1951, the chicken embryology research of Viktor Hamburger and Howard Hamilton set the stage for future developmental biology studies that continue today and directly benefit human medicine, since much of what we know about human limb formation and eye development has been uncovered through studies of chickens. The first oncogene, a gene that triggers cancer, was discovered in the chicken genome, and this research later helped earn Michael Bishop and Harold Varmus a Nobel Prize. One of the isolates of *Streptomyces griseaus* that produced the antibiotic streptomycin was isolated from a healthy chicken (Schatz, 1993). Common fictional lore indicates that streptomycin was isolated during a determination of what was making chickens ill on a New Jersey farm (Schatz, 1993). Finally, chickens serve as important research models for human diseases such as ovarian cancer and muscular dystrophy.

THE HORMONE MYTH

The majority of the public thinks that hormones are used in broiler chicken production. The fact that the birds grow so incredibly quickly, combined with some poultry marketers suggesting—by default—that competitors have hormones in their product when they advertise their own chickens as "hormone free," makes this perception understandable, but nonetheless untrue.

Birds can grow very rapidly. As discussed in the reproduction chapter, many songbirds that are altricial with no feathers and undeveloped eyes at hatch are fully grown fledglings flying from the nest in a matter of two to three weeks. Although broiler chicks are precocious, in captivity they become altricial because they are provided heat, so they do not have to waste ingested energy on keeping warm. They also do not have to forage for food and water, as it is provided for them at a close distance. As a result, broilers are very sedentary and do not wander away from their food and water source. So as in altricial birds, almost all of the ingested food energy can be utilized for growth.

Even if feeding hormones to broilers were legal, it would not be practical or effective. Growth hormone—which many people assume is the hormone fed to chickens—is a protein hormone. As a protein hormone, if ingested it will be converted in the digestive tract into its individual amino acid components, just like all the other protein consumed in the diet. Thus, it would be rendered useless by digestion. This is why diabetics have to inject their insulin, another protein hormone, rather than ingest it. The only option would be to inject growth hormone every day or every couple of days. At first thought this may seem reasonable, until the idea is examined. For example, the population of the state of Georgia, according to the 2011 United States Census Report, is 9.8 million. The number of broilers produced in Georgia in 2011 was 1.375 billion (USDA, 2012). That means every individual in the state would be responsible for injecting about 140 broilers if growth hormone was being injected. Broilers are raised on the floors of broiler houses, so each bird would have to be caught and then injected, so the labor force required to accomplish this would employ most of the state—and the price of your chicken would likely be $100 per pound. Automated injection systems are not employed because again, consider the likelihood of free-ranging broilers in a broiler house willingly walking up to an injection station to get injected every day or even every few days.

Anabolic steroids are the other hormones that people think of as being fed to chickens to promote growth. Structurally, anabolic steroids are hard to digest and could potentially be fed and absorbed across the intestine and enter the bloodstream. Delivery effectiveness would be better with injections. However, even if fed or injected, they would not be effective in broilers. Anabolic steroids are very capable of increasing muscle mass, but this only happens when the animal or person being injected combines this with rigorous physical training. Broilers maintained in broiler houses are not flying, they are not even running around. They are mostly sedentary except when they get up to eat more. They are the classic couch potato, so giving anabolic steroids to broilers, just as giving it to a couch potato, would have no benefit in increasing muscle mass. Furthermore, the cost of anabolic steroids would again make the price of chicken unreasonable even if it did work.

The bottom line: Broiler chickens are not fed steroids.

AVIAN INFLUENZA

Media reports about the avian influenza, or bird flu as related to the H5N1 strain of bird flu, have often created an unreasonable state of fear in the general public. Bird flu is an infection caused by influenza viruses that naturally occur in birds. Wild birds often carry bird flu viruses, but are unaffected by them. But domestic birds such as chickens and ducks often become fatally infected when exposed to some strains of bird flu. Avian flu viruses are classified by a combination of two groups of proteins: the hemagglutinin (H) and neuraminidase (N) proteins. There are 16 H proteins (H1 to H16) and 9 N proteins (N1 to N9). Avian flu strains are classified as low or highly pathogenic, based on their ability to produce disease in poultry. Low pathogenic avian flu naturally occurs in wild birds and can spread to domestic birds through direct contact as it is excreted through feces and through secretions from the nose, mouth, and eyes. It can also be spread indirectly by contact of material that is contaminated with secretions or excretions from contaminated birds. Low pathogenic avian flu causes no signs of infection or only minor symptoms. Highly pathogenic avian flu spreads more rapidly than low pathogenic bird flu and causes a higher death rate in birds. It is often fatal to domestic chickens and turkeys.

Since 2003 through to the end of 2011, about 573 people were infected with the H5N1 virus; of that number, 336 of them died. Most of the deaths have occurred in Indonesia, but many deaths have also occurred in Vietnam, Egypt, and China. There was an uptick in H5N1 avian flu at the end of 2011, and this is feared to be the result of a variant strain of H5N1 that is now spreading in Asia. The Centers for Disease Control indicate that avian flu does not spread easily from birds to humans. The H5N1 strain of avian flu would have to mutate potentially multiple times in order for it to become highly pathogenic in humans, with easy human-to-human transmission. Avian influenza is not transmissible by eating properly prepared poultry. It is important to note that there are cultural differences that make the avian flu more likely to spread from chickens to humans in Southeast Asia. People have much more direct contact with poultry in this region of the world. It is not unusual for poultry caretakers to actually live in the same facility as their poultry. For family backyard chicken operations, it is not unusual for the birds to have access to and actually enter the family residence. Raw duck liver is often consumed in Asia as a favored dish. Furthermore, if a bird becomes ill the family will often kill, dress, cook, and eat it.

The H5N1-pathogenic avian flu virus has not been found in commercial poultry or wild birds in the United States. There have been a few highly pathogenic avian flu outbreaks in the United States in the past, but they were not the H5N1 strain. Avian migrations are mostly north to south and not east to west (from Asia to the United States), so wild bird contact from infected areas should be limited. The United States Department of Agriculture monitors for H5N1 in commercial flocks, migratory birds, backyard flocks, and live bird markets. If any highly pathogenic bird flu of any strain is detected, the United States Department of Agriculture will work with state and industry representatives to quarantine the immediate outbreak area, to eradicate commercial birds in the quarantine area, monitor the region outside the quarantined area, disinfect farms in the quarantine area, and finally to test that the disinfected farm(s) is bird flu virus–free. The U.S. Department of Agriculture also maintains a store of avian flu vaccines that could be used to protect healthy birds.

Legally imported birds coming into to the United States have a mandatory quarantine, as discussed in Chapter 2. Quarantined birds are tested for the H5N1 avian flu. Additionally, all bird imports have been banned for the past few years from countries that have had cases of the H5N1 avian flu. The U.S. Department of Agriculture also bans the importation of all poultry and poultry products from countries that have had confirmed cases of H5N1. Overall, the risk of an H5N1 flu outbreak is small in the United States, as evidenced by the fact there has been no spread of it here since it appeared in Southeast Asia almost 10 years ago.

SUMMARY

Although Galliformes is a large order of birds that encompasses all of the landfowl, many of which have been hunted extensively, surprisingly few species are extinct or even critically endangered currently. Many are beautiful birds with elaborate plumage and are often kept as backyard flocks or pets or for display in zoos and parks. Many Galliformes, especially within the Phasianidae family, have been domesticated and are the basis of the multibillion dollar commercial poultry industries. Within the commercial chicken industry, research conducted at the university and industrial levels has led to tremendous efficiency gains in the production of eggs and chicken meat, as well as contributing greatly to the human medical field.

REFERENCES

Berthouly-Salazar, C., X. Rognon, T. Nhu Van, M. Gely, C. Vu Chi, M. Tixier-Boichard, B. Bed'Hom, N. Bruneau, E. Verrier, J. Maillard, and J. Michaux. 2010. Vietnamese chickens: A gate towards Asian genetic diversity. *BMC Genetics* **11**:53.

BirdLife International. 2012. "IUCN Red List for birds." Accessed on 05/01/2012: http://www. birdlife.org

Brown, Robin. 2007. State's long association with chickens is story worthy of pullet surprise. *News Journal*, May 8, 2007.

Burnet, F. M. 1960. The Nobel Lectures in Immunology. The Nobel Prize for Physiology or Medicine, 1960. Immunologic recognition of self. *Scandinavian Journal of Immunology* **33**:3–13.

Cook, R. E. 1988. Poultry Research Programs in the Future. *Poultry Science* **67**:890–896.

Eriksson, J., G. Larson, U. Gunnarsson, B. Bed'hom, M. Tixier-Boichard, L. Strömstedt, D. Wright, A. Jungerius, A. Vereijken, E. Randi, P. Jensen, and L. Andersson. 2008. Identification of the yellow skin gene reveals a hybrid origin of the domestic chicken. *PLoS Genetics* **4**:e1000010.

Food Safety and Inspection Service. 2011. "Fact Sheets: Meat Preparation: Game from Farm to Table." USDA (United States Department of Agriculture). Accessed 04/15/12: http://www. fsis.usda.gov/Factsheets/Farm_Raised_Game/index.asp#3

Food and Agriculture Organization of the United Nations. 2010. *Poultry Meat and Eggs Agribusiness Handbook*. Food and Agriculture Organization of the United Nations: Rome, Italy.

Foster, K. P. 1999. The earliest zoos and gardens. Pages 64–71 *Scientific American*.

Georgia Poultry Federation. 2012. "Georgia Poultry Facts." Accessed 04/15/12: http://www.gapf. org/

Glick, B., T. S. Chang, and R. G. Jaap. 1956. The Bursa of Fabricius and antibody production. *Poultry Science* **35**:224–225.

Gongora, J., N. J. Rawlence, V. A. Mobegi, H. Jianlin, J. A. Alcalde, J. T. Matus, O. Hanotte, C. Moran, J. J. Austin, S. Ulm, A. J. Anderson, G. Larson, and A. Cooper. 2008a. Indo-European and Asian origins for Chilean and Pacific chickens revealed by mtDNA. *Proceedings of the National Academy of Sciences* **105**:10308–10313.

Gongora, J., N. J. Rawlence, V. A. Mobegi, H. Jianlin, J. A. Alcalde, J. T. Matus, O. Hanotte, C. Moran, J. J. Austin, S. Ulm, A. J. Anderson, G. Larson, and A. Cooper. 2008b. Reply to Storey et al.: More DNA and dating studies needed for ancient El Arenal-1 chickens. Page E100 in *Proceedings of the National Academy of Sciences, USA.*

GPLN (Georgia Poultry Laboratory Network). 2012. "History." Accessed 05/01/12: http://www.gapoultrylab.org/history.html

Horton, T. 2006. 12 Day Wonders. Pages 66 79. *Washingtonian Magazine.* September.

Kanginakudru, S., M. Metta, R. D. Jakati, and J. Nagaraju. 2008. Genetic evidence from Indian Red Junglefowl corroborates multiple domestication of modern day chicken. *BMC Evolutionary Biology* 8:174.

Lerich, S. P. 2012. The North American Wild Turkey. Pages 31–36. *AFA Watchbird.*

Liu, Y.-P., G.-S. Wu, Y.-G. Yao, Y.-W. Miao, G. Luikart, M. Baig, A. Beja-Pereira, Z.-L. Ding, M. G. Palanichamy, and Y.-P. Zhang. 2006. Multiple maternal origins of chickens: Out of the Asian jungles. *Molecular Phylogenetics and Evolution* 38:12–19.

MacDonald, K. C. and R. M. Blench. 2001. Chickens. Pages 496–499 in K. F. Kiple and K. C. Ornelas, editors. *The Cambridge World History of Food.* Cambridge University Press.

NWTF (National Wild Turkey Federation). 2011. The Wild Turkey. Accessed 05/01/12: http://www.nwtf.org/

Parkes, K. S. (1992): [Review of] "Distribution and taxonomy of birds of the world." *Journal of Field Ornithology* 63(2): 228–235.

Perrins, C. 2009. *The Princeton Encyclopedia of Birds.* Princeton University Press, Princeton, NJ.

Peterson, A. T. and I. L. Brisbin. 1998. Genetic endangerment of wild Red Junglefowl Gallus gallus? *Bird Conservation International* 8:387–394.

Plotkin, S. A. 2005. *Vaccines: Past, present and future.* Nat Med.

Plowman, T. 2012. "Billion-dollar poultry industry traces its roots to 1923 error." Accessed 05/01/12: http://www.intercom.net/~terrypl/poultry.html

Peterson, A. T. and I. L. Brisbin. 1998. Genetic endangerment of wild Red Junglefowl Gallus gallus? *Bird Conservation International* (8): 387–394.

Schatz, A. 1993. The true story of the discovery of streptomycin. *Actinomycetes* 4:27–39.

Smith, P. and C. Daniel. 2000. *The Chicken Book.* University of Georgia Press, Athens.

South Dakota Game, Fish and Parks. 2012. "South Dakota Game Harvest Reports: Pheasants." Accessed 05/01/12: http://gfp.sd.gov/hunting/harvest/reports/Pheasant.pdf

Storey, A. A., D. Quiroz, J. M. Ramírez, N. Beavan-Athfield, D. J. Addison, R. Walter, T. Hunt, J. S. Athens, L. Huynen, and E. A. Matisoo-Smith. 2008. Pre-Columbian chickens, dates, isotopes, and mtDNA. *Proceedings of the National Academy of Sciences* 105:E99.

Storey, A. A., J. M. Ramírez, D. Quiroz, D. V. Burley, D. J. Addison, R. Walter, A. J. Anderson, T. L. Hunt, J. S. Athens, L. Huynen, and E. A. Matisoo-Smith. 2007. Radiocarbon and DNA evidence for a pre-Columbian introduction of Polynesian chickens to Chile. Proceedings of the *National Academy of Sciences 104:10335–10339.*

Tixier-Boichard, M., B. Bed'hom, and X. Rognon. 2011. Chicken domestication: From archeology to genomics. *Comptes Rendus Biologies* 334:197–204.

USDA (United States Department of Agriculture). 2011. "U.S. Broiler Industry: Background Statistics and Information." Accessed 04/15/12: http://www.ers.usda.gov/News/broilercoverage.htm

USDA (United States Department of Agriculture). 2012. *Poultry: Production and Value 2011 Summary.* USDA, National Agricultural Statistics Service.

XIII ANSERIFORMES: WATERFOWL

ANATIDAE: DUCKS, GEESE, AND SWANS

With over 160 species worldwide, there is tremendous diversity of species across the Anatidae family. However, their dependence on wetlands at various stages of their lives unifies the group. They inhabit wetlands and coastal areas on every continent, with the exception of Antarctica. Anatids tend to show a great deal of adaptability when faced with changing environments and harvesting by hunters. This family is arguably the most economically valuable wild avian family, with billions of dollars contributed annually by conservation organizations, wildlife-watchers, and waterfowl hunters.

PHYSICAL CHARACTERISTICS

Waterfowl have several adaptive characteristics that equip them for living in an aquatic environment. Since water conducts heat away from the body faster than air, all waterfowl have dense body plumage that insulates them from the cooler water temperatures. Waterfowl have long, flat bills with lamellae along the sides for filter feeding prey from the water, and a slight hook at the tip, often referred to as a bean. Having some variation of webbed feet (refer to Chapter 4 for foot types) set far back on the body relative to other avian species, waterfowl are easily equipped for propulsion in the water. Their legs are positioned to match accordingly with each species' foraging habits.

Many waterfowl species spend part of the year in colder climates and are still able to maneuver comfortably in frigid water, insulated by dense plumage on their bodies, but their legs and feet are still left exposed to the elements. Avian legs and feet are unique in having countercurrent blood flow exchange, which refers to the main artery and vein in the

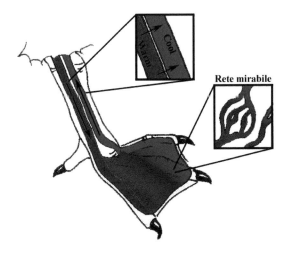

FIGURE 13.1 Avian legs and feet are unique in having countercurrent blood flow exchange, allowing, for example, waterfowl to keep their feet comfortable in nearly freezing water. Because the main artery and vein are adjacent to one another, the returning, cooler blood is warmed by the warm blood coming from the body. This heat exchange prevents the colder blood from lowering the core body temperature of the bird. Birds are also able to dilate and constrict the rete mirable vessels in the foot, controlling the amount of blood shunted to the legs and feet.

FIGURE 13.2 Dabbling ducks will tip over or "dabble" to reach food in shallow waters.

leg lying adjacent to one another, combined with the intertwining of the arteries and veins in the foot (Figure 13.1). Also referred to as rete mirabile—Latin for "wonderful net"—the arrangement of blood vessels moving away from the heart and toward the feet warms the returning, cooler blood flow from the feet in a countercurrent heat exchange. The exchange allows the blood returning to the heart to be warmed, therefore not cooling, but maintaining the bird's core temperature. Birds regulate the amount of heat loss from their legs and feet by varying the amount of blood shunted to the foot. By constricting blood vessels in the foot, blood is shunted more directly back up the leg toward the body, reducing the amount of heat loss. Birds may tuck one leg among body feathers and stand on one leg to reduce the amount of heat loss through unfeathered limbs by half. Conversely, when overheated, birds are able to lose most of their metabolic heat via this exchange by shunting more blood flow through the feet, as a method of cooling (Ricklefs, 1990).

The Anatidae family is represented by two major groups: the true ducks (Anatidae) and the geese and swans (subfamily Anserinae). Whistling ducks are in their own subfamily (Dendrocygninae), but for this book, we will include them with the other ducks. The ducks can be generally divided into dabbling ducks and diving ducks.

DUCKS

DABBLING DUCKS

Dabbling ducks, also called puddle ducks, have legs near the center of their body and get their name from their ability to "dabble" down or tip over headfirst into the water (Figure 13.2). Ducks often feed by sucking in water through their slightly open bill and then, using their tongue, forcing it out of their bill through toothlike serrations called lamellae (Figure 13.3). They are able to leap directly off of the surface of the water, unlike diving ducks, which require a running start in order to take flight.

Whistling ducks are tropical dabbling ducks, and though they are considered ducks, they are placed in their own subfamily, Dendrocygninae, and are more closely related to swans and geese than other ducks. This is apparent when they stretch their neck and legs out for landing, unlike other ducks. Whistling ducks are named for their gregarious whistling calls. They were formerly referred to as "tree ducks," though only a few of the species, such as the Black-bellied Whistling Duck (Figure 13.4), were found perching or nesting in trees. Whistling ducks have long legs, long necks, and relatively large bills, which are all adaptations to an arboreal lifestyle.

Both dabbling and whistling ducks are omnivorous. Their diets change throughout the course of the year, adapting to their seasonal environments. The Mallard (Figure 13.5) is the most widespread duck on earth due to its adaptability and tolerance of human environmental disturbance. Generally, Mallards are tending to migrate less and less each year or only migrate a short distance, especially around urban areas. With plentiful food and comfortable habitats suitable for breeding and wintering, the birds have no reason to make an annual leave.

DIVING DUCKS

Diving ducks tend to be smaller and more compact than dabbling ducks. Their legs are shorter and are set farther back ventrally on the body, which is more advantageous for diving. They have a small, narrow bill, adapted for eating plant material as well as animal prey, such as mollusks, crustaceans, or fish. Diving ducks pursue prey and food sources by diving and swimming underwater, using their strong feet to propel themselves. Some species such as mergansers consume mostly fish, and will often hunt cooperatively to increase their success. Diving ducks, in contrast to the dabblers, require a runway of land or water to taxi on in order to take flight (Figure 13.6). Diving ducks are also called sea ducks or bay ducks because many of the species spend a great deal of their life at sea and are often observed foraging in inshore waters. Some examples of diving ducks include Goldeneyes, Buffleheads, mergansers, and scoters (Figure 13.7 a–d).

DUCK REPRODUCTION

Ducks tend to show strong sexual dimorphism, with the male being more flamboyantly pigmented and the female wearing less conspicuous coloration for camouflage at the nest. There are some exceptions to this rule among ducks. When both sexes share the same plumage patterns and colors such as the Whistling Ducks, Mottled Duck, and American Black Ducks, they will form long-lasting and often lifelong pair bonds. Ducks are philopatric, meaning that they will return to nest at their own birth site. Most ducks are monogamous for a single breeding season, referred to as seasonal monogamy. Unpaired males will exhibit "gang" polygamous reproductive behavior. The male is called the drake, the female is the hen, and the young are ducklings. A few duck species, such as the Muscovy and Ruddy Ducks, are polygamous, where a single male will establish territory in which several females will make their nest and mate with the male. Most duck species will nest on the ground near water, but some species (Wood Ducks, Whistling Ducks) prefer to nest in tree cavities. Ducks lay five to 12 eggs per clutch, but occasionally can lay up to 17 or 18 eggs at a time. After hatch, the young are very precocious and leave the nest almost immediately, only to follow the female while she shows them how to acquire food. Though hours old, the ducklings are able to walk, swim, and forage for food.

FIGURE 13.3 The inside of a duck's bill has small ridges or lamellae that they force water through while feeding.

FIGURE 13.4 Black-bellied Whistling Duck

FIGURE 13.5 Male (foreground) and female Mallard.

FIGURE 13.6 Diving ducks need to taxi on land or water in order to take flight.

FIGURE 13.7 (a) Common Goldeneye

FIGURE 13.7 (b) Male and female Buffleheads

Reproduction is physiologically taxing on waterfowl and is fundamentally linked to food availability. The greatest energy demands are placed on females during the breeding season, due to the additional energy requirements for follicular growth, egg-laying and incubation (Alisauskas and Ankney. 1992; Ankney et al., 1991). During the breeding season, many waterfowl species are known to use stored fat for egg production, and research has suggested that nutrient reserves of fat, protein, and minerals are directly related to clutch size and need to reach a particular threshold before rapid follicular growth may occur (Alisauskas and Ankney, 1994). The extent of the demand on females as well as males varies across waterfowl species. Male ducks are often at a nutritional deficit during the breeding season due to their efforts defending territory or mobile space around their nesting female, allowing her to feed and satisfy the high nutritional demands of reproduction. Male Wood Ducks, for example, use considerable fat reserves during courtship and mate guarding, losing around 70 percent of their fat stores by the time the female begins incubating (Hipes and Hepp, 1995).

DUCK MOLTING

Ducks molt twice a year: after the breeding season in the late summer and again in the early spring, just before the breeding season. In late summer after breeding, almost all anseriformes undergo a complete molt, losing and replacing all of their feathers over a couple of weeks. This is a dangerous time for ducks because this synchronous molt leaves them flightless for a period of two to five weeks. Many bird species undergo a gradual molt where some of the feathers are lost at a time, leaving the bird flighted. When ducks endure this flightless period, they are left vulnerable to predators, and as a result, will often linger in the protection of tall grass or out in open water. This fall molt leaves the ducks with a drab, winter coloration, referred to as basic plumage, similar to the typical female coloration. In the spring before breeding season begins, the males will undergo another, less significant molt, only replacing certain feathers to reintroduce their breeding, or alternate, plumage.

DUCK DOMESTICATION

Romans in Europe and Malays in Asia domesticated Mallards over 2500 years. The Mallard later gave rise to over 20 backyard breeds in Europe and more in Asia, where 75 percent of all domestic ducks are kept. Currently in captivity, there are 14 standard breeds of ducks within four classes. The classes within breeds are titled heavy, medium, light, and bantam. Only five breeds of domestic Mallard have been commercially raised in the Western Hemisphere at a notable degree: the Aylesbury, Pekin, and Rouen (for meat production) and the Khaki Campbell and Indian Runner (for egg

IS FEEDING DUCKS BREAD BAD?

Many animal lovers were first introduced to the joys of avian wildlife by feeding ducks at a local park or pond. For many people, feeding ducks and geese bread is a way to interact with wildlife as well as get rid of old bread. But is bread good for them? It turns out that feeding waterfowl bread is not only unhealthy for them, but potentially harmful to their environment. Bread, crackers, chips, donuts, and popcorn are all great sources of carbohydrates, but they offer little nutritional value for birds. In fact, bread is essentially candy to birds, with excessive consumption leading to unneeded weight gain and malnutrition, heart disease, liver problems, and other health complications. Ducks and geese will naturally seek out an easy food source such as human handouts. If they are given bread in moderation, bread is not harmful; however, this is difficult to judge. Though one family may only feed the ducks every few weeks, there are probably many other families feeding them in between, which can lead to a diet of almost exclusively bread products. This can also lead to young waterfowl preferring bread over a natural diet, becoming nutrient-deprived, and possibly not learning valuable foraging skills. Feeding bread can also lead to local environmental concerns. When too much bread is offered to ducks, the soggy, uneaten pieces can lead to an influx in algae growth, eventually affecting nearby waterways and fish populations (Turner and Ruhl, 2007). A carbohydrate-rich diet also causes an increase in defecation, which harbors bacteria responsible for numerous diseases, including avian botulism. Feeding waterfowl moldy bread can cause various diseases such as aspergillosis, a fatal lung infection that can decimate entire flocks. Disease-harboring pests (rats, mice, and insects) may be attracted to the leftover food as well. Overcrowding as a result of excessive food supply can amplify all of these effects.

Many people and organizations are strongly opposed to providing artificial food to waterfowl and many parks and recreational areas deter or prohibit feeding. It is important to realize that wild waterfowl are capable of foraging for food on their own and do not require human handouts. Birds will live longer, healthier lives by relying on natural food sources rather than taking handouts from well-meaning humans. If you still want to feed ducks and geese, there are some healthier alternatives to bread products. Frozen peas or corn that have been defrosted, cracked corn, barley, oats, birdseed, grapes cut in half, earthworms, chopped lettuce, vegetable trimmings, or duck feed pellets (from farm supply stores) are all better choices than bread. Try to feed infrequently so the birds are not getting too much food that would be unhealthy for them, and stop feeding them if they appear uninterested or are leaving the food uneaten. Be sure to obey local ordinances that restrict or prohibit the feeding of ducks or other waterfowl. Another alternative is to take the family to a petting zoo that allows hand feeding, providing you with specially formulated diets for their animals. Feeding wild birds can be a controversial topic, but it can also be a rewarding one. The activity can be more rewarding for bird-lovers if they know what to feed them as part of a nutritious and responsible diet without inadvertently harming the birds (New York State Department of Environmental Conservation. 2012, Mayntz 2012).

production). Egg-laying varieties usually have brown plumage, while white varieties are farmed for meat (Kear, 2005). The Muscovy Duck (Figure 13.8) is not related to the Mallard and was domesticated separately by pre-Columbian inhabitants of tropical America (Stahl et al., 2006). It was later farmed for its meat and eggs, but the domestic breed, unlike the Mallard, has not changed much from its wild ancestor. Presently, the domesticated Muscovy Duck is larger than its wild counterpart and occurs in a variety of colors, but there are no individually recognized breeds (Kear, 2005).

Feather down is plentiful in waterfowl, especially in those species where the female incubates exclusively in northern temperate regions. The finest down has been farmed from wild colonies of the strictly protected sea duck, the Common Eider (Figure 13.9) in parts of northern Europe for almost 1000 years. In these areas, the wild Eiders are encouraged by the farmers to settle on their land to breed and nest. The female will pluck her down breast feathers to line her nest (Figure 13.10). The farmers often make two collections: one right after the eggs are laid (the female replaces the lost down almost immediately) and a second collection after the nest has been fully abandoned (Kear, 2005). The down is cleaned and used for high-end comforters, pillows, and clothing. This down, called eiderdown, is

FIGURE 13.7 (c) Male Hooded Merganser in breeding plumage.

FIGURE 13.7   (d) A large flock of sea-going Surf Scoters.

FIGURE 13.8   Muscovy Duck

FIGURE 13.9   Common Eider male (left) and female (right).

extremely valuable, and farmers will go to great lengths to provide nesting boxes and protect the nests against natural predators. Although Eider farming is small scale, this practice is sustainable and harmless to the birds, as it can be performed without disrupting the birds' reproduction. Though eiderdown is still harvested in a few areas, the practice has largely been replaced by filling with synthetic material or domestically raised duck or goose down.

GEESE AND SWANS

Geese and swans belong to the same subfamily, Anserinae. Compared to ducks, geese and swans tend to have longer legs to facilitate walking, and longer necks to assist with feeding in shallow water without having to tip over, as dabblers do.

Most geese are highly migratory, forming large flocks in the winter, sometimes numbering in the hundreds of thousands (Harris 2009). Geese tend to be more terrestrial than ducks in their feeding, grazing on green grasses and other foliage. They are larger than ducks but smaller than swans, ranging in length from 22–43 inches (56–110 centimeters). Geese, as well as swans, have a bill lined with lamellae that act like teeth, adapted for grazing on aquatic and ground vegetation.

The largest of the waterfowl, swans are majestic and graceful with their long necks contrasting against their heavy bodies. There are only seven species of swans worldwide, and all adult plumage in the Northern Hemisphere is white. The larger species are some of the heaviest of all flighted birds. Mute Swans (Figure 13.11 a), for example, may weigh around 27 pounds (12 kilograms). Two of the swan species are native to North America, the Trumpeter Swan (Figure 13.11 b) and the Tundra Swan. Mute Swans were originally introduced to North America from Europe in the early 19th century, but presently thrive in several areas such as the Chesapeake Bay region, where they have become a pest species (Baughman, 2003).

REPRODUCTION

As with most species in which both sexes share the same plumage, geese and swans are primarily monogamous, forming pair bonds and often remaining with the same mate for life. This behavior is referred to as perennial monogamy. With geese, the male is referred to as the gander, the female is the goose, and the young are goslings. For swans, the male is a cob, the female is the pen, and the young are cygnets. Both swans and geese have relatively simple courtship displays, which involve a great deal of wing flapping, honking, and trumpeting.

Geese and swans are distinct from ducks, with family groups often remaining intact for the fall migration, wintering, and spring migration. Only when the family arrives back on the breeding ground and the adult pair begins to actively nest do the offspring part ways and often join flocks of non-breeding individuals. At two to three years old, the young may reach maturity, find their own mates, and join the breeding population. Swans and geese lay five to six eggs per clutch, which later hatch precocial young. Both of the parents guard and tend to the fledglings.

THE CANADA GOOSE

The Canada Goose (Figure 13.12) is probably the most widely distributed and best known of all North American waterfowl. This goose was not always as plentiful throughout the United States. There are at least 11 subspecies of the Canada Goose, with the largest, the Giant Canada Goose, once believed to be extinct during the early 1900s as a result of hunting pressures. Populations of Giant Canada Goose were discovered in the mid 20th century, identified by their size with a wingspan of 6 feet and weighing 20 pounds (1.8 meters and 9 kilograms, respectively). Presently, many populations of Canada Geese in the lower 48 U.S. states originated from very successful breeding and introductions of the Giant Canada Goose. Of all waterfowl, geese are particularly opportunistic and can easily become accustomed to people. As a result, some migratory populations of Canada Geese are not flying as far south as they once did. Some populations have become non-migratory altogether due to the changes in farm practices that make waste grain available in fall and winter, as well as changes in hunting pressure and changes in weather (Cornell Lab of Ornithology, 2012). Since the 1960s, resident Canada Goose populations have increased dramatically in many areas of the United States. Non-migratory populations have become nuisances on golf courses, farms, airports, and subdivisions across the country (Figure 13.13). In these urban areas, the geese have become comfortable with landscape features that provide expanses of short grass for food, lack of natural predators, absence of hunting, and hand-feeding by people. Though most people do not mind a few geese, problems arise when a few individuals evolve into a flock of dozens or even hundreds of individuals and lawns are overgrazed or the droppings become excessive (a goose can produce a pound of droppings per day). The geese have become such a recognized issue that federal and state organizations have developed and implemented various protocols for deterring the geese from areas or managing the populations. A few recommended methods are discontinuing feeding or eliminating a food supply, allowing legal hunting, modifying the habitat (adding fencing, barriers, etc.), introducing hazing techniques (flagging, lawn sprinklers, balloons, etc.), applying repellents, among other techniques. Federal permits are required to capture, handle, or kill (within urban areas and/or outside of hunting season) Canada Geese, as well as disturb their nests or eggs. However, property owners may register through the

FIGURE 13.10   Common Eider nest lined with fluffy down feathers.

FIGURE 13.11a   Mute Swan

FIGURE 13.11b   Trumpeter Swan

FIGURE 13.12   Canada Goose.

FIGURE 13.13   The Canada Goose has become a pest species in many urban areas.

USFWS to have resident Canada Goose nests and eggs destroyed (DNR, 2012). Though some may consider it a nuisance, with its gregarious behavior and high tolerance for people, the Canada Goose offers many animal lovers an easy opportunity to get close to nature, encouraging an appreciation for wildlife.

WATERFOWL CONSERVATION AND MANAGEMENT

Though the Anatidae family shows an overall resilience to threats of the changing world, of the 165 species, 27 are vulnerable, endangered, or critically endangered. Six species have already become extinct (BirdLife International, 2012). Overhunting and the drainage and degradation of wetland habitats have contributed to the reduced populations of many waterfowl species.

Another threat to certain waterfowl is the hybridization of species. Introduction of non-native species can bring species together that were previously geographically isolated and had separate gene pools. This is particularly a problem when the introduced species is dominant or aggressive toward native species. The Mallard has adapted to survive and reproduce in countless habitats worldwide. Mallard populations have been introduced to areas where they would not naturally be found for the purposes of farming, sport, and pond beautification. The Mallard has been crossbreeding with other ducks worldwide, threatening species such as the African Black Duck and Yellow-billed Duck in Africa and bringing the New Zealand Grey Duck to near extinction. The Koloa Maoli or Hawaiian Duck (Figure 13.14), a federally endangered species, is found exclusively in Hawaii. The greatest current threat to its future is crossbreeding or hybridization with the introduced Mallard. Resolving the problem has been challenging, as the native Koloa appears visually similar to female Mallards. Hybrids between the two species are difficult to distinguish in the field because hybrid size and plumage can vary so greatly. Fortunately, for this particular species, it is predicted that the population will recover with the natural barrier of Hawaii's isolated, island environment after the Mallards are removed from the island (USGS, 2007).

Lead poisoning has also taken its toll on various avian populations, particularly waterfowl. Lead has been used in various forms for thousands of years, originally in cooking utensils and more recently in many industrial commercial applications. However, lead is a deadly toxin that damages many organs in the body and can affect all animals, including humans. The negative effects of lead shot on wildlife, specifically waterfowl, have been recognized for more than a hundred years, though only in more recent decades has the problem generated controversy and led to the development of federally mandated restrictions. With respect to lead poisoning, the most significant hazard to wildlife is through direct ingestion of spent lead shots and bullets, lost fishing sinkers or tackle, or through consumption of wounded or dead prey containing lead shot, bullets, or fragments. Waterfowl can easily mistake this lead shot or fragments for grit, which is frequently consumed to assist with grinding food in their gizzards. Before the United States banned the use of lead shot for waterfowl hunting in 1991, it was estimated that up to 3 percent of all waterfowl in North America died annually from lead poisoning (Lahner and Franson, 2009). There has also been some concern that, in areas where frequent hunting occurs each year or near shooting ranges, lead may accumulate in the groundwater, potentially causing a hazard to human health.

Lead poisoning is a chronic, slow-acting, and debilitating disease that renders birds more susceptible to natural predators and sometimes causes crippling, which can lead to misdiagnosis. Sick or dead birds are observed infrequently, if at all, due to the birds' nature of hiding when sick and being eaten by predators. In most cases, the birds die after ingesting one or two pellets, their bodies slowly losing mass over a period of several weeks (Sanderson et al., 1986). Though the use of lead shot was banned for waterfowl hunting, it is still used in ammunition for upland hunting, shooting sports, and in fishing tackle. More recently, concern has shifted to lead poisoning in upland game birds (doves and quail), scavengers (vultures, hawks, and eagles), and other waterbirds through exposure by the ingestion of spent lead shot, bullet fragments, or fishing sinkers. Lead poisoning remains a concern for the already critically endangered California Condor, and since 2008, lead ammunition has been prohibited in California within the Condor's range (Lahner and Franson 2009). Additional states have limited the use of lead shot in upland areas and environmentally safe alternatives to lead shot and sinkers exist, but are not widespread. Many states still do not require these alternatives (USGS, 2009).

FIGURE 13.14 Koloa Maoli duck pair.

The Anatidae family may arguably be one of the most valuable wild avian families from an economic point of view. Wildlife-watchers have contributed billions of dollars annually to local economies and conservation organizations, while American hunters have contributed millions of dollars directly to conservation efforts in their pursuit of waterfowl. Much of this revenue is put toward maintaining or reconstructing wetlands, benefiting waterfowl and other species alike. Several programs have been put in place to assist with the conservation of waterfowl. The National Wildlife Refuge System, established in the United States in 1903, presently includes more than 550 refuges and 38 wetland management districts, encompassing over 150 million acres (Ducks Unlimited, 2012). The Duck Stamp was originally established in 1934 as the federal license required for hunting migratory waterfowl. However, the stamps are also a vital tool for wetland conservation. The Migratory Bird Hunting and Conservation Stamp, also established in 1934, declares that funds (ninety-eight cents of every dollar) derived from the sale of federal Duck Stamps could be used only for the acquisition of land for the National Wildlife Refuge System. It has since ensured the collection of over $750 million, which has conserved more than 5.3 million acres of waterfowl habitat in the United States. The Federal Duck Stamp Program has been called one of the most successful conservation programs ever initiated, and it is a highly effective way to conserve America's natural resources (USFWS, 2012). In addition to federal programs, organizations such as Ducks Unlimited—established in 1937 and now the world's largest private waterfowl and wetlands conservation organization—along with other non-governmental associations have preserved, restored, and created hundreds of thousands of wetland acres across the country.

SUMMARY

The Anatidae family includes a wide diversity of waterfowl. Ducks, geese, and swans have various characteristics that enable them to adapt and endure many types of habitat and environmental changes across the globe, sometimes even developing into pests in urban areas. However, facing habitat degradation and destruction, waterfowl can still become vulnerable. It is still necessary to dedicate conservation efforts to preserving wetland areas not only for the benefit of avian species, but for other wildlife as well.

REFERENCES

Alisauskas, R. T. and C. D. Ankney. 1994. Nutrition of breeding female Ruddy Ducks: The role of nutrient reserves. *The Condor* 96(4):878–897.

Alisauskas, R. T. and C. D. Ankney. 1992. The cost of egg laying and its relationship to nutrient reserves in waterfowl in *Ecology and Management of Breeding Waterfowl*. University of Minnesota Press, Minneapolis.

Alisauskas, R. T., Afton, A. D., and C. D. Ankney. 1991. The role of nutrient reserves in limiting waterfowl reproduction. *The Condor* **93**(4):1029–1032.

Baughman, M. 2003. *National Geographic Reference Atlas to the Birds of North America*. National Geographic Society, Washington, DC.

BirdLife International. 2012. "IUCN Red List for Birds." Accessed on 04/01/2012: http://www. birdlife.org

Cornell Lab of Ornithology. 2012. "All About Birds: Canada Goose." Accessed 04/01/2012: http:// www.allaboutbirds.org/guide/canada_goose/lifehistory

DNR (Department of Natural Resources of Maryland) 2012. "When Resident Geese Become a Problem." Accessed 04/01/2012: http://www.dnr.state.md.us/wildlife/Hunt_Trap/waterfowl/ geese/ResGeeseProblem.asp

Ducks Unlimited. 2012. "Milestones in Conservation." Accessed 04/11/2012: www.ducks.org

Harris, T. 2009. *National Geographic Complete Birds of the World*. National Geographic Society, Washington, DC.

Hipes, D. L. and G. R. Hepp. 1995. Nutrient-reserve dynamics of breeding male Wood Ducks. *The Condor* **97**:451–460.

Kear, J. *Ducks, Geese and Swans*. Oxford University Press. 2005

Lahner, L. L. and J. C. Franson. 2009. *Lead Poisoning in Wild Birds*. USGS National Wildlife Health Center, Department of the Interior, U.S. Geological Survey.

Mayntz, M. 2012. "Is Feeding Ducks Bread Bad?" New York Times Company. Accessed 04/11/2012: http://birding.about.com/od/birdfeeders/a/feedingducksbread.htm

New York State Department of Environmental Conservation. 2012. "Stop Feeding Waterfowl." Accessed 04/10/2012: http://www.dec.ny.gov/animals/7001.html

Ricklefs, R. E. 1990. *Ecology, 3rd edition*. Chiron Press and W. H. Freeman. New York.

Sanderson, Glen C. and Frank C. Bellrose. 1986. A Review of the Problem of Lead Poisoning in Waterfowl. Illinois *Natural History Survey, Champaign, Illinois. Special Publication 4.* 34pp. Jamestown, ND: Northern Prairie Wildlife Research Center Online. http://www.npwrc.usgs.gov/resource/birds/pbpoison/index.htm (Version 17OCT97)

Stahl, P. W., Muse, M. C., and F. Delgado-Espinoza. 2006. New evidence for pre-Columbian Muscovy Duck Cairina moschata from Ecuador. *Ibis* **148**:657–663.

Turner, A. M. and N. Ruhl. 2007. Phosphorus loadings associated with a park tourist attraction: Limnological consequences of feeding the fish. *Environmental Management* **39**(4):526–533.

USFWS (United States Fish & Wildlife Service). 2012. "Federal Duck Stamp Office." Accessed 04/11/2012: www.fws.gov

USGS (U.S. Geological Survey). 2007. Hawaiian Duck's Future Threatened by Feral Mallards. *USGS Fact Sheet.* U.S. Department of the Interior.

USGS (U.S. Geological Survey). 2009. "Concerns Rise Over Known and Potential Impacts of Lead on Wildlife." U.S. Department of the Interior. Accessed 04/01/2012: http://www.nwhc.usgs.gov/disease_information/lead_poisoning

XIV   OPPORTUNITIES

THE ECONOMIC IMPORTANCE OF BIRDS

An annual, quantifiable, trillion-dollar-plus bird economy exists in the world, which provides millions of jobs and substantial opportunity for people with an interest in a career involving birds.

BIRD-WATCHING

Bird-watching revenue is probably the largest component of this bird economic commerce. Bird-watching is one of the most common hobbies around the world. In the United States, almost one in four Americans, or 48 million individuals, 16 years or older were active bird-watchers in 2006 (Carver, 2009), and this total does not include casual observers of birds. Of these birders, 88 percent of them actively birded around their homes, while 42 percent of the total number took trips away from home just to watch birds. In 2006, birders within the United States spent about 36 billion dollars directly related to their hobby. The direct expenditures include purchase of bird-observation equipment, including such things as binoculars (Figure 14.1), spotting scopes, cameras and camping equipment, equipment to entice birds for observation, such as bird feeders (Figure 14.2), bird food and nest boxes, and trip-related expenditures, such as food, lodging, and transportation. When the $36 billion from direct expenditures is combined with the indirect expenditures to generate the goods and support the direct expenditures, the total industry output in 2006 for birding was $82 billion in the United States and supported 671,000 jobs (Carver, 2009).

Not all the people in the United States who feed birds are active bird-watchers. In 2006, wild birds were fed by 53.8 million people who spent $3.3 billion on wild bird food

FIGURE 14.1   In the U.S., one in four adult individuals are bird watchers and birding contributes over $80 billion annually to the U.S. economy.

(U.S. Department of the Interior, 2007). The activity of people feeding wild birds is also one of the most widespread, global human activities.

Bird-watching is also a major player in global tourism. The economic impact of global tourism is harder to quantify, but estimates put direct and indirect revenue at about $6 trillion in 2010 (CREST, 2010) and $6.3 trillion in 2011 (UNWTO, 2011). In 2010, travel for leisure, recreation, and holidays accounted for 51 percent (or 480 million arrivals) of all international arrivals, while the other 49 percent of arrivals were based on business, visiting family and friends, religious purposes, etc. (UNWTO, 2011).

Ecotourism is often broken up into categories such as nature tourists (traveling to experience and enjoy nature) and wildlife-related tourists (traveling to a destination specifically to observe wildlife). Filion (1994) and Filion et al. (1992) determined that 40–60 percent of all international tourists are nature tourists, and 20 to 40 percent of all tourists are wildlife-related tourists. A substantial portion of the wildlife tourists are assumed to be bird-watchers, as observing birds is the most common wildlife watched within individual nations. For example, in the United States, in 2006, 71 million residents 16 years of age or older participated in watching wildlife, with 48 million of this total (67.7 percent) watching birds. Therefore, estimates for international bird-watching ecotourism revenue range from $500 billion to $1 trillion annually.

AGRICULTURE

The other major portion of the annual economic value of birds is associated with agriculture. Meat and eggs produced by birds are the largest sources of animal protein produced and eaten by humans. In 2007, a total of 88 million tons of poultry meat was produced globally (Food and Agriculture Organization of the United Nations, 2010). Most of the total meat was derived from chickens (87 percent), followed by turkeys (6.7 percent), ducks (4 percent), and the remaining (2.7 percent) from geese, pigeons, quails, pheasants, Ostriches, and Emus combined. Global egg production in 2007 was 60 million tons produced by an estimated global population of about 5 billion egg-laying hens (Food and Agriculture Organization of the United Nations, 2010). Just in the United States, the direct value of poultry production in 2011 from broilers, eggs, turkeys, and chickens was $35.6 billion (USDA, 2012), and this total does not include what would be the billions of dollars generated by allied industries that support poultry production and the consumption of poultry products. To illustrate the significance of allied industries, in the state of Georgia the direct value of poultry production equals about $4 billion, but its overall contribution to the state economy is estimated at about $18.4 billion. In addition to meat and eggs, many other products are harvested from domesticated birds, such as feathers, oils, leather, and feces, which are highly valuable in the clothing, pharmaceutical, cosmetics, or fertilizer industries.

FIGURE 14.2   The activity of feeding wild birds is one of the most globally widespread human activities.

PETS, PUBLICATIONS AND BIRD CONSERVATION

There are several other major sources of revenue associated with birds. Birds are popular pets across the globe. In the United States, it is estimated that there are 16 to 40 million caged birds kept as pets (Whitaker, 2009; APPA, 2012). As the third most numerous non-aquatic pet—after dogs and cats—birds account for over a billion dollars of direct revenue in the United States alone. In addition, millions of ornamental and backyard chickens and gamebirds are kept by Americans.

Because people worldwide enjoy watching birds and keeping them as pets, hundreds of bird-related publications such as magazines, books, and field guides are produced every year. In 2006, $360 million was spent on magazines and books by wildlife-watchers in the United States.

The U.S. Fish and Wildlife Service is responsible for managing the nation's biological resources and ensuring a healthy environment. It oversees the National Wildlife Refuge System, the Endangered Species Act, and the Migratory Bird Treaty Act. Its total enacted budget in 2012 was almost $1.5 billion (U.S. Department of the Interior, 2012). Of this total, migratory bird management received about $51.5 million for the conservation, monitoring, and habitat preservation of migratory birds. The Endangered Species Program received about $176 million in 2012 for the conservation and recovery of endangered species such as the California Condor, Puerto Rican Parrot, and Whooping Crane. In addition to federal spending, individual states also have departments of natural resources which appropriate state money for similar purposes. More importantly, national governments around the world have similar agencies to our Fish and Wildlife Service, with similar objectives. There is also a multitude of private foundations and organizations such as the Audubon Society and BirdLife International raising and spending money for bird conservation.

ECOSYSTEM SERVICE

Beyond the relatively easily quantified components of the worldwide bird economy is the ecosystem service that birds provide to humans (Şekercioğlu et al., 2004; Whelan et al., 2008) that is infinitely valuable to our well-being. As indicator species to the health of virtually every ecosystem present in the world, birds are essential environmental monitors. As foragers of insects, seed dispersers, and pollinators, birds help maintain ecosystems throughout the world. Granivores consume weed seeds, destroying the seeds in the process and preventing their growth. Raptors help control rodent populations and clean up carcasses, which help prevent disease.

ISSUES TO BE CONFRONTED IN THE FUTURE

CONSERVATION OF BIRDS

As discussed in Chapter 2, there have been steep declines in the overall population of birds and significant increases in the number of birds threatened with extinction. To stabilize wild bird populations, habitat preservation is critical. Habitats associated with migratory routes and those associated with the greatest bird diversity are initially the most important to identify, protect, manage, and even restore, in order to save bird species from extinction, to potentially increase the population of some bird species, and to mitigate the impact of climate change on these identified habitats. Many of these key or critical bird habitats have already been identified around the world by BirdLife International. Another encouraging and necessary trend is the preservation of entire migratory corridors instead of individual stopovers and destination refuges/national parks.

Preservation of island habitats for birds presents a unique challenge. As highlighted throughout this book, the majority of bird extinctions, as well as currently critically endangered bird species, occur on islands. In many cases, the threats on islands are not the loss of habitat, but the impact of introduced invasive species. For example, as previously discussed with the Kakapo and Kiwi species in New Zealand, recovery programs involve placing them on small islands in which introduced invasive predators have been eradicated. As these islands reach their small carrying capacity, will Kiwis and Kakapos from these locations routinely be placed on larger islands to face likely death? Or will tough decisions be made to eradicate predators on these locations? Getting rid of invasive plants and animals like rats and snakes is a pretty easy sell, but eradicating more cuddly animals such as stoats or cats will be more difficult.

Promoting and accomplishing the conversion to clean, efficient, and renewable energy sources have to continue for the long-term maintenance of bird populations and habitats. However, just because it is renewable and/or clean does not mean that it does not come with risk to bird populations. For instance, wind-generated energy has created mortality and habitat disturbances for some bird populations, as reviewed by Drewitt and Langston (2006). Bird deaths from collisions with the windmill turbines (Figure 14.3) occur with increased rates in poorly situated wind farms, located in areas with a high density of birds or in bird migratory routes. Especially concerning has been the propensity of some long-lived but slow-to-reproduce raptors to be killed by collisions with turbines (Drewitt and Langston, 2006; the Peregrine Fund, 2006). Currently proposed wind farms that could impact California Condors and Whooping Cranes continue to attract much debate in the Unites States. It will be essential to make sure that wind farm locations are well thought out and avoid critical bird areas.

Ecotourism provides opportunities for bird and bird habitat preservation, but it must be managed closely to safeguard the very things people are paying to see. A balance has to be struck

FIGURE 14.3   Bird collisions with wind turbines can contribute significantly to annual bird mortality rates.

in providing as much access as possible while preventing stressful disturbances of wildlife that could alter behavior, reproductive success, and mortality rates. Preventing the degradation of the ecosystem at an ecotourism site due to tourist removal of natural attractions (rare plants, seeds, and other natural souvenirs) and minimizing habitat destruction through road/path building and soil erosion—all while accommodating increased foot and motorized traffic—are also important. However, the benefits of ecotourism can be enormous. It heightens visitor awareness and appreciation of natural wildlife and ecosystem resources and the need to protect them. It also can provide revenue for further conservation efforts. It employs local residents and vests them in preserving their local natural habitats rather than degrading them and encourages them to protect local wildlife rather than persecute it. Parrot clay licks in South America are proven tourist attractions, and the attitudes of the local population toward parrots have changed from persecution to protection, because the parrots are now the resource for their economic livelihood (Johnson and Brightsmith, 2003).

The majority of bird species either migrate across multiple countries or have geographical ranges that encompass more than one country. Thus, effective preservation of these species involves international agreements. Additionally, pollution and its effects on habitat preservation typically involve several regional countries or is global in scope. For example, reducing pollution that may be associated with global warming must be confronted collectively. International agreements are incredibly difficult to forge so that a vast majority of countries will commit and sign and abide by the agreement. CITES (Chapter 3), which establishes international controls over trade in wild plant and animal species that are threatened or may be threatened due to excessive commercial exploitation, has 175 countries that have signed and participate in this agreement. Less than 20 countries do not participate in CITES. The Convention on the Conservation of Migratory Species of Wild Animals, which focuses on conserving terrestrial, marine, and avian species throughout their range, currently only has 116 parties (countries) that have signed the agreement since it went into force in 1983. Effective bird conservation will take global effort and commitment, which thus far has not been completely accomplished.

UNITY OF EFFORTS

Given the international nature of bird preservation, it is essential to unify all national bird organizations in umbrella groups—such as BirdLife International—so there is a collective, international consensus and approach to protecting bird species. While there is progress in this merging, further improvement is needed, typically at national levels where unity is lacking. For example, in the United States, there is a plethora of bird-related national organizations representing academia, research, industry (agricultural and pet), conservation, hobby, and pet interests. However, there is not one effective voice that represents the core, shared interests of all of these groups at a national, and thus, international level. Given the overall high regard for birds in the populace and their economic importance, it is surprising that all of these national bird-related organizations cannot form a powerful umbrella organization to promote their shared interests nationally and internationally.

PET BIRDS

Animal welfare issues will continue to intensify, both in the court of public opinion and through regulations that may be imposed under state and federal animal welfare acts. Regretfully, the image broadcast and stories typically reported are the ones dealing with the plight of smuggled parrots, bird-breeding mills, bird hoarders, or birds confiscated from deplorable conditions by officials. The positive stories dealing with the millions of people who have found fulfillment and companionship from their pet birds are not told. While enjoying birds, whether through exhibits at various zoos and bird parks or at home as private owners, people may not appreciate that animal welfare laws affect the displays at these parks, as well as the pet bird kept at home. Additionally, the public also does not typically realize that the knowledge gained from aviculturalists such as falconers, parrot breeders, and exotic pheasant breeders has been essential in saving and preventing the extinction of bird species. Currently, there are bird species that only exist in captivity, and this number will undoubtedly grow in the coming years, with a number of species on the brink of extinction in the wild. Generally, even many ardent animal rights activists are not opposed to captive management when the alternative is extinction.

With the restrictions on bird importation imposed by CITES and the Wild Bird Conservation Act of 1992 (Chapter 3), there continues to be a loss of species and genetic diversity in American aviculture as it applies to parrots, gamefowl, and waterfowl. Even in domesticated birds like ornamental chickens, many of the specific original breeds are being lost over time, reducing genetic diversity. Because there is a business aspect to aviculture, the laws of supply and demand play a huge role in bird breeding. In the caged bird pet industry, for species that sell well, it is often tempting and understandable that breeders sell all of their produced offspring to meet demand and make money. However, by doing this, future breeders are not held back, and ideally, those held back would be parent-raised instead of hand-raised by humans to make them more suitable breeders. Of course, allowing parents to raise the offspring can also mean fewer offspring produced over a given period of time. For species that do not sell well, nest boxes may not be provided or the birds may be sold into non-breeding situations; hence, over time, the number of birds for this species decreases. Some breeders do become very dedicated to preserving species that are not popular in the pet trade, and their valuable contribution to aviculture is highly commended. To ensure future populations, it is imperative that we promote new aviculturalists to replace them as they retire.

Some species of imported birds never adjusted well to captivity and captive breeding. Determining the conditions needed to have them successfully reproduce was never accomplished, and over time, these species are being lost to attrition. Other species simply were not imported in great enough numbers to have a diverse genetic base before legal importation was terminated for the species. Although it is likely that many of these species will eventually be lost forever in the United States, it should be noted that exceptions to the import bans under the Wild Bird Conservation Act can be obtained from the United States Fish and Wildlife Service through cooperative breeding programs. Such exemptions have occurred for a variety of species (LePage, 2011).

Regretfully, for most commercial and hobby breeders of avian species, there has never been a unified, formal registry for banding and recording birds. For species that continue to dwindle in number and for even for those with stable captive populations, having such a registry would help ensure that genetic diversity is being maximized, as future breeders would avoid breeding related birds. This problem of breeding related birds has intensified with the availability of the easy transport of birds within the United States and the fact that people move more frequently. It is always amusing to hear breeders say, "here on the East Coast of the United States"—they are sure their recently purchased breeder bird is unrelated to their current stock because it came from the West Coast.

Unwanted birds—usually caged pet birds—are another problem facing aviculture. As previously discussed in Chapter 8, bird sanctuaries provide invaluable resources to the avian community. The people who staff and operate these facilities are to be commended. However, most of these facilities are bursting at the seams with birds, especially due to the increased relinquishment of birds during the recent recession. It is imperative that mechanisms are put in place to facilitate finding permanent homes for adoptable birds at these facilities. Many very loving pet-quality birds end up at sanctuaries due to their owners having to relinquish them because of changes in family structure, finances, noise ordinances, etc. Getting these birds out of sanctuaries as quickly as possible is paramount to make room for birds that are not pet quality due to behavioral issues or being retired breeders.

THINGS YOU CAN DO TO HELP BIRDS

Avian death resulting from collisions with clear and reflective sheet glass and plastic in windows is estimated to be the second largest human-associated source of avian mortality behind habitat destruction and accounts for billions of bird deaths annually worldwide (Klem Jr., 1990, 2006, 2009). Bird window collisions can be reduced or almost prevented by utilizing stripe and grid patterns of clear UV-reflecting and absorbing window coverings (Klem Jr., 2009) that birds detect with their UV vision capabilities, but do not obstruct the view of humans because of our inability to see in the UV range. Additionally, one-way films that do not obstruct the view out a window, but make it opaque looking in, are also effective at preventing bird collisions, as is placing decals on windows about every 5 to 10 centimeters (Klem Jr., 2009). As a home or business owner, you can take the steps to prevent bird collisions with your windows by following one of the three methods outlined above.

FIGURE 14.4 Domestic and feral cats are responsible for killing hundreds of millions of birds each year in the U.S. alone.

If you have cat(s) as pets, please keep them inside. Domestic cats (Figure 14.4) that are permitted outside kill hundreds of millions of birds each year in the United States alone (American Bird Conservancy, 2012). Pet cats maintained exclusively indoors live longer than those permitted outdoors, as they have less risk of disease, do not get hit by cars or attacked by other cats, dogs, or wildlife (such as coyotes) and are not at risk for theft or poisoning by humans. From the perspective of wild bird conservation, outdoor feral cat colonies should not be trapped, neutered, and released—which has become a common practice—but instead be trapped and then either be maintained in indoor facilities or humanely euthanized.

As a landowner, you can preserve and create favorable environments for birds. Always preserve wetlands already existing on a property, and if a suitable location is available on your land, consider creating a wetland environment. You can create living brush piles in open areas to provide escape cover from predators. If timber has to be harvested on your property, consider selective logging that removes only some of the trees, and thus, simply thins dense forests. In particular, try to preferentially leave food-producing trees and trees with nest cavities, as suitable nesting cavities are typically limiting. You can also allow areas of your property to grow naturally so that different types of habitats coexist on the property and create edges. Where two or more habitats meet is called an edge, such as where a forest meets a meadow, and edges typically support increased biodiversity.

As a home and landowner, you can plant native bird food-producing shrubs and choose not to plant—or even remove—non-native invasive plant species that outcompete and diminish native plants that local birds evolved to depend on in their habitat. You can also plant food plots for birds that contain grain, berry, and/or nut-producing plants. You can choose to strategically place nest boxes for different species of birds on your property, as well as provide constant water sources and supplemental feeding stations for birds. Try to avoid or limit the use of pesticides on your property that are not ecologically friendly.

If you are a bird hunter, consider hunting on a hunting reserve. At these reserves, gamebirds, and at some preserves, waterfowl, have been raised in captivity, with minimal contact with humans and then conditioned using large, prerelease pens simulating living independently in the wild. Once adapted to living in the wild, they are permanently released on the preserve, which typically has very well-developed cover habitat that makes hunting the released birds very challenging. The advantage to the hunter is that the birds are guaranteed to be present on the preserve, but hunting on the preserve does not impact wild populations of game and waterfowl.

Share your interest in birds with others so they can get excited about watching birds, having birds as pets, working with birds, or conserving birds and their habitats. Additionally, do not hesitate to promote the positive accomplishments of aviculture and the importance of birds, whether it is the success of endangered bird species recovery programs, the companionship provided by pet birds, their contribution to our health and well-being, their ecosystem service, or the satisfaction derived from bird-related hobbies, such as racing pigeons or exhibiting ornamental chickens. Finally, support bird-related organizations that promote the bird-related issues you are most passionate about.

IMPORTANCE OF EDUCATION AND RESEARCH

Education is the key to successfully interacting with wild, pet, or hobby birds and to understanding the importance of aviculture and the significance of birds to our everyday lives. An educated public knows the proper husbandry for their bird companions, appreciates the value and how to promote the preservation and restoration of bird habitat, and understands how they can facilitate conserving bird populations and bird species.

Research (Figure 14.5) provides the knowledge that is taught and provides the mechanisms by which to promote bird well-being. It has been—and still is—key in identifying factors that have caused or are causing bird declines, with key examples of this highlighted in the raptor chapter with regard to DDT and diclofenac. Research is also essential for determining how to restore the most critically endangered bird species through direct intervention. It is vital for discovering ways to alleviate bird losses due to human habitat alterations, such as birds

FIGURE 14.5 Research with birds has provided valuable knowledge of their biology, population trends, and habitat use, which is essential in management planning and conservation.

hitting windows and power lines. Additionally, research has been imperative for improving nutrition, preventing disease, and enhancing the welfare of pet and commercial birds.

If you have an interest in pursuing education at an undergraduate or graduate level in avian biology or to be involved with or conduct bird research, there are many educational programs and research opportunities available. The website for the Ornithological Societies of North America (http://www.osnabirds.org/Home.aspx), has a job listing that is updated regularly. It lists research opportunities at all skill levels, as well as graduate educational opportunities. The Ornithological Societies of North America consists of the American Ornithologist's Union, Association of Field Ornithologists, Cooper Ornithological Society, Raptor Research Foundation, Waterbird Society, and Wilson Ornithological Society. These organizations, along with the Association of Avian Veterinarians, are all key organizations supporting student education and research, especially in the United States and the rest of North America.

SUMMARY

Birds are integral components of our lives, and mankind's universal interaction and fascination with them provides a collective unity. Their vital importance to humankind is best illustrated by the fact that there is more economic commerce associated with them than any other animal, except humans. Therefore, protecting bird biodiversity is in mankind's collective interest.

REFERENCES

American Bird Conservancy. 2012. "Cats Indoors." Accessed 04/30/12: http://www.abcbirds.org/abcprograms/policy/cats/index.html

APPA (American Pet Products Association). 2012. "Industry Statistics and Trends." Accessed 04/30/12: http://www.americanpetproducts.org/press_industrytrends.asp

Carver, E. 2009. *Birding in the United States: A Demographic and Economic Analysis*. U.S. Department of the Interior, Fish and Wildlife Service. U.S. Government Printing Office, Washington, DC.

CREST (Center for Responsible Travel). 2010. "Market Trend Series: Responsible Travel: Global Trends and Statistics." Stanford University and Washington, DC. Accessed 04/30/12: www.responsibletravel.org

Drewitt, A. L. and R. H. W. Langston. 2006. Assessing the impacts of wind farms on birds. *Ibis* **148**:29–42.

Filion, F. L., J. P. Foley, and A. J. Jacquemot. 1992. The economics of global ecotourism. *Fourth World Congress on National Parks and Protected Areas, Caracas, Venezuela.*

Filion, F. L. F., J. P., Jacquemot, A. J., and Munasinghe, M. 1994. The economics of global ecotourism. Pages pp. 235–252 *in* M. M. Munasinghe, J., editor. *Protected area economics and policy: Linking conservation and sustainable development.* World Bank, Washington, DC.

Food and Agriculture Organization of the United Nations. 2010. *Poultry Meat and Eggs Agribusiness Handbook.* Food and Agriculture Organization of the United Nations: Rome, Italy.

The International Ecotourism Society. 2000. "Ecotourism Statistical Fact Sheet." Accessed 04/30/12: www.active-tourism.com/factsEcotourism1.pdf

Johnson, A. and D. Brightsmith. 2003. Helping local people value their national treasures. *PsittaScene* **15**:5–7.

Klem Jr., D. 1990. Collisions between Birds and Windows: Mortality and Prevention (Colisiones de Pájaros con Ventanas: Mortalidad y Prevención). *Journal of Field Ornithology* **61**:120–128.

Klem Jr., D. 2006. Glass: A deadly conservation issue for birds. *Bird Observer* **34**:73–81.

Klem Jr., D. 2009. Preventing Bird-Window Collisions. *Wilson Journal of Ornithology* **121**:314–321.

LePage, M. E. 2011. Cooperative Breeding Programs, Legal Importation under the Wild Bird Conservation Act, AFA *Watchbird* **38**(3):9.

The Peregrine Fund. 2006. "Recent Raptor News: Windfarm Wipes Out White-tailed Eagles." Accessed 04/30/12: http://www.globalraptors.org/grin/SiteNews.asp?lNewsType=1

Ruggles-Brise, O. and E. Aimable. 2012. *Travel and Tourism Economic Impact 2012 World.* World Travel and Tourism Council, London.

Şekercioğlu, Ç. H., G. C. Daily, and P. R. Ehrlich. 2004. Ecosystem consequences of bird declines. *Proceedings of the National Academy of Sciences* **101**:18042–18047.

UNWTO (World Tourism Organization). 2011. *UNWTO Tourism Highlights, 2011 Edition.* UNWTO Publications, Madrid.

USDA (United States Department of Agriculture). 2012. *Poultry-Production and Value 2011 Summary.* USDA, National Agricultural Statistics Service.

U.S. Department of the Interior, Fish and Wildlife Service and U.S. Department of Commerce, Bureau of the Census. 2007. 2006 *National Survey of Fishing, Hunting, and Wildlife-Associated Recreation.* Washington, DC: U.S. Government Printing Office, October 2007.

U.S. Department of the Interior, Fish and Wildlife Service. 2012. *Fiscal Year 2013 Budget Justification.* Washington DC: U.S. Government Printing Office.

Whelan, C. J., D. G. Wenny, and R. J. Marquis. 2008. Ecosystem Services Provided by Birds. *Annals of the New York Academy of Sciences* **1134**:25–60.

Whitaker, B. 2009. "The Parrots and People Paradox." Accessed 04/30/12: http://www.cbsnews.com/stories/2009/05/06/eveningnews/main4996913.shtml

IMAGE CREDITS

CHAPTER I

Source: commons.wikimedia.org/wiki/File:Archaeopteryx_American_Museum_of_Natural_History.jpg. Cleared via Creative Commons Attribution-Share Alike 3.0 Unported license.

Source: commons.wikimedia.org/wiki/File:Anchiornis_BW.jpg. Cleared via Creative Commons Attribution 3.0 Unported license.

Source: flickr.com/photos/bruce_mcadam/6393696279. Cleared via Creative Commons Attribution-Share Alike 2.0 Generic license.

Source: commons.wikimedia.org/wiki/File:Confuciusornis_sanctus_skeleton.JPG. Cleared via Creative Commons Attribution-Share Alike 3.0 Unported license.

Source: copyrightexpired.com/earlyimage/bones/display_century1886_ichthyornis.htm. Copyright in the Public Domain.

Source: commons.wikimedia.org/wiki/File:Bec_del_bec_de_serra_gran_(Mergus_merganser).jpg. Cleared via Creative Commons Attribution-Share Alike 2.5 Generic license.

Source: commons.wikimedia.org/wiki/File:Gallus_wingbones_01.JPG. Cleared via Creative Commons Attribution 3.0 Unported license.

Source: commons.wikimedia.org/wiki/File:Bird_and_dino_hand_difference_debate.JPG. Copyright in the Public Domain.

Source: commons.wikimedia.org/wiki/File:Limusaurus_forelimb.JPG. Copyright in the Public Domain.

Source: commons.wikimedia.org/wiki/File:ArchaeopteryxTheUrvogel Feather.jpg. Cleared via Creative Commons Attribution-Share Alike 3.0 Unported license.

Source: flickr.com/photos/dejeuxx/5200491236. Cleared via Creative Commons Attribution-Share Alike 3.0 Unported license.

J. Arthur Thomson, from The Outline of Science, vol. 1. Copyright in the Public Domain.

Source: flickr.com/photos/swolfe/5735497956. Cleared via Creative Commons Attribution 2.0 Generic license.

Source: flickr.com/photos/64565252@N00/1359787741. Cleared via Creative Commons Attribution-Share Alike 2.0 Generic license.

Source: commons.wikimedia.org/wiki/File:ApusHorus_RobertWienand.jpg. Cleared via Creative Commons Attribution-Share Alike 3.0 Unported license.

Source: flickr.com/photos/55826454@N00/3649550997. Cleared via Creative Commons Attribution 2.0 Generic license.

Source: commons.wikimedia.org/wiki/File:Emu_Side.JPG. Cleared via Creative Commons Attribution-Share Alike 3.0 Unported license.

Source: commons.wikimedia.org/wiki/File:Sagittarius_serpentarius_Sekret%C3%A4r.JPG. Cleared via Creative Commons Attribution-Share Alike 3.0 Unported license.

CHAPTER II

Source: digitalmedia.fws.gov. Copyright in the Public Domain.

Source: commons.wikimedia.org/wiki/File:Virginiawachtel_2007-06-16_102.jpg. Cleared via Creative Commons Attribution-Share Alike 3.0 Unported license. Attribution: BS Thurner Hof.

Source: commons.wikimedia.org/wiki/File:Hesperiphona_vespertina_CT3.jpg. Cleared via Creative Commons Attribution-Share Alike 3.0 Unported license.

Source: commons.wikimedia.org/wiki/File:Northern_Pintails_(Male_%26_Female)_I_IMG_0911.jpg. Cleared via Creative Commons Attribution-Share Alike 3.0 Unported license.

Source: commons.wikimedia.org/wiki/File:3813GrandChapeau1911.png. Copyright in the Public Domain.

Source: flickr.com/photos/dariosanches/4794624945. Cleared via Creative Commons Attribution-Share Alike 2.0 Generic license.

Source: flickr.com/photos/28577026@N02/2795125527. Cleared via Creative Commons Attribution 2.0 Generic license.

Source: commons.wikimedia.org/wiki/File:Ko%C4%8Dka_v_krm%C3%ADtku_2.jpg. Copyright in the Public Domain.

Source: geograph.org.uk/photo/1309587. Cleared via Creative Commons Attribution-Share Alike 2.0 Generic license. Attribution: Christine Matthews.

Source: commons.wikimedia.org/wiki/File:1863_17_26_Parakeet.jpg. Copyright in the Public Domain.

Source: commons.wikimedia.org/wiki/File:Pandion_haliaetus_NBII.jpg. Copyright in the Public Domain.

Source: commons.wikimedia.org/wiki/File:Eoliennes_Gaspesie.jpg. Cleared via Creative Commons Attribution-Share Alike 3.0 Unported license.

Source: commons.wikimedia.org/wiki/File:Six_Emperor_Penguins.jpg. Copyright in the Public Domain.

Source: flickr.com/photos/dendroica/5359147340. Cleared via Creative Commons Attribution 2.0 Generic license.

Source: flickr.com/photos/usfwshq/5120918705. Cleared via Creative Commons Attribution 2.0 Generic license.

Source: flickr.com/photos/42244964@N03/5377619453. Cleared via Creative Commons Attribution 2.0 Generic license

Source: commons.wikimedia.org/wiki/File:Condor_in_flight.JPG. Copyright in the Public Domain.

Source: commons.wikimedia.org/wiki/File:Gymnogyps_californianus1.jpg. Copyright in the Public Domain.

CHAPTER III

Source: commons.wikimedia.org/wiki/File:White_Rhino.jpg. Cleared via Creative Commons Attribution 2.0 Generic license.

Source: flickr.com/photos/38518750@N00/4572121441. Cleared via Creative Commons Attribution 2.0 Generic license.

Source: cbp.gov/xp/CustomsToday/2004/Aug/baggage_surprises.xml. Copyright in the Public Domain.

Source: flickr.com/photos/7391668@N03/1540533876. Cleared via Creative Commons Attribution 2.0 Generic license.

CHAPTER IV

Source: flickr.com/photos/86366039@N00/4313766239. Cleared via Creative Commons Attribution 2.0 Generic license.

Source: geograph.org.uk/photo/1776884. Cleared via Creative Commons Attribution-Share Alike 2.0 Generic license. Attribution: ceridwen.

Source: flickr.com/photos/40630886@N03/4113791594. Cleared via Creative Commons Attribution 2.0 Generic license.

Source: flickr.com/photos/29174969@N00/5977884006. Cleared via Creative Commons Attribution 2.0 Generic license.

Source: commons.wikimedia.org/wiki/File:WingMuscles.svg. Cleared via Creative Commons Attribution-Share Alike 2.5 Generic license.

Source: flickr.com/photos/37804979@N00/3938418990. Cleared via Creative Commons Attribution 2.0 Generic license.

Source: commons.wikimedia.org/wiki/File:Pavo_muticus_-_Hai_Hong_Karni.jpg. Cleared via Creative Commons Attribution-Share Alike 3.0 Unported license.

Source: commons.wikimedia.org/wiki/File:Owl_face_closeup.jpg. Cleared via Creative Commons Attribution 2.0 Generic license.

Source: flickr.com/photos/94051094@N00/5158914603. Cleared via Creative Commons Attribution-Share Alike 2.0 Generic license.

Source: commons.wikimedia.org/wiki/File:Red-crested_Turaco_RWD.jpg. Cleared via Creative Commons Attribution-Share Alike 3.0 Unported license.

Source: commons.wikimedia.org/wiki/File:EmperorPenguin_2005_2592.JPG. Cleared via Creative Commons Attribution-Share Alike 3.0 Unported license.

Source: flickr.com/photos/8272102@N04/497208595. Cleared via Creative Commons Attribution 2.0 Generic license.

Source: plus.google.com/photos/118334733218924806356/albums/5341938324922081841/5504132944658939986?banner=pwa. Cleared via Creative Commons Attribution 3.0 Unported license.

Source: commons.wikimedia.org/wiki/File:White-winged_Crossbill_Uropygial.JPG. Cleared via Creative Commons Attribution-Share Alike 3.0 Unported license.

Source: flickr.com/photos/usfwsnortheast/4035465562/sizes/o/in/set-72157622516772109. Copyright in the Public Domain.

CHAPTER V

Source: commons.wikimedia.org/wiki/File:Parus_caeruleus1.jpg. Cleared via Creative Commons Attribution-Share Alike 3.0 Unported license.

Source: commons.wikimedia.org/wiki/File:Stavenn_Eurypiga_helias_00.jpg. Cleared via Creative Commons Attribution-Share Alike 3.0 Unported license.

Source: flickr.com/photos/baxterclaws/5163858168. Cleared via Creative Commons Attribution 2.0 Generic license.

Source: flickr.com/photos/silentkids/471895341. Cleared via Creative Commons Attribution 2.0 Generic license.

Source: digitalmedia.fws.gov/cdm4/item_viewer.php?CISOROOT=/natdiglib&CISOPTR=4852&CISOBOX=1&REC=4. Copyright in the Public Domain.

CHAPTER VI

Source: flickr.com/photos/38972116@N00/439427873. Cleared via Creative Commons Attribution-Share Alike 2.0 Generic license.

Source: commons.wikimedia.org/wiki/File:Brugmansia_(detail).jpg. Cleared via Creative Commons Attribution-Share Alike 3.0 Unported license.

Source: commons.wikimedia.org/wiki/File:Roseatespoonbill.jpg. Cleared via Creative Commons Attribution-Share Alike 3.0 Unported license. Attribution: Matt Edmonds at en.wikipedia.

Source: commons.wikimedia.org/wiki/File:Ibis-5.jpg. Cleared via Creative Commons Attribution-Share Alike 3.0 Unported license.

Source: commons.wikimedia.org/wiki/File:Bartgeier_Gypaetus_barbatus_front_Richard_Bartz.jpg. Cleared via Creative Commons Attribution-Share Alike 2.5 Generic license.

Source: flickr.com/photos/8987759@N07/2702329889. Cleared via Creative Commons Attribution 2.0 Generic license.

Source: commons.wikimedia.org/wiki/File:Carduelis-tristis-002.jpg. Cleared via Creative Commons Attribution-Share Alike 3.0 Unported license.

Source: naturespicsonline.com/photos/13343?q=red+crossbill. Cleared via Creative Commons Attribution-Share Alike 3.0 Unported license.

Source: flickr.com/photos/66284747@N00/3523540568. Cleared via Creative Commons Attribution 2.0 Generic license.

Source: commons.wikimedia.org/wiki/File:Pheucticus_ludovicianus_CT3.jpg. Cleared via Creative Commons Attribution-Share Alike 3.0 Unported license.

CHAPTER VII

Source: digitalmedia.fws.gov/cdm4/item_viewer.php?CISOROOT=/natdiglib&CISOPTR=2354&CISOBOX=1&REC=4. Copyright in the Public Domain.

Source: commons.wikimedia.org/wiki/File:Superb_lyrbird_in_scrub_edit2.jpg. Cleared via GNU Free Documentation License, Version 1.2. Attribution: Fir0002/Flagstaffotos. A copy of this license can be found here: commons.wikimedia.org/wiki/Commons:GNU_Free_Documentation_License_1.2.

Source: commons.wikimedia.org/wiki/File:Cr%C3%ADasHirundorustica.JPG. Cleared via Creative Commons Attribution-Share Alike 3.0 Unported license.

Source: commons.wikimedia.org/wiki/File:Reed_warbler_cuckoo.jpg. Cleared via Creative Commons Attribution ShareAlike 3.0 license.

CHAPTER VIII

Source: commons.wikimedia.org/wiki/File:Platycercus_eximius_3.jpg. Cleared via Creative Commons Attribution-Share Alike 2.5 Generic license.

Source: commons.wikimedia.org/wiki/File:Strigops_habroptilus_1.jpg. Cleared via Creative Commons Attribution-Share Alike 3.0 Unported license.

Source: commons.wikimedia.org/wiki/File:Anodorhynchus_hyacinthinus_-Disney_-Florida-8.jpg. Cleared via Creative Commons Attribution-Share Alike 3.0 Unported license. Attribution: Hank Gillette.

Source: commons.wikimedia.org/wiki/File:Diopsittaca_nobilis_-pet-2-4c.jpg. Cleared via Creative Commons Attribution-Share Alike 3.0 Unported license.

Source: flickr.com/photos/24841463@N00/406830188. Cleared via Creative Commons Attribution-Share Alike 2.0 Generic license.

Source: commons.wikimedia.org/wiki/File:African_Grey_Parrot_RWD.jpg. Cleared via Creative Commons Attribution-Share Alike 3.0 Unported license.

Source: commons.wikimedia.org/wiki/File:Amazona_oratrix_-captive-8a.jpg. Cleared via Creative Commons Attribution-Share Alike 2.0 Generic license.

Source: commons.wikimedia.org/wiki/File:Yellow-naped_Amazon.jpg. Cleared via Creative Commons Attribution-Share Alike 3.0 Unported license. Attribution: Matt Edmonds at the English language Wikipedia.

Source: flickr.com/photos/19731486@N07/2957492457. Cleared via Creative Commons Attribution 2.0 Generic license.

Source: flickr.com/photos/74821452@N00/90544685. Cleared via Creative Commons Attribution 2.0 Generic license.

Source: nymphensittichseite.de. Copyright in the Public Domain.

Source: commons.wikimedia.org/wiki/File:Leadbeater_cockatoo_31l07.jpg. Cleared via Creative Commons Attribution-Share Alike 3.0 Unported license. Attribution: Snowmanradio.

Source: flickr.com/photos/16520061@N08/1917526108. Cleared via Creative Commons Attribution 2.0 Generic license.

Source: flickr.com/photos/26942860@N06/4058340177. Cleared via Creative Commons Attribution 2.0 Generic license.

Source: photos8.org/birds_g33-tanimbar_corella_p1920.html?&resource=view/parrot_2-other.html. Cleared via Creative Commons Attribution 2.0 Generic license. Attribution: Sam Mugraby, Photos8.com.

Source: flickr.com/photos/paulspace/5121718338. Cleared via Creative Commons Attribution 2.0 Generic license.

Source: commons.wikimedia.org/wiki/File:Leucopsar_rothschildi_-_20080420.jpg. Cleared via Creative Commons Attribution-Share Alike 3.0 Unported license.

CHAPTER IX

Source: commons.wikimedia.org/wiki/File:Californian_Condor_50_MC.jpg. Cleared via Creative Commons Attribution-Share Alike 3.0 Unported license.

Source: commons.wikimedia.org/wiki/File:Sharp_shinned_hawk_2.jpg. Cleared via Creative Commons Attribution-Share Alike 3.0 Unported license. Attribution: Abdoozy at en.wikipedia.

Source: shpilenok.livejournal.com/41559.html. Cleared via Creative Commons Attribution 3.0 Unported license.

Source: flickr.com/photos/cscole/5060692957. Cleared via Creative Commons Attribution 2.0 Generic license.

Source: flickr.com/photos/59323989@N00/2962800442. Cleared via Creative Commons Attribution 2.0 Generic license.

Source: commons.wikimedia.org/wiki/File:Sagittarius_serpentarius_Sekret%C3%A4r.jpg. Cleared via Creative Commons Attribution-Share Alike 3.0 Unported license.

Source: commons.wikimedia.org/wiki/File:Northern_Goshawk_ad_M2.jpg. Cleared via Creative Commons Attribution-Share Alike 3.0 Unported license.

Source: flickr.com/photos/9062441@N02/2094073020. Cleared via Creative Commons Attribution 2.0 Generic license.

Source: flickr.com/photos/34887625@N03/3381275214. Cleared via Creative Commons Attribution 2.0 Generic license.

Source: commons.wikimedia.org/wiki/File:Steinadler,_Aquila_chrysaetos_08.jpg. Cleared via Creative Commons Attribution-Share Alike 2.5 Generic license.

Source: commons.wikimedia.org/wiki/File:Gyps_bengalensis_PLoS.png. Cleared via Creative Commons Attribution 2.5 Generic license.

Source: flickr.com/photos/72825507@N00/2351478580. Cleared via Creative Commons Attribution 2.0 Generic license.

Source: commons.wikimedia.org/wiki/File:Coragyps_atratus_(landing).jpg. Cleared via Creative Commons Attribution-Share Alike 3.0 Unported license.

Source: commons.wikimedia.org/wiki/File:PeregrineTubercle.jpg. Cleared via Creative Commons Attribution-Share Alike 3.0 Unported license.

Source: flickr.com/photos/10215007@N00/1218390072. Cleared via Creative Commons Attribution-Share Alike 2.0 Generic license.

Source: flickr.com/photos/94051094@N00/5395800621. Cleared via Creative Commons Attribution-Share Alike 2.0 Generic license.

Source: commons.wikimedia.org/wiki/File:Courting_redtails.jpg. Cleared via Creative Commons Attribution-Share Alike 3.0 Unported license.

Source: commons.wikimedia.org/wiki/File:Baby_Bald_Eagle_in_nest.jpg. Cleared via Creative Commons Attribution-Share Alike 3.0 Unported license.

Source: flickr.com/photos/dariosanches/4794624945. Cleared via Creative Commons Attribution-Share Alike 2.0 Generic license.

Source: commons.wikimedia.org/wiki/File:Steinadler_Augenschlag.jpg. Cleared via Creative Commons Attribution-Share Alike 2.5 Generic license.

Source: flickr.com/photos/28867468@N08/4332964832. Cleared via Creative Commons Attribution 2.0 Generic license.

Source: commons.wikimedia.org/wiki/File:Lytovchenko_Olexandr_Calvucci.jpeg. Copyright in the Public Domain.

Source: commons.wikimedia.org/wiki/File:USAF_falcon.jpg. Copyright in the Public Domain.

Source: geograph.org.uk/photo/970123. Cleared via Creative Commons Attribution-Share Alike 2.0 Generic license. Attribution: Sylvia Duckworth.

Source: flickr.com/photos/25609635@N03/3956977307. Creative Commons Attribution 2.0 Generic license.

Source: commons.wikimedia.org/wiki/File:Northern_Goshawk_ad_M2.jpg. Cleared via Creative Commons Attribution-Share Alike 3.0 Unported license.

CHAPTER X

Source: flickr.com/photos/29231471@N00/3185121177. Cleared via Creative Commons Attribution 2.0 Generic license.

Source: commons.wikimedia.org/wiki/File:Ectopistes_migratoriusAAP042CA.jpg. Copyright in the Public Domain.

Source: naturespicsonline.com/galleries/Nature15/_mg_8449a.htm. Cleared via Creative Commons Attribution-Share Alike 2.5 Generic license.

Source: flickr.com/photos/hisgett/4215602681. Cleared via Creative Commons Attribution 2.0 Generic license.

Source: commons.wikimedia.org/wiki/File:Bus_pigeon_loft.jpg. Copyright in the Public Domain.

Source: arcweb.archives.gov/arc/action/ExternalIdSearch?id=512434&jScript=true. Copyright in the Public Domain.

Source: commons.wikimedia.org/wiki/File:Messenger_pigion_released_from_British_tank_1918_IWM_Q_9247.jpg. Copyright in the Public Domain.

Source: historywired.si.edu/enlarge.cfm?ID=522&ShowEnlargement=1. Copyright in the Public Domain.

Source: commons.wikimedia.org/wiki/File:Trebic_jejkov_chmelova_holubnik.jpg. Cleared via Creative Commons Attribution-Share Alike 3.0 Unported license. Attribution: Nostrifikator.

Source: geograph.org.uk/photo/954663. Cleared via Creative Commons Attribution-Share Alike 2.0 Generic license. Attribution: Alexander P. Kapp.

Source: geograph.org.uk/photo/1457840. Cleared via Creative Commons Attribution-Share Alike 2.0 Generic license. Attribution: Betty Longbottom.

Source: geograph.org.uk/photo/946114. Cleared via Creative Commons Attribution-Share Alike 2.0 Generic license. Attribution: David Wright.

Photos by Roger Wyatt.

Source: commons.wikimedia.org/wiki/File:Galati_Roller_Pigeon.jpg. Cleared via Creative Commons Attribution-Share Alike 3.0 Unported license.

Source: flickr.com/photos/12015033@N00/2035736278. Cleared via Creative Commons Attribution-Share Alike 2.0 Generic license.

Source: flickr.com/photos/12015033@N00/2274791930. Cleared via Creative Commons Attribution-Share Alike 2.0 Generic license.

Source: flickr.com/photos/12015033@N00/1391611833. Cleared via Creative Commons Attribution-Share Alike 2.0 Generic license.

Source: commons.wikimedia.org/wiki/File:Fely_wit.jpg. Cleared via Creative Commons Attribution-Share Alike 3.0 Unported license. Attribution: Fabiovanolst at nl.wikipedia.

Source: flickr.com/photos/12015033@N00/2084137347. Cleared via Creative Commons Attribution-Share Alike 2.0 Generic license.

Source: flickr.com/photos/12015033@N00/1918016949. Cleared via Creative Commons Attribution 2.0 Generic license.

Source: flickr.com/photos/12015033@N00/2236681939. Cleared via Creative Commons Attribution-Share Alike 2.0 Generic license.

Source: flickr.com/photos/12015033@N00/2140912197. Cleared via Creative Commons Attribution-Share Alike 2.0 Generic license.

Source: commons.wikimedia.org/wiki/File:Geopelia_cuneata_1_.JPG. Copyright in the Public Domain.

CHAPTER XI

Source: commons.wikimedia.org/wiki/File:Shoulder_girdle-ostrich.jpg. Cleared via Creative Commons Attribution-Share Alike 3.0 Unported license.

Source: commons.wikimedia.org/wiki/File:Dromaius_novaehollandiae_-zoo_-two_feet.jpg. Cleared via Creative Commons Attribution 3.0 Unported license.

Source: commons.wikimedia.org/wiki/File:Ostrich_foot.jpg. Cleared via Creative Commons Attribution-Share Alike 3.0 Unported license. Attribution: Tony Wills.

Source: flickr.com/photos/55826454@N00/3649550997. Cleared via Creative Commons Attribution 2.0 Generic license.

Source: commons.wikimedia.org/wiki/File:Double-wattled_Cassowary.jpg. Cleared via Creative Commons Attribution-Share Alike 3.0 Unported license.

Source: commons.wikimedia.org/wiki/File:Cassowary_feet_closeup.png. Cleared via Creative Commons Attribution-Share Alike 3.0 Unported license.

Source: flickr.com/photos/28577026@N02/2795125527. Cleared via Creative Commons Attribution 2.0 Generic license.

Source: drvector.blogspot.com/2007/02/my-afternoon-with-apteryx.html. Copyright in the Public Domain.

Source: flickr.com/photos/64565252@N00/451883177. Cleared via Creative Commons Attribution-Share Alike 2.0 Generic license.

Source: flickr.com/photos/91237943@N00/192523900. Cleared via Creative Commons Attribution 2.0 Generic license.

Source: commons.wikimedia.org/wiki/File:Emu_Side.jpg. Cleared via Creative Commons Attribution-Share Alike 3.0 Unported license.

Source: commons.wikimedia.org/wiki/File:Yaen002.jpg. Cleared via Creative Commons Attribution-Share Alike 3.0 Unported license.

Source: commons.wikimedia.org/wiki/File:3813GrandChapeau1911.png. Copyright in the Public Domain.

CHAPTER XII

Source: flickr.com/photos/27446776@N00/612578942. Cleared via Creative Commons Attribution-Share Alike 2.0 Generic license.

Source: commons.wikimedia.org/wiki/File:Tragopan_satyra,_ZOO_Praha_197.jpg. leared via Creative Commons Attribution-Share Alike 3.0 Unported license.

Source: flickr.com/photos/39871249@N07/6728838119. Cleared via Creative Commons Attribution 2.0 Generic license.

Source: commons.wikimedia.org/wiki/File:Lady_Amherst%27s_Pheasant,_Chrysolophus_amherstiae_cropped.jpg. Cleared via Creative Commons Attribution 2.0 Generic license.

Source: flickr.com/photos/odfw/5179520616. Cleared via Creative Commons Attribution-Share Alike 2.0 Generic license.

Source: commons.wikimedia.org/wiki/File:Pavo_muticus_-_Hai_Hong_Karni.jpg. Cleared via Creative Commons Attribution-Share Alike 3.0 Unported license.

Source: commons.wikimedia.org/wiki/File:Gall-dindi.jpg. Copyright in the Public Domain.

CHAPTER XIII

Source: commons.wikimedia.org/wiki/File:Anas_platyrhynchos_upending_JdP.jpg. Copyright in the Public Domain.

Source: commons.wikimedia.org/wiki/File:Neck_and_bill_of_a_White_Duck.jpg. Cleared via Creative Commons Attribution-Share Alike 3.0 Unported license.

Source: commons.wikimedia.org/wiki/File:Anas_platyrhynchos_-_Ka%C4%8DIca_div%C3%A1.jpg. Cleared via Creative Commons Attribution-Share Alike 3.0 Unported license.

Source: flickr.com/photos/72825507@N00/438045208. Cleared via Creative Commons Attribution 2.0 Generic license.

Source: flickr.com/photos/davehamster/3575650951. Cleared via Creative Commons Attribution 2.0 Generic license.

Source: naturespicsonline.com/photos/12943?q=hooded+merganser. Cleared via Creative Commons Attribution-Share Alike 2.5 Generic license.

Source: fotocommunity.de/pc/pc/mypics/862897/display/12641545. Cleared via Creative Commons Attribution-Share Alike 3.0 Unported license.

Source: commons.wikimedia.org/wiki/File:Somateria_mollissima_male_female.jpg. Cleared via Creative Commons Attribution-Share Alike 2.5 Generic license. Attribution: Andreas Trepte, www.photo-natur.de.

Source: commons.wikimedia.org/wiki/File:Common_eider_nest.JPG. Cleared via Creative Commons Attribution-Share Alike 3.0 Unported license.

Source: flickr.com/photos/19663529@N00/111538678. Cleared via Creative Commons Attribution-Share Alike 2.0 Generic license.

Source: naturespicsonline.com/photos/13334?q=trumpeter+swan. Cleared via Creative Commons Attribution-Share Alike 2.5 Generic license.

Source: commons.wikimedia.org/wiki/File:Canada_Goose_Cape_May_RWD.jpg. Cleared via Creative Commons Attribution-Share Alike 3.0 Unported license.

Source: commons.wikimedia.org/wiki/File:Canada_Goose_Albany.jpg. Cleared via Creative Commons Attribution-Share Alike 3.0 Unported license. Attribution: Matt H. Wade.

Source: commons.wikimedia.org/wiki/File:Hawaiian_duck.jpg. Copyright in the Public Domain.

CHAPTER XIV

Source: commons.wikimedia.org/wiki/File:Eoliennes_Gaspesie.jpg. Cleared via Creative Commons Attribution-Share Alike 3.0 Unported license.

Source: flickr.com/photos/7955467@N03/3488673676. Cleared via Creative Commons Attribution-Share Alike 2.0 Generic license.

Illustrations by Matthew Kirkland Jones.

CPSIA information can be obtained
at www.ICGtesting.com
Printed in the USA
LVIC04n2355070616
491623LV00005B/7